★★★

ALL-STAR GAZING

50 Years of the GAA All-Stars

*To Billy
Enjoy!*

by Moira Dunne and Eileen Dunne

Eileen & Moira

Copyright © Moira Dunne & Eileen Dunne
The right of Moira Dunne & Eileen Dunne to be identified as the owners of this work has been asserted
in accordance with the Copyright, Designs and Patents Act, 1988.
All Rights Reserved.
No part of this publication may be reproduced.

First published in 2021 by Dunne Publishing.
ISBN: 978-1-3999-0772-9

Editor: Donal Keenan
Graphic Design: DBA Publications Ltd.

Photographic acknowledgements:
Most of the photos in this book come from Mick Dunne's archive.
The authors wish to thank the following for the use of their photographs: Ray McManus, Sportsfile, Jim O'Sullivan,
Jack Ryan, Pat Doab, Pat Hartigan, Iggy Clarke, The Kearins Family, John Mullane, Pat Hartigan, John Downey,
John Purcell, Frank McGuigan, Eddie Keher, Aidan Ryan, The Jacob Family, Colm O'Rourke, Jack Cosgrove,
Mickey Quinn, Rory O'Connell, The GAA, Mark Restan, Shea Fahey, Kevin O'Brien, Paddy Reynolds,
Ray Cummins, Tom Spillane, The Kelleher Family, Tommy Smyth, Pat Critchley,
Pádraig Faulkner, Dylan Vaughan and Conor McKeown.

Every effort has been made to obtain the necessary permissions with reference to copyright material,
both illustrated and quoted. We apologise for any omissions in this respect and will be pleased to make
the appropriate acknowledgements in any future edition.

The compilation of this book has required substantial research.
The publishers would welcome any additional information and observations that our readers have.

CONTENTS

FOREWORD BY LARRY McCARTHY, UACHTARÁN CHUMANN LÚTHCHLEAS GAEL 4

INTRODUCTION 6

ALL-STAR TIME IN THE SUNSHINE STATE 7

HOW THE ALL-STARS BEGAN IN 1971 10

THE FIRST ALL-STAR TEAMS 17

WHO ARE THE ALL-STARS? 27

THE GAA OSCARS 45

LEAVING ON A JET PLANE 67

ANNUAL TRIP IN THE SEVENTIES 78

INTO THE EIGHTIES 98

PASTURES NEW IN THE NINETIES 106

A GOLDEN SPELL IN THE NOUGHTIES 116

SELECTING THE ALL-STARS 134

GAZING INTO THE FUTURE 147

HURLING ALL-STAR LISTS (1971-2020) 149

FOOTBALL ALL-STAR LISTS (1971-2020) 172

ACKNOWLEDGEMENTS 197

All-Star Gazing

Foreword

Is cúis mhór bród duinn mar eagraíocht go bhfuil ceiliúradh 50 bliain bainte amach ag scéim na Réalta agus an togra fós ag dul ó neart go neart.

The All-Stars is the most prestigious sporting awards scheme in Irish society and has gone from strength to strength since its inception in 1971.

Few of the pioneering journalists who looked to the United States for inspiration to honour the best of our games, could have known how the genesis of an idea would take root and become one of the most coveted accolades in Gaelic Games.

This year we celebrate a half a century of excellence in our cherished games of football and hurling.

The names of those honoured over the five decades trip off the tongue and represent the best our games have to offer. Crucially, the allure of an award remains as attractive today as it did during the early days of the initiative.

There are various elements to what it is that helps the All-Stars occupy a special place on the Irish sporting landscape:

- the speculation and anticipation that accompanies the announcement of both the nominations and the eventual winners
- the glitz and glamour of the awards night itself; and of course
- the tall tales of international travel that has seen award winners bring our games far and wide, while making an important connection with our GAA clubs around the globe.

In the early days, during those international trips, the players were often accommodated in the homes of Irish families, another novel element of a storied scheme.

While the GAA and various sponsors – current partners PwC among them – have played a central role in running the scheme, one of the most important pillars of the All-Stars has been its independence and integrity, provided by the role of GAA journalists making the all-important selections of both nominees and overall winners.

To that end, it is fitting that the Dunne sisters, Eileen and Moira, should be the driving force behind this excellent publication to mark the 50th anniversary.

Daughters of founding member, and renowned broadcaster, Mick, who was beamed into our homes thanks to RTÉ and The Sunday Game, they have overseen a trawl of material and imagery, some of which has never been published before.

In so doing, they have done the GAA and people with an interest in our games and the All-Stars a true service.

One measure of success for any undertaking in life is staying power and an ability to remain relevant and valued as one generation passes the baton to the next.

In this regard the All-Stars has been a resoundingly positive addition to the GAA family.

Here's to the next 50 years.

Le gach dea ghuí,

Labhrás Mac Carthaigh
Uachtarán
Chumann Lúthchleas Gael

Contributors

HURLERS	COUNTY
Aidan Ryan	Tipperary
Bobby Ryan	Tipperary
Brendan Cummins	Tipperary
Brian Lohan	Clare
Brian Whelahan	Offaly
Charlie McCarthy	Cork
Cian Lynch	Limerick
Ciarán Barr	Antrim
Colm Bonnar	Tipperary
Conal Bonnar	Tipperary
Cormac Bonnar	Tipperary
DJ Carey	Kilkenny
Damien Martin	Offaly
David Kilcoyne	Westmeath
Declan Carr	Tipperary
Dónal Óg Cusack	Cork
Éamonn Cregan	Limerick
Eddie Keher	Kilkenny
Eoin Kelly	Tipperary
Francis Loughnane	Tipperary
Frank Cummins	Kilkenny
Frank Lohan	Clare
Gary Kirby	Limerick
Ger Henderson	Kilkenny
Henry Shefflin	Kilkenny
Iggy Clarke	Galway
Jack Ryan	Tipperary
Jimmy Cooney	Galway
Joe Canning	Galway
Joe Connolly	Galway
Joe Cooney	Galway
John Connolly	Galway
John Fenton	Cork
John Henderson	Kilkenny
John Mullane	Waterford
John Quigley	Wexford
Martin Quigley	Wexford
Michael 'Babs'	Tipperary
Mick Bermingham	Dublin
Mick Jacob	Wexford
Noel Skehan	Kilkenny
Ollie Canning	Galway
Pádraic Maher	Tipperary
Pat Critchley	Laois
Pat Fleury	Offaly
Pat Hartigan	Limerick
Pat Henderson	Kilkenny
Peter Finnerty	Galway
Ronan Maher	Tipperary
Séamus Callinan	Tipperary
Seán Óg Ó hAilpín	Cork
Tadhg O'Connor	Tipperary
Tony Maher	Cork

DUAL ALL-STARS	COUNTY
Jimmy Barry Murphy	Cork
Ray Cummins	Cork

FOOTBALLERS	COUNTY
Aidan O'Shea	Mayo
Alan Brogan	Dublin
Andy McCallin	Antrim
Anthony Tohill	Derry
Barney Rock	Dublin
Bernard Brogan	Dublin
Bernard Brogan Jnr	Dublin
Billy Morgan	Cork
Brian Fenton	Dublin
Brian McGuigan	Tyrone
Charlie Redmond	Dublin
Colm Browne	Laois
Colm Cooper	Kerry
Colm Kavanagh	Tyrone
Colm O'Rourke	Meath
Conor Mortimer	Mayo
Danny Culloty	Cork
Darragh Ó Sé	Kerry
Dean Rock	Dublin
Declan Browne	Tipperary
Denis 'Ogie' Moran	Kerry
Dermot Earley Jnr	Kildare
Donie O'Sullivan	Kerry
Eoin Liston	Kerry
Eugene Mulligan	Offaly
Frank McGuigan	Tyrone
Fr. Nick Clavin	Offaly
Gay O'Driscoll	Dublin
Ger Lynch	Kerry
Ger Power	Kerry
Greg Blaney	Down
Jack Cosgrove	Galway
Jack O'Shea	Kerry
James McCartan Jnr	Down
Jimmy Keaveney	Dublin
Johnny Carey	Mayo
Keith Barr	Dublin
Kevin O'Brien	Wicklow
Kevin O'Neill	Mayo
Kieran McGeeney	Armagh
Larry Tompkins	Cork
Liam Irwin	Laois
Liam O'Neill	Galway
Liam Sammon	Galway
Marc Ó Sé	Kerry
Martin Furlong	Offaly
Matt Connor	Offaly
Matty Forde	Wexford
Maurice Fitzgerald	Kerry
Mick O'Dwyer	Kerry
Mick Spillane	Kerry
Mickey Kearins	Sligo
Mickey Quinn	Leitrim
Mikey Sheehy	Kerry
Ollie Brady	Cavan
PJ Smyth	Galway
Paddy Cullen	Dublin
Paddy Keenan	Louth
Paddy Reynolds	Meath
Pádraic Joyce	Galway
Pádraig Faulkner	Cavan
Pat Reynolds	Meath
Pat Spillane	Kerry
Paul Earley	Roscommon
Paul Flynn	Dublin
Peter McGinnity	Fermanagh
Raymond Munroe	Tyrone
Richie Connor	Offaly
Robbie Kelleher	Dublin
Rory O'Connell	Westmeath
Séamus Leyden	Galway
Seán Cavanagh	Tyrone
Seán O'Neill	Down
Shane Ryan	Dublin
Shea Fahy	Cork
Tadhg Kennelly	Kerry
Tom Spillane	Kerry
Tomás Connor	Offaly
Tomás Ó Sé	Kerry
Tommy Carr	Dublin
Tommy Dowd	Meath
Tony Hanahoe	Dublin
Tony McTague	Offaly
Willie Bryan	Offaly
Willie Joe Padden	Mayo

OTHER	CONTRIBUTORS
Alan Milton	GAA Director of Comms.
Dermot Kelly	Ex RTE
Dermot Power	Ex Bank of Ireland
Donal Keenan	Journalist
Frank Murphy	Cork GAA
Humphrey Kelleher	Ex Bank of Ireland
Jarlath Daly	Sculptor
Jim O'Sullivan	Journalist
Jim Whitty	Ex Bank of Ireland
John Downey	Son of Paddy Downey
John Purcell	Son of Pádraig Puirséal
Liam Mulvihill	GAA Iar Ard Stiúrthóir
Liam O'Donohue	Lár na Páirce Museum
Martin Breheny	Journalist
Michael Lyster	Journalist
Noel Coughlan	Ex RTE
Paddy Gormley	New York GAA
Paddy Hickey	Son of John D. Hickey
Páraic Duffy	GAA Iar Ard Stiúrthóir
Pat Doab	Austin GAA
Pat Griffin	London GAA
Pat Heneghan	Ex Carrolls
Rowan Gillespie	Sculptor
Seamus King	Lár na Páirce Museum
Seán Harte	Toronto GAA
Tim Murphy	San Francisco GAA
Tom Parsons	GPA CEO
Tom Ryan	GAA Ard Stiúrthóir
Tommy Smyth	New York GAA

Introduction

The discovery of a dusty old cardboard box one day in late 2016 led to the writing of this book. Inside the box was a treasure trove of All-Star files that belonged to Mick Dunne, our father, GAA journalist and one of the founders of the long-running scheme.

In 2010 we had donated Dad's 60-year collection of GAA match reports and other records to the GAA Museum, so the discovery of the All-Star material in his small home office was a great surprise. He had retained 25 years' worth of official documents in his capacity as secretary of the All-Star scheme, as well as many personal photos and mementos from the All-Star trips to the US and Canada. There were also letters from Seán Ó Síocháin, Jack Lynch, and many legendary hurlers and footballers. As a result of this wealth of information, we decided to compile everything into a commemorative book to celebrate the 50th anniversary of the much-loved award scheme in Autumn 2021.

With the GAA's endorsement, we began to research the history of the All-Stars. We spoke to 136 All-Stars - hurlers and footballers from across the five decades. They helped us piece together the facts as they shared their memories of All-Star banquets, tours and the many friendships made. We often met two or three players together, and as one memory sparked another, the anecdotes would flow.

It was a privilege to meet each All-Star, legends of the game, young and old. We were greeted with great interest and encouragement everywhere we went. We heard about the impact of All-Star recognition on those first All-Stars in the 1970s and how the opportunity to travel abroad was valued through the 1980s and early 1990s. When we met the younger All-Stars, we heard how much it meant to them to be part of their county's All-Star Roll of Honour, following in the footsteps of their heroes.

We were welcomed in many players' homes with lots of stories as well as copious cups of tea, sandwiches and scones. Family members chipped in with their All-Star memories too. We enjoyed every encounter whether at a potato farm in Meath, the Men's Shed in Tullamore, Templenoe on a balmy summer night or a special evening spent in Kinsale.

Our only regret is that we could not meet every All-Star, but with almost 800 recipients, it was never going to be possible. To reduce the list, we focused primarily on the All-Star record holders, All-Star family connections and the first or only All-Star from a county. Fortunately, when Covid-19 arrived in early 2020, our All-Star research was almost complete. Zoom allowed us to complete some of the interviews online, but we still missed a few players.

As well as telling the history of the scheme we also present the All-Stars statistics from the last 50 years. The name of every player nominated since 1971 is also included to complete the All-Star story.

One of the best discoveries was an article in Dad's records that he wrote in 1973, a year after the first All-Star tour to San Francisco. We start this book with his version of how it all began.

By Moira Dunne and Eileen Dunne

All-Star Time in the Sunshine State

Written by Mick Dunne in 1973 for *Our Games Annual*

It was late into a Californian night as hundreds of Irish and Irish Americans swarmed around the arrivals gate at San Francisco International Airport. They were there to greet the 707 jet that had just flown the 1971 All-Ireland champions Tipperary and Offaly, the Carrolls All-Star hurlers and footballers, their officials and supporters, over 5,500 miles from Ireland.

An air of high excitement and great expectancy hovered over the terminal. As we surveyed this happy scene through an aircraft window, Paddy Downey – the Gaelic Games editor of *The Irish Times* – was moved to remark: "It's a far-cry, fellows, from a miserable, wet day back in Belfield". But only his fellow sports journalists who were among the travelling party recognised the significance of his words.

Only we understood fully that this arrival in the Sunshine State was the culmination of something which began – half in jest, whole in earnest – on an appalling day in UCD sportsground at Belfield 11 months before.

That was the occasion of the first All-Ireland seven-a-side club football championship, organised by the UCD club and sponsored by PJ Carroll & Company Ltd. Paddy Downey was being mild when he recalled it as a "miserable day" because it was a Saturday afternoon of April 1971 ruined by torrential rain and high winds. Yet, on such an inauspicious occasion was the idea for the Carrolls GAA All-Star Awards scheme born.

To complete the full background, it is necessary to go back to the early 1960s. That is when the sports journalists who cover Gaelic games regularly banded together as the Association of Gaelic Sports Journalists in order, among other things, to establish a scheme of annual awards to hurlers and footballers. This was to be a gesture of our appreciation to players in general – although we were presenting individual awards – for the entertainment they provided for us throughout the playing season. For let no one believe that the Gaelic sports journalists are men with hearts of stone unable to enjoy themselves even as they do their day's work, which is reporting matches up and down the country.

At that time, we presented awards to Liam Devaney (Tipperary), John Doyle (Tipperary), Gerry O'Malley (Roscommon) and Mick O'Connell (Kerry); awards, I might add, which we like to think these players did not deposit in the dustbin at the first opportunity. However, impecunious

Mick Dunne in the Balboa Stadium Press Box in San Francisco in 1973

labourers that we sports journalists are, we were, regrettably, unable to continue the scheme in 1963. But let me assure you, this did not stop us talking about it…..and talking about it…..and talking…..

Indeed, as John D. Hickey (*Irish Independent*), Paddy Downey (*Irish Times*), Pádraig Puirséal (*Irish Press*) and myself travelled throughout the country, or met socially, it did not take long to get around to the subject of annual awards. It happened so frequently, as my colleagues will confirm, that the conversation usually ended with one or other of us – expressing himself rather emphatically – exhorting the group: "Well, let's do something about it". But for years, I must confess, we talked a lot…. and did little.

And so, we talked on and on. Until that dismal day at

All-Star Gazing

Belfield. Messrs. Hickey, Downey, Puirséal and I were at the seven-a-side championship so naturally, as had now become our habit, where two or three of us were gathered we began bemoaning the fact that we had let the award scheme drop.

This time, though, we did something. And I must say we were prompted by the fact that PJ Carroll and Co. were sponsors of the seven-a-side matches. So, during a break from the elements, we 'chatted-up' Pat Heneghan, the livewire Promotions Manager of Carrolls. "How about it, Pat?", we say. "How about what?" retorted a puzzled Mr H. "Going the whole hog and sponsoring the Gaelic sports journalists who'll pick a hurling and football team for you?" Oh, nothing bashful about these boys, you must agree.

Sometime in early summer Pat Heneghan, when I met him in Galway, expressed interest….and wanted details. So, a set of proposals for the Carrolls GAA All-Stars was prepared and submitted to Pat and also forwarded to Pat Fanning, the President of the GAA, and to the General Secretary Seán Ó Síocháin. The latter submission was an essential as far as the sports journalists were concerned because - and it's no harm to reveal it now – we had been somewhat disappointed with the reaction of the GAA, as a body, when we had our own awards in the 1960s.

As was made clear to Carrolls, we would go ahead only with the official approval of the Central Council (C.C.). And that, I am happy to say, came quickly after Pat Fanning and Seán Ó Síocháin showed their interest. (Aside – so maybe the C.C. aren't such ruffians after all!).

Thereafter, things started "humming" and a meeting in July 1971 formed the Steering Committee of John Hickey, Pádraig Puirséal, Paddy Downey, Pat Heneghan and yours truly. At that meeting my colleagues – with tremendous magnanimity and admirable unanimity – decided I should be the secretary of said committee. (And, until then, I had regarded them all as good friends.)

That, I might add, was about the last thing that was unanimous between us – as can be vouched for by Messrs. Fanning, Ó Síocháin and Heneghan who have had the "rare pleasure" of sitting in as non-voting observers when we select the All-Star teams. However, it is not true that for weeks after the selection meetings the sports journalists refuse to talk to each other at matches; we are all big enough to say "hello" – however frostily- to those of the committee who have the audacity to hold opposite views!

The scheme reaches its fitting climax at a presentation banquet of immense splendour in December. That is a night for renewing old friendships, making new friends among players and officials gathered from the 32 counties but, most important of all, it is a night of concentrated glory for 30 hurlers and footballers who have richly entertained so many thousands of us during the playing season.

And that, primarily, is the reason for the Carrolls GAA All-Stars; that is why the sports journalists – those of us who are selectors or nominators from the daily and provincial press and from RTÉ – continue to be actively engaged in carrying the scheme through. This is our way of saying "thanks" and we only regret that the awards have to be confined to 30 players.

It is also fair I suppose that journalists who spend some of their time criticising the decisions of county and provincial selectors should "get some of their own medicine back". And does that happen?

Of course, the scheme could not exist without the active interest of the P.J. Carroll management and their representative, Pat Heneghan, whose dedication to the scheme over the past two years has been far and away above the call of his duty to his employers – and maybe that is not unexpected from one who was educated at St. Mary's College in Galway.

Neither would Carrolls nor the sports journalists continue their interest without the unbounded support and enthusiasm of Pat Fanning and Seán Ó Síocháin, support and enthusiasm that does not go unappreciated.

Furthermore, the interest of the United Irish Societies and St. Patrick's Fathers of San Francisco – joint organisers of the annual spring trip to California – has added a "new dimension" as Pat Fanning called it recently, to the whole idea of All-Star awards. So, when the All-Stars step off their jet on the U.S. West Coast next March they will know "it's a darned far cry from a miserable wet day in Belfield!".

Our Games Annual 1973 and on next page the original article by Mick Dunne

ALL-STAR TIME IN THE SUNSHINE STATE

... a far cry from a wet day at Belfield

by

MICK DUNNE

*of Radio Telefís Éireann
Sports Department*

IT was late into a Californian night as hundreds of Irish and Irish-Americans swarmed around the arrivals-gate at San Francisco International Airport. They were there to greet the 707 jet that had just flown the 1971 All-Ireland champions, Tipperary and Offaly, and the Carroll's All-Star hurlers and footballers, their officials and supporters, over 5,500 miles from Ireland.

An air of high excitement and great expectancy hovered over the terminal. As we surveyed this happy scene through an aircraft window, Paddy Downey — the Gaelic Games editor of "The Irish Times" —was moved to remark: "It's a far-cry, fellows, from a miserable, wet day back in Belfield." But only his fellow sports journalists who were among the travelling party recognised the significance of his words.

Only we understood fully that this arrival in the Sunshine State was the culmination of something which began—half in jest, whole in earnest—on an appalling day in the U.C.D. sportsground at Belfield 11 months before.

That was the occasion of the first All-Ireland seven-a-side club football championship, organised by the U.C.D. club and sponsored by P. J. Carroll and Company. Paddy Downey was being mild when he recalled it as a "miserable day" because it was a Saturday afternoon of April '71 ruined by torrential rain and high winds.

Yet, on such an inauspicious occasion was the idea for the Carroll's G.A.A. All-Star Awards scheme born.

This was to be a gesture of our appreciation to players in general—although we were presenting individual awards—for the entertainment they provided throughout the playing season. For let no one believe that the Gaelic sports journalists are men with hearts of stone unable to enjoy themselves even as they do their day's work, which is reporting matches up and down the country.

At that time we presented awards to Liam Devaney (Tipperary), John Doyle (Tipperary), Gerry O'Malley (Roscommon) and Mick O'Connell (Kerry); awards, I might add, which we like to think these players did not deposit in the dustbin at the first opportunity. However, impecunious labourers that we sports journalists are, we were, regrettably, unable to continue the scheme in 1963. But let me assure you, this did not stop us talking about it . . . and talking about it . . . and talking. . . .

Indeed, as John D. Hickey ("Irish Independent"), Paddy Downey ("The Irish Times"), Padraig Puirséal ("Irish Press") and myself travelled throughout the country, or met socially, it did not take long to get around to the subject of annual awards. It happened so frequently, as my colleagues will confirm, that the conversation usually ended with one or other of us —expressing himself rather emphatically —exhorting the group: "Well, let's do something about it." But for years, I must confess, we talked a lot . . . and did little.

And so we talked on . . . and on. Until that dismal day at Belfield. Messrs. Hickey, Downey, Puirséal and myself were at the seven-a-side championship . . . so naturally, as had now become our habit, where two or three of us were gathered, we got back again to bemoaning the fact that we had let the award scheme drop.

This time, though, we did something. And I must say we were prompted by the fact that P. J. Carroll and Co. were sponsors of the seven-a-side matches. So during a break from the elements we "chatted-up" Pat Heneghan, the livewire Public Relations Manager of Carrolls.

Sometime in early summer Pat Heneghan, when I met him in Galway, expressed interest . . . and wanted details. So a set of proposals for the Carrolls G.A.A. All-Stars was prepared and submitted to Pat and also forwarded to Pat Fanning, the President of the G.A.A., and to the General Secretary, Seán Ó Síocháin. The latter submission was an essential as far as the sports journalists were concerned because —and it's no harm to reveal it now—we had been somewhat disappointed with the reaction of the G.A.A., as a body, when we had our own awards in the 'Sixties.

As was made clear to Carrolls, we would go ahead only with the official approval of the Central Council. And that, I am happy to say, came quickly after Pat Fanning and Seán Ó Síocháin showed their interest. (Aside—so maybe the C.C. aren't so dense after all !).

Thereafter, things started "humming" and a meeting in July '71 formed the Steering Committee of John Hickey, Padraig Puirséal, Paddy Downey, Pat Heneghan and yours truly. At that meeting my colleagues—with tremendous magnanimity and admirable unanimity — decided I should be secretary of said committee. (And, until then, I had regarded them all as good friends.)

The scheme reaches its fitting climax at a presentation banquet of immense splendour in December. That is a night for renewing old friendships, making new friends among players and officials gathered from the 32 counties, but most important of all it is a night of concentrated glory for 30 hurlers and footballers who have richly entertained so many thousands of us during the playing season.

And this, primarily, is the reason for the Carrolls G.A.A. All-Stars; this is why the sports journalists—those of us who are selectors or nominators from the daily and provincial press and from R.T.E.—continue to be actively engaged in carrying the scheme through. This is our way of saying "thanks" and we only regret that the awards have to be confined to 30 players.

Of course, the scheme could not exist without the active interest of the P. J. Carroll management and their representative, Pat Heneghan, whose dedication to the scheme over the past two years has been far and away above the call of his duty to his employers—and maybe that is not unexpected from one who was educated at St. Mary's College in Galway.

Neither would Carrolls nor the sports journalists continue their interest without the unbounded support and enthusiasm of Pat Fanning and Seán Ó Síocháin; support and enthusiasm that does not go unappreciated.

Furthermore, the interest of the United Irish Societies and St. Patrick's Fathers of San Francisco—joint organisers of the annual spring trip to California—has added a "new dimension" as Pat Fanning called it recently, to the whole idea of All-Star awards. So when the All-Stars step off their jet on the U.S. West Coast next March they will know that "it's a darned far cry from a miserable day in Belfield !"

All-Star Gazing

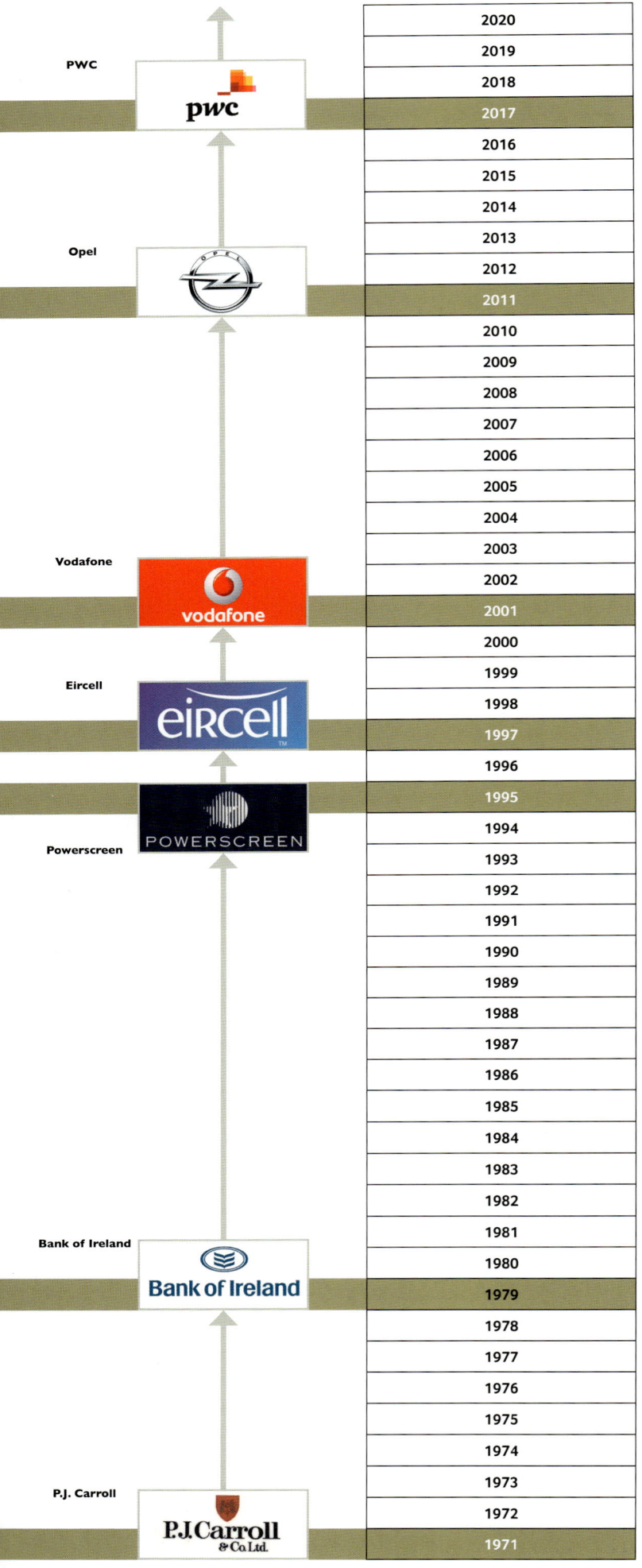

How The All-Stars Began in 1971

Five decades later, the founding GAA journalists would surely be delighted that their idea to recognise the best hurlers and footballers each year not only endured but became the longest-running sports awards scheme in Ireland.

At the end of each season, the hurling and football All-Star announcements are keenly anticipated. New All-Stars are selected, the records are updated, and the All-Star history continues to expand. As the years roll by, a new generation of players takes pride in joining their county's All-Star Roll of Honour.

The All-Star teams are selected by a panel of journalists, and although some rules have changed, the basic principles of the scheme remain the same as those set out in 1971. Six companies have provided financial backing for the All-Star scheme over the 50 years. The Bank of Ireland, who took over from Carrolls at the end of 1978, sponsored the awards for the longest period of 17 years. Known as 'title sponsors', the scheme's name is updated with each change in sponsor. Since PwC began their sponsorship in 2017, the title of the scheme has been the PwC All-Stars.

Feargal O'Rourke, PwC Managing Partner, said: "We would like to congratulate the GAA/GPA on the 50th anniversary of the All-Stars celebrating young Irish sporting talent. Over the years we have seen superb displays of talent, teamwork and sheer determination. Supporting people to fulfil their maximum potential is very much at the core of how we run our business. We look forward to lots more excitement on the field in the years to come".

The All-Star awards are presented jointly by the GAA and GPA since the merger of the All-Star scheme with the GPA's own awards in 2011. For five years prior to that, the player representative body had picked its own Gaelic Team of the Year but the amalgamation of the two awards schemes was a significant part of the negotiations that saw the GPA officially recognised by the GAA that year.

GPA CEO Tom Parsons said, "There is no doubt about it, our Gaelic games are all about being part of a team, representing your family, community and, in the case of our inter-county players, your county. The All-Stars recognise the impact an individual player's performance has for their team and they are one of Ireland's most prestigious sporting awards. They are a symbol of a player's effort, excellence and performance and brings a huge sense of pride for, not only the player, but also their family, team and community. The GPA would like to recognise the vision of those who originally championed the scheme, led by the late Mick Dunne, and congratulate the players who received All-Star awards since the scheme's inception in 1971. Here's to the next fifty."

In 2020, after a season like no other due to the global Covid-19 pandemic, the GAA was determined to continue the All-Star tradition. The announcement of the 2020 All-Stars in February 2021 completed the 50-year All-Star record with Waterford hurler Stephen Bennett becoming the 1,500th All-Star to be named.

THE BEGINNING

The All-Star scheme was started in 1971 by the four leading GAA journalists of that time, Paddy Downey, Mick Dunne, John D. Hickey and Pádraig Puirséal. Passionate about the hurling and football games they covered, the men had great respect for the GAA players and wanted to find a way to honour them each year. Mick Dunne was a keen follower of American sports, and the annual recognition there of a sport's top performers in the 'All-Star games' had inspired him. In 1961 and 1962 the journalists clubbed together to present a trophy to their top hurler and footballer. However, as they funded the initiative themselves, they could not continue it on an annual basis.

In 1963 the Cú Chulainn Awards honouring the best players in each position on a hurling and football team were sponsored by Gaelic Weekly magazine. The players were selected by the Association of Gaelic Sports Journalists of which Puirséal, Downey, Dunne and Hickey were members. The chosen players were presented with awards, but the scheme was discontinued in 1968, again due to lack of funding.

ENTER CARROLLS

The four men persisted with their idea into the 1970s. In April 1971, they found a perfect opportunity to progress it when they attended a seven-a-side football tournament in UCD, organised by Eugene McGee, who was the UCD manager at the time. Significantly, tobacco manufacturer Carrolls sponsored the event.

While taking refuge from bad weather in a tea caravan, they approached the Carrolls Public Relations Officer, Pat Heneghan, to enquire if the company would sponsor an annual award scheme. To their delight, he expressed immediate interest.

Carrolls already sponsored major sports events like the Irish Open Golf and Tennis tournaments. Pat Heneghan recalls, "I was immediately interested in the idea of the All-Stars. The attraction for Carrolls was getting involved in a sport with a broader appeal than golf or tennis.

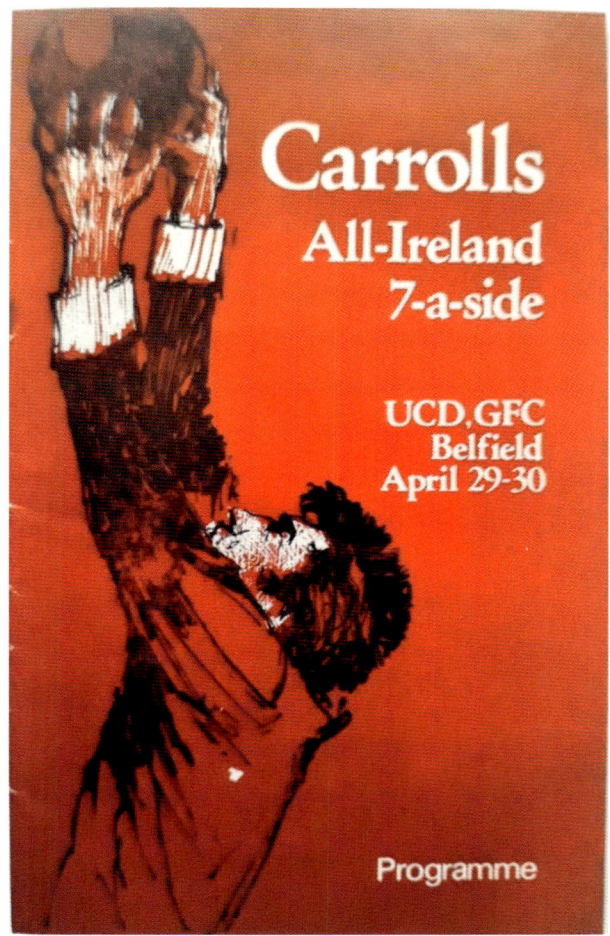

Programme for the tournament in UCD where it all began

The GAA covered all social demographics. We all got excited talking about a new awards scheme, we abandoned the caravan and took the party across to the Montrose Hotel. I said to the barman, 'give me a large bottle of whiskey to celebrate'".

From there, things began to move quickly. Just weeks later, Pat had secured the backing of Carrolls. The only stipulation was that the scheme would be known as the 'Carrolls GAA All-Stars'. With a sponsor confirmed for the All-Star scheme, the journalists' next step was to approach the GAA.

GAA APPROVAL

In 1971 there were many reasons why the GAA might not have supported the scheme. Firstly, it represented a form of player recognition which was viewed with suspicion within the Association, once described as a "glorification of the individual to the detriment of team spirit".

Then there was the tricky subject of sponsorship, which had yet to be accepted by the GAA. Later that year, a report by the McNamee Commission would recommend "cautious engagement" with sponsors.

PRIVATE AND CONFIDENTIAL

CARROLLS ALL STARS

Minutes of meeting held at Carrolls, Grand Parade on 28th July 1971

PRESENT: Paddy Downey   - Irish Times
          Mick Dunne   - R.T.E.
          John D. Hickey - Irish Independent
          Paddy Puirseal - Irish Press
          Pat Heneghan   - Carrolls

The following items were discussed:

1. **SCHEME OUTLINES**

   Two Carrolls G.A.A. All-Star teams will be chosen, one for hurling and one for football. The period will cover the 1971 Championship season and the Carrolls All-Star hurling team will be announced in October, the football team in November. A panel of full time G.A.A. journalists will be asked to nominate fifteen men for each team. These nomination papers will then be examined by a selection committee who will make the final decision on the teams to receive awards. Presentations to the winning teams will be made at a banquet in Dublin in December. A further extension to the scheme is the distinct possibility that the G.A.A. will nominate the Carrolls All-Star teams to play in U.S.A. (football) and in London (hurling).

2. **G.A.A. APPROVAL**

   Mick Dunne told the meeting that the executive of the Central Council of the G.A.A. gave full approval to the scheme as it did not involve direct sponsorship to the G.A.A. as such but sponsorship through G.A.A. journalists. The executive appointed P. Fanning (President) and S. O Siochain (General Secretary) to act on committees with the G.A.A. writers and the sponsors.

3. **COMMITTEES**

   It was decided to have three committees or groups to carry out the scheme and they are:-

   1. Nomination Panel   This would consist of recognised G.A.A. writers from the National Dailies, Evenings, Sundays, Belfast Dailies, R.T.E. and B.B.C. All of which would have the right to nominate the man of their choice for each position on the Carrolls G.A.A. All-Star teams.

      The Nomination Panel will consist of:-

      Independent Newspapers - J.D. Hickey, Con Kenealy, Tom O'Riordan, Michael Cogley, Bob Hyland, Donal Carroll, Tommy Kelly, John Comyn.

      Irish Press Group - Padraig Puirseal, Gerry McCarty, Peadar O'Brien, Sean Og O Ceallachain, Eugene McGee, Michael Fortune.

      Irish Times - Paddy Downey, Ned Van Esbeck, Peter Byrne.

      Cork Examiner - Jim Sullivan, Val Dorgan, Michael Ellard.

      Belfast Telegraph - Gerry McGuigan

      Newsletter - Eoin McQuillan

      Irish News - Denis O'Hara

      R.T.E. - M. O'Hehir, Mick Dunne, Maurice Reidy

      B.B.C. - Liam MacDowell

      All of the above are journalists and are regular attenders at G.A.A. games throughout the Championship season.

cont/...2

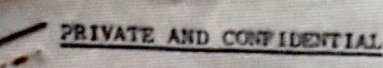
Minutes of the first All-Star meeting in 1971

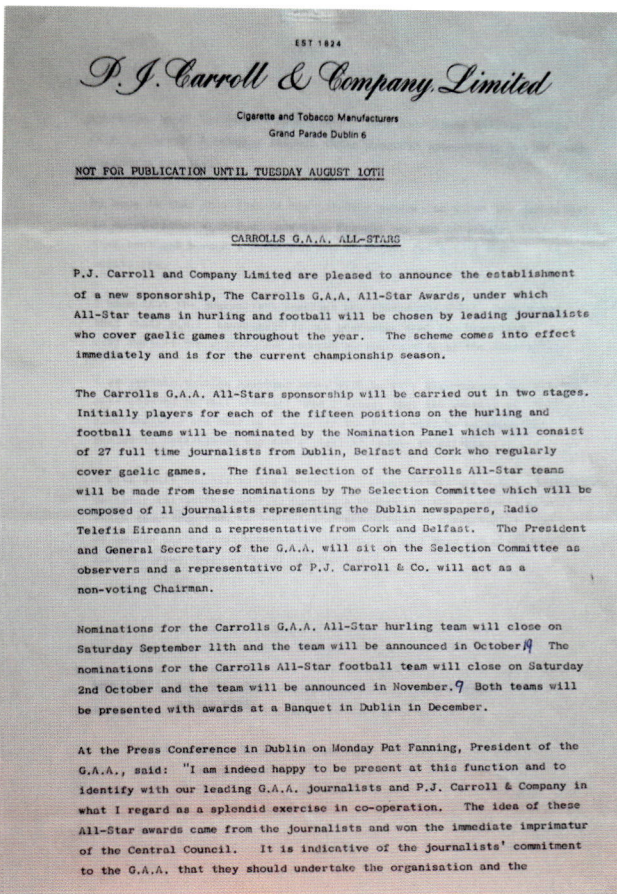
Press release announcing the All-Star scheme in 1971

Added to that was the complication that the sponsor in question was a tobacco company. Looking back now, you would expect this to be a stumbling block. However, in the early 1970s, smoking was still considered a glamorous pastime. The associated health risks were only emerging, so the Carrolls involvement did not raise much concern at the outset.

The journalists outlined in their proposal that, "as sponsorship from Carrolls would be given to a scheme to be run and organised by journalists, it would not embarrass the Central Council of the GAA with anyone who might not be completely favourable to sponsorship".

As the players would not benefit directly from the scheme, the GAA felt they could support it. "It was the first major sponsorship the GAA ever embraced", reported Paddy Downey in *The Irish Times*.

A TIME FOR CHANGE

The timing turned out to be just right for the four journalists who had a great ally in the GAA's Director General, Seán Ó Síocháin, then known as the 'Ard Rúnaí'. He knew that Irish society was changing rapidly in the early 1970s and that the GAA needed to evolve with it. The Association had already taken an enormous step forward just weeks earlier when the controversial Rule 27 was abolished at the annual GAA Congress in Belfast.

Rule 27, otherwise known as 'The Ban', had been in place since the founding of the organisation in 1884. The rule banned GAA members from playing, promoting, or watching so-called foreign games. GAA scouts regularly attended local soccer and rugby games to report if Association members were playing or even in attendance. It was an ongoing cause of disquiet among GAA players.

Lifting the ban represented a significant shift for the GAA towards a more inclusive organisation. Gone were the days where large crowds at matches could be taken for granted. Mobility was increasing with car ownership and, as a result, people had more choice when it came to their free time. Interest in other sports and different types of entertainment was growing too, as more homes around the country got access to their first television.

"Our games are in competition with other games and pastimes and the battle for the allegiance of young people is being waged with mounting intensity", said GAA President Pat Fanning at the time. The McNamee Report would later express the need for "improved contacts with the press, coverage of Gaelic games on television, and publication of year books and youth magazines". In supporting the new All-Star scheme, the Association had already taken a step to strengthen its relationship with the journalists.

FIRST ALL-STAR MEETING

The first All-Star meeting took place on 28th July 1971 in the Carrolls headquarters on Grand Parade in Dublin. It was attended by Pat Heneghan and the four journalists.

Together they worked out the details of the new scheme and established three committees:

1. A Steering Committee to govern the scheme - consisting of the four founding journalists along with Pat Heneghan and Seán Ó Síocháin.
2. A Nomination Panel to nominate players for selection as All-Stars – consisting of 26 recognised GAA writers from the national newspapers, RTÉ and the BBC.
3. A Selection Panel to select the final 15 players in each code – consisting of 11 GAA writers who were fully involved in the Championship season.

Mick Dunne was appointed Secretary of the Steering Committee, a role he held for the next 25 years. At the press conference to announce the All-Stars in August, GAA President Pat Fanning pledged the Association's support. "My hope is that the idea of All-Star Awards will take root and become a permanent and important feature of GAA activities".

All-Star Gazing

Paddy Downey expressed his optimism too. "A plan has been formulated to select Ireland teams annually in hurling and football and this time it is virtually certain to become a permanent and glamorous feature of the Irish sporting scene".

GLITZ AND GLAMOUR

From the outset, the journalists wanted to establish a prestigious and glamorous award scheme, and this aligned perfectly with Pat Heneghan's way of working. When the All-Star awards became a reality later that year, it was clear that the sponsors would spare no expense.

Carrolls commissioned Gary Trimble, the country's leading sculptor, to design a unique All-Star trophy for the chosen players.

A formal banquet was held that December to present the All-Star trophies to the players. The Taoiseach of the day, Mr. Jack Lynch, was invited as the guest of honour. Pat Heneghan is proud of the fact that the All-Star banquet was the first black-tie event ever held in the GAA.

This new level of glamour caused great excitement, and GAA people were pleased that the games could be viewed differently by those outside the sport. Some were surprised and even intimidated by the splendour. Pat recalled the reaction of the traditional musicians who came to entertain the guests, "they initially refused to go into the banquet hall when they saw everyone formally dressed. I had to persuade them that the assembled guests were just a regular GAA crowd!".

Seán Ó Síocháin congratulated the organisers after the first All-Star banquet. In a letter to Mick Dunne, he said the scheme had "added fresh lustre to the games". Pat Heneghan recalled fondly how much Ó Síocháin had contributed to the establishment of the All-Stars. "He was friendly, gentle and helpful, he was one of the people".

JOURNALISTS' VISION

The founding journalists had finally done something about their long-held wish to thank the players. The players were delighted with the recognition they received, as it was a new experience for them, but they also valued the opinion of those journalists. In fact, many of the All-Stars selected in the early 1970s spoke about the special relationship that existed then between the journalists and players.

"The All-Star award meant a lot as there was a lot of respect for the journalists at that time", said Liam Sammon. "They were at every match and wrote about the game itself and how it was played, rather than focusing on controversies". Eugene Mulligan recalled fondly that "the journalists were your friends in those days. You would even call to their house. I played handball with Mick Dunne in San Francisco on the first tour in 1972 - that wouldn't happen now". Donie O'Sullivan shared similar sentiments, "in those days you could trust the journalists. You got to know them".

Letter from Seán Ó Síocháin after the first banquet

Seán Ó Síocháin

For Pat Henderson: "Those journalists were a very honourable bunch of people. They would rarely let you down by printing something you didn't want them to". Martin Quigley recalled, "Pádraig Puirséal was a gentleman, Mick Dunne too. You felt very comfortable when they were interviewing you".

Mikey Sheehy shared his views on the four founders. "Starting the All-Stars was massive foresight by those first journalists in 1971".

COMRADES IN ARMS

So, who were the men who started the All-Star scheme in 1971? First and foremost, they were great friends; described affectionately by *Irish Times* journalist Keith Duggan many years later as "comrades in arms". Four different characters, from a pioneer to a whiskey lover, who got to know each other during the 1960s travelling the country together, reporting on matches for their newspapers.

Paddy Downey was born in 1929, in Goleen in West Cork. On moving to Dublin in the 1950s, he became editor of *The Gaelic Echo* magazine before joining *The Irish Times* in 1957. He was appointed Gaelic games correspondent in 1962, he later became Gaelic games editor and continued in that role until his retirement in 1994.

A tall man, he walked with a stick, having suffered from polio as a child. He was famed for his bow ties and suave demeanour. *Irish Times* sports editor Gerry Noone painted the following picture of his colleague: "with paper in typewriter, catchline and by-line already scribed, he'd sit back, light pipe and puff away while masterminding those silky words that made your All-Ireland hurling and football finals so memorable". He died in 2013, aged 84.

Mick Dunne was born in Clonaslee, Co. Laois in 1929. He began his career in *The Irish Press* in 1947, initially working in the library before being appointed Gaelic Games correspondent 10 years later. Following his move to RTÉ in 1970, he became a well-known voice on radio and television. Each Saturday he presented Gaelic Stadium; the first Gaelic games preview programme shown on RTÉ.

A perfectionist in every aspect of his work, Mick had in-depth knowledge of hurling and football. His love of American sport grew from his early trips there in the 1960s, covering GAA matches. In an interview with Seán Moran many years later, Paddy Downey credited Mick with the original idea of the GAA All-Stars. He died in 2002, aged 73.

Sports journalist and novelist Pádraig Puirséal was born in Mooncoin, Co. Kilkenny in 1914. He graduated from UCD with an MA in English literature and worked initially in Cahill's publishing

John D Hickey, Pat Heneghan, Mick Dunne and Paddy Downey on the occasion of Hickey's retirement from the Steering Committee in 1976

All-Star Gazing

Pádraig Puirséal and Úna Bean Uí Phuirséil on Fifth Avenue, New York during the All-Star tour of 1977. Úna was President of the Camogie Association at the time

house. During that time, he wrote four novels under the English version of his name, Patrick Purcell. Renowned for his knowledge of GAA history, he spent a brief spell in *The Irish Independent* before moving to *The Irish Press* in 1953, becoming that paper's GAA and Coursing correspondent in 1970. In 1950, he founded and published *The Gaelic Sportsman* newspaper, which was dedicated to reporting on all aspects of Gaelic Games.

At the time of his death in 1979, he was working on a book called *The GAA in its Time*. The book was subsequently completed by his sister Mary and published in 1982.

John D Hickey was the veteran of the pack. A proud Tipperary man, he was born in Templemore in 1911, before his family moved to Thurles, where he attended Thurles CBS. His first job was with *The Tipperary Star* newspaper. An opportunity with *The Irish Press* brought him to Dublin. He later moved to *The Irish Independent*, where he combined sub-editing with writing duties. From 1962 he began writing exclusively on GAA affairs.

After his retirement, he enjoyed spending time in his garden in Churchtown. He died in June 1977, just two months after his 66th birthday.

ALL-STAR FOUNDERS HONOURED

Throughout their careers, the journalists devoted considerable time and energy to ensure that the All-Star scheme maintained its importance and relevance year after year.

At the 25th All-Star banquet in 1995, the two surviving founders Paddy Downey and Mick Dunne were honoured by the GAA with a special All-Star trophy sculpted by Jarlath Daly. He recalls the commission. "Those All-Star trophies were unique as they are the only ones I ever created that combined both a hurler and footballer together".

All-Star founders Mick Dunne and Paddy Downey are presented with a specially commissioned All-Star trophy by GAA Ard-Stiúrthóir Liam Mulvihill and President Jack Boothman in 1995.

The First All-Star Teams

Players from seven different counties made up the first All-Star hurling team: four each from All-Ireland finalists Tipperary and Kilkenny, two players from Cork and Limerick and one from Dublin, Galway and Offaly.

In football the county representation on the first All-Star team showed a wider spread. The two All-Ireland finalists Offaly and Galway received four awards each, while one player was selected from each of Antrim, Cork, Down, Kerry, Mayo, Meath and Sligo.

carrolls GAA allstars
1971 HURLING TEAM

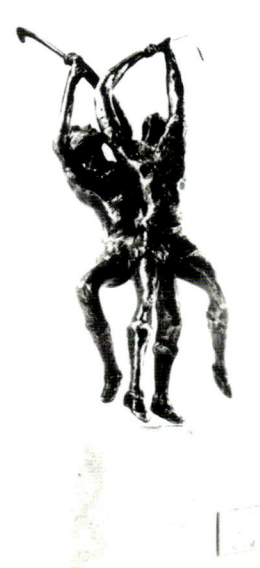

Damien Martin (Offaly) — Tony Maher (Cork) — Pat Hartigan (Limerick) — Jim Treacy (Kilkenny) — Tadhg O'Connor (Tipperary)

Mick Roche (Tipperary) — Martin Coogan (Kilkenny) — John Connolly (Galway) — Frank Cummins (Kilkenny) — Francis Loughnane (Tipperary)

Michael Keating (Tipperary) — Eddie Keher (Kilkenny) — Mick Bermingham (Dublin) — Ray Cummins (Cork) — Eamonn Cregan (Limerick)

The Carroll's All-Star Hurling team in 1971

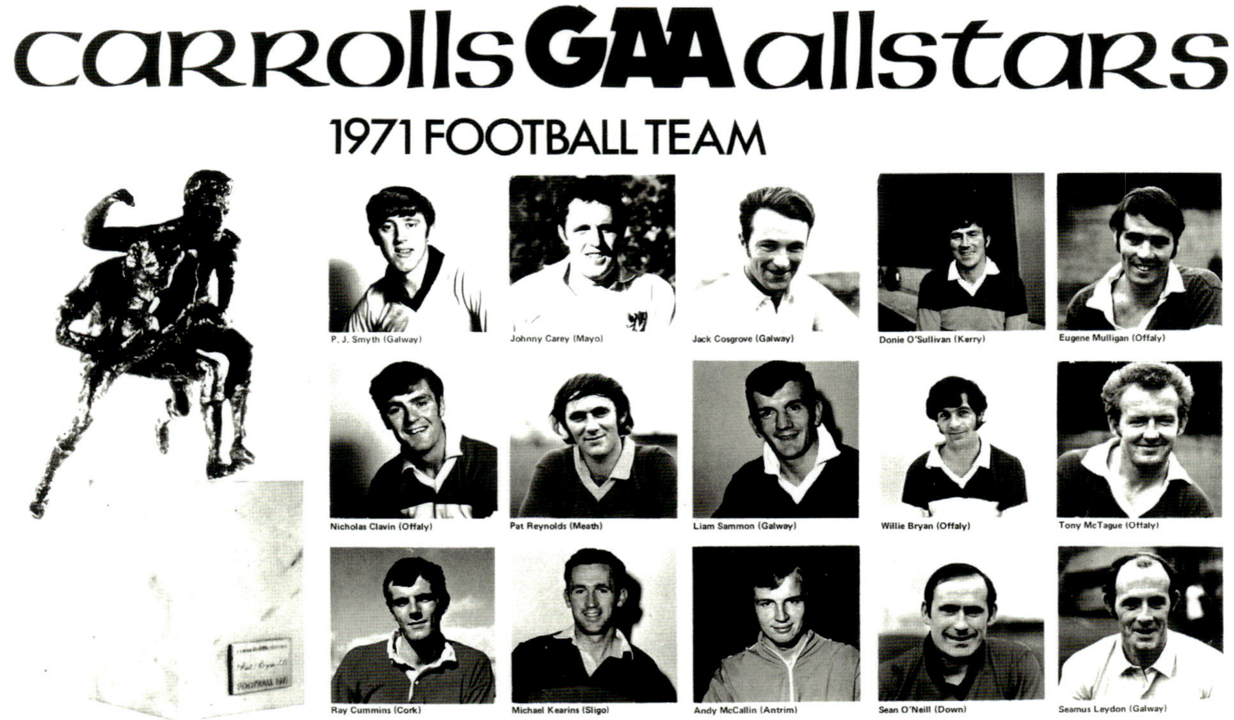

carrolls GAA allstars
1971 FOOTBALL TEAM

P. J. Smyth (Galway) — Johnny Carey (Mayo) — Jack Cosgrove (Galway) — Donie O'Sullivan (Kerry) — Eugene Mulligan (Offaly)

Nicholas Clavin (Offaly) — Pat Reynolds (Meath) — Liam Sammon (Galway) — Willie Bryan (Offaly) — Tony McTague (Offaly)

Ray Cummins (Cork) — Michael Kearins (Sligo) — Andy McCallin (Antrim) — Sean O'Neill (Down) — Seamus Leydon (Galway)

The Carroll's All-Star Football team in 1971

All-Star Gazing

When the first All-Star teams were announced in autumn 1971, there was little build-up or anticipation. At that stage, not many people had heard of the new awards scheme and, unlike today, the list of nominated players was not published in advance.

The hurling All-Star team was announced on Monday October 18th on RTÉ television and radio sports bulletins. The team was published the next day in the national newspapers. Two weeks later the first All-Star football team was announced in the same way.

Only 29 players were honoured that first year because dual player Ray Cummins was selected on both the All-Star hurling and football teams. This fantastic achievement has never been replicated during the 50-years of the scheme.

In the first year, many of those selected had no idea that they were in the running for an award. In today's world of instant communication and media build-up, it is fascinating to hear how the first All-Stars heard the news.

Tony Maher says, "I heard I was getting an All-Star award and I asked, what's that? I was told that there was a new award being given out, but I didn't know what it was at that stage".

Hurler Mick Bermingham, Dublin's first All-Star said, "I didn't take too much notice of the nomination initially because we didn't really know what this new scheme was. We definitely didn't realise what it would become".

Pat Reynolds recalled, "I was in the pub on the Monday night and some fella told me I got an award. I said, an award for what? I hadn't heard about the All-Stars at that stage". He added, "in those days there would be lots of different Irish selections picked for various exhibition matches so you didn't take any notice".

Irish Press **newspaper clipping of the Football All-Star announcement from Jack Cosgrove's personal file**

Jack Cosgrove said, "We had lost the All-Ireland final in 1971 so an All-Star was the last thing on our minds. It was new so there were no previous winners. You were selected in your position in those days. The team was announced on a Monday night on TV after the news in the sports section. Just a listing of the names, no photos".

Damien Martin found out about his All-Star selection on his return from a trip to New York. "When I landed at Shannon Airport, I bought a newspaper and that's when I found out I had won an All-Star".

THE FIRST ALL-STAR

The prestige of receiving an All-Star grew quickly over the next few years. But who has the honour of being the first-ever All-Star? The hurling team was the first to be announced, so the record books show that goalkeeper Damien Martin was the first All-Star.

However, it could be argued that Offaly footballer Eugene Mulligan was the first All-Star as he was nominated unanimously for the right half-back position. Teammate and All-Star, Fr. Nick Clavin recalled, "everyone knew, once the nominations came out, that Eugene had won an All-Star".

As there were 26 journalists on the Nomination Panel in 1971, this was an impressive achievement. For other positions that year, up to 13 players were nominated. "It was amazing to be the only name nominated by such a large number of journalists", Eugene told us. "But Damien is the first All-Star".

Cork's Ray Cummins is still the only player to be selected on both the hurling and football All-Star teams in the same year

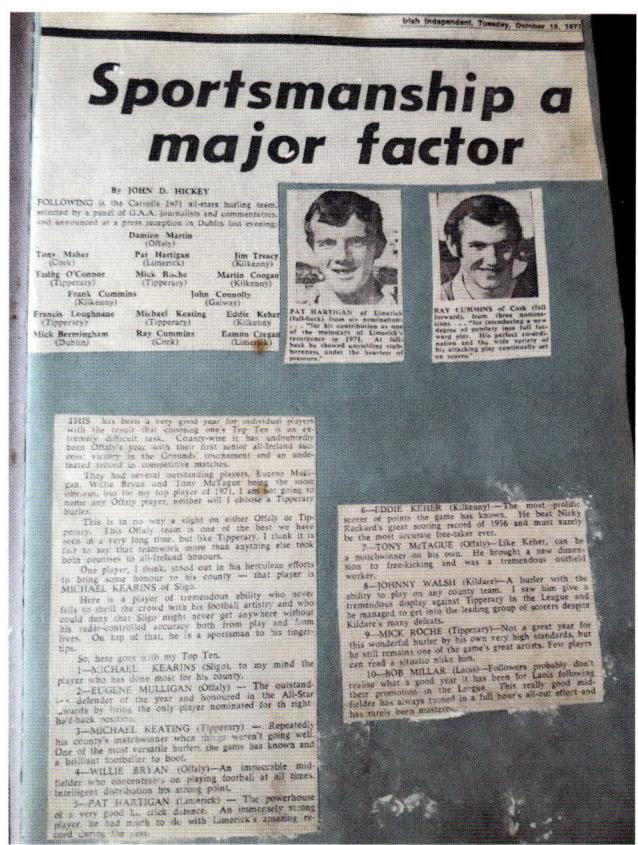

Announcement of the first All-Star teams in the *Irish Independent* from Pat Hartigan's personal file. *Note: the photos and names are mixed up!*

Decades later Cian Lynch examines the first Carrolls All-Star poster hanging in Quinn's De Bucket bar, County Limerick

Galway football goalkeeper PJ Smyth added to the debate when he pointed out that the footballers were first to be presented with their trophies on the night of the inaugural banquet. So, he takes pride in the fact that he was the first recipient of an All-Star award.

Eugene magnanimously defers to Damien but let us leave the final word to Fr. Nick. "Of course, it's Eugene Mulligan – Eugene was chosen by God!".

ALL-STAR POSTERS

As part of the marketing for the first All-Star scheme, the Carrolls PR department produced a poster with a picture of all the All-Stars.

Photographs of players were not widely available in 1971, so the sponsors sent a local photographer to each player's home. Taken in advance of the team announcements, the photographers gave nothing away, insisting that they were visiting all the nominees.

In fact, for many of those first All-Stars, the arrival of the local photographer was the first they heard about being nominated.

Pat Hartigan remembers it clearly, "I was out farming when a telegram came to the Creamery in Drumbarra asking if I was available for a photograph. A local photographer arrived but he wouldn't say who else he was visiting". Pat was reluctant to mention the photographer to the other nominees in case they hadn't heard anything.

Jack Cosgrove recalled the freelance photographer arriving in a big car to take the photo. "He assured us that he was taking everyone's photo, that it wasn't to be taken as an indication that I had won".

Michael 'Babs' Keating said, "the All-Star selection committee called to say they were sending the photographer. I remember he expected me to have a Tipperary jersey to wear". Babs didn't have one as players were not allowed to keep their jerseys at the time. "So, I had to pull on a Munster jersey instead".

However, Babs was not alone. A check of that first poster shows the All-Stars sporting a selection of county jerseys, provincial jerseys and regular clothes.

For Babs it wasn't just the jersey that caused problems. He made a special trip to the dentist the morning the photograph was being taken, to get a temporary crown for his tooth as he had lost the crown in a match the previous weekend. It was important to look good for the posters.

John Connolly also had concerns after picking up a facial injury in an inter-factory match the previous weekend. On his return from Kilkenny, his mother said, "someone was here from the All-Stars to take your photo and he's staying overnight so he can come back again tomorrow.

"I was horrified as my face was black and blue from the match. So, I ended up turning sideways for the photo so that the bruising wasn't visible. If you look at the poster, you will see me doing my best impersonation of Pádraig Pearse – the iconic sideways pose!".

All-Star Gazing

The first Carroll's All-Star poster

50 Years of the GAA All-Stars

The players were right to be concerned about how they looked. At the All-Star banquet in December, poster-size versions of the photos hung around the banquet hall. Jimmy Barry Murphy recalled, "the lads got a great kick out of seeing posters of themselves. I remember lads taking them home on the train to Cork the next day".

The All-Star posters included a citation for each player, written by Mick Dunne, which outlined the reason for their selection. The individual recognition meant a lot to the players, as demonstrated by Jimmy, who in 2018 could still remember his citation from 1973, when he was selected for his first All-Star. 'For the grace and skill of his football and his ability to take and make scores from broken play'.

Peter McGinnity recalled fondly, "the posters were a huge thing. The All-Star banquet was great, but the poster lives on forever! It was the public view of the All-Star award. Imagine walking in somewhere and seeing your photo on the poster.

That was the big publicity for the All-Stars more so than the banquet itself".

Adding to the glamour of the scheme, the All-Star posters have been produced every year since. In years gone by, many GAA fans, young and old, collected them, and they adorned the walls of pubs and schools around the country. Three-time All-Star Greg Blaney recalled, "growing up in the 1970s, I had about four or five posters on my bedroom wall. I could tell you how many All-Star awards each county won each year".

A collection of the printed All-Star posters from 1971 to 2016 is on display in the Lár na Páirce museum in Thurles, Co. Tipperary. Electronic versions can be viewed in the GAA museum, and the posters can be purchased from the GAA Museum website.

In 2017, new sponsors PwC introduced a dedicated All-Star app which provides a digital listing of the All-Star teams plus lots of additional statistics.

Cian Lynch features in the 50th All-Star poster published in 2021

All-Star Gazing

LAVISH LUNCH IN CARROLLS

The first All-Star banquet took place in the InterContinental Hotel (known to most as Jurys Hotel) in Dublin in December 1971. On the day of the banquet, the players were also invited to a lavish lunch at the Carrolls headquarters. As this was the first time the All-Star teams got together, there was huge interest from the assembled press and photographers.

Each player was given green playing gear for the All-Star tour to America the following spring. Jack Cosgrove remembers, "The green togs and jerseys were given out in Carrolls at the lunch and a team photo was taken. We felt like leprechauns in the all-green strip".

Fr. Nick Clavin said, "we didn't get any boots with the kit, so if you look at that photo, half of us, the ones in the back row, are in our stocking feet. Imagine a team photo

A unique All-Star poster on the wall of St Patrick's Classical School in Navan, honouring the school's six All-Stars including school principal, Colm O'Rourke

The first photo of the Carroll's All-Star Football team in Carroll's in December 1971
Back L to R: Seamus Leydon, Pat Reynolds, Nick Clavin, Ray Cummins, Jack Cosgrove, Donie O'Sullivan, Liam Sammon, Willie Bryan
Front L to R: Eugene Mulligan, Tony McTague, Michael Kearins, Johnny Carey, PJ Smyth, Seán O'Neill, Andy McCallin

and you are standing in your stocking feet! We got a lot of slagging for that photo over the years".

But despite the lack of boots, the players were delighted to receive the free gear. Francis Loughnane explained, "in those days we didn't even get to keep our county jersey. In fact, you would be in trouble with the County Board if you didn't return the jersey to the pile in the middle of the dressing room after a match".

Eddie Keher remembers, "This was huge because we never got anything in those days". Frank Cummins added, "you'd nearly be shot for trying to keep a Kilkenny jersey back then". Johnny Carey said, "getting the All-Star gear – it was the first time I got anything free from the GAA".

Many of the players spoke about the first-class hospitality at that lunch in Carrolls. In fact, listening to the stories of how much they enjoyed themselves, you would wonder how the 29 All-Stars made it to the banquet later that evening!

FIRST ALL-STAR BANQUET

The inaugural banquet was well promoted in advance by Carrolls. Frank Cummins recalled the build-up. "When my invitation arrived, my brother said, 'you are getting so much publicity about the All-Stars, it's like you are getting an Oscar'".

Pat Hartigan and Éamonn Cregan with Pat's first All-Star jersey

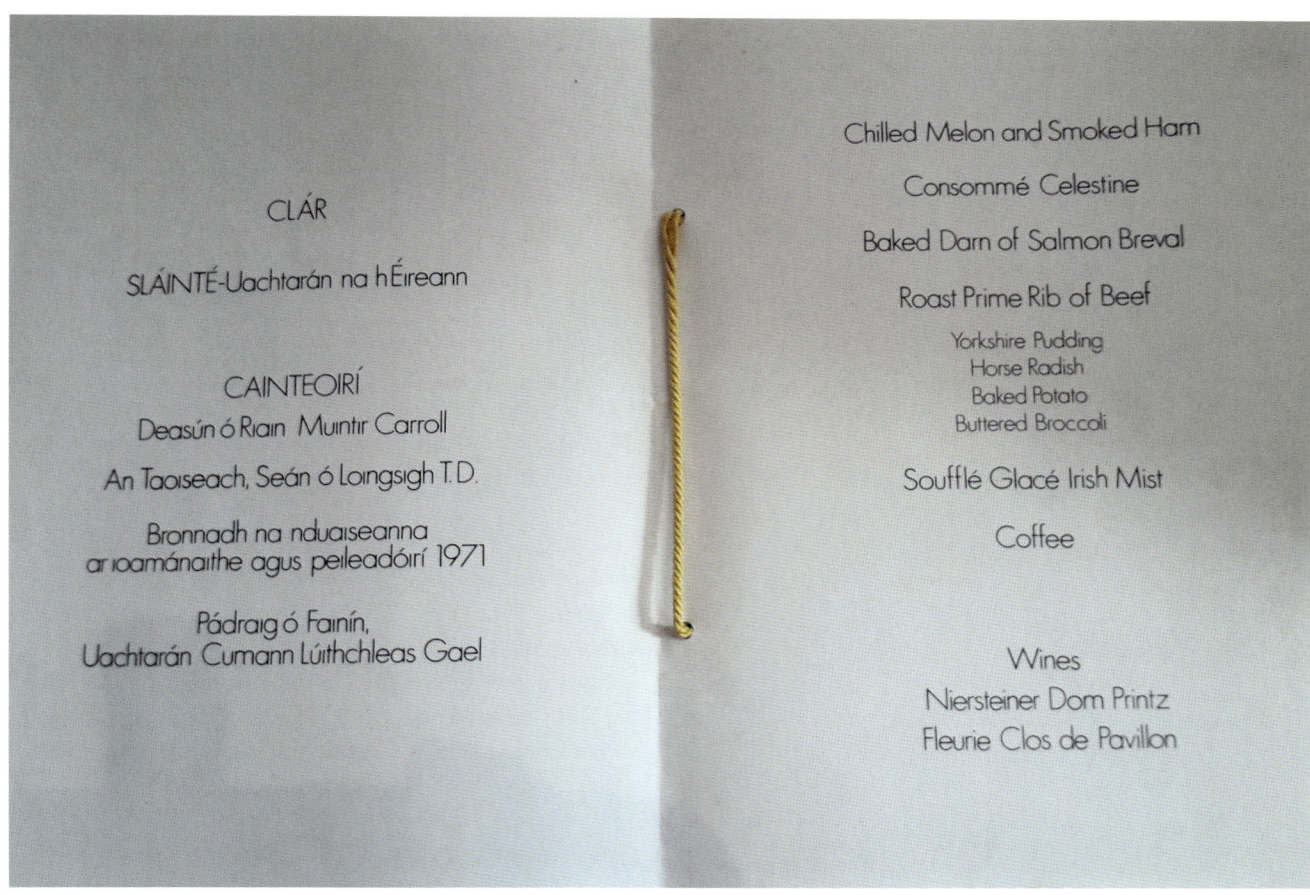

The Menu from the first All-Star banquet in 1971

All-Star Gazing

An Taoiseach Jack Lynch poses with the first teams of hurling and football All-Stars after presenting them with their trophies.

Letter from An Taoiseach Jack Lynch

ROINN AN TAOISIGH
DEPARTMENT OF THE TAOISEACH
BAILE ÁTHA CLIATH 2
DUBLIN 2

22 September 1971

Dear Mick,

Thank you for inviting me to the Carroll's G.A.A. All-Stars Banquet on Wednesday December 15. I am glad to accept but, as this is a Dáil night and in view of the uncertainty of present events, you will understand that I must accept with reservations.

Yours sincerely,

Jack Lynch

Mr. Mick Dunne,

Éamonn Cregan remembered, "The evening of the banquet was something special".

The All-Star Steering Committee did not confirm the date for the first banquet until An Taoiseach Jack Lynch was consulted, as he was to be the guest of honour. Mick Dunne wrote to him explaining that, "December 15th has been booked, but should you not be free on the night mentioned, but were available on another date before Christmas, we would endeavour to make arrangements for a banquet that would fit in with your engagements".

Lynch replied, "as this is a Dáil night and in view of the uncertainty of present events, you will understand that I must accept with reservations".

allstars

50 Years of the GAA All-Stars

The 'uncertainty of present events' was a reference to the ongoing conflict in Northern Ireland (known at the time as The Troubles). Mick Dunne goes on to wish him "every success for a fruitful conclusion to the weighty affairs of State in which you are immersed at the present time".

Jack Lynch soon confirmed his attendance and to the players' delight, he presented the first All-Star trophies. His presence was significant as Jack Lynch was a multiple All-Ireland winner himself, having won six All-Ireland medals for Cork in both football and hurling in the 1940s.

Jack Cosgrove recalled, "Jack Lynch was a member of the club I played for in Cork (Glen Rovers), so he had an extra few words for me when he presented the trophy". For Pat Heneghan an abiding memory of that first banquet is, "Jack Lynch going around to every single table to shake hands with every single guest".

Jack Lynch was the guest of honour at many of the early banquets. The fact he had a special connection with the GAA and the All-Stars was in no doubt. In December 1979, he announced his resignation as Taoiseach, just two days before the All-Star banquet, which he was due to attend.

Jim Whitty of Bank of Ireland recalled, "there was big media hype about the resignation. He was shafted and wasn't going to stay around. So, we didn't know if he would still come to the banquet". Come he did and he was greeted by a standing ovation. "The wheel has come full circle", he told

Mickey Kearins with the All-Star trophy he won in 1971

Seán O'Neill with his first All-Star trophy from 1971

the assembled guests. "At my last official function, I'm back with my own ….the GAA".

Jim continued, "Each year, Jack would ask myself and Mick (Dunne) around for tea in his house a few days before the banquet. I would have a couple of whiskeys with Jack, and Mick would drink his Diet Coke. That was access to a Taoiseach that no other scheme had".

Lynch might have been selected for many All-Stars himself had the scheme been in place during his playing career. The All-Star Steering Committee honoured him in 1981, when he was the second recipient of the All-Time hurling award.

So what did it mean to players to be selected on the All-Star team in 1971? Eddie Keher put it quite simply, "It was massive".

At 20 years of age, Andy McCallin was the youngest player to receive the award. He remembers lots of excitement and being interviewed by RTÉ. "I was overawed going down to Dublin to the banquet. The only other player I knew was Seán O'Neill". A keen hurler too, Andy said, "I was probably most excited about meeting the hurlers".

Andy brought his fiancée, now wife, to the banquet. "We weren't married yet, so we were given separate rooms. Two big suites in the Intercontinental Hotel". On the bed in each room was a carton of 200 Carrolls cigarettes. Andy's fiancée didn't smoke, but Andy did, so his joy of being selected as an All-Star was boosted by receiving 400 free cigarettes. "The only downside was that I couldn't bring more people to the banquet. It would have meant a lot to me to bring my father".

After an inter-county career that started in the late 1950s, Seán O'Neill had received many awards by the time the first All-Star team was picked in 1971. Of the All-Star award, he says, "it was the ultimate accolade. It had much higher value than the Cú Chulainn awards I had previously received. When the word came out about the new scheme, you didn't want to be left out". Pat Hartigan agreed, "getting an All-Star was the ultimate".

Ray Cummins was never a big fan of individual awards, but when it came to the All-Stars, "I managed to convince myself that this was okay! It was special because you felt that you were part of a national team".

For Éamonn Cregan it was fantastic because "we had lost the Munster final that year, so it was a great boost. After the All-Ireland, it was the most important thing".

"In those days you didn't expect much, so we were honoured", said Séamus Leyden. Johnny Carey concurred, "there was a novelty about it all".

Willie Bryan felt that the All-Stars, "was a terrific idea. Any fella that said he didn't want to win one is lying".

Mickey Kearins explained the significance of the All-Star. "It was a great honour, especially for a player like me. At the time, we (Sligo) were winning nothing".

Liam Sammon felt that the scheme brought the GAA to a new level. "There had been previous awards schemes, but this was very upmarket. It created a lot of excitement because of the newness of it all". Donie O'Sullivan, a recipient of a Cú Chulainn award in the 1960s, said, "the All-Star banquet was a huge contrast to the previous awards dinner in the Gresham Hotel".

To this day, some players are still trying to figure out why they were selected on that first All-Star team. Andy McCallin attributes his surprise inclusion to playing for Ulster alongside Seán O'Neill in that year's Railway Cup final. "Seán was absolutely out of this world. I think that performance won me my All-Star".

Distribution of Awards by County (1971 - 2020)

HURLING ALL-STARS

County	Awards
Kilkenny	188
Cork	112
Tipperary	104
Galway	96
Limerick	64
Clare	53
Offaly	42
Waterford	42
Wexford	33
Dublin	8
Antrim	5
Down	1
Laois	1
Westmeath	1

FOOTBALL ALL-STARS

Kerry	145
Dublin	139
Cork	64
Mayo	51
Meath	49
Tyrone	49
Galway	38
Donegal	34
Offaly	30
Derry	27
Armagh	24
Down	23
Roscommon	15
Kildare	15
Monaghan	13
Cavan	5
Westmeath	5
Laois	5
Fermanagh	4
Sligo	4
Tipperary	4
Leitrim	2
Wexford	1
Clare	1
Wicklow	1
Antrim	1
Louth	1

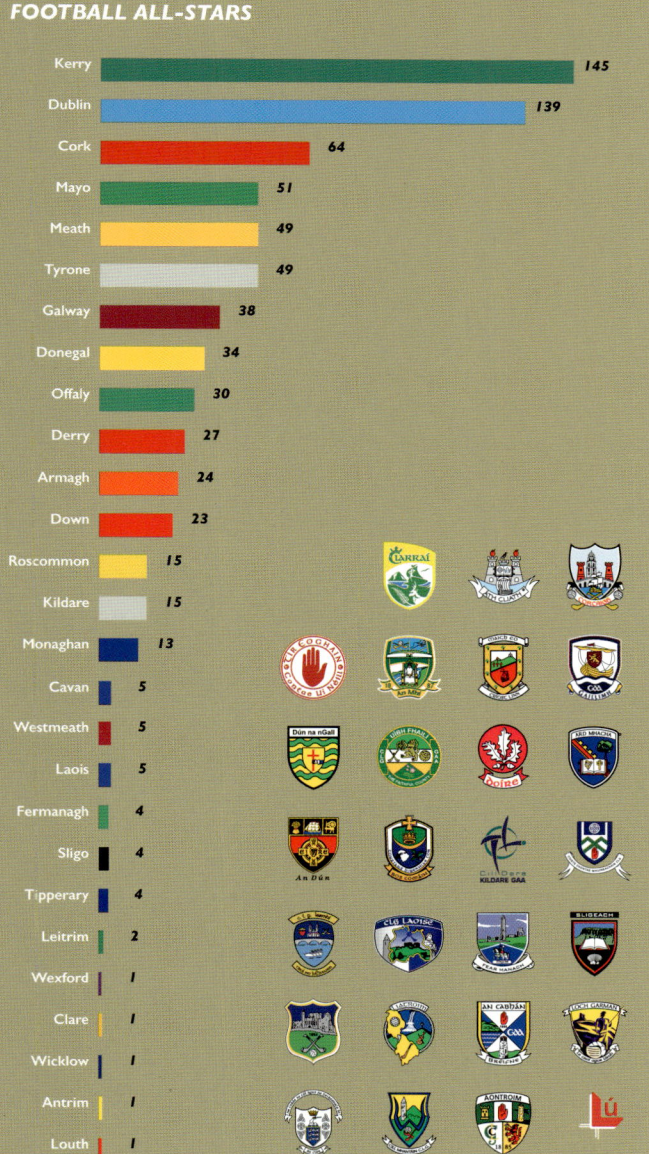

Who Are The All-Stars?

Since 1971, 1,500 All-Star awards have been presented to 799 players (369 hurlers and 430 footballers) with many receiving multiple awards. As four players have been honoured in both codes the actual number of players selected as All-Stars over the 50-year period is 795.

A player's All-Star record places his career achievements in context. When players are introduced in the media or at an event, the number of All-Stars they have received comes second only to their All-Ireland medals.

Aidan O'Shea said, "I grew up hearing the All-Star folklore. My dad, from Kerry, was like an encyclopaedia. He would always be referencing players by, 'he won five All-Irelands and three All-Stars'. It was ingrained; the awareness of all the people before me who had done it, so I definitely wanted to win All-Stars".

"I am very proud of my All-Stars. I am always introduced first as an All-Ireland winner, second as a five-time All-Star winner", said Tomás Ó Sé.

Anthony Tohill summed it up, "Once you have it that's what you are – you are an All-Star. When I won my first in 1992, my midfield partner Brian McGilligan, an All-Star himself, said to me 'you are a marked man now, Tohill'. I thought it was a really good way of saying it: the journalists had marked me as a sufficient standard to be an All-Star, opposition teams now started paying more attention to me in games. For my own teammates, and our own supporters, I was a marked man because every time I went out to play, they expected me to perform like an All-Star".

Fifty years of All-Star records make for fascinating reading for anyone with a statistical mind. Here is a summary of these records. The full list of players nominated and selected since 1971 is provided later in the book.

Players from 14 counties have been honoured with All-Star hurling awards, while players from 27 counties have been honoured in football. While Longford and Carlow have had no players selected on All-Star teams, both counties received many football nominations over the years, and Carlow's Paddy Quirke was nominated three times in hurling. In 2013 London GAA was recognised for its progress in that year's football championship when Lorcan Mulvey was included in the list of All-Star nominees.

All-Star Gazing

Kilkenny tops the All-Star hurling list with 188 awards, while Kerry players have received the most football awards, 145. When the All-Star records for both codes are combined, dual counties Cork, Galway and Offaly jump right up the honours list. Offaly ranks seventh in the overall All-Star awards table, a strong position for a small county.

THE HURLING ALL-STARS

The list of hurling All-Stars is led by Kilkenny and Tipperary players. A snapshot of players with the most awards (five or more) is given below, the complete list of all hurling All-Stars is provided later in the book.

Player	No. of Awards	County
Henry Shefflin	11	Kilkenny
DJ Carey	9	Kilkenny
Tommy Walsh	9	Kilkenny
JJ Delaney	7	Kilkenny
Noel Skehan	7	Kilkenny
Nicholas English	6	Tipperary
Eoin Kelly	6	Tipperary
Pádraic Maher	6	Tipperary
Joe McKenna	6	Limerick
Jimmy Barry Murphy	5	Cork
Joe Canning	5	Galway
Joe Cooney	5	Galway
Brendan Cummins	5	Tipperary
John Fenton	5	Cork
Peter Finnerty	5	Galway
Pat Hartigan	5	Limerick
Ger Henderson	5	Kilkenny
Joe Hennessy	5	Kilkenny
Eddie Keher	5	Kilkenny
John Mullane	5	Waterford
Tony O'Sullivan	5	Cork
TJ Reid	5	Kilkenny
Daithí Burke	5	Galway

Henry Shefflin is the most decorated hurling All-Star with 11 awards. Eight of those awards came in consecutive seasons, an achievement that reflects his consistency as a hurler. He was also voted Hurler of the Year by his peers three times during that period.

"2000, the first year I won, was a rollercoaster. I was still only a young fella. I felt like a boy and winning the All-Star meant I was joining the other great players who had won it. They were men. I was up there with Anthony Daly, Johnny Dooley thinking, I have arrived. Then in 2002 winning the All-Star gave me a great lift as I was quite down after losing the All-Ireland. I remember hearing I had won on the Wednesday, and it made me believe, we can come back".

Henry continued, "winning each year, you are kind of in a flow. You have tunnel vision and you come home and put the trophy away. But when you are finished it takes pride of place. I started to appreciate the awards more towards the end. I was aware that I was catching up with DJ and Pat Spillane. Towards the end of my career, I knew that I was running out of time! One of my fondest memories was coming home on the Saturday after winning the first award. I can distinctly remember stopping outside the door of my parents' house, taking the All-Star out of the Vodafone bag, and bringing it in to my parents. They were so proud. I felt I was giving something back to them after all they had done for me".

Henry shared how in later years he and his wife Deirdre would drive back down the night of the banquet and have the All-Star trophy on the table the next morning for the kids.

DJ Carey has nine hurling All-Stars and held the record for many years until Henry surpassed him in 2011. Eddie Keher and Pat Hartigan, both selected on the first team in 1971, went on to receive five All-Stars in a row during the early years of the scheme.

| Henry Shefflin, the most decorated All-Star in the 50-year history of the scheme, with his collection of trophies

More recently, in 2011, Tommy Walsh joined DJ Carey on nine All-Stars. Remarkably his nine awards came in consecutive seasons from 2003 to 2011 and in five different positions: left half-forward, midfield, left full-back, left half-back and right half-back.

Four other hurlers have been selected in both defence and attack: Brian Whelahan, Ken McGrath, Michael Walsh and Brian Corcoran. The first player to achieve this was Whelahan having been chosen at full forward in 1998 as well as at right half-back in 1992, 1995 and 1999.

Henry Shefflin shares a record with Brian Corcoran for the longest year span between awards. Brian received his third All-Star in 2004, 12 years after his first in 1992.

Player	Span between Awards	First	Last
Brian Corcoran	12	1992	2004
Henry Shefflin	12	2000	2012
Frank Cummins	12	1971	1983
DJ Carey	11	1991	2002
JJ Delaney	11	2003	2014
Noel Skehan	11	1972	1983

Eoin Kelly was selected for his fifth All-Star award by the age of 24 matching Pat Hartigan's achievement in the 1970s.

THE FOOTBALL ALL-STARS

The list of football All-Stars is topped by Kerry players. A snapshot of players with the most awards is given below, the complete list of all football All-Stars is provided later in the book.

Player	No. of Awards	County
Pat Spillane	9	Kerry
Colm Cooper	8	Kerry
Mikey Sheehy	7	Kerry
Peter Canavan	6	Tyrone
Stephen Cluxton	6	Dublin
Jack O'Shea	6	Kerry
Ger Power	6	Kerry
Seán Cavanagh	5	Tyrone
John Egan	5	Kerry
John O'Keeffe	5	Kerry
John O'Leary	5	Dublin
Páidí Ó Sé	5	Kerry
Tomás Ó Sé	5	Kerry
Brian Fenton	5	Dublin

Pat Spillane is the most decorated football All-Star. He received nine awards between 1976 and 1986. Pat does not dwell on the statistics of his glittering career, however. When asked what it means to hold the football All-Star record, he replied, "I should have got another one in 1991, in my last year".

Pat's memories of being an All-Star centre on the fun had at All-Star banquets and on trips with his Kerry teammates. "Winning the All-Star comes after the All-Ireland medal, but it is the second biggest achievement. The award was special because it was: a) an individual award and b) the equivalent of winning an Oscar. For that night, or really the two days and the night of the All-Star banquet, no stone was left unturned. You were given the five-star glitz and glamour of an Oscar night".

Pat continued, "the night was special back then because it

Pat Spillane (middle row, fifth from left) lines up with his fellow All-Stars after receiving his second award in 1977

All-Star Gazing

was an occasion for the chosen few. The trophy was special too and Carrolls spared no expense on the banquets and the trips. When the Bank of Ireland took over, they continued that too".

He described how he heard the news of his second All-Star selection in 1977. "I remember that the announcement was very secretive. When I won my second All-Star, I was teaching for a year in Ballyvourney. I was supervising study and the principal came in to interrupt the class to say it had just been announced on television news that I had won an All-Star. It was always a big news story. Even the nominations generated great debate".

Pat feels that the prestige of the All-Star award has diminished somewhat, as there are more awards around now. "But back then it was huge".

Colm Cooper came close to Pat when he garnered eight All-Stars between 2002 to 2013. Jack O'Shea was presented with six awards in consecutive years. Páidí Ó Sé was selected five years in a row and more recently, Paul Flynn was awarded in four consecutive years from 2011 to 2014. Seven footballers have been honoured on All-Star teams in both defensive and attacking positions: Graham Geraghty, Ger Power, Eugene Hughes, Anthony McGurk, Paddy Moriarty, Seán Lowry and Ryan McHugh. McGurk was the first to achieve this when he was named centre half-back on the 1975 All-Star team, following his selection in the left full-forward position in 1973.

Dublin's most decorated All-Star, Stephen Cluxton, moved ahead of his fellow goalkeeper John O'Leary in 2019 when he received his sixth award. Stephen's achievement is remarkable as it spans a 17-year period from his first award in 2002 to his sixth in 2019.

Player	Span between Awards	First	Last
Stephen Cluxton	17	2002	2019
Peter Canavan	11	1994	2005
Colm Cooper	11	2002	2013
Greg Blaney	11	1983	1994
Martin Furlong	11	1972	1983
Dermot Earley Jnr	11	1998	2009
John O'Leary	11	1984	1995
Ger Power	11	1975	1986

Cluxton holds two other All-Star records; in 2019, at the age of 38, he became the oldest player ever selected on an All-Star team and he is also the football goalkeeper with the most All-Star awards. Noel Skehan holds the goalkeeping record in hurling having been recognised seven times in that position.

Stephen Cluxton receives his sixth All-Star award in 2019

THE DUAL ALL-STARS

Offaly has a rich All-Star history due to its success in both codes throughout the 1970s, 1980s and 1990s. For many years Offaly was the only county that could boast All-Star awards in every position in both hurling and football. Galway achieved the same feat in 2015. Cork players have All-Stars in all 15 hurling positions, but two further football awards are required (left half-forward and left full-forward) to complete the set.

Since the inauguration of the All-Star scheme, just four players have been selected in both codes.

Player	Combined	Hurling	Football
Jimmy Barry Murphy	7	1976 1977 1978 1983 1986	1973 1974
Ray Cummins	5	1971 1972 1977	1971 1973
Brian Murphy	4	1979 1981	1973 1976
Liam Currams	2	1981	1982

Ray Cummins holds a unique All-Star record, having been selected on both the hurling and football teams in 1971. Also, that year, Michael 'Babs' Keating was nominated in both codes and took his place on the hurling All-Star team.

Jimmy Barry Murphy is the leading dual All-Star. He excelled seven times in 13 years, with five All-Stars in hurling and two in football. "It was a huge honour to win an All-Star, almost as big as winning an All-Ireland medal. It meant a huge amount to my family too. My mother kept all the souvenirs from the All-Star banquets, the menus, the napkins, etc. And the trophies were all in her house until she died a few years ago".

Jimmy liked the fact that the selectors always tried to honour players from counties who might not have a chance to win an All-Ireland. "I thought this was great as there is a lot of luck that can influence what you win when you are playing". He added modestly, "I had plenty of success just because I was born in Cork".

The All-Star records reflect the family legacy within the GAA, and All-Stars have been awarded to brothers, twins and cousins. From the 1990s onwards, the sons of All-Stars also began to receive awards.

THE HURLING ALL-STAR BROTHERS

In hurling 29 sets of brothers have received All-Star awards. In the case of the Henderson, Dooley and Bonnar families, three brothers have been honoured. In many years two of the three brothers from each family were selected on the same All-Star team.

County	Family	Total	Brother	Year
Kilkenny	Henderson	8	Pat	1973, 1974
			Ger	1978, 1979, 1982, 1983, 1987
			John	1983
Offaly	Dooley	6	Johnny	1994, 1995, 2000
			Billy	1994, 1995
			Joe	1998
Tipperary	Bonnar	5	Colm	1988
			Conal	1989, 1991
			Cormac	1989, 1991

Leading dual All-Star Jimmy Barry Murphy (fourth from left, middle row) features in the All-Star group photo and autographs from 1978

All-Star Gazing

Colm was the first Bonnar brother to be selected in 1988. His younger brother Conal recalled the impact this had on him. "Looking at the people who had won All-Stars, you are thinking, 'they must be unbelievable people, they must be Gods, I could never win one'. They would be the people you looked up to on the All-Star posters, the likes of Ger Henderson. Then when my brother walked in with an All-Star, I thought, well, maybe I could win". He added, "I was jealous too, I was determined to win a heap of them".

County	Family	Total	Brother	Year
Kilkenny	Walsh	11	Tommy	2003, 2004, 2005, 2006, 2007, 2008, 2009, 2010, 2011
			Pádraig	2016, 2019
Galway	Canning	9	Ollie	2001, 2003, 2005, 2009
			Joe	2098, 2009, 2012, 2017, 2018
Tipperary	Kelly	8	Eoin	2001, 2002, 2004, 2005, 2006, 2010
			Paul	2002, 2005
Tipperary	Maher	8	Pádraic	2009, 2011, 2014, 2016, 2017, 2019
			Ronan	2016, 2019
Galway	Cooney	7	Joe	1985, 1986, 1987, 1989, 1990
			Jimmy	1980, 1981
Cork	Cashman	5	Tom	1977, 1978, 1983
			Jim	1990, 1991
Kilkenny	Comerford	5	Andy	1999, 2000
			Martin	2002, 2003, 2006
Kilkenny	Fennelly	5	Liam	1983, 1985, 1987, 1992
			Ger	1983
Clare	Lohan	5	Brian	1995, 1996, 1997, 2000
			Frank	1999
Kilkenny	O'Connor	5	Willie	1992, 1997, 1998, 2000
			Eddie	1993
Cork	O'Connor	5	Jerry	2004, 2005, 2006
			Ben	2005, 2008
Wexford	Quigley	5	Martin	1973, 1974, 1975, 1976
			John	1974
Kilkenny	Fennelly	5	Michael	2010, 2011, 2015
			Colin	2014, 2019
Tipperary	McGrath	4	Noel	2009, 2010, 2019
			John	2016
Cork	Ó hAilpín	4	Seán Óg	2003, 2004, 2005
			Setanta	2003
Tipperary	Ryan	4	Bobby	1986, 1988, 1989
			Aidan	1987
Waterford	Shanahan	4	Dan	2004, 2006, 2007
			Maurice	2015
Galway	Connolly	3	John	1971, 1979
			Joe	1980
Galway	Mannion	3	Cathal	2015
			Pádraic	2017, 2018
Wexford	Doran	2	Colm	1973
			Tony	1976

The three Bonnar brothers, Conal, Cormac and Colm, with their All-Star memorabilia – trophies, jackets and jerseys

Martin Quigley got four All-Stars in-a-row from 1973 and when his brother John was selected in 1974, they became the first brothers to be presented with hurling All-Stars and the first pair to be selected on the same hurling team. The O'Connor brothers from Cork, Ben and Jerry, are the only twins to have All-Star awards.

Brian Lohan reflected on the number of All-Star awards he and his brother have received. "Frank should have won more. Maybe the fact that I was being picked meant that he wasn't. The selectors may have thought well, there is one going to that family anyway". Frank said, "it means a lot to be on the list of brothers who have won hurling All-Stars. I thought there would have been a lot more names on the list".

Ollie Canning, who was selected on the same team as his younger brother Joe in 2009, told us, "Winning an All-Star with Joe in 2009 was one of the highlights of my hurling career. I always felt that he had the potential to win All-Stars as I watched him coming up through the ranks, but to actually win one together in 2009 was a really special achievement and an occasion that I'm very proud of for myself, Joe and our family. It was brilliant to receive All-Stars together when he was really only starting his senior inter-county career and I was nearing the end of mine".

"It's a great honour personally to receive an All-Star award", said Joe. "It's something that's really special for our club – Portumna has the most All-Star hurling awards of any club in Galway and for us that's a great achievement. For me, to follow in the footsteps of Seán Tracey, Ollie and Damien Hayes is nice because when I was growing up playing

Henderson brothers, John, Ger and Pat

Dooley brothers, Billy, Joe and Johnny

All-Star Gazing

underage, these were the guys that I looked up to and aspired to be like.

"It was really special to receive an All-Star with Ollie in 2009 and a great night for Mam and Dad. If I'm honest, you don't really appreciate these things fully when you are still playing because you are too invested in the next game or next training".

Ollie also spoke about the role his parents played in their hurling success, "I know they are very proud of our hurling careers - whether we won an All-Star or not - but I feel winning an All-Star together was a real bonus and reflected the encouragement and support our parents gave us when we were young". He shares Joe's view about time and perspective. "It's only looking back now I appreciate the significance of 2009, having two brothers on an All-Star team. I probably didn't appreciate it fully at the time".

Joe retired from inter-county hurling following Galway's exit from Championship 2021. In his final game he scored 0-9 and overtook Henry Shefflin to become the championship's leading all-time scorer.

More recently, brothers Pádraic and Ronan Maher were both honoured for the first time in 2016, in Ronan's debut season on the Tipperary senior team. Pádraic explained what the award meant to him. "The All-Star is a personal goal, a motivator to get that bit better each year. It is nearly a greater achievement nowadays as there are more matches and more players getting exposure. So, the selectors have a greater pool of players to pick from".

Ronan added, "it was great to be selected because you felt your contribution to Tipp's year was recognised. Then to win with my brother too was special. The family and the club (Thurles Sarsfields) were very proud". Pádraic has been honoured six times which sees him at the top of Tipperary's All-Star Roll of Honour, along with Eoin Kelly and Nicky English. Surprised to see his name among such hurling legends, he reflected, "it makes me feel lucky to have been selected on even one of these All-Star teams. Only 50 All-Star teams ever selected, and I was on one of them". In 2019 the Maher brothers repeated their achievement when they were both selected again on the All-Star hurling team.

Brothers Ollie and Joe Canning are selected on the same hurling All-Star team in 2009

Brothers Ronan and Pádraic Maher are selected on the same hurling team in 2019

THE HURLING ALL-STAR FATHERS AND SONS

The Larkins from Kilkenny were the first father and son to receive hurling All-Stars, when in 2002 Philly emulated his father Phil's achievement.

The Powers joined them in 2010, and when goalkeeper Brian Hogan got his first All-Star in 2019, he and his father Ken became the first father and son to succeed in the same position. Remarkably the same feat was achieved the following year, when Nickie Quaid was selected in goal for Limerick, as was his late father Tommy in 1992.

County	Family	Total	Father	Year	Son	Year
Kilkenny	Larkin	5	Phil 'Fan'	1973, 1974, 1976, 1978	Philly	2002
Kilkenny	Power	4	Richie	1982, 1986	Richie Jnr	2010, 2011
Tipperary	Hogan	2	Ken	1987	Brian	2019
Limerick	Quaid	2	Tommy	1992	Nickie	2020

Richie Power Snr and his son Richie Power Jr, Kilkenny

Phil 'Fan' Larkin and his son Philly, Kilkenny

Tommy Quaid and his son, Nickie, Limerick

Ken Hogan and his son Brian, Tipperary

All-Star Gazing

THE FOOTBALL ALL-STAR BROTHERS

In football 16 sets of brothers have received All-Star awards. In the case of the Spillane and Ó Sé families, three brothers have been honoured. The Spillane brothers boast 13 All-Star awards, an impressive haul that narrowly beats the Ó Sé family's total of 12. Pat and Tom were the first brothers to be named on the same football team in 1984.

County	Family	Total	Brother	Year
Kerry	Spillane	13	Pat	1976, 1977, 1978, 1979, 1980, 1981, 1984, 1985, 1986
			Tom	1984, 1986, 1987
			Mick	1985
Kerry	Ó Sé	12	Darragh	2000, 2002, 2006, 2007
			Tomás	2004, 2005, 2007, 2008, 2009
			Marc	2006, 2007, 2011

The Ó Sé brothers, Tomás, Darragh and Marc in action for Kerry

Pat Spillane | Tom Spillane | Mick Spillane

Marc, Darragh and Tomás Ó Sé receiving their All-Stars in 2007

The Ó Sé family hold a unique record however, as all three brothers were selected on the same All-Star team in 2007. Colm Cooper recalled, "there was something special in the air that night as the three names were called out at No 3, No 6, No 8. You could feel it, you could tell history was being made".

"There is a picture of the three of us winning together up on the wall in our club, An Ghaeltacht. That means a lot", said Tomás. Marc's award that night also marked the 100th All-Star ever awarded to a Kerry footballer.

The remaining sets of All-Star brothers are listed below.

County	Family	Total	Brother	Year
Dublin	Brogan	7	Alan	2006, 2007, 2011
			Bernard	2010, 2011, 2013, 2015
Tyrone	Cavanagh	7	Seán	2003, 2004, 2005, 2008, 2013
			Colm	2017, 2018
Offaly	Connor	4	Matt	1980, 1982, 1983
			Richie	1981
Offaly	Lowry	3	Seán	1979, 1982
			Brendan	1981
Derry	McGurk	3	Anthony	1973, 1975
			Johnny	1993
Donegal	McHugh	3	Martin	1983, 1992
			James	1992
Donegal	McHugh	3	Mark	2012
			Ryan	2016, 2018
Mayo	Mortimer	3	Kenneth	1996, 1997
			Conor	2006
Roscommon	Earley	3	Dermot	1974, 1979
			Paul	1985
Offaly	Connor	2	Tomás	1978
			Liam	1982

The Connors from Offaly were the first brothers to receive football All-Stars when Richie was selected on the team in 1981, just a year after his brother Matt. Their cousin Tomás Connor had already been awarded in 1978 and he was joined by his brother Liam in 1982.

The Mortimer brothers, Kenneth and Conor, are the only brothers from Mayo who have All-Star awards. "I never gloated about my All-Star because my third brother, Trevor, didn't have one. He was nominated in 2004 but didn't win. I thought he deserved one", said Conor. "There is a sense of achievement for family and friends when you win. They would be on the phone, congratulating you, even when you are nominated. The individual award is weird because your prime focus as a player is the All-Ireland. I wasn't focused on a personal accolade, and you won't win it without the 14 guys behind you".

He continued, "When I won in 2006, I was doing a Masters in DCU and sharing a house with Ross McConnell, Dick Clerkin and Bernard Brogan. I remember it was such a big deal to those lads. They were much younger, and they hadn't started playing county yet". Conor concluded, "you will always have an All-Star – they can't take it away from you".

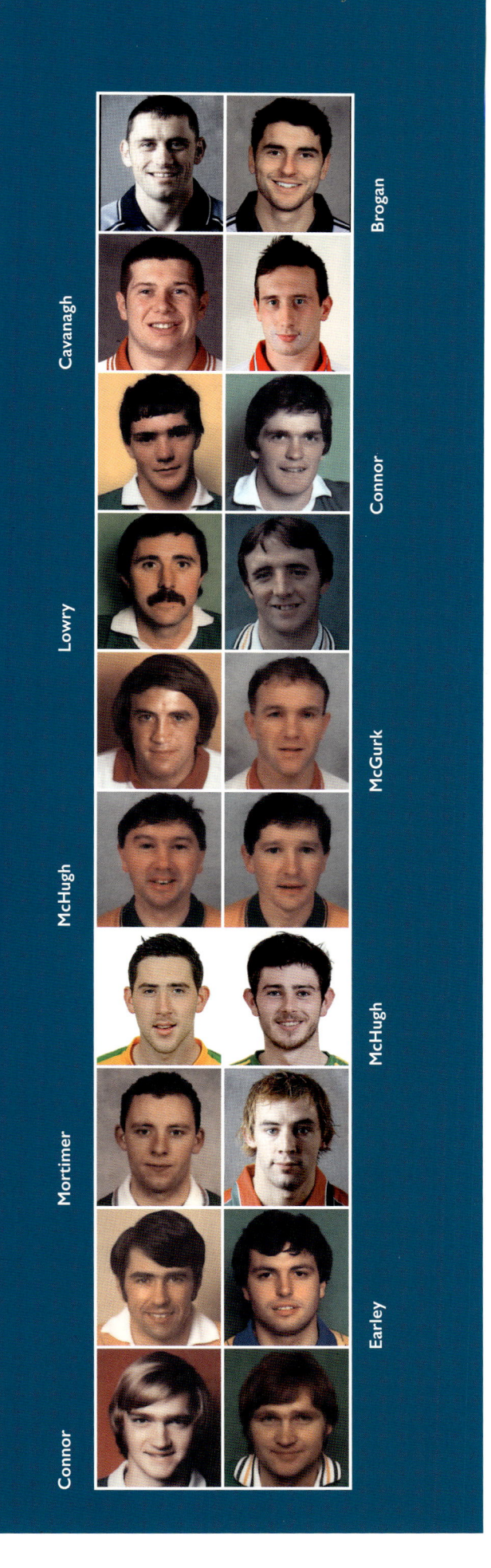

All-Star Gazing

Perhaps the Carr brothers, Declan and Tommy, hold one of the most interesting All-Star records as they were selected playing for different counties in different codes.

County	Code	All-Star	Year
Tipperary	Hurling	Declan Carr	1989
Dublin	Football	Tommy Carr	1991

When asked about the significance of getting an All-Star when his brother already had one, Tommy joked, "it meant a lot, particularly as I deserved it much more than Declan did!".

THE FOOTBALL ALL-STAR FATHERS AND SONS

In football 12 fathers and sons have been honoured with All-Star awards. The Brogan and McHugh families share a similar record as two sons have emulated their father's achievements.

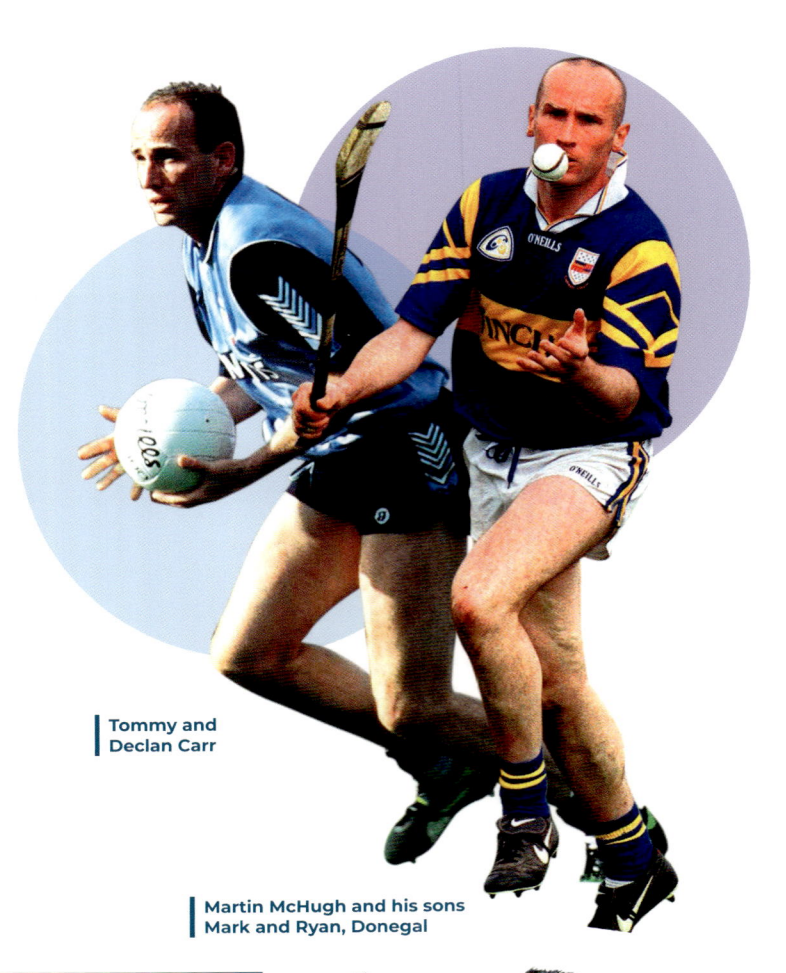

Tommy and Declan Carr

Martin McHugh and his sons Mark and Ryan, Donegal

County	Family	Total	Father	Year	Son 1	Year	Son 2	Year
Dublin	Brogan	8	Bernard	1979	Alan	2006, 2007, 2011	Bernard	2010, 2011, 2013, 2015
Donegal	McHugh	5	Martin	1983, 1992	Mark	2012	Ryan	2016, 2018

The Brogans line up with a sample of the family All-Star trophy collection

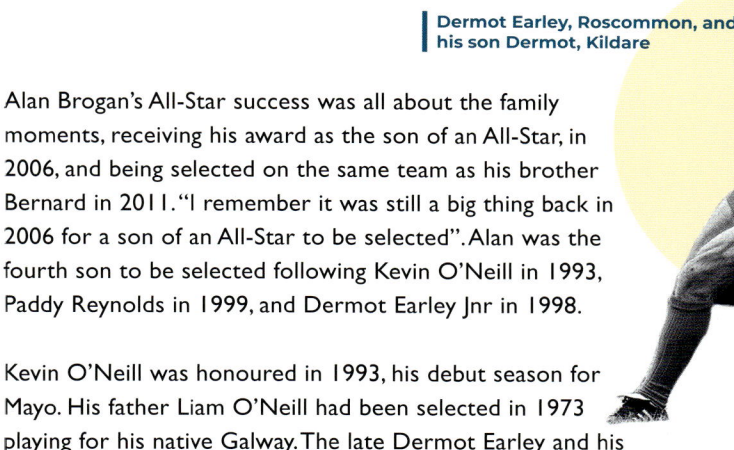

Dermot Earley, Roscommon, and his son Dermot, Kildare

Alan Brogan's All-Star success was all about the family moments, receiving his award as the son of an All-Star, in 2006, and being selected on the same team as his brother Bernard in 2011. "I remember it was still a big thing back in 2006 for a son of an All-Star to be selected". Alan was the fourth son to be selected following Kevin O'Neill in 1993, Paddy Reynolds in 1999, and Dermot Earley Jnr in 1998.

Kevin O'Neill was honoured in 1993, his debut season for Mayo. His father Liam O'Neill had been selected in 1973 playing for his native Galway. The late Dermot Earley and his son Dermot were also recognised as All-Stars playing for different counties; Dermot Jnr. received two awards playing for Kildare, while his father was honoured twice during his illustrious career with Roscommon.

Liam O'Neill said, "winning the All-Star was the next best thing to an All-Ireland, and it was some compensation after losing the All-Ireland in 1973. But I got a bigger kick out of Kevin winning in 1993. I was so proud of him; he was a massive talent. Kevin could win games the way Micky Kearins or Ciarán McDonald could - me, I was a grafter".

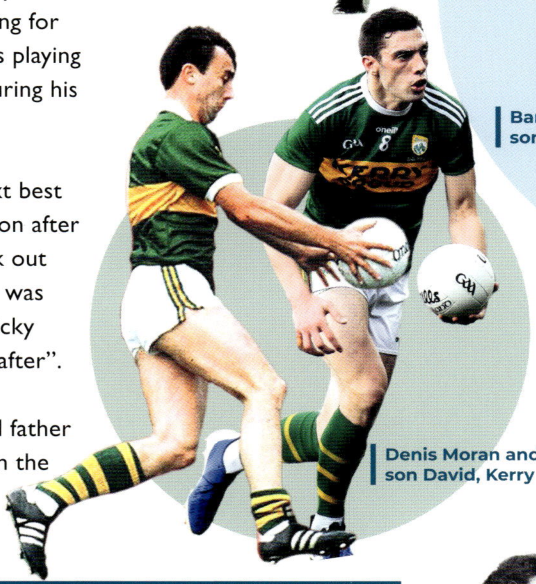

Barney and Dean Rock became the most honoured father and son All-Star pairing when Dean was selected on the team in 2020.

Barney Rock and his son Dean, Dublin

Denis Moran and his son David, Kerry

County	Family	Total	Father	Year	Son	Year
Dublin	Rock	6	Barney	1983, 1984, 1985	Dean	2016, 2017, 2020
Dublin	McCaffrey	5	Noel	1988	Jack	2015, 2017, 2018, 2019
Roscommon/ Kildare	Earley	4	Dermot	1974, 1979	Dermot	1998, 2009
Kerry	Kennelly	3	Tim	1979, 1980	Tadhg	2009
Kerry	Moran	3	Denis	1981	David	2014, 2019
Tyrone	McGuigan	2	Frank	1984	Brian	2003
Galway/Mayo	O'Neill	2	Liam	1973	Kevin	1993
Meath	Reynolds	2	Pat	1971	Paddy	1999

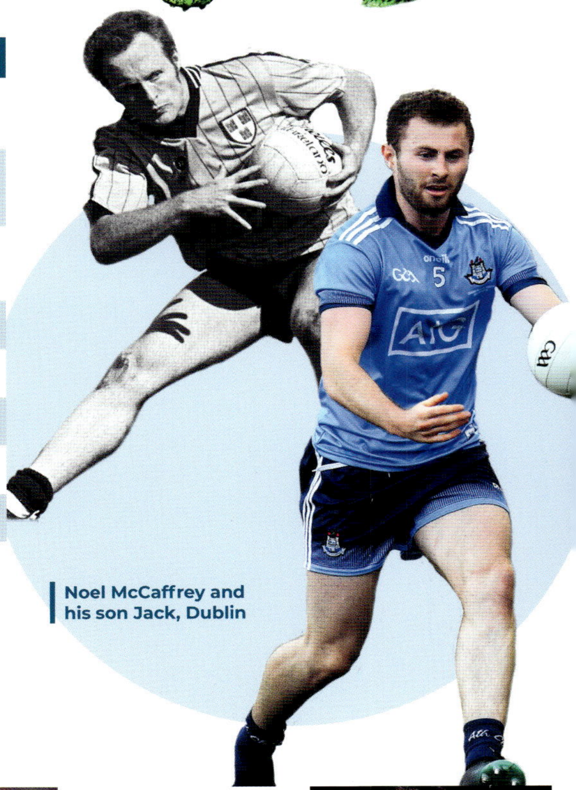

Noel McCaffrey and his son Jack, Dublin

Tim Kennelly and his son Tadhg, Kerry

Frank McGuigan and his son Brian, Tyrone

Liam O'Neill, Galway, and his son Kevin, Mayo

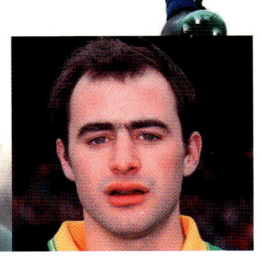

Pat Reynolds and his son Paddy, Meath

All-Star Gazing

Pat and Paddy Reynolds with their All-Star trophies, won in 1971 and 1999

Dean said, "it is really nice to top that leader board and share that with Dad. Both his legacy and his career with Dublin was something I was very aware of growing up. It was nice to have someone like that to look up to, but it did bring some pressure during my childhood. It is easy to look back now and say it was always going to happen, but it was tough along the way. Getting the first All-Star was a huge monkey off your back. Once I got that I was trying to equal Dad and get the three. That was always a goal of mine to get the same as him". He added, "my mother looks after the All-Star trophies. They are her pride and joy".

Barney chipped in, "the All-Star trophies are up on top of the cupboard - three on either side. I will be ticked off when he wins his fourth!" Dean concluded, "everything from here is a bonus".

Dermot Earley Jnr has fond memories of the All-Star banquet in 1998. "I was delighted to be there with Dad. I was only 20 and I thought it would be like this every year, so I probably didn't appreciate it enough. I valued the second All-Star more, when I won 11 years later in 2009. I was nominated in 2002 and my sister Noelle won an All-Star that year too so that meant a lot to the family".

Tadhg Kennelly fulfilled an ambition when he was selected in 2009. "I always wanted to win an All-Star as I was thinking Dad has one. At the banquet, that year, I was sitting beside Dermot Earley Jnr, we had both won, and both our fathers had won together 30 years previous in 1979".

It was a remarkable achievement for Tadhg in a season where he returned from Australia to play for Kerry and help them win the All-Ireland. "It was a very special year. I haven't reflected on the All-Star win until now, as I went straight back to Australia to resume my career". The trophy has pride of place, alongside his dad's on the mantelpiece at home in Kerry.

THE PLAYERS OF THE YEAR

Every year since 2004 one hurler and footballer has been named Player of the Year (POTY). A young player of the year is also chosen in both codes. Three nominees are agreed by the All-Star selectors and the POTY is then chosen by the players.

The winner is usually a player from that year's All-Ireland champions or finalists. Bernard Brogan's POTY award in 2010 was noteworthy as he was recognised in a year when Dublin did not reach the All-Ireland final. His brother Alan received the same accolade the following year in 2011 making the Brogans the only brothers to both have POTY awards.

50 Years of the GAA All-Stars

When Séamus Callanan and Stephen Cluxton were named hurling and football POTYs in 2019, it was the first time that both recipients had captained their counties to All-Ireland success.

In 2020 Brian Fenton became only the second footballer after Trevor Giles to be picked twice as POTY. He also received his fifth All-Star for his performances for Dublin at midfield, placing him just one All-Star behind Kerry midfield legend Jack O'Shea. The 2020 playing season, and subsequent All-Star presentation, was restricted by the Covid-19 pandemic but there was a special moment for Brian after he received his award. "That night I glanced at my phone and there was a congratulatory text from Jack O'Shea. It was a standout text, a touch of class. For him to think 'I am going to text that young fella from Dublin,' it was just lovely. He went to the effort to do that, and it lifted me completely".

Brian continued, "in Dublin we talk about team success. Individual success is secondary, and you don't gloat about it. But I won't lie to you, it means everything to me. Winning an All-Ireland is amazing but to win an All-Star at the end of the year is unreal. It is the perfect year. That is because I know how much it means to my family, my club and young kids. I would love to think that whenever my Dublin career is finished up, in years to come I might be that player who texts the modern POTY to say congratulations. That would be unreal because it just means so much.

"It is nights like that that you realise you are being compared to legends. Being named on The *Irish Independent* All-Star team of the last 50 years in midfield with Jacko, and Spillane on the same team. I know how highly they are regarded and to be in that company is just unbelievable".

Brian Fenton, Dublin, with his 2020 Footballer of the Year trophy

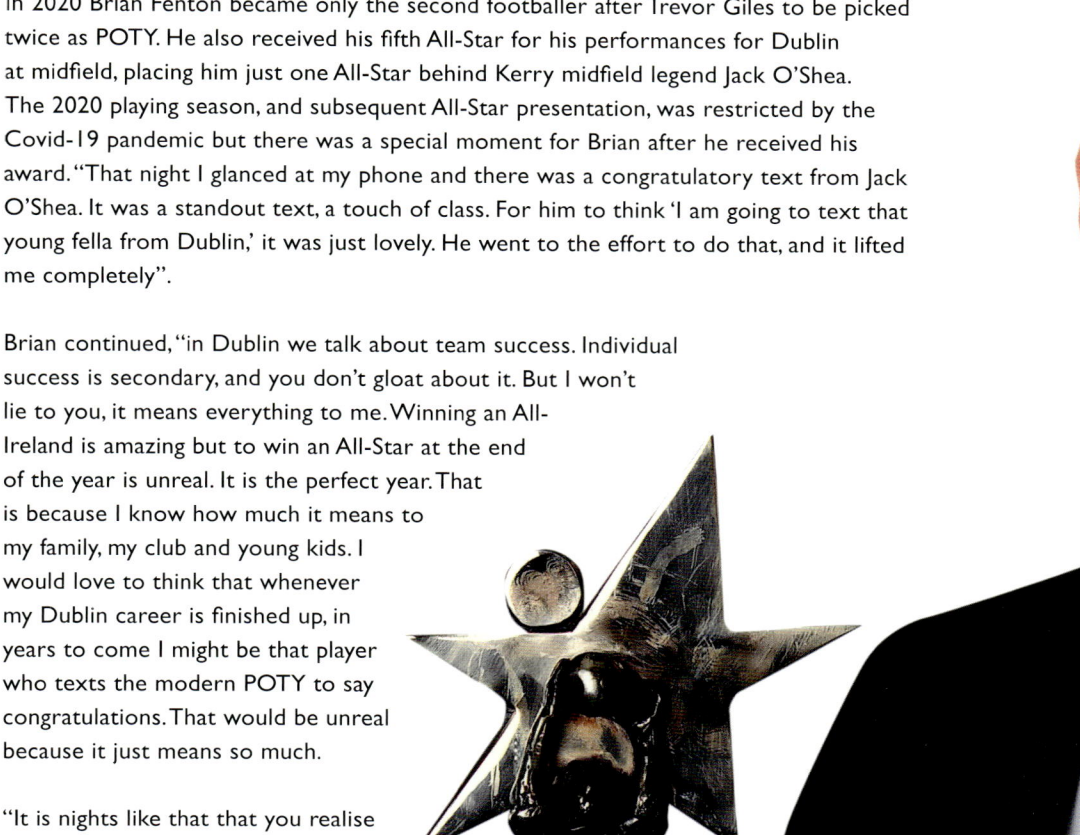

Brian Fenton is named in midfield alongside Jack O'Shea in the Irish Independent's 50 year 'Supreme Team'.

All-Star Gazing

ALL-STAR HURLER OF THE YEAR

1995	Brian Lohan	Clare
1996	Martin Storey	Wexford
1997	Jamesie O'Connor	Clare
1998	Tony Browne	Waterford
1999	Brian Corcoran	Cork
2000	DJ Carey	Kilkenny
2001	Tommy Dunne	Tipperary
2002	Henry Shefflin	Kilkenny
2003	JJ Delaney	Kilkenny
2004	Seán Óg Ó hAilpín	Cork
2005	Jerry O'Connor	Cork
2006	Henry Shefflin	Kilkenny
2007	Dan Shanahan	Waterford
2008	Eoin Larkin	Kilkenny
2009	Tommy Walsh	Kilkenny
2010	Lar Corbett	Tipperary
2011	Michael Fennelly	Kilkenny
2012	Henry Shefflin	Kilkenny
2013	Tony Kelly	Clare
2014	Richie Hogan	Kilkenny
2015	TJ Reid	Kilkenny
2016	Austin Gleeson	Waterford
2017	Joe Canning	Galway
2018	Cian Lynch	Limerick
2019	Séamus Callanan	Tipperary
2020	Gearóid Hegarty	Limerick

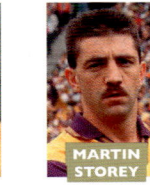

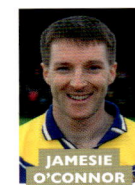

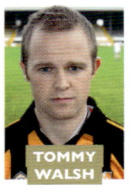

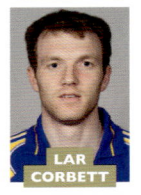

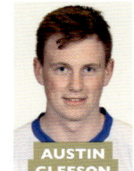

ALL-STAR FOOTBALLER OF THE YEAR

1995	Peter Canavan	Tyrone
1996	Trevor Giles	Meath
1997	Maurice Fitzgerald	Kerry
1998	Jarlath Fallon	Galway
1999	Trevor Giles	Meath
2000	Seamus Moynihan	Kerry
2001	Declan Meehan	Galway
2002	Kieran McGeeney	Armagh
2003	Steven McDonnell	Armagh
2004	Tomás Ó Sé	Kerry
2005	Stephen O'Neill	Tyrone
2006	Kieran Donaghy	Kerry
2007	Marc Ó Sé	Kerry
2008	Seán Cavanagh	Tyrone
2009	Paul Galvin	Kerry
2010	Bernard Brogan	Dublin
2011	Alan Brogan	Dublin
2012	Karl Lacey	Donegal
2013	Michael D. Macauley	Dublin
2014	James O'Donoghue	Kerry
2015	Jack McCaffrey	Dublin
2016	Lee Keegan	Mayo
2017	Andy Moran	Mayo
2018	Brian Fenton	Dublin
2019	Stephen Cluxton	Dublin
2020	Brian Fenton	Dublin

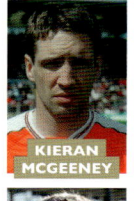

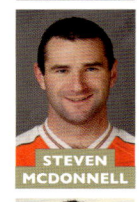

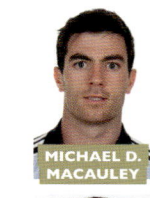

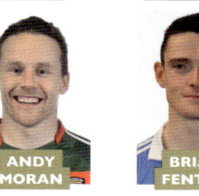

THE ALL-TIME ALL-STARS

To celebrate 10 years of the All-Star scheme in 1980, the members of the Steering Committee decided to expand the awards to include two former GAA stars who would, in their opinion, "have undoubtedly been All-Stars had the scheme been in operation during their playing careers".

Year	Hurling recipient
1980	Mick Mackey, Limerick
1981	Jack Lynch, Cork
1982	Garrett Howard, Limerick and Dublin
1983	Pa 'Fowler' McInerney, Clare, Dublin and Tipperary
1984	Jim Langton, Kilkenny
1985	Eudie Coughlan, Cork
1986	Tommy Doyle, Tipperary
1987	Christy Moylan, Waterford
1988	Paddy 'Fox' Collins, Cork
1989	MJ 'Inky' Flaherty, Galway
1990	John Joe 'Goggles' Doyle, Clare
1991	Jackie Power, Limerick
1992	Billy and Bobby Rackard, Wexford
1993	Pat Stakelum, Tipperary
1994	Martin White, Kilkenny

Year	Football recipient
1980	Larry Stanley, Kildare
1981	Tommy Murphy, Laois
1982	Paddy Moclair, Mayo
1983	Jim McCullough, Armagh
1985	JJ 'Purty' and Tim 'Roundy' Landers, Kerry
1986	Alf Murray, Armagh
1987	Mick Higgins, Cavan
1988	Kevin Armstrong, Antrim
1989	Peter McDermott, Meath
1990	Eddie Boyle, Louth
1991	Seán Purcell, Galway
1992	Seán Flanagan, Mayo
1993	Jimmy Murray, Roscommon
1994	Bill Delaney, Laois

The recipients were invited to the banquet and received a specially designed statuette. The award was not continued when Powerscreen took over as sponsor in 1995. The All-Time All-Star Roll of Honour (above) is an impressive list of hurling and football legends who played in previous decades as far back as the 1910s.

All-Time winners Eugene 'Eudie' Coughlan and brothers Tim 'Roundy' and JJ 'Purty' Landers receive their awards from Jack Lynch at the All-Star banquet in 1985

All-Star Gazing

After Jack Lynch was honoured at the banquet in 1981, he sent a letter of thanks to the All-Star steering committee. "It was with disbelief that I learned that I had been selected for the Bank of Ireland All-Time Sports Award in Hurling for 1981", he wrote, "in the course of my senior Inter County Hurling career from 1938 to 1951 I played with, and against, so many hurlers who I genuinely feel would have deserved to receive this honour instead of me. May I convey ……..to the Sports Writers Committee my sincere thanks and appreciation for the great honour that they have conferred on me".

Tommy Murphy, who played for Laois and Carlow, was also honoured in 1981. Unfortunately, Tommy could not attend the banquet to receive his All-Time award due to ill health. He died a few years later in 1985.

Letter from Jack Lynch

Letter from Tommy Murphy

The GAA Oscars

Since that first night of splendour in December 1971, the All-Star banquet night has become one of the highlights of the year and one of the most popular and important events in the GAA calendar. With the season usually concluded, the players can relax and enjoy themselves. Although generally a formal black-tie event, the atmosphere at the All-Stars is always one of celebration and fun as the heroes of the day mingle and chat. Footballers and hurlers get a chance to meet each other. Rivalries on the pitch are ignored, for one night at least.

LAVISH BANQUET

The high standards set by Carrolls, at the first banquet, continued throughout the 1970s and into the next decade during Bank of Ireland's sponsorship. Dermot Power, who coordinated the bank's All-Star activities for many years, told us, "We decided that it was going to be really well done. It was the GAA putting its best foot forward. We wanted the event to be prestigious".

Generally held in a top Dublin hotel, venues have included the InterContinental (known to most as Jurys), the Burlington and Citywest Hotels. In 2013, the banquet took place in the Croke Park Conference Suite, but logistical issues hampered the night. The following year it was moved to the Convention Centre in Dublin, where it has remained ever since.

In the early years, the guest list was very select, with only 500 people invited. Invitations were limited to the All-Stars and their partners, county board officers, GAA officials, sponsor representatives and the All-Star selectors.

The formal dress code presented a challenge for many because they had never dressed in 'black-tie' before. But for most it added to the glamour of the evening. "The banquet was fantastic, it was like Hollywood", said Charlie McCarthy, reminiscing about the events of the early 1970s. For Ray Cummins, "it was great because it happened at a time of year when everything was quiet. The night was fabulous".

Jimmy Barry Murphy recalls the excitement of getting fitted for a suit and then getting the train up to Dublin. "I remember the very lavish lunch in Carrolls, which ran into the banquet. The first year I was only 19 and I didn't have a girlfriend at the time, so I brought a buddy".

The Dublin Convention Centre lit up for the PwC All-Star Awards in 2018

Many players invited friends or family as their 'plus one'. When Mickey Quinn became Leitrim's first All-Star in 1990, he brought his mum. "It was very special to have her there as she was fanatical about football". He added, "the function was a great occasion for meeting all the players and the media personnel too".

The Kerry players often brought a gang of pals up to Dublin. The pals would hang out in the hotel bar during the formal part of the evening and then join in for the craic later in the night.

Eoin Liston remembers the excitement that surrounded the All-Star banquets. "Going up to Dublin to get your award was huge. It was great to meet the other stars, from hurling especially".

All-Star Gazing

Cork All-Star Hurlers Tony Maher, Ray Cummins, Charlie McCarthy and their wives Veronica, Ber and Pauline at the banquet in 1972

Seán Óg Ó hAilpín said, "the banquet is a big night for the partners as success doesn't come alone. My wife Siobhán used to love the big night in Dublin, getting her dress, getting ready and then maybe stopping for some shopping in Kildare Village on the way home. It was a payback for the sacrifices during the year".

But for some younger players the banquet could be a bit daunting. Colm Cooper was selected in his first year playing senior football for Kerry. "I was only 19 going up to my first All-Star banquet in Dublin. I was very shy. I had only ever worn a formal suit once before to my debs".

Fellow Kerry man, Maurice Fitzgerald, also received an All-Star in his first year with Kerry. "I was only 18-years-old, so I found the banquet a real challenge". Maurice brought his parents to the event. "It means more to me now that I had that experience at the All-Star banquet with my parents particularly as my dad has now passed away".

In the early years, guests received a specially designed All-Star guest list and menu on arrival at the banquet. The list included a seating plan, which helped to locate others as the night progressed.

The food was top-class, no effort was spared. Baked Alaska, the dessert du jour in the 1970s, was regularly on the menu.

Mick Jacob recalls, "amazing food - there were pheasant feathers and pigs' heads". Linen napkins on every table were embroidered with the All-Star logo.

Not surprisingly, as Carrolls sponsored the event, there was an abundance of cigarettes available at every table.

ENTERTAINMENT

Ireland's leading musicians, such as The Chieftains and The Furey Brothers, entertained the guests once the formal proceedings were over. However, the guests were usually more interested in chatting among themselves, and these top acts were often ignored.

By the mid-1980s, the organisers decided to dispense with the formal entertainment. Dermot Power recalled Managing Director Frank O'Rourke announcing diplomatically, "this

The menu from the Carrolls All-Star banquet in 1973

carrolls GAA allstars 1973

FOOTBALLERS	HURLERS
GOALKEEPER	
BILLY MORGAN (CORK)	NOEL SKEHAN (KILKENNY)
RIGHT FULL BACK	
FRANK COGAN (CORK)	FAN LARKIN (KILKENNY)
FULL BACK	
MICK RYAN (OFFALY)	PAT HARTIGAN (LIMERICK)
LEFT FULL BACK	
BRIAN MURPHY (CORK)	JIM O'BRIEN (LIMERICK)
RIGHT HALF BACK	
LIAM O'NEILL (GALWAY)	COLM DORAN (WEXFORD)
CENTRE HALF BACK	
T. J. GILMORE (GALWAY)	PAT HENDERSON (KILKENNY)
LEFT HALF BACK	
KEVIN J. O'SULLIVAN (CORK)	SEAN FOLEY (LIMERICK)
CENTREFIELD	
JOHN O'KEEFFE (KERRY)	LIAM O'BRIEN (KILKENNY)
CENTREFIELD	
DENIS LONG (CORK)	RICHIE BENNIS (LIMERICK)
RIGHT HALF FORWARD	
JOHN COONEY (OFFALY)	FRANCIS LOUGHNANE (TIPPERARY)
CENTRE HALF FORWARD	
KEVIN KILMURRAY (OFFALY)	PAT DELANEY (KILKENNY)
LEFT HALF FORWARD	
LIAM SAMMON (GALWAY)	EAMON GRIMES (LIMERICK)
RIGHT FULL FORWARD	
JIMMY BARRY MURPHY (CORK)	MARTIN QUIGLEY (WEXFORD)
FULL FORWARD	
RAY CUMMINS (CORK)	KIERAN PURCELL (KILKENNY)
LEFT FULL FORWARD	
ANTHONY McGURK (DERRY)	EDDIE KEHER (KILKENNY)

CLÁR
SLÁINTE - Uachtarán na hÉireann

CAINTEOIRÍ
Deasún Ó Riain Muintir Carroll
An Taoiseach, Liam MacCosgair T.D.
Bronnadh na nduaiseanna ar iomanaithe agus peileadóirí 1973
An Dr Dónal Ó Cianáin
Uachtarán Cumann Lúthchleas Gael

Melon & Smoked Ham
Consommé au Sherry
Baked Darn of Salmon Breval
Roast Prime Rib of Beef
Yorkshire Pudding
Horseradish Sauce
Parsley Potatoes
Glazed Carrots
Buttered Broccoli
Baked Alaska
Coffee

Wines
Moselle Kloster Prinz (white)
Nuits St Georges (red)

50 Years of the GAA All-Stars

Paddy Reilly supported by The Artane Boys Band entertains the guests while guest of honour President Mary Robinson and Uachtarán CLG Peter Quinn look on. Inset - Kerry's Maurice Fitzgerald picks up Footballer of the Year and his third All-Star in 1997.

year the entertainment will be the company of friends". While Bank of Ireland had continued many of the Carrolls traditions, they added a few new ideas too. As Donal Carroll reported in the *Irish Independent*, The Artane Band played 'Salute to the All-Stars' during the presentation ceremony. This was a piece of music specially commissioned from leading composer and teacher, Dr. A.J. Potter.

As a way of involving Bank officials from all over the country, a hostess was assigned to each table. Coordinator Jim Whitty recalled, "people who were interested in the GAA, were delighted to get a trip to Dublin for the weekend". "Oh jeez, we loved the hostesses", recalled Pat Spillane. "They looked after you all night".

Some of the new ideas were not so popular such as the introduction in 1985 of boxes for the All-Stars to sit in as they were announced to the audience. Pat remembered, "it was hilarious. We looked like chimpanzees in the Zoo sitting in those feckin' booths".

Barney Rock was sitting near Spillane and laughed as he recalled, "the presentation that year was a bit funny. We were put into boxes, 15 boxes, beside and above each other. I was number 10 and Pat Spillane was number 12 that year, so he was one door away from me. All of a sudden, when your name was called the lights around the box would go on! We were all wondering what would have happened if the bulbs blew".

"However, it was a great honour to get an All-Star award. It was something you would always be looking at and wondering if it would happen to you".

Jim Whitty got the novel idea for the boxes at a show in New York during one of the All-Star trips. He explained, "the challenge was to come up with new ideas for the stage set each year to keep the banquet fresh and interesting". The Bank of Ireland commissioned Jack Restan to design the set each year. His son Mark told us, "Each year Dad took pride in coming up with something more elaborate than the previous year".

The player booths at the All-Star banquet in 1985
(Top L to R) - John O'Leary, Páidí Ó Sé, Gerry Hargan, Mick Spillane, Tommy Doyle, Ciarán Murray, Dermot Flanagan.
(Bottom L to R) - Eugene Hughes, Paul Earley, Kevin McStay, Pat Spillane, Tommy Conroy, Barney Rock,

All-Star Gazing

LIVE TV BROADCAST

The guest list for the All-Star banquet gradually increased and by 1990 it had grown to 800. By 2019, more than 1,300 were in attendance at the last All-Star banquet before the Covid-19 pandemic.

The first big increase came in 1986, when RTÉ began to broadcast the awards presentation live on TV. Keen to introduce a surprise element to the proceedings, the RTÉ producers asked if the All-Star teams could be revealed on the night. Not surprisingly, the newspaper journalists, who traditionally announced the teams in their columns, were not in favour. As a compromise, the All-Star organisers agreed that one team would be announced in the print media in advance, while the other team would be revealed on the night.

As a result, the guest list had to expand to include all players nominated in each position. These players were delighted to attend the banquet even if they did not receive All-Stars. But some found it hard dealing with the uncertainty on the night. "It is very tough on the nominees", said Jimmy Barry Murphy. "For amateur players, it can be a level of embarrassment". He preferred the way it was in his day when the players found out beforehand.

Despite receiving nine All-Stars, DJ Carey admits he was very anxious at the banquets each year, waiting to hear if he had been selected. "I think it would be better if players knew beforehand".

Brian McGuigan has mixed views. "It is nice to get the surprise on the night rather than knowing beforehand. Although, it is obviously easier if you know when you don't win. When you win the All-Ireland, you feel for any teammates who miss out on an All-Star. On the night, you can see how disappointed they are".

Liam Irwin has clear memories of the banquet he attended. "I was there in 1985, it was the first year that the nominees were invited. The next year when I won my All-Star, I was on crutches. I remember Mick Dunne announcing, 'and here we have Liam Irwin on crutches', but I had hidden them behind the curtain, so I walked out without them".

For many years, the All-Star nominees were seated together, which led to some awkward moments as the teams were announced. Brendan Cummins recalled his first experience of the banquet in 1997. "I was sitting with Davy Fitzgerald and Damien Fitzhenry, my two goalkeeping rivals who had also been nominated. It was my first year, so I wasn't expecting to win but when Damien was announced there was a bit of tension between the two lads. I remember looking at these two hurling legends thinking, wow, this All-Star award really means a lot to these guys".

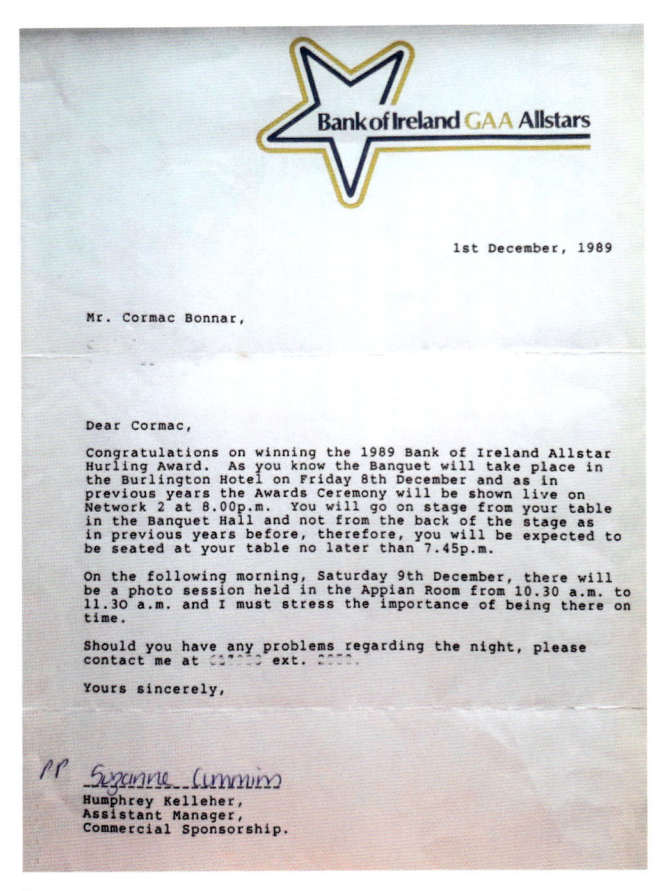

Letter to Cormac Bonnar outlining the format for the awards presentation in 1989

Bobby Ryan recalled, "The first year I won an All-Star, I was sitting at the table with the two other nominees in my position - John Taylor and Dermot McCurtain. When I won, my legs were like jelly walking up to collect the award. I was genuinely shocked; I thought the other two lads had a great year that year. I felt bad coming back to the table with the trophy, so I put it under the table, as I didn't want to rub it in", adding, "it is a pity John never went on to win an All-Star. He really deserved it that year".

Metal plaque given to all nominees during the Vodafone sponsorship years

Tipperary's 1987 All-Stars Aidan Ryan, Pat Fox, Nicholas English and Ken Hogan

WATCHING ON TV

The live broadcast from the All-Star banquet continued each year, apart from 1992, when RTÉ staff were on strike. The programme may have inspired future All-Stars watching at home. Tomás Ó Sé remembers watching the banquets during the 1990s. "It was a time when Kerry weren't going well. Meath and Cork were winning lots of All-Stars. I remember picking the team beforehand with my mates in school. Then the All-Star night was like a movie night. All of us sitting on the couch at home, you would have the treats out. Those were the days when there wasn't much on TV", he laughed.

Seán Óg Ó hAilpín also has fond memories of watching the banquets on TV as a child, after moving with his family from the Fiji Islands, via Australia to Cork City in 1988. Hurling and football became a big part of his life, and he went on to play in both codes for Cork. He captained the hurlers, won three All-Ireland hurling medals and three hurling All-Star awards.

"On All-Star nights we would all be helping out at the bingo, working the board up in the club (Na Piarsaigh)". He remembers the year that his clubmate Tony O'Sullivan got his third All-Star. "There was breaking news in the middle of the bingo; everything stopped as the word was coming through from the Burlington that Tony had won. I was inspired by Tony, and I grew up wanting to beat his haul of All-Stars". Seán Óg received three hurling All-Stars during his dual career which didn't quite match Tony's five, but when his brother Setanta was selected in 2003, the Ó hAilpíns joined that select group of brothers who have been chosen on the same All-Star hurling team.

HEROES AND IDOLS

For the younger players the chance to meet GAA legends they may have looked up to, on All-Star nights, brings a realisation that they have joined an elite group. Séamus Callanan said, "at my first banquet in 2008 I was sitting with other Tipperary players, like Eoin Kelly, idols that I had looked up to. Henry Shefflin was at the next table. I remember thinking, I am actually in this room with all these people. I am in this bunch now".

Eoin Kelly recalled, "I won an All-Star in my first season when I was only 19. Going to the banquet and seeing players there that you had watched on TV, your heroes and idols, like DJ Carey and Peter Canavan, to meet them and then when they say hello and acknowledge you, it's unbelievable for your confidence as a player". Eoin went on to receive six All-Star awards in 2001, 2002, 2004, 2005, 2006, 2010, while his brother Paul was honoured twice during those years.

RTÉ colleagues Eileen Dunne and Michael Lyster co-present at the banquet in 1989

All-Star Gazing

Shane Ryan said, "at the All-Stars, there is a lot of mutual love between players that have never met before. Lads telling each other, 'I think you are great'. I remember people I admired coming up and saying they were delighted to meet me, footballers and hurlers as well". Shane enjoyed meeting his hero Chris Lawn from Tyrone.

Greg Blaney reminisced about his first All-Star banquet in 1983. "It was such a thrill. I had grown up watching the Dublin and Kerry teams, and a few of those players were there. It was great to meet them. I met Jimmy Barry Murphy, and he had been a hero of mine too".

He added, "it was even a thrill to meet the journalists. In those days, they were real hard core GAA men, the likes of Mick Dunne and Paddy Downey. So, it meant more that they were picking you. Nowadays, you get the impression that a lot of the journalists cover other sports too. I remember Paddy Downey was very polished and very well-read".

BREAKING DOWN THE BARRIERS

Martin Quigley said, "the banquet was an opportunity to meet your peers. It broke down the barriers between counties". He remembers socialising with the Kilkenny players at the banquet, something he would not otherwise get a chance to do.

Dónal Óg Cusack says the All-Star night is fantastic. "There was always great prestige and glamour around it. Everyone that goes to it says, 'this is a serious night'. And the amount of people at it. You could say to someone, 'I will see you there', and you would never see them. My parents ended up going one year and they loved it. My mother loved to get dressed up. It is a sports event, but also an important event in the Irish calendar".

Dónal recalled the first year he was selected, "I wasn't going to go as I didn't think I would get the award. I was happy enough to be nominated. But I headed up to Dublin with Diarmuid O'Sullivan, we played together in Cloyne, and his mother and my grandmother were sisters.

"The event is so big and so formal; I was very young and wide-eyed. I assumed that all the Cork lads would be sitting together. I can remember looking at the table listing, and saying, 'Oh my God, I'm with a load of Clare lads by myself'. But I was sitting with Anthony Daly and Jamesie O'Connor, and they couldn't have been nicer". Dónal reflected, "It was a surprise when I won. Davy Fitzgerald probably felt that he deserved the All-Star that year. Mind you, in 2005, he got an award that I should have won, so it evened out".

Charlie Redmond went to many banquets in the 1990s. "The All-Star banquet was always a great night. The matches were all over, so it was a great way to end the season. It was an opportunity to chat to guys in other counties as we didn't

Cloyne All-Stars Dónal Óg Cusack and Diarmuid O'Sullivan

meet them in college back then. It was a night of its own. It had its own dynamic, even if you only got nominated. You were doing well even to be nominated".

"I loved mixing with the players", said Kieran McGeeney. "Being with people who really love football. I loved talking to them - people who have the same passion. We might have butted heads on the pitch, but everyone is there for the same reason. Everyone understands".

SPECIAL NIGHT FOR THE CHAMPIONS

"When you win the All-Ireland, the All-Star banquet is like a team night out because so many of you are there", said Eoin Kelly. "It is such a great night it motivates you for the next year. You are thinking, I want to be here again next year with my team".

Tomás Ó Sé feels the same, "The All-Star Banquet is a great night for the champions. On the night of the All-Ireland final night when you win, it all gets stretched. At the All-Stars everyone is back together again. In 2013, the year I retired, I was asked to present the POTY award to Michael Darragh

Champions Kerry at the All-Star Awards Banquet in 2008. L to R: Colm Cooper, Declan O'Sullivan, Tommy Walsh, Kieran Donaghy and Tomás Ó Sé

Macauley. That was a huge honour, being asked back. The banquet is still very glitzy in fairness to the GAA".

His brother Marc said, "it is a winner's night. It tops off your season. When you have lost the All-Ireland you don't actually want to be there", though Marc said he appreciates how big the All-Star night is for players from smaller counties too.

For Colm Cooper the All-Star banquet is the All-Ireland winners' night. "The champions are shown at the opening of the show, so it's all about them. When your county wins the All-Ireland, and you get the All-Star, you feel you were one of the reasons that your county won. It copper-fastens you. It cements your year as a player. It's the cherry on top of the cake".

"They are great nights, the shackles are off, it puts closure on the whole season", according to Cian Lynch. When newly-crowned hurling champions Limerick received six All-Star awards in 2019, the entire team was nominated. Cian, who was also named Hurler of the Year, said, "so, we were all there together that night. Seeing your friends getting their All-Stars too was special. The night was unbelievable. To mingle and chat away with the likes of Joe Canning and to see each other's viewpoints. Players I would have looked up to before playing senior".

He continued, "and the footballers too. Brian Fenton was the Footballer of the Year, so we spent a lot of time together. He was so humble. You wouldn't think the footballers would be watching the hurling. It shows we are all the same. You form a special bond at the banquets and on the All-Star trips,

making friends with lads that you never thought you would be friendly with".

Cian enjoyed meeting legends of the game too, "football players you had watched growing up. You just never thought you would be part of it".

"The whole narrative around the All-Stars is around friendship", said Brian Fenton. "The Limerick lads in 2018 and, in particular, getting to know Cian Lynch that day, you are kind of in their circle now. With the hurlers you want to be best friends with them straight away but with your biggest competitors in football, you are slower to let

Players of the Year Cian Lynch and Brian Fenton at the All-Star banquet in 2018

your guard down. You are thinking, I will have a drink with you, but I don't want to get too close to you! There is an awkwardness at the beginning of the night at the drinks reception. You have the Dublin players and the Kerry players, the Tipp hurlers and the Limerick hurlers and it is all 'chest out, shoulders back' type of stuff. But that lessens as the night goes on, you have the awards and then you end up in Coppers at 5am and sure you don't care!".

Brian continued, "There is a reassurance going there with your teammates. For a player who is the only one nominated from a county, you would be nervous going in, not knowing anyone. It can be an intimidating place for that first half an hour. Those nights at the banquet are unreal. It is done so well, the glitz and the glamour. You look at the Grammys and the Oscars, it's almost like our own version of that in Ireland. And to be part of that, and to be winning and then to be called up on stage, it's a lovely moment, ah, it's unbelievable, so special. It is a very special moment for our families too. I know how much my dad and my sisters love it. It is a privilege to be there on a yearly basis for Dad".

As the All-Stars are called up to receive their awards they are often interviewed on stage. Sometimes they seem reluctant to say much about their achievement. Séamus Callanan explained, "going up on stage is daunting. Even in 2019 when I knew in advance that I had won an All-Star and the POTY award, I was still really nervous going up to Dublin. When you are growing up playing the game, the emphasis from day one is on the team. So, the interviews are hard because you are being asked questions about your own performance, whereas usually after matches you are talking about the team".

When Paul Flynn was awarded his fourth All-Star in succession in 2014, he was the first footballer to achieve this since Páidí Ó Sé in 1985. "2011 was the first year I was nominated. I was kind of a bit player before that. Then Pat Gilroy (the Dublin manager) worked with me to help me develop my game. I remember being in college in DCU and there were fellas ahead of me getting All-Star nominations. At the time, all I wanted was to get a nomination and go to the All-Stars as a nominee. Even in 2011, although I had a good year, I was still surprised when I won".

Paul was on the same college course as Michael Murphy. "We were living together, so we were very close. I remember clearly one day sitting on the windowsill in one of the dorms, and he was lying on the bed, saying to him, 'what would you give to have one All-Ireland and one All-Star? You would just retire the happiest man in the world'. We still joke about it because, in 2011, I won an All-Star and All-Ireland, and then in 2012, he did the same with Donegal. It was a dream that became a reality very quickly.

"2011 was so special. We (the Dublin footballers) were in a whirlwind after winning the first All-Ireland in 16 years.

| Séamus Callanan on stage at the All-Star banquet in 2019

| Paul Flynn with his housemate Aidan Walsh on the red carpet at the 2012 All-Stars

Everything was new and so special; we were just so excited. That excitement then led into the All-Stars as the banquet was the next formal gathering for all of us. The pride I got from winning the award was when I saw how happy my mam and dad, and brother, were".

Flynn was the only Dublin player selected the following year. "There was a unique moment at the banquet in 2012. Myself, Michael Murphy from Donegal and Aidan Walsh from Cork were all living together at this stage. The three of us left from DCU, went for a drink, and went to the All-Stars together.

The amount of people that still ask me about that - three guys living together winning All-Stars".

Along with Martin O'Connell, Tommy Dowd heads Meath's All-Star Roll of Honour. "I am very proud to have been selected in four different positions – numbers 12, 13, 14 and 15. It was a huge thing to be around all those great footballers. A great occasion - going to 'The Burlo' in Dublin. It capped off the year after all the training and hard work".

Meath beat Mayo in a replay of the All-Ireland final in 1996. In a contentious match, each team had a player sent off after a brawl involving most of the players. Tommy captained the side and played a crucial role in Meath's win, scoring 1-3 on the day. He reflected, "there was something more special about winning an All-Star when you won the All-Ireland as well. But it was tense at the banquet in 1996. The row in the final took away from it".

He added, "being captain of Meath, it still meant a lot. It was great for my club too, as Dunderry is only an Intermediate club. The All-Star is highly valued. It is something for the grandchildren to look back on".

EARLY PHOTO CALL

The tradition of taking photographs for All-Star posters in advance could not continue once the live announcements on the night commenced. Instead, Sportsfile started taking the players' photos the morning after the banquet. Humphrey Kelleher of Bank of Ireland recounted, "I was the lucky one who had to get the players out of bed the following morning. Believe me, it wasn't easy".

Eoin Kelly laughed, "you would be fearful of Ray McManus, looking for a photo the morning after the banquet".

Did the photos still mean as much as they did in the early years? Conal Bonnar confirmed that they did. "In 1991, the club wanted me back early the next day for a match, but I told them I had to wait for the photo for the poster because I hated the photo used the previous year. I was afraid they would use it again if I didn't turn up".

Brendan Cummins loved the photo shoot. "The status of waking up the next morning and going to be photographed for the poster by Brendan Moran (of Sportsfile). Putting on the county jersey. That's when it hits you that you have won an All-Star".

Due to the success of Ballyhale in the club championship, Henry Shefflin would often be "minding himself" the night of the banquet. He remembers one year getting up early to get back for a match. "I went to get my photo taken before I left and was surprised when Ray McManus said, 'you are the second one in. Your teammate has been here already'. It turns out Cha (James Fitzpatrick) had been to Coppers till 5am and got his photo taken when he got back at 7am on his way to bed!".

In 2007 when the Ó Sé brothers received their three awards, there was a long night of celebration. Tomás described the scene the next morning. "It had been a great

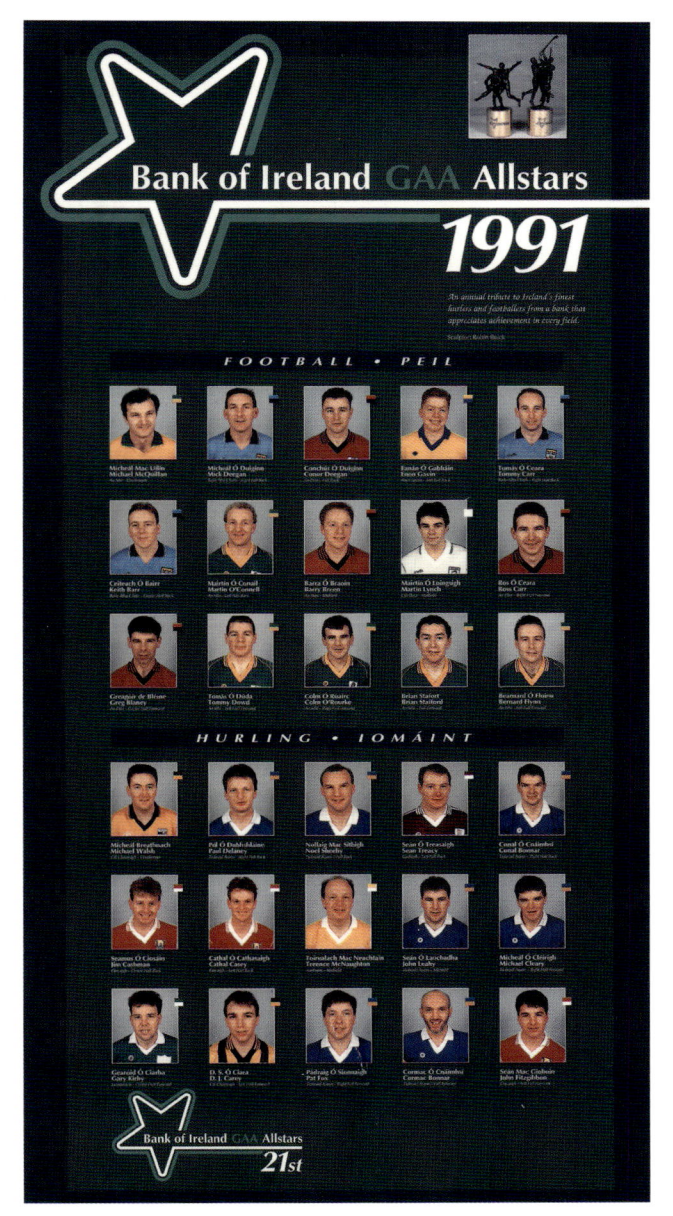

The 1991 All-Star poster

night. Éamonn Fitzmaurice's wedding was the next day in Kerry. Me and Darragh were standing outside the Citywest Hotel talking to Ciarán Whelan. I said, 'Jesus lads, how are we getting home?'. Next minute, a chopper arrives out of nowhere to collect us and take us to the wedding. Whelan was just shaking his head at us".

Ciarán Whelan still laughs at the memory. "I remember it well. The chopper arriving for the Ó Sé brothers the next day after the banquet. It was the Celtic Tiger gone mad".

PERSONAL MOTIVATION

Bernard Brogan used his early experience at All-Star banquets as motivation to become an All-Ireland Champion. He was POTY in 2010, the season before Dublin made their breakthrough in 2011.

"The All-Stars was a real night of celebration for the All-Ireland winners. Winning the POTY was a great personal accolade but there was a bitter sweetness to it. It's all about the team for me. I remember thinking, I would swap this to win an All-Ireland. I want to be here celebrating All-Stars with six or seven of my teammates as All-Ireland Champions, having a pint and having the craic. I decided that I was definitely coming back here as an All-Ireland winner. The All-Stars gave me that drive and motivation".

Brendan Cummins also used the All-Stars as a personal motivator during his career. "I didn't win an All-Star in 2007. I had been dropped by Babs (the Tipperary manager at that time). On the night of the banquet that year, I went up to my club (Ballybacon-Grange). I trained on the pitch on my own while the banquet was on television. I was determined to get back the next year and win an All-Star". Brendan achieved his goal the following year. "I won in 2008, and the next night after the banquet, I went back up to the club and repeated the training session with the All-Star trophy plonked in the centre of the pitch". Brendan went on to claim his fifth All-Star in 2010.

BELIEF AND RECOGNITION

Being chosen as an All-Star gave Alan Brogan belief at a time when the Dublin team was struggling to make a breakthrough. "When I won in 2006, it was a case of really believing I was now as good as the guys who had won All-Stars in the past. We had a couple of bad years in 2003 and 2004. In 2005 we won Leinster, and when Tyrone beat us, we still had doubts. So, winning in 2006, suddenly you are up there with the Darragh Ó Sé's of the world. Then you think, this is my level now; this is where I deserve to be".

For Willie Joe Padden, it was nice to get the recognition. "If you didn't win an All-Ireland, at least by winning an All-Star, you were close enough. In 1985, it was my consolation".

Kieran McGeeney says an All-Star is something that every player feels is achievable. "It holds something special for most county players. Even an All-Star nomination holds something, as it is a recognition. The reality is that a lot of players have zero chance of winning an All-Ireland medal.

| A proud moment for Brendan Cummins (back row, third from left) as he returns to the All-Star hurling team in 2008

But an All-Star award or a nomination is something they can win".

Pádraic Joyce says he was too young to understand the prestige of it when he got his first All-Star in 1998. "I was the first All-Star in Killererin, and there was a celebration in the local pub the following night. When I won in 2000 and 2001, we had lost to Kerry, so for me, it was nice to win one". He added, "it is a huge honour and a bonus when you win the All-Ireland".

Anthony Tohill told us, "It's a great accolade and once you have it, that's what you are, an All-Star. "The All-Stars are the elite players", muses Ciarán Barr, "role models for the next generation". Seán Cavanagh says, "You only need to win one to be an All-Star!". Dermot Earley Jnr summed it up perfectly, "I always feel privileged to be forever called an All-Star".

Gary Kirby received four hurling All-Stars playing for Limerick. "My first award in 1991 was the 25th All-Star for Limerick and the first since the mid-1980s. There was great excitement. I was on the radio. To win the first All-Star was special. I got loads of congratulations cards from people. It was a big thing back then".

He talked about the anticipation each year before the All-Star teams were announced. "Once the All-Ireland final is over, you would be waiting anxiously to see who is nominated for the All-Stars. You would be conscious of the guys in your position, especially in the earlier years when three players were picked per position. Then at the banquet, it was easier the year you knew, especially if you didn't win. You had time to get used to the news. The All-Star is a big thing. It is the next thing after the All-Ireland, which is the ultimate goal. It is a dream for any young fella. It tells you that you can compete with your peers; you are up there".

Reflecting on past Limerick All-Stars, Gary said, "to be mentioned among those names meant a lot. They would have been my heroes; now, you were among them". He has great memories of the banquets. "It was less of a show back then, more of a celebration. My mum came to the first one, and she kept all the stuff from the banquet. When my wife started coming, mum would tell her, make sure you bring everything home! She has the four All-Star posters up at home from the years I won".

Aidan O'Shea was the first All-Star from his club Breaffy. "The club is only about 60 years old, so that was very important for me. They have pictures up in the club, of me receiving the awards at the banquets".

Aidan continued, "Everyone wants to be an All-Star. When you start out, you want to win one, then you get greedy. I am proud that my three awards are all in different positions".

A photo of All-Star Aidan O'Shea on display in the Breaffy clubhouse

Looking at the All-Star Roll of Honour for Mayo, he added, "I am proud too that this generation of players has multiplied the number of Mayo All-Stars significantly. Hopefully, it will inspire a young generation in Mayo. I grew up watching Kerry, as Mayo weren't winning much in those days. My dad had the All-Star posters around the house. Mike Frank Russell was a hero. When I saw them winning All-Stars, I wanted to emulate those guys".

At Aidan's first All-Star banquet, he was sitting beside Paul Galvin, who had won Footballer of the Year. "It was before he was into fashion, but I remember him asking me about my suit and where I got it. He was telling me he just got his in Tullamore on the way up. I remember Tom O'Sullivan was wearing gold shoes that night on stage! The banquets are a great occasion. Particularly the earlier ones in Citywest, which were more inclusive. Now that it is opened up, it gets lost, and it is not so intimate".

Aidan O'Shea examines the 1971 football All-Star lineup

All-Star Gazing

Charlie Redmond receives his second All-Star award from Pat Molloy, Bank of Ireland in 1994

SPECIAL MEMORIES

Charlie Redmond got his first All-Star in 1993. "That year, the football team was announced live on the night. I was pulled into a room with all the other nominees beforehand, and we were told who won". He told his wife Gráinne but asked her to keep the secret. She popped out to the lobby in the Burlington to call her dad with the news. She swore him to secrecy and her father, who owned a pub in Cavan, had great fun when all the lads assembled later to watch the All-Stars. "I think Charlie will win it. Does anyone want to put a bet on it?" The banquet revived a special memory for Charlie as, sadly, Gráinne passed away in 2016.

Keith Barr loved the banquets too. "I kept all the menus and napkins from all the banquets I was at". "You did not!" said Charlie.

When Iggy Clarke first became an All-Star in 1975, he was studying to be a priest in Maynooth College, as well as playing hurling for Galway. "At 23, it was great to get an individual award. The announcement came through mid-week. Seán Silke from Galway was in Maynooth at the time as a lay student, and we took off out of the college to celebrate. A fella drove us to Kilcock to Lyons pub, where we started drinking whiskey. It was late when we got back, and the gates of the college were closed. So, we had to climb a wall to get back in, waiting for the security guard to do his rounds before we moved. Silke lifted me over, and I still have a memory of sitting on top of that wall".

Clarke went on to be selected three more times during his career. "In 1980, it was a particular honour. Because of the shoulder injury I got in the semi-final that year, I only played 30 minutes in the final. I felt the All-Star selectors remembered me for my year before the injury. It was a lovely acknowledgement after a tough experience".

FIRST ALL-STAR IN THE COUNTY

The achievement takes on a different significance for players who receive the first or only All-Star for their county. Mickey Quinn explained, "an All-Star is something every player wants to win. I was privileged to be the first person

Iggy Clarke receives his third award from An Taoiseach Jack Lynch in 1979 and right, pictured with his four All-Star trophies

in Leitrim to win one. Leitrim people are great supporters of the county team and are football mad. Back in 1990, the county team was going really well. There was a lot of excitement at the time. And I still get a lot of recognition because of it around the county now".

Kevin O'Brien was also selected on that football team in 1990, and he too was the first player from his county to be honoured.

On being Wicklow's first All-Star Kevin said, "I don't love the label, there is plenty of slagging about it. You would like to think that someone else could get one in Wicklow. Little did I know that I would ever be in the reckoning for an All-Star. When you won you felt you were representing the players that you played with, and it was nice to represent the club and the county too. You don't forget those players and you feel a bit of it is theirs too. You think of the coaches who dragged you out training and helped you; calmed you down when you had your little tantrums. You feel you are representing them and look back and say it was all worthwhile".

Kevin continued, "Mick Dunne was great. He was always very encouraging for a young fella like me. I remember at the banquet saying to him that maybe it was looking after all the reporters during the trip to Australia that did it! He said to me, 'don't you ever say that - you totally deserved to win'. I will never forget that".

The previous month Kevin had played a significant role in helping an Irish team win the Compromise Rules series in Australia. The month-long trip had topped a fantastic season for Kevin where he had excelled at midfield.

He sparkled in an Irish squad full of established players like Jack O'Shea and Robbie O'Malley along with Dubliner and Aussie Rules star Jim Stynes.

"We were away for a month, and we all became great friends. At the end of the tour, we had to say goodbye, but we knew the All-Star banquet was coming up in December and that the majority of the panel would be nominated. Jim was coming home for Christmas, and we were both thinking, 'God, we will miss the guys, they are all going to be together'. So, Jim, God rest him, and myself, we spent a whole night trying to get two tickets for the banquet from Dermot Power from Bank of Ireland. We said to him, 'we'll sit at the back of the television cameras, no one will know we are there'. He just laughed at us.

"Then I was nominated so we were laughing - I was going to bring Jim as my girlfriend! Little did we know that I would get the All-Star. I was driving along one day, and Des Cahill announced it and I nearly drove into the ditch. Jim got an invitation in the end, so I was able to bring my wife. It was a great night, but we (Baltinglass) were playing a Leinster Club Final against Paul Curran's Thomas Davis two days later, so we behaved ourselves!".

Mickey Quinn proudly poses at home with his All-Star trophy

Kevin O'Brien, Bernard Flynn, Eamonn Heery and the late Jim Stynes hold the winner's trophy in Australia in 1990

Nicholas English congratulates Mickey Quinn at the All-Star banquet in 1990

All-Star Gazing

Wexford All-Stars Damien Fitzhenry and Matty Forde at the banquet in 2004

Kevin reflected, "Poor Jim, he made the party after all. He was a great guy. How much he was adored out in Australia is incredible. A massive loss for Australian football and what he did for charity was incredible. He made such a difference in young people's lives and instilled such confidence in them. That was something he didn't have to do if he didn't want to".

Jim's brother Brian was selected in midfield on the football All-Star team in 1995 having helped Dublin win the All-Ireland that year.

In 2010 Paddy Keenan became Louth's first All-Star in a year when he captained his team to reach the Leinster Final against Meath. "Because I am from a smaller county, it was special to get that recognition. Players can get forgotten about when you are not winning on a regular basis. The team isn't competing at the latter stages of the championship, so your games are not on television. But 2010 was a high-profile year for Louth".

There was lots of pride in Louth when Paddy received his award. "No one really knew how to go about things as it was the first All-Star for Louth. Karen, my wife, came to the banquet as well as my parents. They would have gone to every match; they were very invested in all the games. They were nearly more excited than me. It was a great night talking one-to-one with other players and having a drink with some heroes. It was great for my family to meet the players too, like the Brogans and Henry Shefflin".

Back in Louth, there was a celebration in Paddy's club (St Patricks GFC) after the next league match. "Everyone made a big song and dance about it. We had food, I had the trophy with me, and I said a few words. The place was packed; people had come from all over the place. I was overwhelmed by all the good wishes by text, by phone and in person". Paddy concluded, "you probably don't appreciate it all until you finish playing. Outside of winning a Leinster title, the All-Star would come first. It is the biggest individual accolade for a player".

Matty Forde got Wexford's only football All-Star in 2004. "I was very surprised when I was nominated as Wexford didn't go far in the championship that year". Matty was the top scorer of the year with 8-36 in the League and 3-34 in the Championship. But he still wasn't expecting to be selected. "I got a phone call from a journalist a few days before the banquet. I wasn't prepared for it at all".

He went up to Dublin early the day of the banquet as he was also receiving the Top Scorer award from eir. "I was sharing a room in Citywest with Kerry's Tom O'Sullivan. I was asleep when he arrived. He apologised for waking me up, but I said to him, 'it's fine, you kept Conor Mortimer scoreless in the final, so I had a better chance of winning the All-Star'. I was delighted to meet Damien Fitzhenry at the banquet as he was a hero of mine over the years in Wexford. When I came back the next day, all my family was waiting to celebrate my award. It was a lovely night. I also got an award from my club, Kilanerin–Ballyfad, at the end of year function".

Laois hurler Pat Critchley was selected on the All-Star hurling team in 1985. He recalled how he heard the news. "I remember I was in a phone kiosk, and it was a phone call from Mick Dunne, who was a Clonaslee man. Mick said, 'It is great as a Laois man to tell you that you are the first player from our county to win an All-Star'. I remember the emotion and pride".

Laois had reached the final of the Centenary Cup the previous year and advanced to the Leinster semi-final the year Pat was selected. "We played a match five Sundays in-a-row. So, we were in the limelight. Offaly were our bogey team at that time. I felt the All-Star was a reward for that 1980s Laois team. It was a big thing for the supporters too". Then Pat reflected, "it was a huge honour for me, but I would have preferred if the team won a Leinster rather than me winning an All-Star. John Taylor lost out that year as he had been sent off. I know the All-Stars have to be role models but that was harsh. I haven't met a hurling person since, from inside or outside the county, who didn't agree that he should have received an All-Star too. Indeed, I feel he should have had several".

A year later in 1986, when the Laois footballers won the county's second National Football League title, Colm Browne and Liam Irwin were selected on the All-Star team. "Colm is the second All-Star from Laois as he was picked at left half-back", laughed midfielder Liam. Colm thinks the All-Stars is a quality scheme. "It has purchase. Even a nomination is special".

He was nominated three times, in 1978, 1980 and 1981, before his selection in 1986. "I remember being picked as a replacement on the All-Star tour in 1982. It was amazing, within 12 months I was on the All-Star tour, a team trip with Laois to America and then my honeymoon".

Hurler David Kilcoyne remembers the excitement in Westmeath in 1986 when he became the county's first All-Star. "I was being invited to book launches and pub openings. I was a guest at all kinds of clubs, even pitch and putt clubs!". He feels that his All-Star was a recognition for the team and their achievements. "It was a reflection of the team's success that year".

Rory O'Connell became Westmeath's first football All-Star in 2001. "I had never been to anything like the banquet before. When I got to Citywest, I remember beforehand the reporters saying, 'you've won it'. But I didn't want to believe it. It was a huge occasion for all the family. My mum

Pat Critchley with fellow Laois man Michael Carroll at the All-Star banquet in 1985

and dad, brothers and cousins, were all outside in the bar of the hotel. They were drinking champagne when I won. They nearly had better craic!", he laughed.

On the significance of being selected as an All-Star, Rory added. "It is only now when you get older, and you look back that you realise the achievement. I always wanted to win an All-Star growing up. But at the time, it's all about the team. You won it because of them. You can look back, and not a lot of people have an All-Star out of all the people who have played the game. For years afterwards I was still invited to loads of things. I got a free car for a year from Seán Whytes in Athlone. That was huge because back then, there was no car sponsorship for players. I have great memories; I am one of the lucky ones".

Fermanagh footballer Peter McGinnity got his county's first All-Star in 1982. "I wasn't expecting to win as I had been through the process before when I was nominated in 1975. My family were delighted and all the boys I played with too. After the banquet, I was presented with my All-Star many times! The chairman of the Fermanagh County Board presented it again when the club won the championship in 1982".

Peter reflected, "When you started playing, you had a pathway, things you wanted to achieve: MacRory Cup in

All-Star Gazing

Fermanagh's first All-Star Peter McGinnity poses with his trophy in front of his family tree

college, county minor, county senior, play Railway Cup. I really valued the Railway Cup; it was a great chance to meet other players. It was the highest accolade I could hope to get.

"Then in the 1970s, there was this new thing called an All-Star award. It became a new goal. When you won, it was great to be mixing with other players, especially those in other provinces you wouldn't meet playing provincial. You were now of equal status. I remember meeting Billy Morgan and Jimmy Barry Murphy.

"We were clearing out my mum's house recently, and we found a Bank of Ireland linen napkin. I probably took it from the All-Star banquet as we didn't have linen napkins at home back then!".

Peter concluded, "in the quiet moments now; it means more than it did then. You were busy at the time; you didn't think much about it. You just got on with the next thing that was coming along".

ABSENT ALL-STARS

Only a handful of All-Stars have not attended the banquet to receive their award in person. Some exceptional circumstances have caused players to be absent. Others have gone to great lengths to return home for the event; Martin O'Doherty flew in from California after he had emigrated to LA and John Fitzgibbon returned from New York. More recently in 2019, Brian Hogan returned with his girlfriend from Dubai to pick up his award, spending less than 48 hours in the country.

In 1988 five members of the All-Ireland winning Meath team were named on the All-Star football team. The Meath players were set to miss the banquet, as it clashed with the team holiday in the Canary Islands. Bank of Ireland arranged to fly the All-Stars home via Madrid and London, the day of the banquet. The players encountered a delay in Madrid, which caused them to miss the connection to Dublin. Colm O'Rourke rang Dermot Power from the bank who recalled, "I get this call from O'Rourke to tell me they are stuck in London, that they are not going to make it. So, I said, 'we'll charter a plane'. To which Colm replied, 'we'll need two'".

O'Rourke organised two planes in London and the group arrived just in time, thanks in part to a garda escort from Dublin Airport to the Burlington Hotel. But they had no suits, and there was no time to source any. Power said, "they ended up borrowing shirts, trousers, everything they could, from the waiters in the Burlington". Michael Lyster laughed, "I am pretty sure some of the Meath lads were in their stocking feet receiving their award that year".

The bank picked up the bill for the two planes, which Dermot estimated to be about £5,000.

When Pete Finnerty was selected for his third award in 1987, he was living in New York and could not travel home

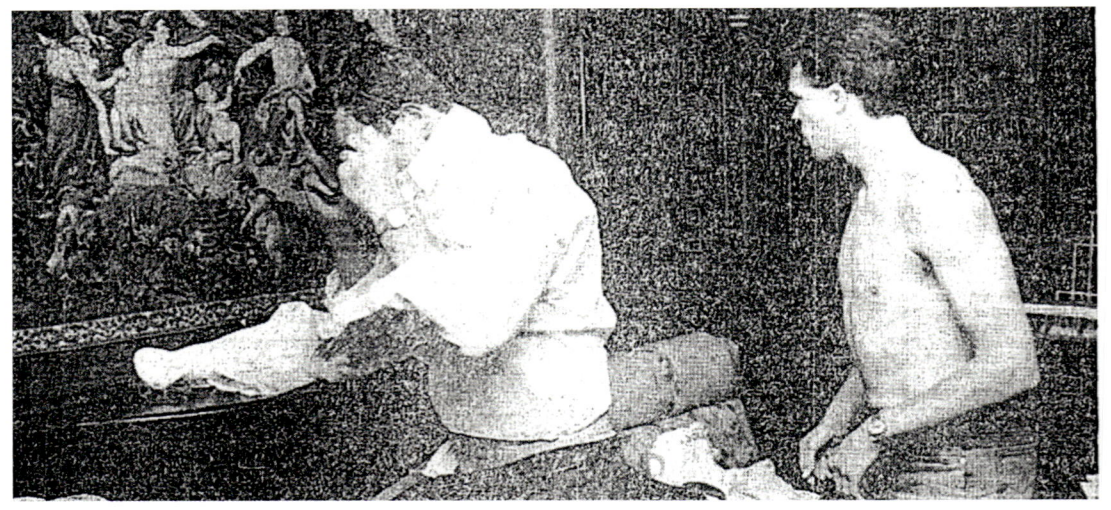

The Irish Independent covers the story as Colm O'Rourke and Liam Hayes "tog out" backstage in the Burlington in 1989

Ultimate dressing room!

A CHARTERED airplane, customs co-operation and a police escort brought Meath's five football all stars to last night's presentation banquet at Dublin's Burlington Hotel in dramatic fashion. But it still left the Meath men with a race against time to get "togged out" for their big night as our picture shows. Quite a change for Colm O'Rourke (left) and Liam Hayes from some of the dressing rooms they've used in the past!

The players had cut short their holiday in the Canary Islands to attend the banquet but a delayed arrival in London's Heathrow Airport meant they missed their connection to Dublin.

50 Years of the GAA All-Stars

Lt. John Maughan chats to Mick Dunne and Shea Fahy at the celebration

for the banquet. The Bank of Ireland liaised with their New York office to arrange a special presentation of the All-Star trophy.

Pete recalled, "I was presented with my award by Cardinal O'Connor in the sacristy in St. Patrick's Cathedral after 8 am Mass. I remember that I had no suit at that time, so I borrowed clothes from a friend of mine. But he was about six inches smaller than me! Afterwards, the bank guys took the trophy with them, which was just as well as we went off and spent the day celebrating". The trophy was taken back to Dublin and Pete's dad accepted it on his behalf at the All-Star banquet a few days later.

In 1989 Shea Fahy was presented with his All-Star trophy in Lebanon while on peace-keeping duty with the Irish Army. Shea was part of the Cork team who lost to Meath in the All-Ireland final the previous September. He was announced on the All-Star football team after his departure for Lebanon. The following February, five days before the All-Star banquet, Mick Dunne flew out to Lebanon, on behalf of the Bank of Ireland, to deliver the trophy.

At a ceremony at the UNIFIL Headquarters in Naquora, on the border between Israel and Lebanon, Lieutenant Colonel Pat McMahon, the Commanding Officer of the Irish 64th Inf Battalion and former Louth footballer, made the presentation. An Israeli film crew was hired to record the presentation, which was then played at the All-Star Banquet in Dublin the following Friday.

The visit meant a lot to Shea and his colleagues, though as he explained, it might never have happened. "When I was contacted by the bank initially, I was reluctant to receive the award. Cork had just been beaten in the All-Ireland final by Meath, and now that I was away, I kinda wanted to forget all about it".

However, Lt Colonel McMahon, encouraged him to accept the award pointing out that it would be a welcome distraction and morale boost for the entire battalion, which was in lockdown at the time. "A local guy had recently been kidnapped and shot, and the Irish troops were being blamed. The troops were on high alert and could not go out as normal. When they did, they had to be escorted by armoured cars".

The camera crew prepare for the All-Star presentation to Shea Fahy

Shea Fahy poses with his All-Star trophy alongside Mick Dunne and Lt Colonel McMahon

All-Star Gazing

When Mick Dunne arrived at Tel Aviv airport, the security was high. Officials took every item out of his baggage, and he had a tough time explaining to the puzzled security guards the significance of the All-Star trophy.

He then travelled with a security escort to Naquora for the presentation to Shea. "There was great excitement. Many people with Irish connections were invited to the ceremony and everyone wanted to meet Mick and talk to him", said Shea. The following Saturday a GAA night was held back at the Battalion base to mark his All-Star. "We all wore our county colours, and it was a rare chance to relax and celebrate".

The original plan was for Dunne to travel to the Battalion base in Lebanon, but news came through in advance of his trip that the Israeli camera crew was unwilling to cross the border "because of the grave dangers there".

Shea concluded, "Mick Dunne was amazing to make the trip to Tel Aviv on his own at such a tense time".

Mick, having witnessed first-hand the interest and passion for the games, proposed that RTÉ start broadcasting major GAA games to the troops abroad. In September that year, both All-Ireland finals were shown live in the base in Lebanon.

In October 2003, Setanta Ó hAilpín flew out to Australia to start his AFL football career with Carlton Football Club, just three weeks after his selection as an All-Star. At the banquet in November, his mother Emilie accepted the All-Star trophy on his behalf. His brother Seán told us, "Then when Setanta came home that Christmas, Mum gathered the family, made Setanta's favourite dinner, and afterwards presented the trophy to him in the kitchen".

In 2014 footballer Paul Flynn missed the All-Star banquet because he was serving as best man for Darren Daly, at Darren's wedding to Paul's sister Sarah. "I knew I had won the All-Star in advance, and I was trying to figure out how I could do both. It was difficult as I didn't want to seem any way arrogant that I wasn't going to the banquet. In fairness to my sister and 'Butsy' they tried to move things around to make it work. But it would have meant I missed doing my speech and a good chunk of the night. It was my closest sister, so in the end, it was family first".

A few months later a night was arranged at Paul's club Fingallians, to present him with his award. Clubmate and fellow All-Star Kieran Duff made the presentation in front of Paul's family and friends.

Kieran Duff presents fellow Fingallian Paul Flynn with his All-Star in 2014

Emilie Ó hAilpín receives her son Setanta's All-Star award from GAA President Seán Kelly

50 Years of the GAA All-Stars

THE ALL-STAR TROPHIES

An All-Star award is a recognition of excellence on the playing field that is given to the chosen few each year. It is also a physical trophy, a statuette, a unique piece of sculpture. Each year 30 trophies are specially crafted for presentation at the All-Star banquet. Since the first Carrolls awards in 1971, top Irish sculptors have been commissioned to design these unique works of art.

Alan Brogan spoke about the All-Star trophies. "I think the actual awards, the trophies, have stood the test of time. That is a crucial part of it, keeping the quality of the actual awards. They are something that will be passed on from generation to generation, they will always stay on the mantelpiece for as long as they survive". Looking at the impressive collection of All-Star trophies the Brogans have accumulated, he added "they are beautiful trophies, really beautiful".

Many have compared the All-Star banquet to 'The Oscars' and in some cases the trophy too. Darragh Ó Sé wrote in *The Irish Times* about a trip to LA with his uncle Páidí when they visited the home of actor Gregory Peck. "There was a neighbour of ours from Ventry who was a curate in Los Angeles, Fr. James Kavanagh. In his time over there, he became friendly with Gregory Peck, who had ancestors from West Kerry", explained Darragh.

"One day he took myself and Páidí up to Gregory Peck's house, this mansion in Hollywood. Gregory gave us the grand tour, showed us around the place and was telling stories. He was halfway through some story about how he bought the house when he was filming Moby Dick and he was reciting lines for us in character as Captain Ahab when, all of a sudden, Páidí stopped him in his tracks. 'You have nothing like a bottle of Miller or something handy there, Gregory?' he asked.

"Basically, Páidí was getting bored of this man and his stories, and it was a hot day in LA. I asked him at one point did he want his picture taken with Gregory's Oscar and he said, 'nah, I'm grand. Sure, haven't I five of them at home?'".

Páidí was selected five years in-a-row, from 1981 to 1985, having played for Kerry since 1975. His nephew Tomás said, "Páidí would have felt he should have got an All-Star earlier than he did in his career, so I knew how hard-earned they were".

In 2002 Tomás was very disappointed not to be selected himself even though, on reflection, he understands why he didn't get one that year. "At the time, I was raging, and I wasn't going to go to the banquet. But Páidí encouraged me to go. He said to me, 'Go to the banquet. You show up, and you show it respect'. So, I did". Tomás added, "Páidí would go up every year. He loved it. He always knew the team beforehand, before it was announced. He took great pride in knowing, being 'in the know' with all the journalists".

Leading Dublin sculptor Gary Trimble was commissioned by Carrolls to design the first All-Star trophies in 1971. Inspired by Rodin and Donatello, he was known for his religious works.

The trophies were cast in bronze and set on a white marble base. Of the hurling trophy, Gary said at the time, "I have tried to portray the poise and grace of hurling but also the tension and the wonderful physical prowess that is so much part of the sport. It is perhaps the most difficult piece of sculpture I have ever undertaken, but it has also been one of my most satisfying commissions". The castings were made by John Behan at the Dublin Art Foundry.

Johnny Carey, Mayo, with one of the first All-Star Football Trophies from 1971

Páidí Ó Sé

Gary Trimble's sketches for the first All-Star trophies in 1971

All-Star Gazing

Gary Trimble reveals the design of the first All-Star hurling trophy to J. H. D. Ryan, managing director Carroll's, John D. Hickey, GAA editor *Irish Independent* and GAA Ard Rúnaí Seán Ó Síocháin

Each piece was individualised with the player's name engraved on the marble base by Weirs Jewellers on Grafton Street. Gay O'Driscoll said, "it meant a lot to me to win one of John Behan's trophies as he was from Marino like me, and his brothers Paddy and Simon Behan had played for Dublin". Johnny Carey remembers being told in 1971 that the trophies were worth 200 pounds. "At the time, that was a lot of money".

Tony McTague says, "I spoke to Gary Trimble about the trophies at the first All-Star banquet. He told me that he tried to ensure that each trophy was different from the other; either a leg or arm would be in a slightly different position". Trimble continued to design the All-Star trophies throughout the Carrolls sponsorship years until he died in a car crash in 1978, still in his artistic prime.

In 1979 Rowan Gillespie was chosen to make the Bank of Ireland All-Star trophies. Rowan was born in Dublin and had moved with his family to live in Cyprus and then York, where he studied art. "My wife and I had returned to Ireland in 1977, attracted by the artists' tax exemption scheme. I was a struggling artist, but my good friend Suzanne McDougal displayed some of my pieces in various exhibitions in the Lad Lane Gallery on Baggot Street".

The gallery was just across the road from the Bank of Ireland headquarters. "One day Donal O'Donovan called me from the bank to ask if I would be interested in making the All-Star trophies. I jumped at the chance". said Rowan. He made the All-Star trophies for the next 12 years and went on to gain international recognition for his bronze casting. He has worked on major public commissions in Ireland and abroad. His most famous work is the Famine Trilogy which includes three commemorative sculptures on Custom House Quay in Dublin, Ireland Park in Toronto and Hunter Island in Tasmania.

Rowan explained how his career as a sculptor took off with the Bank of Ireland commission. "It was the chance of a lifetime. It gave me a guaranteed living as an artist. I often think if I hadn't received that commission for the All-Star trophies in 1979, I may never have made it as an artist".

As Rowan worked on the All-Star trophies, he developed an approach he would continue to use throughout his career. "That first year I researched the GAA to come up

Rowan Gillespie with two uncompleted All-Star trophies in his Clonlea Studios in 2019

Declan Doyle, Bank of Ireland Sponsorship Manager examines one of Robin Buick's All-Star trophies.

with design ideas. I had been educated in the UK, so I hadn't been taught anything about the GAA in school. I found it fascinating and it gave me an opportunity to learn more about my own country. It also gave me a way of working throughout my career, researching a topic extensively before I started to design".

Rowan passed the All-Star assignment to Robin Buick in 1991 as he felt he needed to take on other types of commissions. But he has great memories of making the trophies, which he handcrafted from start to finish.

"I had no equipment or technology in those days. My kids all helped out – it was brilliant. We made the trophies during the summer months. We had a swimming pool, so many of the neighbours' kids used to gather and help too. It was like a summer art class!".

Robin Buick designed the All-Star trophies from 1991 until 1994, when the Bank of Ireland sponsorship came to an end. During that time, he created a special trophy to mark the 20th year of the All-Stars in 1991.

When Powerscreen took over sponsorship in 1995, artist Jarlath Daly spotted an opportunity. He approached managing director Shane McKeown about designing the trophies and got the commission. He has made the All-Star trophies ever since, except for a couple of years in the early 2010s.

Today Jarlath designs trophies for many leading sports organisations in Ireland and the UK. He recognises the impact the All-Star commission had on his career. "Securing the All-Stars afforded me the opportunity to take a risk. I left secondary school teaching after 19 years' service. Thankfully, it was a wise decision as I now have a successful career as a Fine Art Sculptor".

Jarlath creates his pieces in the Brown Street Dublin Foundry. The All-Star design differs from year to year, but each year all 15 trophies for each code are the same.

Leo Higgins, who works with Jarlath, worked on the first Carrolls trophies in the Dublin Foundry. He is very proud of his long association with the All-Stars. "What struck me over the years was how much the players valued the awards".

Jarlath Daly and Leo Higgins in Brown Street Foundry with the 2019 Footballer of the Year trophy.

All-Star Gazing

Kieran McGeeney's parents, Pat and Brigid, proudly display all his trophies in their home

Breda and Gus Lohan display their sons' All-Star trophies with pride

One of Larry Tompkins All-Star trophies displayed in the pub in Cork.

The All-Star trophies take pride of place in the homes of the recipients, though in many cases, the awards reside with their parents. Brigid and Pat McGeeney proudly display their son Kieran's vast collection of medals, awards and trophies. Brigid told us, "I keep saying to Kieran that they all should be in his house now, but he says, 'Mum, you keep them. You and Dad are the reason I won them all'".

Frank and Brian Lohan's five All-Star trophies are showcased by their parents Breda and Gus in the Lohan family home. Gus received two All-Star nominations himself in the early 1970s when he hurled for both Galway and Clare.

Colm Cooper's trophies are kept by his parents too. "My mum has a trophy room, and all eight All-Stars are together on a shelf. Each year I bring them down to the summer festival day at the club (Dr Crokes). It is interesting to see how the kids are much more excited to see the All-Star trophies than the All-Ireland medals". He reflected, "I hope one of the kids goes on to win an All-Star one day and that they were inspired seeing my trophies in the club when they were younger".

Aidan O'Shea's trophies are "in Mam and Dad's house. In the good room. They are deadly". In Johnny Carey's house in Galway, his All-Star trophy from 1971 resides on the mantlepiece performing an important contemporary job – it guards a slip of paper with the Wi-Fi code!

Larry Tompkins has one of his All-Star trophies on display in his sports pub in Cork City. "The All-Star trophy is very defining. It makes people stop and look, as it's so amazing. People often walk past it in the pub and go back again to see it. They really want to hear all about it and talk about what it means. It was an honour to get it".

"If you go into the sitting-room in my parent's house, it is like a bloody shrine to my career!", said Paul Flynn with a laugh. "You've got the four All-Star awards up on the mantelpiece along with every other vase and Man of the Match award. And it is not a big sitting-room. I am one of eight kids; the other seven don't get a look in!

"My mam always says to Fiona, my wife, 'you are welcome to take it all,' but Fiona says, 'no, you keep it, there is no room for it in our house'. I don't know if it is beaten into us to be humble. But still, there isn't a day that I don't walk into the sitting-room in my mam's house and feel a sense of pride at the same time".

Pete Finnerty, who was selected five times, said, "I will probably give one trophy to each of my five children".

In some cases, players have used their awards as a significant way of saying thank-you. Paddy Cullen gave one of his five trophies to publican Liam Dillon years after Liam had given him 100 dollars spending money before his first trip in 1974.

In sadder circumstances, Ger Power chose one of his All-Star trophies as a way of saying thank-you to businessman Michael O'Flynn who helped him significantly when his daughter Jane was ill. She passed away in 2007.

ALL-STAR TOURS FROM 1972 TO 1991

1971
1st All-Star Hurling and Football Teams Selected

1972 San Francisco
(H) 1971 All-Stars vs 1971 All-Ireland Champions Tipperary
(F) 1971 All-Stars vs 1971 All-Ireland Champions Offaly

1973 San Francisco
(H) 1972 All-Stars vs 1972 All-Ireland Champions Kilkenny
(F) 1972 All-Stars vs 1972 All-Ireland Champions Offaly

1974 San Francisco, LA
(H) 1973 All-Stars vs 1973 All-Ireland Champions Limerick
(F) 1973 All-Stars vs 1973 All-Ireland Champions Cork

1975 San Francisco, LA, New York
(H) 1974 All-Stars vs 1974 All-Ireland Champions Kilkenny
(F) 1974 All-Stars vs 1974 All-Ireland Champions Dublin

1976 LA, San Francisco, New York
(H) 1975 All-Stars vs 1975 All-Ireland Champions Kilkenny
(F) 1975 All-Stars vs 1975 All-Ireland Champions Kerry

1977 Chicago, LA, San Francisco, New York
(H) 1976 All-Stars vs 1976 All-Ireland Champions Cork
(F) 1976 All-Stars vs 1976 All-Ireland Champions Dublin

1978 New York (F), Boston (H), San Francisco (All), LA (All)
(H) 1977 All-Stars vs 1977 All-Ireland Champions Cork
(F) 1977 All-Stars vs 1977 All-Ireland Champions Dublin

1979 New York, Chicago, San Francisco, LA
(H) 1979 All-Stars vs 1979 All-Ireland Champions Kilkenny
(F) 1979 All-Stars vs 1979 All-Ireland Champions Kerry

1980 New York, Chicago, LA
(H) 1980 All-Stars vs 1980 All-Ireland Champions Galway
(F) 1980 All-Stars vs 1980 All-Ireland Champions Kerry

1981 No tour

1982 New York, San Francisco
(H) 1981 All-Stars vs 1981 All-Ireland Champions Offaly
(F) 1981 All-Stars vs 1981 All-Ireland Champions Kerry

1983 New York, San Francisco
(H) 1982 All-Stars vs 1982 All-Ireland Champions Kilkenny
(F) 1982 All-Stars vs 1982 All-Ireland Champions Offaly

1984 No tour due to GAA Centenary Year Celebrations

1985 San Francisco, New York
(H) 1984 All-Stars vs 1984 All-Ireland Champions Cork
(F) 1984 All-Stars vs 1984 All-Ireland Champions Kerry

1986 New York, LA
(H) 1985 All-Stars vs 1985 All-Ireland Champions Offaly

1987 San Francisco, Chicago
(H) 1986 All-Stars vs 1986 All-Ireland Champions Cork
(F) 1986 All-Stars vs 1986 All-Ireland Champions Kerry

1988 Boston, San Francisco
(H) 1987 All-Stars vs 1987 All-Ireland Champions Galway
(F) 1987 All-Stars vs 1987 All-Ireland Champions Meath

1989 New York
(H) 1988 All-Stars vs 1988 All-Ireland Champions Galway

1990 New York, San Francisco
(F) 1989 All-Stars vs 1989 All-Ireland Champions Cork

1990 Toronto
(H) 1989 All-Stars vs 1989 All-Ireland Champions Tipperary
(F) 1989 All-Ireland Semi-Finalists Dublin vs Tyrone

1991 Toronto
(H) 1990 All-Stars vs 1990 All-Ireland Champions Cork
(F) 1990 All-Stars vs 1990 All-Ireland Champions Cork

Leaving on a Jet Plane

A significant part of the All-Star story has been the opportunity given to players, to travel and play abroad. The purpose of the trip is two-fold: to reward the selected players and to strengthen the links with Irish communities overseas. All-Star tours are primarily funded by the sponsors with some assistance from the GAA at home and in the host cities. The tours usually involve an exhibition match for the All-Stars. In the first two decades of the scheme, the reigning All-Ireland hurling and football champions were included in the tour to provide opposition for All-Star teams.

So how did the first All-Star tour come about? The early discussions centred around an exhibition match in Ireland between the All-Stars and a 'Rest of Ireland' team. This idea was based on the American All-Star model of annual games in the major sports. The committee documented that, "the All-Stars would be keen to prove they were the best and the Rest of Ireland players would be attracted to play as a means of showing that they should not have been passed over by the All-Stars selectors". The match in Ireland never came off and the GAA soon began to discuss a foreign trip with sponsors Carrolls.

Earlier in 1971, a GAA contingent had travelled to San Francisco to play an exhibition match as part of the city's St Patrick's Day festival. The Kerry football team with stars like Mick O'Connell, Donie O'Sullivan and Mick O'Dwyer played a selection of other top players like Seán O'Neill, Billy Morgan and Liam Sammon.

That trip had been a great success and when planning started for a return visit in 1972, Seán Ó Síocháin was keen to bring the football All-Ireland champions. There was interest in San Francisco in seeing the All-Stars too because of the parallel with the US All-Stars model. Carrolls offered to fund a trip for the All-Star footballers, then this was soon extended to include the hurling All-Stars and the All-Ireland champions.

Up to then, the East Coast of America had been the established destination for visiting GAA teams. From the 1920s there was a tradition of GAA teams travelling to New York and during the 1960s the National League final was hosted annually by New York GAA.

However, by 1971 the relationship between the GAA Central Council and New York GAA had become strained. In the 1970 National League final played in New York, an incident that left referee Clem Foley needing hospitalisation, deepened the rift. Following this the GAA imposed a two-year suspension on New York GAA.

All-Star Gazing

CARROLLS GAA allstars

FOR IMMEDIATE RELEASE

The Carrolls G.A.A. All-Star Football team will play against the All-Ireland Champions Offaly in San Francisco on March 26th and April 2nd 1972. This was announced by Mr Pat Fanning, President of the G.A.A. at a reception for the four All-Ireland football teams in Dublin on Monday 26th September.

The Carrolls G.A.A. All-Star football and hurling teams will be chosen by leading journalists who cover gaelic games throughout the year. The hurling team will be announced on October 19th and the football team on November 8th. Players will also have to be picked to fill positions on the Carrolls G.A.A. All-Star football team to replace any of the Offaly men who may be on that team as Offaly will have prior claim on their men for the 10 day visit to the United States.

The visit to America is organised by the United Irish Societies in California and this development adds greatly to the Carrolls G.A.A. All-Star Awards which are sponsored by Carrolls of Dundalk, the well known firm of cigarette manufactures. Both the Carrolls G.A.A. All-Star teams will be presented with their awards at a Banquet to be held in Dublin in December.

ENQUIRIES: P.D. Heneghan

28th September 1971

NEWS

p.j.carroll & company limited
cigarette and tobacco manufacturers est.1824
grand parade, Dublin 6

All-Star Hurling Line-Up

Damian Martin

Tony Maher, Pat Hartigan, Jim Treacy

Niall Wheeler, Justin McCarthy, Martin Coogan

John Connolly, Frank Cummins,

Jimmy McNamara, John Quigley, Eddie Keher,

Mick Bermingham, Ray Cummins, Eamonn Cregan.

Subs: Denis Coughlan and Pádraic Fahy.

All-Star Football Line-Up

P.J. Smyth

John Carey, Jack Cosgrove, Donie O'Sullivan,

Brian McEniff, Mick Carolan, Pat Reynolds

Liam Sammon, Ray Carolan

Eamonn Coleman, Ray Cummins, Jimmy Hannify

Andy McCallin, Seán O'Neill, Seamus Leydon.

It was confirmed that the first All-Star tour would visit San Francisco in March 1972, again to coincide with the St Patrick's Day festival. The trip was organised locally by two groups, the Saint Patrick Fathers and the United Irish Societies (UIS). The president of the UIS was Irishman Andy McKenna who ran a travel agency in San Francisco and played a huge role in organising the trip. Many successful business people in the Irish community also supported the tour.

The travelling party included the two All-Star teams plus football champions Offaly and hurling champions Tipperary. As some of the All-Stars selected were also All-Ireland champions, additional players were required to fill in as replacements on both All-Star teams.

Niall Wheeler, Justin McCarthy, Jimmy McNamara and John Quigley replaced the four Tipperary hurlers.

Brian McEniff, Mick Carolan, Ray Carolan and Eamonn Coleman replaced the four Offaly footballers. Jimmy Hannify replaced All-Star Mickey Kearins who could not travel. Pádraic Fahy and Denis Coughlan were brought as substitutes.

Kilkenny County Board chairman Nicholas Purcell and Galway County Board secretary John Dunne were asked by the GAA to manage the two All-Star teams. Jimmy Hatton and John Moloney refereed the hurling and football matches, respectively.

The excitement began to build once the tour was announced. Pat Hartigan remembers that "there was lots of speculation that first year because initially, the hurlers weren't due to travel".

Many of the players had never been abroad before. Even for those who had, the chance to travel to San Francisco was special. Jack Cosgrove said, "the West Coast of America was a whole different ball game. Not many Irish people had been there at that time. Slowly but surely, it dawned on us what was happening. There were phone calls about the All-Stars, measurements for blazers. Then you realised that you were going to San Francisco. Wow! The excitement kicked in after Christmas".

Ray Cummins had been to New York for the National League final with Cork in 1970. "So, I had travelled abroad before. But this was unbelievable, it was incredible to get to the West Coast".

"I had only been on a plane once before. That was to Ibiza", recalls Andy McCallin, "but I had never been on a transatlantic flight, on such a huge plane".

50 Years of the GAA All-Stars

The first All-Star Touring Party departs from Shannon Airport March 1972

Donie O'Sullivan with Paddy Downey in Downtown San Francisco March 1972

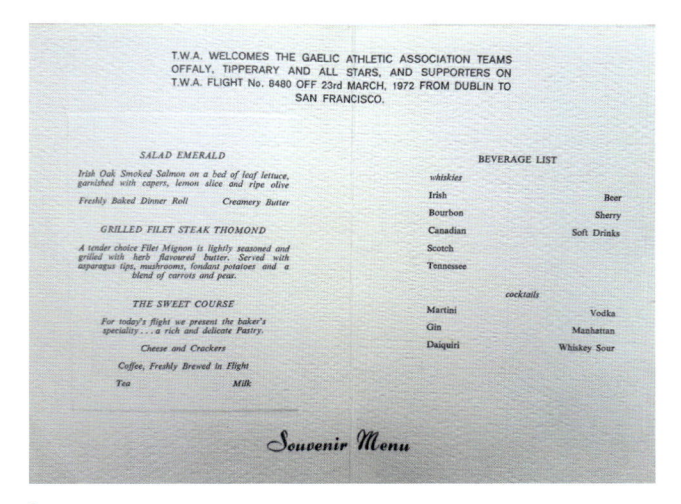

FLOWER POWER IN SAN FRANCISCO

San Francisco in the 1970s was known for the 'flower power' movement and bohemian street life. Most of the Irish community lived near the Irish Centre located beside the Golden Gate Park in downtown San Francisco. Tadhg O'Connor recalled, "there were lots of hippies around the place, people chanting and spaced out".

"I remember the characters in downtown Market Square", recalls Donie O'Sullivan. "The smell of marijuana from all the hippies".

BOMB BLAST IN BELFAST

By contrast, the atmosphere back in Ireland was tense at that time. Seán O'Neill almost missed the All-Star trip as he was injured in the Donegall Street bombing in Belfast, three days before the departure of the tour. The incident was part of the ongoing 'troubles' in Northern Ireland. A car bomb was detonated on the city centre street crowded with shoppers, schoolchildren and office workers. Seán, who worked nearby in his Solicitors practice, was knocked unconscious. His only lasting impact from the blast was glass in his ear, but his doctor strongly advised him not to fly. However, Seán stressed the importance of the All-Star tour and got the go-ahead.

SPENDING ALLOWANCE

The players received an allowance of $60 to cover the entire trip. Some players had this supplemented by their clubs or county boards, such as Damien Martin, whose club St. Rynagh's presented him with £50.

TWA In-Flight Menu 1st All-Star Trip 1972

However, the Offaly footballers were upset about the trip expenses, and many threatened not to travel. "We got a higher allowance on previous trips to New York so to us, $60 was very low", said Tony McTague.

The GAA was not sympathetic and issued an ultimatum to the players to "withdraw their demand for extra personal expenses". Paddy Downey reported in *The Irish Times,* "the GAA Executive felt that this demand was not in accord with the amateur status of the Association and that if not withdrawn another team will be invited to take their place on tour". In the end, the issue was resolved, and most of the Offaly players travelled.

In March 1972, the first All-Star party crossed the Atlantic on a TWA 707 jumbo jet, departing from Dublin and then Shannon on Thursday, March 23rd and returning home 10 days later, on April 4th.

All-Star Gazing

Described by Downey as, "the biggest ever promotion of Gaelic games abroad", the 175-strong travelling party included players, team managers, county board officials, GAA dignitaries, representatives from Carrolls, the All-Star Steering Committee and other journalists. Some relatives and friends of the players travelled too, plus guests including Wexford hurling legend Nickey Rackard.

In a letter to those travelling Seán Ó Síocháin outlined, "TWA is providing first-class service on this Charter, including a feature film between Shannon and Pittsburgh and another between Pittsburgh and San Francisco".

The airline may have provided first-class food and films, but the abiding memory for most players is the abundance of free cigarettes provided by Carrolls. "Cigarettes were thrown everywhere", says Donie O'Sullivan. "I remember Pat Heneghan giving them out on the plane and John Dowling from Offaly giving out Tullamore Dew whiskey".

However, as reported by Paddy Downey, "most of the passengers were sleeping peacefully and, there was not a flower to be seen in anyone's hair when the lights of San Francisco became visible".

The party arrived in San Francisco at 8pm local time and was greeted by hundreds of Irish Americans plus the Mayor of San Francisco, Joseph L. Alioto. The party then travelled to City Hall for a reception.

HOST FAMILIES

To keep the tour costs down, the players did not stay in hotels. Instead, they were hosted individually by local families from the Irish American community.

The players were told, "there will be no question of paying your hosts for the accommodation or meals but, it would be a gesture very much appreciated if each member of the party took out an appropriate present for his host".

The hosts would look after the players and bring them wherever they needed to go. In most cases this worked out very well and provided a 'home away from home' for the players.

"I was hosted every year by Kevin Downey", said Seán O'Neill. Kevin, a successful businessman in San Francisco, was originally from County Down and was one of the trip's organisers. Seán felt that in general hosting was a great idea as, "it meant the players mixed and formed great friendships whereas if they stayed in a hotel, they would have kept to themselves.

It was a fantastic experience to spend time with an influential character like Kevin Downey, who made every effort to give us a fantastic time".

Pat Hartigan of Limerick, a member of the Carrolls G.A.A. All-Stars hurling team, greeted by Mr. Thomas Mellon, San Francisco City Administrator, when the teams visited San Francisco City Hall.

Newspaper report of the first All-Star tour

Andy McCallin and Eamonn Coleman were hosted by the Spears, originally from Co. Down, and it worked out very well. "On leaving I gave one of my two All-Star jackets to the son of the family", recalls Andy, "though I still have the green one".

The host families were scattered all over the city and the suburbs. Jack Cosgrove stayed with a grand-aunt who lived out in the Sunset area of San Francisco. "I had never met her before. She went to bed at 6pm every evening and I was only 22 at the time! But she was delighted to have me stay and organised a party to introduce me to her Irish friends. They all came with presents for me: books, maps and plenty of envelopes filled with dollars".

Jack soon made alternative plans. "I met a girl I knew from Clifden; she was working in a bank downtown. Her partner was a cop in the San Francisco Police Force. She invited me to stay with them in the city. It was fantastic. They took me to Alcatraz, and her partner got special access to San Quentin prison, which was amazing".

For Pat Hartigan, things worked out well with his host Teresa Halligan. "We became great friends and stayed in touch afterwards. I travelled over to San Francisco for her 90th birthday party there a few years ago".

Michael 'Babs' Keating tells a different story. "Hosting could be a disaster because San Francisco was so spread out you could be way out in the wilds". Babs was assigned a host family outside the city near his mother's cousin, who was a nun. "My mother wanted me to stay close to the convent so I could go to 7 o'clock mass every morning". The hosts collected Babs from City Hall and brought him to all the matches. But he never saw the nun. One day he rang his pal, the late Mick Roche, and asked, 'how's everything going?' Mick said, 'awful, they (the hosts) have been fighting all night'. Fr. Nick Clavin was due to stay in the same house as Willie Bryan, but as Willie had brought his new wife Millie on the

50 Years of the GAA All-Stars

Seán Ó Siocháin, Kevin Downey, Seán O'Neill and John Duffy in San Francisco and below, Invitation to a welcoming party at Harrington's Bar, San Francisco

Welcoming Party
ALL IRELAND TEAMS
Friday Evening, March 24, 1972 at 8:00 p.m.
Harrington's
9 JONES STREET — SAN FRANCISCO
COMPLIMENTARY
TEAM DINNER & GUEST
PAT CLANCY TRIO
CORNED BEEF & CABBAGE

trip, there was no room for Nick. He ended up staying with Séamus Darby and John Smith. The three of them shared one room with two beds. "We rotated so that every third night you slept on the floor", said Fr. Nick. Despite the sleeping arrangements, "we all made good friends with the family. That was a real advantage to the hosting. We continued to be friends over the years".

The night before the first All-Star matches there was a party for the visitors in Harrington's Bar downtown. It was a very Irish affair, with traditional entertainment and food. The venue became a meeting point for the players during that and subsequent trips.

ALL-STAR MATCHES

The All-Star hurling and football matches took place over two weekends in Balboa Stadium, a soccer pitch in downtown San Francisco. The scores of each match would be combined and the team with the highest aggregate score would win the series.

The organisers had worked hard to lengthen the hot dry Balboa pitch by moving back the surrounding banks, but it was still much shorter than a GAA field which particularly affected the hurling matches.

Damien Martin who was selected MVP, 'the most valuable player' for the tournament remembers, "I made a save against Babs in the match. The ball hit me in the chest, and everyone thought it was an amazing save, but it was only because the pitch was so short".

The selection of an MVP for each code, was a new concept for the Irish lads, years before the GAA introduced the 'Man of the Match' award back home. Fr. Nick Clavin was named football MVP.

There was a live commentary during the matches on the loudspeaker in the ground. Known locally as, 'calling the game,' Eugene Mulligan still remembers snippets he heard while playing the match, "Eugene was a unanimous All-Star selection, and now we know why".

MICK DUNNE

United Irish Societies
and
Saint Patrick's Fathers
present

GAELIC FOOTBALL
OFFALY, ALL IRELAND CHAMPIONS
&
CARROLLS G.A.A. ALLSTAR
AWARD WINNERS 1971

HURLING
TIPPERARY ALL IRELAND CHAMPIONS
&
CARROLLS G.A.A. ALLSTAR
AWARD WINNERS 1971

1972

Match Programme for the first All-Star match

All-Star Gazing

| The first All-Star match about to throw-in at Balboa Stadium in March 1972

| Hurling referee Jimmy Hatton and spectators on the grassy slopes

| Séamus Ó Riain (middle) with All-Star hurling manager Nicholas Purcell (left) as the All-Star and Tipperary players parade at Balboa Stadium

| All-Star Plaque

| Eddie Keher receives the Perpetual trophy from Tim Cahill

Tipperary won the first ever All-Star match by a score of 6-10 to 6-7. All-Star Mick Bermingham recalls, "I thought it would be an exhibition match, but it was quite competitive. The referee Jim Hatton let a lot go, he wasn't handing out any cards".

Mick remembers Séamus Ó Riain coming into the dressing room to talk to the All-Stars before the first match. A former GAA President, Ó Riain was there as part of the Tipperary delegation. "I remember that he stressed the importance of the match and how 'we needed to give an exhibition of hurling for the locals and to play the game in the right spirit'. So we went out for the first half and took him at his word. We came back in at half-time black and blue! We had loads of injuries. Eddie Keher needed stitches in the back of his head. I had a bruised eye. We realised Tipperary were not doing as Ó Riain had asked so in the second-half we stood up to them".

The All-Stars decided they weren't going to be caught off guard again and they did extra training in advance of the second match.

The following weekend the hurling All-Stars, helped by dual star Ray Cummins, won the second match comfortably (5-17 to 2-16), making them overall winners of the series. Cummins had opted to play for the footballers the first week, but he was asked to play both matches the second weekend.

Eddie Keher, captain of the All-Star hurlers, received the winners' trophy from United Irish Societies' Thomas Cahill. Cahill originally from Kilkenny himself, was also the former Chief of Police in San Francisco. Not realising that The Cahill Cup was to be a perpetual trophy, Eddie brought the cup home and kept it. "I remember when we returned without it in 1973, the Commissioner went mad", laughed Eddie.

The All-Star football matches were also competitive. The first weekend, the All-Stars beat champions Offaly by a point (0-12 to 0-11). Liam Sammon, captain of the football All-Stars, remembers, "there was a lot of competition between Offaly and Galway at that time. The first match ended with the All-Stars scoring a controversial late point. Offaly narrowly lost, so they were a bit sore about that. They were determined to win the second match, and there were rumours that they trained all week". Martin Furlong recalled, "well, there were no niceties anyway".

Offaly won the second match by four points (1-15 to 1-11) which meant they won the series on aggregate. They were presented with the Tom O'Sullivan Cup, which had been donated by the local Kerry society in memory of one of their players Tom 'Kerry' O'Sullivan.

Jack Cosgrove remembers the high temperatures at the stadium. "We were training one day in the searing heat. The

Tipperary players (visible Len Gaynor, Liam King, Dinny Ryan and Séamus Hogan) and the hurling All-Stars (visible Pat Hartigan and Nicky Purcell) behind the cheerleaders in Balboa Stadium in San Francisco in 1972

Match official Jimmy Hennessey, Tipperary players (L to R), Jack Ryan, Babs Keating, Roger Ryan, and replacement Jimmy McNamara take to the field in San Francisco in 1972

Tipperary players (L to R) PJ Ryan, Noel Lane, Jim Fogarty, Noel O'Dwyer, Paul Byrne, Frances Loughnane and All-Star Éamonn Cregan in the pre-match parade in San Francisco in 1972

All-Star Gazing

On the road to Lake Tahoe - L to R: Mick Ryan, Denis Coughlan, Orla Ní Shíocháin, Dinny Ryan, Jack Ryan, Ray Cummins, Anne Sheehy, Anne Carroll and Sheila Brosnan

ground was rock hard, and the sprinklers were on. Yet there was John Dunne still wearing his traditional hat and braces. It is an image I will never forget".

Each player received a wooden plaque as a memento of the inaugural All-Star matches.

A reported 6,000 spectators watched the first two games, but the crowd was lower the following weekend, possibly because the matches were held on Easter weekend. The *San Francisco Chronicle* reported, "the spectators who overflowed the stands onto Balboa's grassy slopes enjoyed the games immensely".

LOCAL REACTION

The visit of the All-Stars and the All-Ireland Champions generated a lot of local interest. People with Irish connections travelled from all over the West Coast of America to see their hurling and football heroes in action. "There were massive crowds around the city the week of the All-Star tour. I remember the nights in Harrington's Bar and John Connolly singing and playing music", said Mick Bermingham.

There were many official events in the Irish Centre during the 15-day trip and the players were the guests of honour as they mingled with the locals. "We were like Gods in San Francisco with those green All-Star blazers", reflected Andy McCallin.

Kevin Downey invited Andy to play golf at the Olympic Club, one of the most prestigious golf resorts in the area. "I wasn't a golfer, and when Kevin realised this, he gave me a swipe card to access the sauna and steam rooms instead. I brought a few of the lads and we were delighted with ourselves".

"It was all matches, dances and functions", recalled Johnny Carey. The Galway Society organised additional functions so that their members could meet the Galway players. The profit from the event was divided between the players at the end of the night. "Everyone wanted to be part of it. We were treated like royalty", recalled Jack Cosgrove.

Jack remembers the three McDonagh brothers, originally from Clifden, who owned a drapery store in San Francisco. "They took us to their shop and told us to take whatever we wanted. Then they took us to a restaurant where they were well known, so the red carpet was out". He still remembers the meal, the steak overflowing on the plate. "By the time we got to the main course, it seemed like we had eaten 12 courses already".

Jack continued, "then a stretch limousine arrived to take us to the Playboy Club, where the brothers were keyholders. There was plenty of champagne. It was such an experience". Jack was given a Playboy calendar before he left. "I didn't bring that souvenir home to my mother!", he added with a smile.

Jack was so well looked after in San Francisco that he came home with extra money. "Nobody could believe it. In fact, I had enough money to buy a car".

Kevin Ger O'Sullivan, Billy Morgan, Ray Cummins, Jim O'Sullivan, Seán O'Neill and Donie O'Sullivan in San Francisco

LAKE TAHOE

There was an official trip to a casino in Lake Tahoe, Nevada where, unlike California, gambling was legal. Some players missed the official trip, so they went by Greyhound bus instead. Others were driven there by their hosts.

Eugene Mulligan recalled, "we played the slot machines and Mick Ryan won $1,100. We scooped up Mick's winnings and left the casino immediately. The girl who paid out the money couldn't believe that we didn't want to stay and play on. But we were afraid that we would lose the money which was a small fortune. Mick used his casino winnings to pay for half the house he built when he got back home".

TIJUANA

There was also a visit south to Tijuana, just across the tightly controlled Mexican border. Eddie Keher recalled a day trip with his host. "We made a visit to Tijuana and on the way back into the US there was a police check at the border. One of the Irish lads had no passport with him, and they were not going to let us through".

Eddie explained to the border policeman that they were over from Ireland to play GAA matches in San Francisco but he "wasn't having any of it", laughed Eddie. "Then I remembered that I had the programme from the All-Star match with me and that did the trick".

FRIENDSHIPS

The first All-Star tour gave players from different counties and different provinces a chance to spend time together. It was also a unique chance for footballers and hurlers to mix. Babs Keating got to know footballers like Antrim's Andy McCallin. "I met him on the plane on the way out. We stayed in touch after the trip and Andy came to stay in my brother's hotel (The Kilcoran Lodge) many times since 1972".

"The trip in 1972 was a great chance to meet players from other counties", said John Connolly. "I got to know the Kilkenny lads, Jim Treacy and Frank Cummins. We became great friends and are still friends to this day. I was also excited to meet the footballers, lads like Colm McAlarney and Seán O'Neill". John was amazed that footballers put the hurlers up on a pedestal.

Ray Cummins recalled how at that time players from different counties only met for Railway Cup matches. "The Cork lads would go up and back on the train the day of the match. There was no time to get to know each other. So, it was great to socialise and to train together. There was a different atmosphere when you met the players on tour compared to meeting them at home".

Frances Loughnane agreed, "you didn't have as much contact with other players back then, you would have your meal after a game and go your separate ways".

"Today fellas meet in college but back then there were no opportunities to meet players from other counties", said Eddie Keher. "I became friends with Pat Hartigan". An additional highlight for Eddie on that first trip was the chance to meet hurling legend Nickey Rackard.

Tony Maher spoke about getting to know the legendary hurler Jimmy Doyle as they were both hosted in San Francisco by Corkman Don Cummins. Tony wrote after Jimmy's passing in 2015, "we formed a bond on that All-Star trip that lasted for years. Any time Tipperary played a game in Páirc Uí Chaoimh, Jimmy would come over to the house for a cup of tea, and I often met him off the train. We were great friends. Every year, I would get a Christmas card from him with the comment, 'old friends are best'".

For Frank Cummins getting a chance to meet Seán O'Neill, "was a highlight of my GAA career as he was my hero. I remember watching him in the 1960 All-Ireland Final, a historic day when Down beat Kerry to win their first football All-Ireland".

Donie O'Sullivan recalled, "The first All-Star trip in 1972 was really magnificent. Everything was so different out there. The people in San Francisco were wonderful. There were so many officials and press that year, compared to the previous trip in 1971. I got to know Dave Guiney the journalist, as well as his good friend Nickey Rackard, who was on the trip as a supporter. It was great to meet the hurlers too because we were usually kept apart at home. Meeting the likes of Jimmy Doyle was fantastic".

Andy McCallin said, "I knew Eugene Mulligan and Seán O'Neill already, but I got to know Pat Reynolds, Mick Ryan, Eamonn Coleman and Ray Cummins".

Jack Cosgrove said it was great to see people like Andy McCallin from Antrim and Mickey Kearins from Sligo being honoured that first year. "Guys from counties that wouldn't have a chance to win the All-Ireland, people you wouldn't have met. I still meet Willie Bryan and Pat Reynolds as they come to Clifden regularly. Mick Roche was a great player and one of the great characters on the trip in 1972".

"GAA teams didn't socialise back then", said Séamus Leyden. "Teams even dined separately after matches. In San Francisco, the camaraderie generated was great". For Babs Keating, a treasured memory from that first All-Star trip is the time he spent with his great friend Mick Roche, who passed away in 2016. Mick worked for sponsors Carrolls at that time.

The players got to know the journalists too. Eugene Mulligan remembers playing handball with Mick Dunne in the Olympic Club in San Francisco. Jim O'Sullivan of The Irish Examiner (then called The Cork Examiner) travelled on the trip to Lake Tahoe with Ray Cummins, Tony Maher and Jimmy Doyle. He wrote years later that he had the privilege to know Jimmy as a friend, having first met him on the inaugural All-Star trip. "I got to know Jimmy the person, who was kind, considerate and humble".

O'Sullivan was on the All-Star selection committee from 1971 until his retirement in 2009. He reflected, "while I didn't appreciate it at the time, the decision to reward the chosen All-Stars with trips abroad would prove invaluable to me and others. It wasn't just the fact of getting the opportunity to travel to San Francisco, Los Angeles, Chicago and New York - a delightful prospect in your late 20s –but the more tangible benefit of getting to know players from different counties which not only established friendships but facilitated interviews in the longer term".

SUCCESSFUL TRIP

After 10 days in San Francisco, the first All-Star trip came to an end. The party continued for many on the flight back home. Séamus Leyden remembers the singsong on the way back, "lads singing 'Me and Bobby Magee'".

Bad weather on the approach to Ireland made for a rough landing. The plane was hit by lightning as it flew in over Achill Island. Séamus said, "the lads who weren't drinking were terrified". When they all disembarked at Shannon, "the sober lads wouldn't get back on the plane. They took a coach to Dublin instead".

The inaugural All-Star trip generated tremendous interest along the West Coast of America and plenty of excitement at home too. The Irish in San Francisco were delighted to meet the GAA stars and to see them in action in an era that predated the broadcast of Gaelic games in the US. "To see the players in real life was incredible", said Tim Murphy, who had moved to San Francisco in the 1950s and was one of the United Irish Society organisers. "In those days we had no access to Gaelic games on TV or radio. The only way to know what was happening in the All-Ireland Final was to ring someone at home and listen to the radio commentary down the phone line!".

Seeing the huge interest in the games in San Francisco, the GAA organised the first transmission of an All-Ireland Football Final to the city by satellite the following September. When the final between Kerry and Offaly ended in a draw, the replay in October was also transmitted. Tim said, "I can remember the screams of joy and tears of excitement when the big screen showed Croke Park for the first time. People danced in the streets when Willie Bryan accepted the Sam Maguire from President Pat Fanning in the replay on October 15th". Tim believes the transmission was a direct result of the strengthening of relations that occurred during those first visits in 1971 and 1972.

In an interview after the first All-Star trip, Andy McKenna said, "the Irish in San Francisco were determined to make a success of it. The various county associations got together and got things organised. But the real heroes of this success story have been the families who have acted as hosts to the players. Friendships have been established for life because of the tours. All the players have been great ambassadors, there has never been a complaint about their behaviour and the tears that were shed at San Francisco airport on the morning of departure are testimony to the success of the tour".

Plans for a return trip to San Francisco in 1973 were soon put in place. This time the two All-Star teams, hurling champions Kilkenny and for the second time, football champions Offaly were in the travelling party.

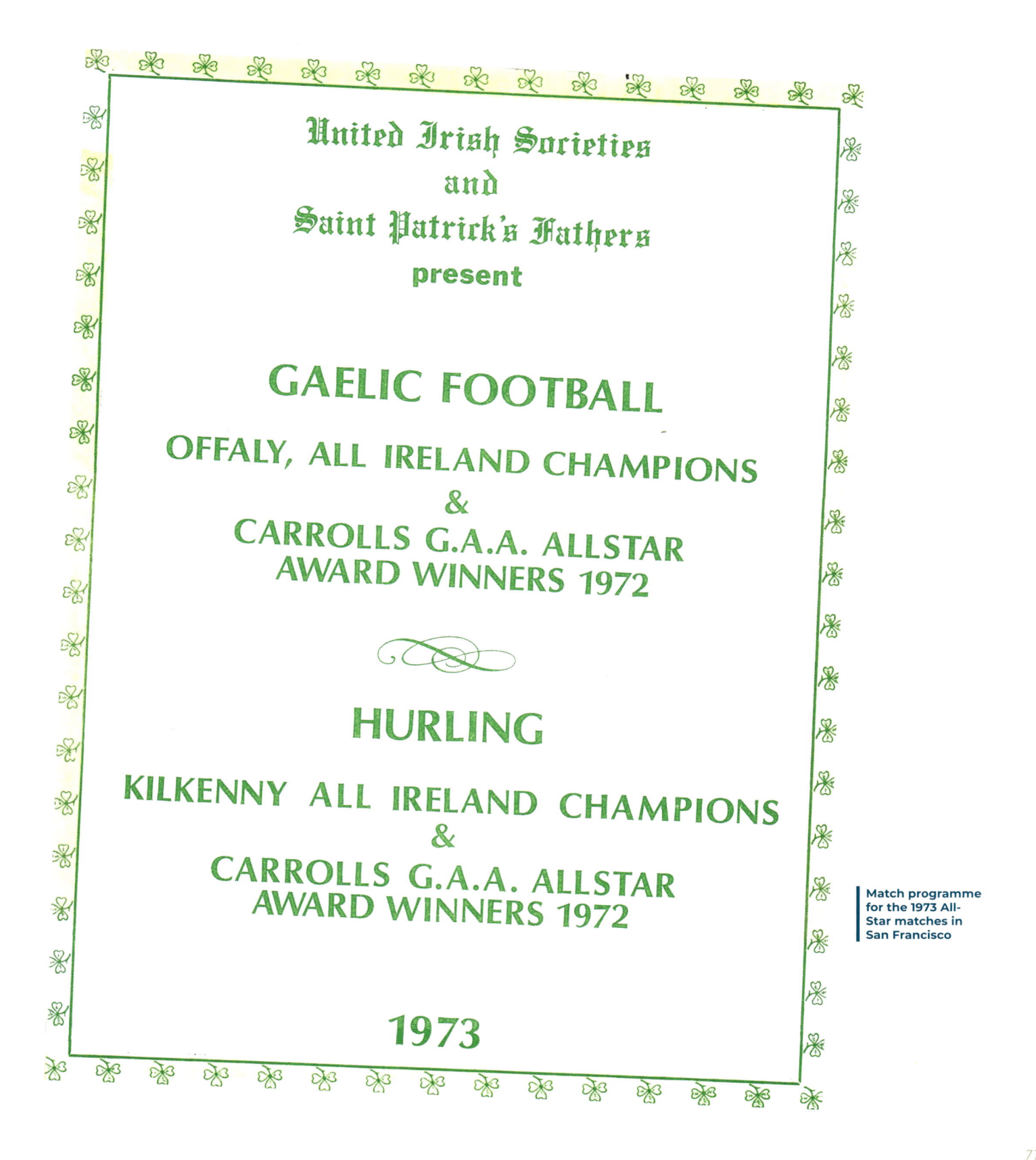

United Irish Societies
and
Saint Patrick's Fathers
present

GAELIC FOOTBALL

OFFALY, ALL IRELAND CHAMPIONS
&
CARROLLS G.A.A. ALLSTAR AWARD WINNERS 1972

HURLING

KILKENNY ALL IRELAND CHAMPIONS
&
CARROLLS G.A.A. ALLSTAR AWARD WINNERS 1972

1973

Match programme for the 1973 All-Star matches in San Francisco

All-Star Gazing

Annual Trip in the Seventies

As the All-Star trips to America became an annual event, each year the players would return with great stories that circulated among the players back home. As the tours grew in popularity, many friends and supporters travelled at their own expense and the touring party often required two jumbo jets. Jim Whitty, who co-ordinated the All-Star activities within Bank of Ireland, recalled, "there was lots of arranging in those trips. Chicago did it best; there was no nonsense. There was always a row with John Kerry O'Donnell in New York".

The itinerary was soon extended; LA was added in 1974 and New York was included in 1975. In 1977 the All-Star tour went to four US cities: Chicago, LA, San Francisco and New York. Boston was visited for the first time in 1978. In 1979 the first Bank of Ireland sponsored trip to America lasted three weeks.

There was considerable prestige associated with the All-Star trip back then. It generated lots of excitement, as the opportunity to travel abroad was still quite rare and in an era before team holidays it was the only chance for the players to travel together.

"Winning an All-Star became a target for players largely because they wanted to go on the trip", said Jimmy Barry Murphy. In 1973 when the Cork footballers won the All-Ireland, he remembers one of his teammates turning to him as they climbed the steps of the Hogan Stand and saying excitedly, "this means we will get to go to San Francisco!".

When Jimmy went on the All-Star trip in 1974, it was his first time abroad and an exciting prospect for a 19-year-old. "Going to San Francisco, I felt like I was going to the end of the world. That trip really broadened my horizons, having to mix with the hosts and the players from other counties".

Martin Quigley said, "The excitement of winning the All-Star award was about going on the trip. I would have had no chance of travelling apart from the All-Star tour. I was a young student, only 22, when I went on my first trip in 1974. It was really nice having people looking after you. Mick Dunne was very friendly with us all". For Noel Skehan, "the trip to San Francisco was monstrous. It was a great chance to meet the footballers, and to get to know the journalists too".

Joe Connolly was the captain of the All-Star Hurling team in 1979. That year his brothers John, Michael and Pádraig were on the trip too. He described how much the tour meant to them. "We had a very ordinary upbringing. Ten kids and our parents, living in a house with three bedrooms. So, for us the All-Star trips were extraordinary. To go on tour for three weeks and visit four American cities was amazing. The Yanks were another level of sophistication compared to us in those days". While Michael and Pádraig never received All-Star awards, Michael was nominated an impressive seven times and was often teased by his brothers, 'always a star, but never an All-Star'.

The brothers have many great memories. Joe recalled the post-match All-Star function in New York one year. "The speeches went on and on and on. So, five of us sneaked out the back and headed off downtown. We ended up in the red-light district around Times Square". With them was Iggy Clarke, who was a priest at the time. He was wearing his

Mick Dunne interviews John Kerry O'Donnell, the owner of Gaelic Park in New York. Dunne noted, "Mr New York GAA sparkles during an interview"

Éamonn Grimes, Charlie McCarthy and Mick Malone in Balboa Stadium

Jimmy Barry Murphy (seventh from left) with the All-Star party in Shannon in 1974

collar and was spotted by a dude on the street who said, "hey Padre, do you want to see how the other half lives?" Iggy laughed at the memory, "I think they took me out to show me the other side of life!".

Iggy travelled on many All-Star trips in the 1970s. One year, while he was still studying at Maynooth, he had to get special permission to go. "It meant I missed the exams and had to sit them in September. Some of the professors complained; they thought I shouldn't have the freedom to go on the trip. But Tomás Ó Fiaich was the president of the college at the time, and he understood".

"I was gobsmacked meeting all the Kerry lads, the likes of Ogie Moran. It was magic. To realise they were just ordinary fellas like ourselves. But I remember going to Gaelic Park for the first time and the bare pitch with dust rising up. I was expecting something better; I couldn't believe it".

ALL-STAR REPLACEMENTS

The tradition of bringing additional players to replace the All-Ireland champions, who had been named on the All-Star teams, continued. It gave many players an unexpected opportunity to travel to America. The All-Star Steering Committee usually chose players who had been nominated for an All-Star and they prioritised players from the smaller counties. For these players, being chosen as an All-Star replacement was a significant honour.

The organisers made a slight distinction between the All-Stars and the replacements as Billy Morgan recalled. "During the Carrolls sponsorship the replacements got the green All-Star jacket, but it had no All-Star crest on it. I was delighted because it meant I could wear the jacket again when I came home, as I had no other jacket at the time".

John Quigley was a replacement on the first trip in 1972. "Even though I didn't win an All-Star that year, I am very honoured to be the first Wexford man to ever go on an All-Star trip". John described in impressive detail the moment he heard the news. "I was in Poulpeasty trying to buy a gun off a farmer called Murphy when the postman came with the letter from the Carrolls All-Stars telling me that I was a replacement for Pat Delaney. It was exciting because it was just three weeks before the trip departed".

When Mickey Kearins was not free to travel one year, Seán Ó Síocháin asked him to select another Sligo man to replace him. Mickey rang his teammate Barnes Murphy to ask if he would like to go to San Francisco with the All-Stars. Barnes replied, "How would I get on the All-Star trip?" Mickey was delighted to be able to say, "I am giving you my place".

All-Star Gazing

Mick O'Dwyer travelled as a replacement on the second All-Star trip in 1973. Despite never being selected as an All-Star, Mick holds a unique All-Star record:
- In 1973 he was an All-Star replacement
- In 1976, 1979, 1980, 1982, 1985, 1987 he travelled on All-Star tours as Kerry manager
- In 1990 he was coach of the All-Star football team in San Francisco and New York
- In 1990 he co-commentated for RTÉ at the exhibition match in Toronto
- In 1998 his son Karl O'Dwyer was selected as an All-Star while playing for Kildare

Mick played well in San Francisco in 1973 and, in fact, was named the football MVP. "That was despite hitting my head off the sprinklers at the side of the pitch and having to go to the hospital after one of the matches", chuckled O'Dwyer.

Paddy Cullen travelled on his first All-Star trip in spring 1974 as a replacement for Billy Morgan, who was lining out for All-Ireland champions Cork. Paddy had not been nominated because Billy was a unanimous choice in goals on the 1973 All-Star team. "It was a huge surprise. Suddenly there I was going into the tailor getting fitted for the green All-Star jacket".

Billy recalled, "when Paddy Cullen was picked as a replacement for me in 1974, he was the only Dub going on the trip. Jimmy Keaveney, who I was good friends with, rang and asked me to look after Paddy". The two goalkeepers have been good friends ever since. As Jimmy recalled that phone call to Billy he added, "Paddy still needs looking after whenever we go on a trip!".

Paddy may have been the only Dublin player on that trip to San Francisco, but he loved every second of it. "I brought a 3.5lb Limerick ham in my suitcase as a gift for my host. Going to San Francisco then was like going to the moon".

It was a few months before Kevin Heffernan's Dublin team burst onto the GAA scene. Cullen explained, "we were nothing at the time. Fellas were embarrassed to say they played for Dublin. When I met my host in San Francisco, a guy called Bartlett, he said, 'so are you the gurrier from Dublin? Nobody else wanted to take you".

Not a great start, but Paddy said it all worked out well in the end. "We played some darts in his basement and soon got to know each other. We went on to become great friends. He came to visit me in Ireland, and we still exchange Christmas cards".

| The All-Star Hurlers pose for the team photo under the passing train in Gaelic Park, New York in 1975

| The All-Star hurlers and footballers decked out in their blazers in 1975

50 Years of the GAA All-Stars

On the Balboa pitch in 1973 (L-R) Donal Monaghan, Kevin Jer O'Sullivan, Donie O'Sullivan, Kevin Downey, Mick O'Dwyer and Eugene Mulligan

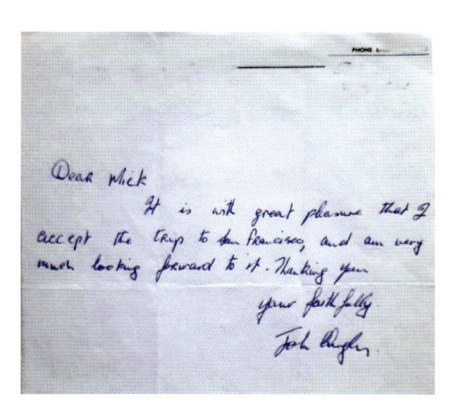

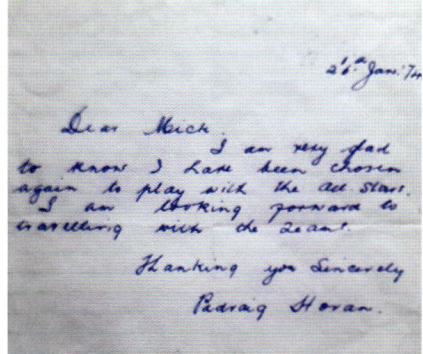

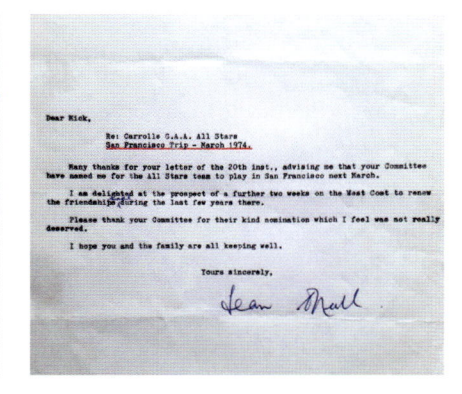

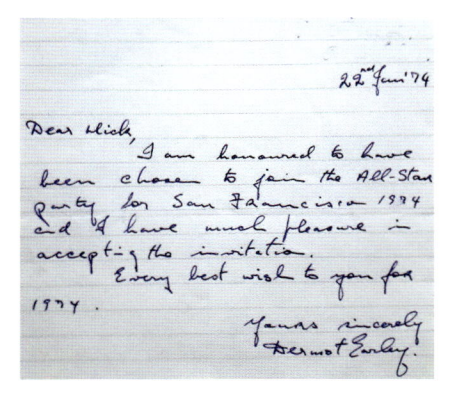

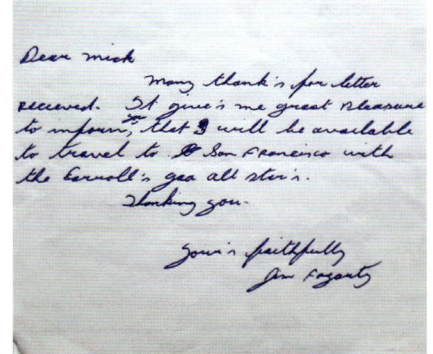

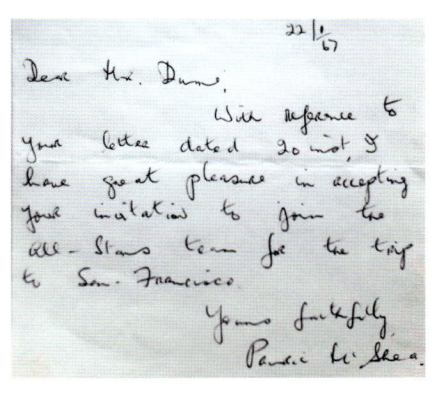

Some letters of acceptance to travel on the All-Star tour as a replacement. Clockwise from top left - John Quigley, Pádraig Horan, Seán O'Neill, Dermot Earley, John Fogarty and Pauric McShea

When Paddy returned to San Francisco just 12 months later in 1975 with Dublin, now the reigning All-Ireland champions, his host was incredulous. "What did you do when you got back from San Francisco?"

He was joking, but Paddy did in fact use his All-Star experience as a motivator for the Dublin footballers in 1974. Gay O'Driscoll remembers the training sessions that Spring. "Parnell Park was on the flight path to Dublin Airport and Paddy used to point to the Aer Lingus planes passing overhead saying, 'lads that will be us if we win the All-Ireland. We can all be on the trip together'. We had heard Paddy's stories about that All-Star trip in 1974, and we all wanted to go".

John Quigley's welcome letter from the Mayor of Los Angeles

All-Star Gazing

Back Home in Shannon Airport in April 1974, (L-R) - Frank McGuigan, Liam Sammon, John Quigley, Pauric McShea, Donie O'Sullivan, Jimmy Duggan, Liam O'Neill, Brian McEniff, Dermot Early, Paddy Cullen, Anthony McGurk, referee Clem Foley and Mick Dunne

DUAL PLAYERS

The GAA limited the size of the All-Star squad to keep the tour costs down. When injuries occurred, teams often had no back-up. In 1973 Brian McEniff was injured and could not play on, so Kevin Ger O'Sullivan had to play with a broken finger. Fr. Nick Clavin recalled being at an All-Star match as a spectator after he had moved to San Diego and when the All-Star team was a player short, he was asked to line out.

From 1974 onwards a dual player was included in the travelling party to provide cover for injured players. Selection as a dual player was an honour awarded by the All-Star selection committee to a player "who had reached a high standard of excellence in both hurling and football".

All-Star	Dual Player
1974	John Quigley (Wexford)
1975	Tommy Carew (Kildare)
1976	Denis Allen (Cork)
1977	Pat Dunny (Kildare)
1978	Michael Kilcoyne (Westmeath)
1979	Mick Holden (Dublin)
1980	Paddy Quirke (Carlow)
1982	Cyril Hughes (Carlow)
1983	Willie Lowry (Westmeath)

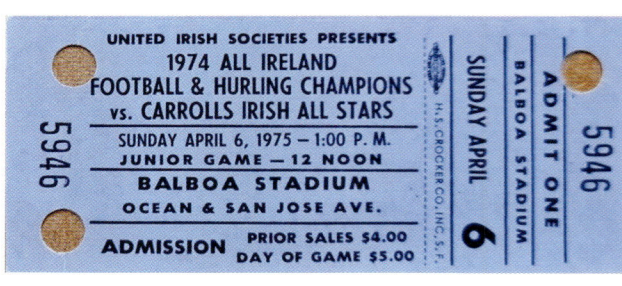

Colm McAlarney and Frank McGuigan are selected as All-Star replacements in 1975

Top: A list of dual players chosen for the All-Star tours

Above: Ticket for the games in San Francisco in 1975

Left: Match report in the *San Francisco Chronicle* in 1975

HOSTING CONTINUES

The tradition of players staying with host families continued for most of the trips during the Carrolls sponsorship years. As in 1972, it worked out well in most cases, and many lasting friendships resulted.

Ogie Moran was hosted by Peggy and Phil Murphy in San Francisco. "I remember the young son coming down to the basement to see me". Ogie kept in touch with the family who returned to Kerry in later years. Their son Mike now works at Waterville House and Golf Links.

Ger Power stayed with a businessman who was originally from Tralee, along with John O'Keeffe and Dinny Long. "It worked out well", said Ger, "The first year we went out he was doing okay in business, then when we went back a few years later he was a millionaire". His teammate Jack O'Shea forged a great friendship with his host in San Francisco, Neil Casey, an electrician from Killarney, who gave Jacko the run of his house and a loan of his BMW. "I got to know him and got on so well that I used to go and stay with him even when the players started staying in hotels".

Pat Henderson spoke about his first host, Dick Harrington, who really rolled out the red carpet. "When I didn't stay with Dick on the next trip, he was quite upset, so I had to go and visit him. I suppose that showed us how much it meant to the hosts to have the All-Stars stay with them. I formed a life-long friendship with Harrington".

Cork County Board Secretary Frank Murphy went on many All-Star trips involving Cork during the 1970s. "There was a big Cork community in San Francisco at the time, they formed a group called 'Rebel Cork'. All the Cork hosts used to come back home for the championship matches each summer, and the friendships that had formed in San Francisco continued".

Ray Cummins thought hosting was a fabulous idea. He stayed every year with Corkman Dan Culloty. "We didn't realise it at first but the whole family gave up their bedrooms for the players. They all slept in temporary beds in the basement". Ray remembers spending time with Dan's son Danny. "He was nine or 10 at the time, a really tall kid and he was into basketball. Me and Jimmy Barry Murphy used to play outside with him, and we were fascinated because we had never seen a basketball hoop before".

The families hosting the Cork players all lived near each other in San Francisco. As Ray tells it, "There seemed to be parties for us every night in different houses".

At one of those parties, Ray met another host, Corkman Don Cummins, who by coincidence owned a site in Kinsale that Ray had tried to purchase earlier that year. Ray had been unable to track down the owner at the time, but they made the connection at the party in San Francisco. Ray built his house on the site, and he and his wife Ber still live there today. The two Cummins families became friends as Don used to return each year to his own holiday home beside Ray and Ber's house.

Charlie McCarthy stayed with the Cummins. "Don took us everywhere. He did everything for us, took us on trips to Sausalito and Redwood". Charlie remembers the split-level house downtown near Golden Gate Park. "It was an open house. Guys who were staying far out of the city would be brought back by the Cork lads and were welcome to stay overnight".

Martin Furlong said he and his wife were "blessed" with their hosts, Jack and Kitty Murphy. "Jack was from Birr. He was self-employed, but he took off work for the whole time that we were there. A lot of the lads wouldn't have been that lucky. He drove us up to the wine country, to see the Redwoods and down the shore to Monterey. He wined and dined us. He also included Damien Martin and his wife on these trips, as their hosts (the Hennessy girls from Tullamore) were working during the day. We all still keep in touch".

INSPIRATION FOR A FUTURE STAR

Many years on in 1982, Ray's hosts, the Cullotys, moved back home to Cork. Having met Jimmy Barry Murphy, Ray Cummins and Billy Morgan as a child, their basketball-loving son Danny, who was now 18, dreamt of playing football for Cork. He began by playing for Newmarket. "I was very raw when I got back home. But I was tall (6 foot 2 inches) and good in the air, so I got noticed playing for the club".

L to R, Michael O'Neill, Con Murphy and Frank Murphy with host Jerry Linehan in Golden Gate Park, San Francisco

All-Star Gazing

When Billy Morgan was appointed Cork manager, he took Danny under his wing, coaching him in the skills of Gaelic football. Danny made the breakthrough onto the Cork senior team, and when he came on as a substitute in the All-Ireland Final in 1989, he achieved his dream.

"My pals in San Francisco all grew up dreaming of winning the Superbowl, but all I wanted to do was win an All-Ireland for Cork. Dad had come out from Cork in 1954 and married my mother, who was from San Francisco. There were people constantly coming over from Cork when I was young". He remembers the Cork legends playing basketball with him. "They had never seen the outdoor basketball hoops before. They were fascinated by my Scalextric too!", he laughed.

Danny became known as 'Danny the Yank' around Cork. Speaking on the Second Captains radio show on RTÉ in 2016, he attributed the nickname to Mícheál Ó Muircheartaigh who used it once in a radio commentary.

The All-Star story came full circle when Danny returned to San Francisco with All-Ireland champions Cork in 1990. In the match against the All-Stars, Danny staked a claim for a starting position in the championship later that year. "I had a good game and I made it onto the Cork team from there". He went on to win a second All-Ireland medal in 1990, this time as one of the starting 15. He was nominated for an All-Star that year. "But Shea Fahy won it!", laughed Danny. He was captain of the Cork team on the All-Star trip to Toronto the following spring in 1991.

The tradition of players staying with host families continued until the Bank of Ireland introduced hotels in 1979 though rumour has it that the odd Dublin legend may have given his host the slip long before then.

Tony Hanahoe revealed, "In Chicago in 1977 I checked myself into a hotel instead of staying with my host. I had a drink with him but then when I didn't stay with him, he complained to the GAA about me". Tony explained how the Dubs felt. "It was supposed to be a team holiday and we thought we should all be together. Our first year in San Francisco I was hosted by a mother and daughter in San Rafael with one of the lads. The mother took a shine to us both. One day we looked at each other and I said, 'I dunno about you, but I'm out of here'.

"I was 29, a bachelor, a professional guy. I wanted to stay on my own. After that first trip in 1975 we approached Seán Ó Síocháin to ask if we could stay in hotels from then on". The response from Croke Park was negative, so the Dubs held a fundraiser to create a holiday fund for the next All-Star trip. "We raised a fortune", said Tony. "Then I was asked to do a promotional event with Eddie Macken and John Giles for the Guaranteed Irish brand. I asked that my fee be given to the Dublin County Board towards the holiday fund. I insisted that I got the same fee as the two professional sportsmen".

Left, Danny Culloty playing for Cork, and above, Danny Culloty and his wife Catherine with Paddy Hayes at Niagara Falls in 1990

Pat Spillane thought that hosting was a lovely idea in theory; bonding with the diaspora, the first and second generation Irish. "The hosts were magnificent; they couldn't do enough for you. But their main aim was to see if they could get their daughter married off to some Irish sports star. Ah, Jesus, I must have met 6,000 Colleens or Erins that you were supposed to fall madly in love with. For lunch it was always bacon and cabbage. We were thinking; we don't eat this in Ireland". His brother Mick added, "hosting was a great idea, but they mollycoddled you. Staying in hotels was fantastic – we all got a chance to sit around the pool chatting together. With hosting, the players never met each other between the matches".

PARTY IN SHANNON

The All-Star trips always originated in Dublin with a stop in Shannon before heading west. This is where the mingling began. In 1979 when the departure from Shannon was delayed by three hours due to technical difficulties, sponsors Bank of Ireland arranged a free bar for the travelling party. Joe Henderson remembers everyone enjoying themselves. "Some fellas got fairly drunk and had to be carried onto the plane. When the plane was ready to depart the pilot actually threatened not to go".

"The flight kept being put back so they couldn't close the bar", recalled Pat Spillane, "After a few hours we got on the plane but there was some problem, so we had to get off again. The Bomber (Eoin Liston) had fallen asleep on the plane. Before we got off again, we woke him up and told him we were in America, but we were still in Shannon!".

Mick Spillane continued, "when you would arrive in Shannon all the other players would know you. It was a real surprise particularly that the hurlers would all recognise you. Joe Connolly would know you. It made you feel that we're all in this together".

During that delay in Shannon Airport in 1979, Joe Connolly enjoyed meeting Mikey Sheehy, Seánie Walsh, Ogie Moran and Eoin Liston. "I really valued the opportunity to meet the other players, the legends of the game, both hurlers and footballers".

Joe had just been named captain of the Galway hurlers. "There was a lot of pressure at the time because it had been 57 years since Galway won the All-Ireland". He asked Mikey for advice about being a captain.

Later in the trip Joe had a similar chat with Tony Hanahoe. "I remember Tony said, 'win every match, every challenge match, every club match, every county match. Every week win everything'". Joe took his advice and captained the Galway hurlers to All-Ireland success the following year.

Joe and Tony became great friends. "I got to know Jimmy Keaveney too on that trip and spent time with him and Tony in Rosie O'Grady's pub in New York. I still think of Tony as the 'King of Captains'".

Mick Spillane (centre) spending time with Eugene Coughlan, Tony O'Keeffe, Ger Power and Frank King

Breakfast at Shannon Airport for Ger Feeney, Mick Jacob and John Quigley

Brian Cody and John D Hickey share a cup of tea in Shannon

All-Star Gazing

CHAMPIONS ON TOUR

The All-Ireland champions continued to travel with the All-Stars each year. At a time when there was very little travel abroad, the trips became the unofficial team holiday. Pat Henderson said, "the All-Star trip allowed the All-Ireland champions to travel together. In those days that was a big deal. To travel to the West Coast was unthinkable at that time".

Tony Hanahoe has great memories of the Dublin team being together. "One year we arrived in the hotel in New York and Anton O'Toole and Tommy Drumm were given the wrong room key. When they got up to the room, it was a massive suite with a free bar. They settled in and enjoyed a few drinks before inviting Colm O'Rourke to join them. When Colm arrived his reaction to the suite was, 'effing Dubs, always getting special treatment'".

"I remember it well", recalled Colm. "It was an early check-in after a late night. I was sharing with Tony McManus, so we got our room keys and lay down for a rest. Then came this call from 'Tooler' to come down quick to their room. We get down and it says, 'The Presidential Suite' on the door. You want to see the place. The guys ordered food and drink and we all spent the day lazing around. We all had a nap then ordered more food and drinks.

| **Frank King, Ger Power and Ann Sheehy enjoy some strawberries in San Francisco sunshine**

| **Eoin Liston watches an All-Star match from the sideline in Gaelic Park, New York**

"By evening time, the table in the middle of the room was full of plates and glasses. Next thing we hear a key in the door and in walks Peadar McCanna from the bank with his wife. We were very sheepish, but Peadar said 'don't worry about a thing'". Colm reflected, "everything was paid for by the bank and I always appreciated how well Peadar reacted. He didn't make us feel bad".

The Kerry team were All-Ireland Champions so often in the 1970s and early 1980s that the All-Star trip was almost an annual event. For Ger Power, "those trips in the Spring were a chance to unwind because as soon as we got back home, it was down to serious training". He added, "the matches weren't a big deal. Nobody was minding themselves".

The trip to LA and New York in May 1976 was Ogie Moran's first. "I was studying for exams at the time and brought all the books thinking I would get loads done but of course I didn't do anything". He cut short his trip to get back for the exams. "I didn't go on to New York with the rest of the lads and flew back from LA. I remember seeing Roger Moore in the airport. He was 'James Bond' at the time, so I thought this was amazing. It really added to the glamour of the trip for me". Ogie remembers all the Kerry lads going to Disneyland together. "It was brilliant. Jaws the Movie was out at the time and it was a big deal back home. I remember the shark shows depicting the movie".

For Eoin Liston the thrill of the trips was about meeting players from other counties. "I became friends with people from counties that Kerry never played against like the footballers from Wexford or the hurlers from Kilkenny. We kept in touch and I went to a few of their weddings in later years".

Mikey Sheehy also talked about the friends he made from other counties. "I am still very friendly with Dinny Allen from Cork and that stems from the All-Star trip in 1976. I got to know Matt Connor over the years, Frank McGuigan and Ollie Brady too. The older you get, the more you appreciate those friendships that you made on the All-Star tours".

John Fenton first travelled in 1977 when Cork were All-Ireland champions. "The All-Star trips were fantastic. That year, when we arrived in New York, former Cork hurler Eddie O'Brien, who had emigrated there in 1972, met the plane. He worked in corporate security and had organised a police escort for the bus into the city. Suddenly all the lads who were having the craic down the back of the bus wanted to be up the front for the excitement of this motorcade from JFK Airport into New York City".

In 1980 John got a late call-up as a replacement. He and his wife Christine had just returned from their honeymoon. "We had to choose between going on the All-Star trip or buying a new suite of furniture". said John. "There really was

50 Years of the GAA All-Stars

John Fenton with his Bank of Ireland All-Star jersey and one of his five All-Star trophies

no choice", said Christine. "We figured we could always buy a sofa, but there may not be another chance to go on an All-Star trip".

ALL-STAR MATCHES

The attendance figures for the All-Star matches in San Francisco increased during the 1970s peaking around 8,000 in 1976. There was usually some coverage in the local press but, in general, the US media didn't take much notice. In 1975 the All-Star Steering Committee asked Michael O'Hehir to travel out in advance of the tour to help publicise the games. He was well known in the US due to his horseracing commentaries and appearances on ABC's 'Wide World of Sport'.

When the All-Star tour visited other cities, similar crowds came to the matches. John Fenton felt that the intensity of the All-Star matches often depended on when they were played. "At the start of the tour, the county rivalries were still at the forefront, so the games were tougher". However, Billy Morgan reckons, "there was always quite a rivalry between the All-Star teams and the Champions". He particularly remembers the Dubs taking it more seriously, "doing training sessions when everyone else was drinking". Robbie Kelleher had a strategy when it came to the matches. "At the reception the night before, I would always find out who I was marking in the match the next day and then make sure that guy had plenty to drink!".

Mikey Sheehy recalled, "there was always a bit of needle in the matches". Jack O'Shea enjoyed the All-Star matches and said, "I always liked to perform". For Eoin Liston, "the matches were serious, but they were a bit of fun too. I remember going in goals one year".

Players from different counties often got a rare chance to play together. However when Willie Bryan was selected on the All-Star team in 1972 alongside Mick O'Connell, the two players didn't get to line out together in midfield the following Spring. While Mick played on the All-Star team, Willie had to play for the Champions Offaly. He regretted that. "We had played against each other in many championship matches over the years. We always thought highly of each other, and I would have loved the chance to play with him".

The All-Star Footballers line up in Balboa Stadium in 1973
Back L to R: Pat Mangan, Tommy Joe Gilmore, Mick O'Dwyer, Dermot Earley, Mick Freyne, Mick O'Connell, Paud O'Donoghue
Front L to R: Paddy Moriarty, Frank McGuigan, Donal Monaghan, Anthony McGurk, Donie O'Sullivan, Seán O'Neill, Billy Morgan, Kevin Ger O'Sullivan

87

All-Star Gazing

Frank McGuigan remembers the games being very competitive. "Guys wanted to win but really only for bragging rights in the bar later. The pitch in Balboa was small, 11-a-side would have been better but then you would be leaving fellas out and everyone wanted to play. The trips were brilliant, fellas were all there for the craic".

Some years the matches got heated. "I recall the first year that the tour visited LA in 1974", said Jim O'Sullivan. "The match was so competitive between Cork and the All-Star footballers that the then GAA President Donal Keenan had to go down onto the pitch to calm things down!".

KERRY VS THE PITTSBURGH STEELERS

Mick O'Connell received his only All-Star in 1972 towards the end of a remarkable playing career. Who can guess how many awards he would have if the All-Star scheme existed in the 1960s?

Although he had retired by 1975, he was flown out to Gaelic Park during the All-Star tour to participate in a kicking contest with American football star Roy Gerela of the Pittsburgh Steelers. Dan Rooney, later US Ambassador to Ireland, was manager of the Steelers and son of its founder Art Rooney. He organised the competition which took place before the All-Star matches. The two players took turns kicking a Gaelic football and an American football.

The New York Times reported, "O'Connell, a 37-year-old fisherman from the Irish island of Valentia, beat the Steelers kicking specialist seven conversions to six. The only one not surprised by this result was O'Connell who had spent the previous month practising with American footballs".

Pro kicker Gerela said, "getting the round ball airborne is not as easy as it looks. But give me a little more practice and maybe I could get good enough to have the Irish offer me a contract". The *Irish Examiner* (then called The *Cork Examiner*) reported back home, "the unverified talk around New York GAA circles was that the Steelers were interested in signing Valentia's greatest".

In the Super Bowl final, the following January against the Dallas Cowboys, Gerela almost cost his team their second title when he uncharacteristically missed his first two kicks. Perhaps the defeat at the hands of the Valentia fisherman in Gaelic Park that day had a lasting effect on his confidence!

Roy Gerela watches the All-Stars in action in Gaelic Park

Mick O'Connell with journalists and All-Star selectors Paddy Downey and Mick Dunne

Frank McGuigan gets a mention in the match report in the San Francisco Chronicle in 1975

POLITICAL CONTROVERSY

In May 1977 football champions Dublin were due to travel on the upcoming All-Star trip to Chicago, San Francisco, LA and New York. In advance of their departure David Hickey and John McCarthy were banned by the North America Board of the GAA from participating in any games within their jurisdiction.

The ban resulted from an incident in the National League Final between Kerry and Dublin at Croke Park a few weeks earlier. During that match, some protesters entered the pitch in support of the ongoing IRA hunger strike in Portlaoise prison. Tom O'Donoghue, Chairman of the North America Board, claimed that Irish Americans were "shocked and outraged at photographs in newspapers showing Hickey and McCarthy violently attacking persons pleading for mercy for the hunger-strikers at Portlaoise Prison". John Kerry O'Donnell said that "in his opinion, the players would be ill-advised" to appear at the New York venue.

Tony Hanahoe described what had happened in the league match. "John McCarthy and Páidí Ó Sé were both gardaí at the time and they tackled the protesters who came on the pitch. David Hickey got involved too". After the match, the Dublin players went to Meagher's pub nearby. Tony's brother arrived to tell him that there had been threatening phone calls to their house. "People thought David and I looked alike on the pitch", explained Tony. "Lots of meetings took place behind the scenes so that David could travel".

Paddy Downey wrote that "calling off the tour would have been a disaster and might well have split the GAA irreparably because of the highly emotive and delicate political issues involved". He added "the Association must be seen to observe its own rules – and one of those rules states very explicitly that the organisation is non-political and non-sectarian".

In the end the ban was lifted but the controversy continued in America. Tony recalled an incident in San Francisco. "There was a police escort for the Dubs coming out of the Irish Cultural Centre when an armed gang turned up looking for Hickey. There was also a banner in the crowd in Gaelic Park over the incident".

Pat Hartigan remembers the controversy too. "Protesters turned up one night at a function in the Irish Centre. I can recall Hanahoe in a white suit getting a police escort out of there with the rest of the Dubs".

David Hickey's ban makes front page news in April 1977 and below, relief as David Hickey makes the All-Star trip

The kick-off between Mick O'Connell and Roy Gerela in Gaelic Park, New York in 1975

All-Star Gazing

The crowd examine a banner that reads 'Hoodlum Hickey' during the Dublin vs All-Stars match in Gaelic Park in 1977

DUBLIN AND KERRY RIVALRY

During the All-Star trip of 1978, a charity match was organised between Kerry and Dublin in New York, to raise funds for the Sister Consilio Rehabilitation Unit in Co. Kildare. Dublin were on tour as All-Ireland champions and the Kerry team was flown out for the weekend to play in the fundraiser.

The match came at the height of the Kerry-Dublin rivalry. Kerry were the victors, but as reported by Paddy Downey, "it was an ill-tempered match that, due to a freak rainstorm, should never have been played".

"Gaelic Park was like a river that day with water flowing all over the place", recalled Paddy Gormley of New York GAA. "The rain started the day before, and it rained all night. And the charity match was the second match. I went up to the press box to get cover and I was sitting beside Mick Dunne doing the commentary".

Gay O'Driscoll remembers it well, "Gaelic Park was a dirt track in those days. On the day of the match, there was torrential rain that made the pitch unplayable. By then we (Kerry and Dublin) had played each other so much the matches had a lot of needle. I remember that three players were sent off and it turned into a nasty match".

Coming just a few months after Dublin had beaten them for the second year running in the All-Ireland final, the Kerry players say their win marked a turning point in the rivalry. Later that year, they beat Dublin. "Nonsense", says O'Driscoll. "Kerry beat us in 1978 because we were too old, not because of any marker laid down in New York".

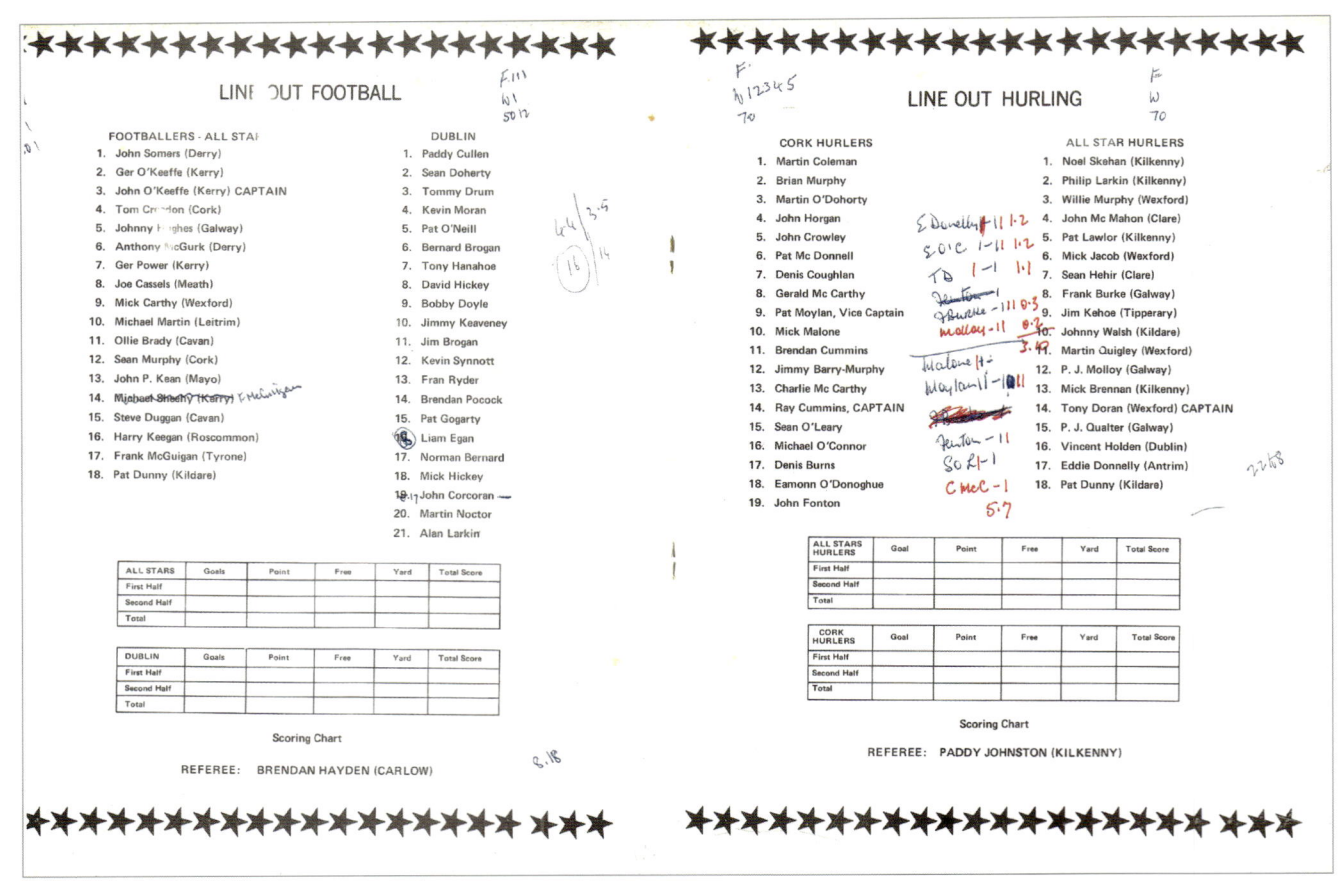

LINE OUT FOOTBALL

FOOTBALLERS – ALL STAR
1. John Somers (Derry)
2. Ger O'Keeffe (Kerry)
3. John O'Keeffe (Kerry) CAPTAIN
4. Tom Creedon (Cork)
5. Johnny Hughes (Galway)
6. Anthony McGurk (Derry)
7. Ger Power (Kerry)
8. Joe Cassells (Meath)
9. Mick Carthy (Wexford)
10. Michael Martin (Leitrim)
11. Ollie Brady (Cavan)
12. Sean Murphy (Cork)
13. John P. Kean (Mayo)
14. Michael Sheehy (Kerry)
15. Steve Duggan (Cavan)
16. Harry Keegan (Roscommon)
17. Frank McGuigan (Tyrone)
18. Pat Dunny (Kildare)

DUBLIN
1. Paddy Cullen
2. Sean Doherty
3. Tommy Drum
4. Kevin Moran
5. Pat O'Neill
6. Bernard Brogan
7. Tony Hanahoe
8. David Hickey
9. Bobby Doyle
10. Jimmy Keaveney
11. Jim Brogan
12. Kevin Synnott
13. Fran Ryder
14. Brendan Pocock
15. Pat Gogarty
16. Liam Egan
17. Norman Bernard
18. Mick Hickey
19. John Corcoran
20. Martin Noctor
21. Alan Larkin

REFEREE: BRENDAN HAYDEN (CARLOW)

LINE OUT HURLING

CORK HURLERS
1. Martin Coleman
2. Brian Murphy
3. Martin O'Doherty
4. John Horgan
5. John Crowley
6. Pat Mc Donnell
7. Denis Coughlan
8. Gerald Mc Carthy
9. Pat Moylan, Vice Captain
10. Mick Malone
11. Brendan Cummins
12. Jimmy Barry-Murphy
13. Charlie Mc Carthy
14. Ray Cummins, CAPTAIN
15. Sean O'Leary
16. Michael O'Connor
17. Denis Burns
18. Eamonn O'Donoghue
19. John Fenton

ALL STAR HURLERS
1. Noel Skehan (Kilkenny)
2. Philip Larkin (Kilkenny)
3. Willie Murphy (Wexford)
4. John Mc Mahon (Clare)
5. Pat Lawlor (Kilkenny)
6. Mick Jacob (Wexford)
7. Sean Hehir (Clare)
8. Frank Burke (Galway)
9. Jim Kehoe (Tipperary)
10. Johnny Walsh (Kildare)
11. Martin Quigley (Wexford)
12. P. J. Molloy (Galway)
13. Mick Brennan (Kilkenny)
14. Tony Doran (Wexford) CAPTAIN
15. P. J. Qualter (Galway)
16. Vincent Holden (Dublin)
17. Eddie Donnelly (Antrim)
18. Pat Dunny (Kildare)

REFEREE: PADDY JOHNSTON (KILKENNY)

The match day programme for the All-Star matches in Chicago on tour in 1977

Match programme for the Sister Consilio charity match in New York

The billboard for the match specifies the match will go ahead "rain or shine"

Pat Spillane laughed at the memory. "It was two teams of alcoholics raising money for a home for the bewildered!". He does not doubt the significance of the match. "That was the defining moment in the making of the Kerry team. We were on the back of being beaten in 1976 and 1977 and had lost a league game to the Dubs as well. It was the first time that O'Dwyer analysed things to find a way of beating the Dubs".

Pat went on to explain the strategy. "What we decided to do that day was lay down a marker. No more 'Mister Nice Guys'. We said we will fight fire with fire, and it was filthy. I don't know how many players were sent off. A load of players had broken noses including Jimmy Deenihan and me. But we won the match and the fight".

Bernard Brogan shared his memories of that match. "Something had happened between Pat O'Neill and Páidí Ó Sé in the previous All-Ireland final. During the match in New York, Pat was on the ground and he saw a pair of boots behind him. Thinking it was Páidí, he turned around and whacked him, breaking his nose in the process. It turned out to be Jimmy Deenihan. Jimmy went off into the dressing room and at half time one of the Kerry lads came into Pat O'Neill and said, 'look Pat would you mind coming in to have a look at Jimmy's nose?' Pat replied, 'I didn't come out here to practice medicine' and your man says to Pat, 'well you didn't come out here to play football either'".

Bernard concluded, "It was a different time. When you look back at the replays on television of what happened in some of the older matches, like the 1975 All-Ireland Final, you go, Jesus, you'd be in court today if you did that".

The Kerry players may have won the battle, but they returned home regretful, nonetheless. As Ogie Moran recalls, "we were mad jealous of the Dubs. They had all the All-Star gear - the jackets and the suntans. They went on out to the West Coast to continue the All-Star tour, and we had to come home".

Future All-Star Greg Blaney used to follow the reports of the tours in the Irish newspapers. "I remember reading all about that match as a kid. It was reported in the papers that there had been a lot of fighting between the two teams. Everyone was talking about it at home".

By 1978 the All-Star matches in San Francisco had moved from Balboa Park to Candlestick Park, home of the San Francisco Giants baseball team. The Irish teams were invited to play an exhibition match before a National League game between the Giants and the Chicago Cubs. Matt Connor remembers the experience. "That All-Star trip was the first time I had ever played under lights. We had to wear black paint on our eyes to deal with the floodlights".

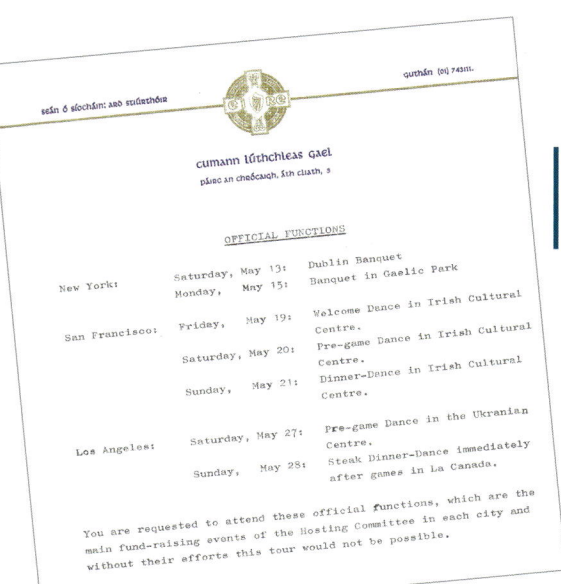

The list of official functions for the players on tour in 1978

All-Star Gazing

The All-Stars and the Cork footballers line out in LA in 1978

In 1979 the timing of the All-Star tour was changed from Spring to Autumn. The teams visited four cities that year: New York, Chicago, San Francisco and LA. Hurling champions Kilkenny had beaten Galway a few weeks earlier in the All-Ireland final and there were five Galway players on the All-Star hurling team. Eddie Keher and Pat Henderson were joint managers of Kilkenny at that time. The final match of the tour in Chicago was played under lights on a small pitch and the atmosphere was intense as the crowd was very close to the action.

John Connolly explained. "The All-Star games were always competitive. I don't know what it is about hurling, but it's impossible to just go out and go through the motions. In Chicago we had all been partying together the night before that match yet the next day, the match was very competitive. We all wanted to win. We all wanted to beat each other".

A big row broke out during the match. "There was absolute mayhem because the players were all in on top of the crowd", said his brother Joe. "Things were very tense for a long time in the bar afterwards. It could have gone either way. Next thing Mick 'Cloney' Brennan made a wisecrack that broke the ice. Soon enough we were all getting on 'singing for Skibbereen' for the rest of the night".

Pat's brothers, Ger and John, were also on that tour in 1979. It was an unforgettable experience for the three brothers travelling together, something they got to repeat on subsequent All-Star trips in the 1980s. Ger remembers the hurling match in Chicago when "things got a bit nasty". Joe and Jimmy Cooney summed it up, "the supporters would want to see a good game. The managers always said beforehand that we needed to put on a show".

Paddy Cullen is interviewed by Mick Dunne in Candlestick Park

The match day programme for the San Francisco leg of the All-Star tour in 1979

United Irish Societies
SAN FRANCISCO

present

GAELIC FOOTBALL

KERRY ALL IRELAND CHAMPIONS
&
IRISH ALL STARS
AWARD WINNERS 1979

HURLING

KILKENNY ALL IRELAND CHAMPIONS
&
IRISH ALL STARS
AWARD WINNERS 1979

50 Years of the GAA All-Stars

GAA President Paddy McFlynn starts the hurling match between the All-Stars and Kilkenny below graffiti covered trains in Gaelic Park, New York in 1979

General Manager of Bank of Ireland Frank O'Rourke starts the football match between the All-Stars (with Bernard Brogan at No. 9) and Kerry in Gaelic Park, New York in 1979

ALL-STAR TOUR

BY PAT QUIGLEY

On arrival at O'Hare International Airport in Chicago, the Allstar party was welcomed by Jim Masterson, chairman, and Harry Costello, secretary Chicago Divisional Board and Hugh McEneany and Michael Ryan, Bank of Ireland.

On to the Holiday Inn in Oaklawn, under the genial managership of Limerick-born Joe English, which was the tour headquarters again in the Windy City. That evening Aer Lingus and Bord Fáilte hosted a welcoming reception for the touring party.

Tuesday morning saw the vast majority of the party head downtown for shopping and sight-seeing; needless to say the Sears Tower was a must for most of the tourists. The tallest building in the world, 1456 ft. high which can be climbed in 55 secs. by express lift to its Skydeck, 12,000 people work in offices, shops, restaurants and bar and, on a clear day, you look out over six states.

Back to the hotel for a quick fresh-up before the Bank of Ireland reception. Out to board the coaches and off to Ango High School in Summit for the games. Galway proved, if proof was needed, that they had men on the substitutes bench who could win a permanent place on the side if the first choices weren't playing up to standard.

Gerry Glynn and Paraic Connolly played in the defence as if their lives depended on their performances — Glynn showing dash and determination as well as considerable skill. Michael King was drafted into goal and can be very pleased with his efforts.

For the Allstars, Paddy Quirke showed that he was worthy of selection as a replacement on the team and would find a place on most inter-county sides. The highlight of the game was the sideline cutting of Cork's John Fenton — he scored three of his eight points from line balls.

For the record, Galway won by 3-16 to 2-15 to go into an aggregate lead of six points (5-32 to 5-26).

Brendan Bermingham, left, and Tomas Connor, both of Offaly.

Inspired by return of Eoin Liston, Kerry blitzed the Allstars in the football game despite the absence of Ger Power, Mike Sheehy and John Egan. The All-Ireland champions treated the 2,000 crowd to an exhibition of high-catching, fast running and scoring.

Having taken the lead after 30 seconds they never looked like being beaten and ran out easy winners by 4-15 to 1-11 and go into a 10-point lead on aggregate (5-25 to 3-21).

The following day began with a "Kerry" breakfast at which Mick O'Dwyer was presented with a plaque honouring his contribution to Kerry's great football story. Back to the sightseeing or golf for a few hours and then the Banquet in Glendora House, at which the winners of the games, the team captains and team managers received trophies.

Another early start to leave Chicago at 9 p.m. for Los Angeles, where the sun shon brilliantly in welcome as Fr. Bernie Leheny and Kathy Wisdom headed the welcoming party. On to the Holiday Inn in Long Beach where Pat Lynch was in charge of arrangements. Off to the rooms, cases unpacked for the last time and another look at the shopping list. Feet up and relax before a welcoming party in the Hotel. Friday — a free day — and Andy McKenna and Aine Sheehy have organised a trip to Disneyland and if you've been told its a paradise for children then don't believe it. The Matterhorn, The Carribean, America the Beautiful, Adventureland, and the many other attractions turned the tourists back a decade or two or more. Mickey Mouse Hats, glasses, pens, souvenirs, photographs — you name it they got them and the Disneylanders returned to the Holiday Inn tired and happy children.

Saturday was another shopping day — and the money was spent fast and furiously. If what was ordered couldn't be got, well get its first cousin. Another dance. Mass was concelebrated by Fr. Bernie Leheny and Fr. Iggy Clarke in the hotel on Sunday morning with the leading officials reading the lessons and making the offerings.

Off to Veterans Memorial Stadium for the final game of the tour. The Bank of Ireland Allstar hurlers held on to gain their only victory by a single point (1-15 to 1-14), thanks mainly to the accuracy of John Fenton and a grim determination. The football game ended all square (Allstars 4-8, Kerry 2-14) after a Matt Connor free was signalled wide to the surprise of most spectators.

The Bank of Ireland aggregate awards were presented to Kerry and Galway at the Banquet that evening — a banquet that was enlivened by the presence of the Bishop of Galway (ex Kerry), Most Rev. Dr. Eamonn Casey, who paid musical tribute to both counties.

Monday another free day — and Andy McKenna had organised a tour to Los Angeles, Hollywood and Farmers' Market. More film for the cameras, more last minute bargains and more problems for the cases. Back to the hotel, late, and the group had left for Hollywood for the Mike Douglas T.V. show — another first for the Allstar Tours.

Tuesday — up and out at 6.30 a.m. (yawn) and off to the Airport. Silence was golden. Cross the states, land in New York, a few hours to kill in Kennedy Airport and then our flight home was called. The comfort on the flight was welcome (thanks Shay Mitchell), all through the night and home, sweet home, on Wednesday with memories to brighten many dark days.

Gaelic World 5

All-Star tour report written by GAA Public Relations Officer, the late Pat Quigley

IMPACT ON THE DIASPORA

While the All-Star trips provided the players with great experiences and memories, it was also a special time for the Irish people living in the host cities. "We were really privileged to see the All-Stars play together because, if you remember, the people at home in Ireland didn't see them play any matches", said Tommy Smyth of New York GAA. "The All-Star visit was always such a big occasion. As soon as the selections were made each year back home, there would be a great buzz. We would know how many replacements would be needed and everyone would be speculating about which players might come out".

Tommy emigrated from Louth in 1963. "It meant so much to the guys living out here particularly from the smaller counties. That they could go and see their players; sometimes, they were even from the same club. They knew they would never see these players in an All-Ireland final but would get to see them play in Gaelic Park. You would hear people in the crowd saying, 'do you see him, he's ours'. To see the likes of Frank McGuigan, what a player! And he was in his heyday when he was over here".

One day in the early 1970s Tommy was asked to help out 'calling the game' in Gaelic Park. He became a regular commentator at GAA

All-Star Gazing

Left, Wexford's Pat Nolan and Mick Jacob with their host Jackie Kavanagh before an All-Star match in San Francisco.
Below, Pádraig Horan and Pat Hartigan at the Balboa Stadium

matches and the experience helped him get a job as a soccer commentator with ESPN many years later. "I cut my teeth as a commentator in Gaelic Park. Years later in 1994, when the World Cup was coming to the US, I approached ESPN and got a job as a commentator. I went from working as a house painter to covering 19 Champions League finals for the station. I have met all the big soccer players in the world".

Paddy Gormley, also of New York GAA, remembers the excitement generated by the All-Star matches. "At that time, all you saw on television was the football All-Ireland final. But it wasn't live, you had to wait until the Monday night to see it. And we never saw the hurling".

The Leitrim man expanded, "the All-Star matches in 1975 brought the biggest crowd that I had seen since the 1960s. There were no county teams coming to New York at the time. So, seeing the stars really brought people out. I remember the Down society had a big function for Colm McAlarney. In fact, all the county societies would hold events for their players".

Game announcer Tommy Smyth (in red) poses with the Kerry team in Gaelic Park

THE PEOPLE YOU MEET

The trips to Lake Tahoe in Nevada continued each time the All-Star teams visited the West Coast. Martin Quigley remembers winning on the slot machines in the casino. "The bells started going nuts, and I thought I had broken the machine. But it turned out I had won $100. It was a lot of money at the time, so I took it and left straight away".

One year Martin's brother John was brought by plane to the Santa Anita racecourse in California by his host, Jackie Kavanagh. "There was no expense spared by Jackie", John recalls. "We stayed in a motel overlooking the Pacific Ocean. At the races, we had access to the VIP area. Jackie encouraged me to put all my money on one particular horse which won. I bought a suit and a really wide tie with a picture of a horse on it. My mother couldn't stop looking at me in the gear when I came home".

John kept in touch with Jackie and met up with him many years later when he came to Ireland in 2006 for the Ryder Cup.

The players who travelled on the All-Star trips during the 1970s still talk about the friendships they formed. "I really enjoyed having the opportunity to meet fellas from other counties that Cork wouldn't meet in the Championship", said Jimmy Barry Murphy. "Playing and mixing with players like Colm McAlarney and Peter McGinnity".

"It is not the places you go; it's the people you meet", reflected Peter McGinnity. "I wouldn't give away the memories of my three All-Star trips for anything. Mixing with players from the other provinces, meeting Jimmy Barry Murphy and Billy Morgan. The craic we had on those trips. To get a chance to play with Seán O'Neill. He was the master at

The All-Star touring party line up with GAA President Con Murphy before take-off in 1976

that time. His Down team had broken Cavan's monopoly on Ulster football. You can't imagine how much it meant to play in the All-Star matches with him".

Pat Hartigan said the All-Star players became very united as a group, even those who were great rivals back home. "One year Noel Skehan lost his wedding ring during a match and a bunch of players went out and combed the pitch until they found it", said Pat, "I still meet fellas all around the country now that I got to know on those All-Star trips".

Billy Morgan enjoyed meeting Frank McGuigan, Johnny Tobin and Éamonn O'Donoghue. Frank was delighted to meet Mickey Freyne and Ollie Brady. "I got to know Jimmy Barry Murphy as well", he said.

Eddie Keher and Pat Hartigan travelled on many All-Star trips together in the 1970s. Both recalled an incident one night in LA after an All-Star function in the Irish Centre. Eddie began the story, "my host had to leave early to get up for work the next day. He arranged for some other guy, who we didn't know, to drive us home". Pat picked it up. "On the way home, this guy was stopped on the highway by the LA Cops for drunk driving. The cops had guns and got us out of the car. They had us spread-eagled with our hands up". Not used to seeing police carry guns, the two Irish lads were nervous in case one false move caused the guns to fire. The driver was arrested, and the lads were left stranded on the LA highway. "After walking for miles, we found a phone box and called my host who in fairness got out of bed and brought us home".

In 1978 Tom Prendergast travelled on the All-Star trip as a replacement. His host Tom Lawlor, a fellow Laois man, worked with the NYPD. One night, Prendergast was staying with friends when another guest in Lawlor's house was murdered. For the next few days, Tom was a suspect in the murder case until the police established that he was elsewhere on the night in question.

Peter McGinnity was on that trip too. "It was a bit of a wake-up call for us all. It made us realise that serious stuff could happen out here".

In 1977 the match in Gaelic Park was played on the last day of the trip. The players had to leave for the airport straight after the match. Replacement Frank McGuigan recalls, "we were all in Gaelic Park drinking after the match when we had to go to JFK to catch the plane home. I thought, I don't want to rush, I'll just stay! So, I stayed for six years. I played with Tyrone in New York and got married out there in 1978. Tyrone and my club (Ardboe) brought me home in October 1983 to play here. The next year I won my All-Star at the age of 30".

Ollie Brady was on that trip as a replacement for Tony Hanahoe. "I was with Frank when he made that decision not to return to Ireland", he said, laughing at the memory.

WEMBLEY BOUND

The early All-Stars also got a chance to play in 'The Wembley Games', an annual tournament played in Wembley Stadium. The games usually involved the All-Ireland finalists playing a selection of players from counties with a large diaspora in London. In 1973 London GAA invited the All-Star hurlers to play Tipperary and the All-Star footballers to play Kerry. The London County Board insisted that the All-Star teams lined out as selected, which meant that unusually, some of the players like Frances Loughnane and Donie O'Sullivan played against their own counties.

A Donegal team played against a 'Great Britain' selection in a curtain-raiser. London GAA's Pat Griffin, one of the umpires for the first match said, "there was a lot of coverage in the newspapers. The *London Evening Standard* ran a special four-page feature".

The Football All-Stars were beaten heavily by Kerry, but the hurling match was much closer, with the All-Stars winning by just two points (1-18 to 1-16). The turnout was disappointingly low, however, so unlike the successful All-Star trips to America, the All-Star visit to London was not repeated.

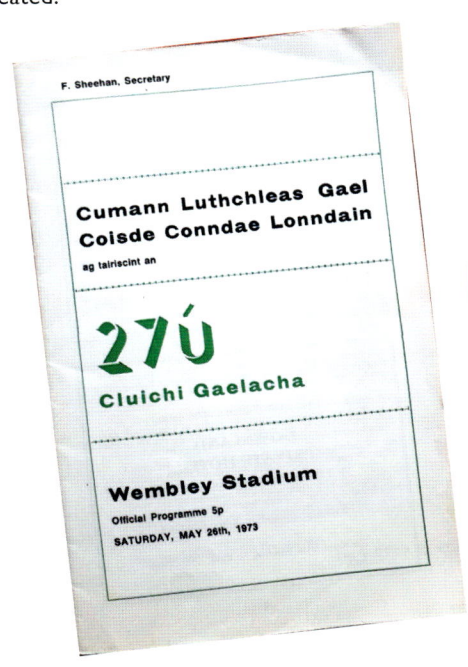

Wembley Games Match Programme

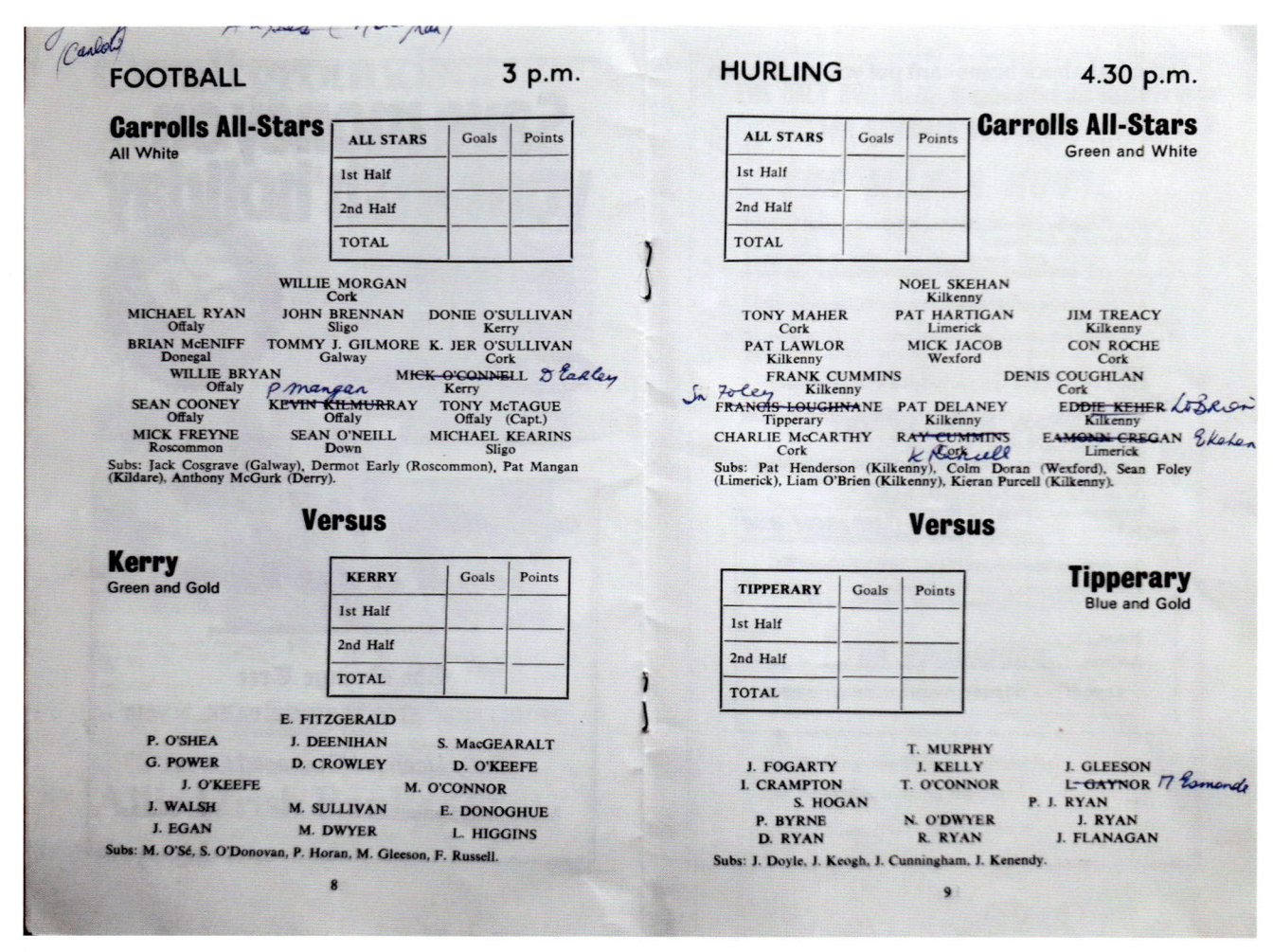

Team line-ups for the Wembley Games

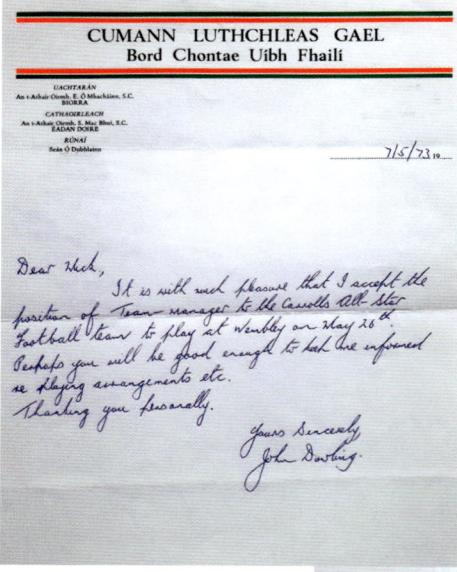

FOOTBALL   3 p.m.

Carrolls All-Stars — All White

ALL STARS	Goals	Points
1st Half		
2nd Half		
TOTAL		

WILLIE MORGAN (Cork)
MICHAEL RYAN (Offaly) — JOHN BRENNAN (Sligo) — DONIE O'SULLIVAN (Kerry)
BRIAN McENIFF (Donegal) — TOMMY J. GILMORE (Galway) — K. JER O'SULLIVAN (Cork)
WILLIE BRYAN (Offaly) — MICK O'CONNELL (Kerry)
SEAN COONEY (Offaly) — KEVIN KILMURRAY (Offaly) — TONY McTAGUE (Offaly) (Capt.)
MICK FREYNE (Roscommon) — SEAN O'NEILL (Down) — MICHAEL KEARINS (Sligo)

Subs: Jack Cosgrave (Galway), Dermot Early (Roscommon), Pat Mangan (Kildare), Anthony McGurk (Derry).

Versus

Kerry — Green and Gold

KERRY	Goals	Points
1st Half		
2nd Half		
TOTAL		

E. FITZGERALD
P. O'SHEA — J. DEENIHAN — S. MacGEARALT
G. POWER — D. CROWLEY — D. O'KEEFE
J. O'KEEFE — M. O'CONNOR
J. WALSH — M. SULLIVAN — E. DONOGHUE
J. EGAN — M. DWYER — L. HIGGINS

Subs: M. O'Sé, S. O'Donovan, P. Horan, M. Gleeson, F. Russell.

HURLING   4.30 p.m.

Carrolls All-Stars — Green and White

ALL STARS	Goals	Points
1st Half		
2nd Half		
TOTAL		

NOEL SKEHAN (Kilkenny)
TONY MAHER (Cork) — PAT HARTIGAN (Limerick) — JIM TREACY (Kilkenny)
PAT LAWLOR (Kilkenny) — MICK JACOB (Wexford) — CON ROCHE (Cork)
FRANK CUMMINS (Kilkenny) — DENIS COUGHLAN (Cork)
FRANCIS LOUGHNANE (Tipperary) — PAT DELANEY (Kilkenny) — EDDIE KEHER (Kilkenny)
CHARLIE McCARTHY (Cork) — RAY CUMMINS (Cork) — EAMONN CREGAN (Limerick)

Subs: Pat Henderson (Kilkenny), Colm Doran (Wexford), Sean Foley (Limerick), Liam O'Brien (Kilkenny), Kieran Purcell (Kilkenny).

Versus

Tipperary — Blue and Gold

TIPPERARY	Goals	Points
1st Half		
2nd Half		
TOTAL		

T. MURPHY
J. FOGARTY — J. KELLY — J. GLEESON
I. CRAMPTON — T. O'CONNOR — L. GAYNOR
S. HOGAN — P. J. RYAN
P. BYRNE — N. O'DWYER — J. RYAN
D. RYAN — R. RYAN — J. FLANAGAN

Subs: J. Doyle, J. Keogh, J. Cunningham, J. Kenendy.

John Dowling accepts the invitation to manage the All-Star Football team in Wembley in 1973

CUMANN LUTHCHLEAS GAEL — Bord Chontae Uíbh Fhailí

Dear Mick,
It is with much pleasure that I accept the position of Team manager to the Carrolls All-Star Football team to play at Wembley on May 26th. Perhaps you will be good enough to let me be informed re playing arrangements etc.
Thanking you personally.
Yours Sincerely,
John Dowling

Nicholas Purcell accepts the invitation to manage the All-Star Hurling team in Wembley in 1973

8/5/73

Dear Mick, I am both pleased and honoured to accept your kind invitation to manage the Carrolls GAA All-Star Hurling Team, which plays Tipperary in Wembley Stadium on 26th inst. Please also convey my appreciation and thanks to your colleagues on the Steering Committee for this fine gesture to me.
I presume Alec Finn will send me details of flight times etc. later.
Kindest regards,
Yours Sincerely,
N. Purcell

The Wembley All-Star games may not have captured the imagination of the fans, but the players were delighted to play in the famous soccer stadium. Pat Hartigan recalled, "I had only ever seen Wembley on TV watching the FA Cup final. I remember Eddie Keher breaking all these little windows around the pitch with his shot. The matches were very competitive, and the pitch was so short that the puck outs would be straight back immediately". Pat who captained the All-Star hurlers added, "it was fantastic walking up the famous steps in Wembley to get the trophy".

ALL-STAR ROMANCE

Many players turned the All-Star trip into their honeymoon, planning their wedding day around the tour dates. Mick Jacob married Breda the day before the tour in 1978. "We went on the trip as our honeymoon", said Breda. "I enjoyed the tour as I was interested in camogie and hurling. I used to go along to all the training sessions".

Ger Henderson proposed to his wife at the All-Star banquet in 1978. "I was very motivated the following year to help Kilkenny win the All-

Ireland so that the All-Star trip could be our honeymoon". Kilkenny duly won in 1979 so his plan worked perfectly.

Inevitably, romance blossomed on tour too. At a function for the All-Stars in San Francisco in 1975, Robbie Kelleher met local girl, Florence, whose parents were originally from Ireland. The pair kept in touch after Robbie flew home and Florence visited Ireland the following summer.

They got married in San Francisco in 1977 just one week before the All-Ireland semi-final between Dublin and Kerry. Robbie flew back home a few days after his wedding. When his mother-in-law questioned why he was leaving his new bride so soon, Robbie explained to her that, "there is a very important football match to be played in Dublin".

Dublin beat Kerry in the semi-final and progressed to play Armagh in the All-Ireland final. In September, Florence moved to Dublin, arriving the day before the final, to be greeted by reporters at Dublin Airport. On the morning of the match the papers reported, "Star's Bride Flies in for Match".

Florence's sister, Trish, had previously met Tipperary hurler Jim Fogarty in San Francisco when he travelled as a replacement on the 1974 trip. Jim returned on the trip the following year and later the couple married and settled in San Francisco where they still live.

Gay O'Driscoll mentioned some liaisons from All-Star tours that didn't turn out so well. He remembers an American girl turning up with her suitcase at a training session in Parnell Park to see a Dublin player she had met in America. Gay laughed, "all the lads were saying to him coming off the pitch, 'you are on your own now!'". When Bernard Brogan recalled that story his sons Alan and Bernard shook their heads in disbelief. Did they not have similar stories from their All-Star tours? "Well, nobody followed us home, that's for sure!", quipped Bernard.

Robbie and Florence Kelleher on their wedding day in San Francisco, and above, an article in the *Sunday Press* on All-Ireland Final Sunday, September 1977

Above - Newlyweds Mick and Helen Jacob at the post-match meal and trophy presentation on the All-Star trip in 1978.

Left - A display of seven All-Star trophies in the Jacob house - Mick's three awards and his daughter Ursula's four awards

All-Star Gazing

Into the Eighties

The All-Star trips continued each year during the 1980s with a couple of exceptions: in 1984, there was no trip as the GAA focused on the centenary celebrations at home and in 1986, only the All-Star hurlers went on tour as an International Rules football team visited Australia.

In 1980 Martin Furlong got a late call-up as an All-Star replacement for the trip in April. He played in goal against the champions Kerry in a tight match in New York. Matt Connor and Anton O'Toole traded scores with Mikey Sheehy and Pat Spillane before Kerry were awarded a penalty. Martin got a hand to Sheehy's penalty kick, deflecting it off the crossbar. Nobody took much notice, but if this sounds familiar, it's because two years later, Martin made a similar save against Mikey in the All-Ireland final in 1982. This time it was significant as it played a part in Offaly's dramatic win over Kerry, which ended their historic five-in-a-row bid.

Did the previous penalty kick go through Furlong's mind when Mikey stepped up in 1982? "Well, the only thing is I knew where he put it the last time", said Martin. And did Mikey do the same thing second time around? "He did, yeah. It was nice to save that penalty, but poor old Mikey got a lot of stick over it. He would have been a hero if he scored it, as it would have put a nail in our coffin that day".

Offaly's Richie Connor travelled as an All-Star in 1982 with football champions Kerry and hurling champions Offaly. "I really enjoyed the opportunity to meet the hurlers on those trips, even the Offaly hurlers, as we are from different ends of the county so we would never meet back home". His brother Matt agreed, "meeting the other players was the best part".

One year on tour in LA, Richie and a few others were invited by a millionaire from Offaly to his house in Pebble Beach. "He had a BBQ in his house for us and gave us passes to play golf in Pebble Beach. No one played golf back then; we had never heard of it. So, we didn't even take the passes", laughed Richie at the memory before adding, "the tour was important for people over there. We had to be careful not to diminish it. We were very conscious of that".

FANTASTIC TRIPS

Bobby Ryan recalled the trips during the 1980s. "They were still relatively poor times in Ireland and there was still very little travel back then. I got to see America with the All-Stars. Some of the best friends I ever made was on those trips. Guys like Ger Cunningham, Mick Lyons and Brian McGilligan. I remain lifelong friends with Niall Cahalane, and we meet anytime I am in West Cork".

Bobby first travelled in 1986 as an All-Star replacement. "The replacements were a great idea. You got a magical phone call. When you saw the 01-number coming up, that meant it was from Bank of Ireland in Dublin. It was always at short notice too which made it more exciting. That year I was the only Tipperary player on the trip. That brought you out of your comfort zone; it encouraged you to mix. The All-Star award was great, but the trip was fantastic. The journalists made it. Big jumbo double-decker planes and everyone smoking!".

Bobby continued to reminisce. "The trips took place in May back then which was very close to the start of the Championship. I remember lads from Wexford trying to get Liam Fennelly drunk on the way home on the plane, as they were playing Kilkenny the following Sunday in the first round of the Championship!".

| All-Star party including Martin Furlong (centre) and Bank of Ireland's Jim Whitty (second from right) outside San Francisco International airport

| A trip to the races for the All-Stars is reported in the *San Francisco Chronicle* in 1983

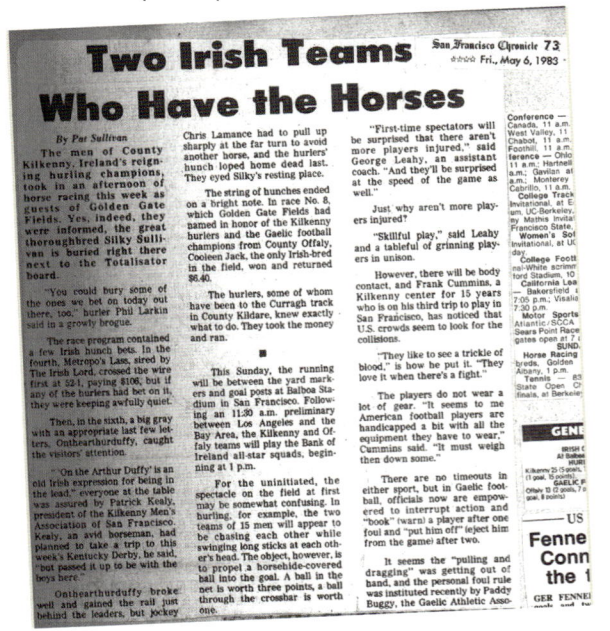

50 Years of the GAA All-Stars

Paddy Kennedy, Richie Connor, Séamus McHugh, Mick Kennedy, Michael O'Toole and Anton McCaul after a training session in San Francisco in 1982

The 1982 All-Star Teams with champions Offaly and Kilkenny ready for take-off at Shannon in 1983

Larry Tompkins went on tour many times in the 1980s. "I was a replacement in 1985 while I was still playing for Kildare. You couldn't beat those trips. There were so many Irish people there supporting the matches. Mixing with players from other counties was special. And making friends with the hurlers too. I am still great mates with many of them".

And what about the matches? "The All-Star games were tough. An exhibition? Sometimes they were like a championship match! You didn't want to disappoint the Irish people who came to see you. There was pride. So, you enjoyed yourself, but you trained, and you took the matches seriously too". Tompkins returned to New York and played for many years during the 1980s. He came home in 1987 and continued his football career in Cork, a move that came about due to connections made in New York. He went on to win two All-Ireland medals and two All-Stars playing for his adopted county.

Having received a third consecutive All-Star in 1985, Barney Rock was asked to captain the football team on tour to America the following year. "There were so many Irish people over there then, it was unbelievable. When you got your All-Star, you knew you were going away for a few weeks. It was a fantastic trip to look forward to. There was more prestige to it back then".

All-Star Gazing

Pete Finnerty, Brendan Lynskey, Paudge Courtney and Liam Fennelly enjoy the sunshine in LA in 1986.
Inset - A young fan seeks an autograph from Pat Spillane in Balboa Stadium in the 1980s

David Kilcoyne was picked as an All-Star replacement in 1985. "It was a big honour. I remember thinking that was as much as I would get". David became the first Westmeath All-Star later that year and travelled on tour again in 1986. He stayed in New York after the tour and played for Clare that summer. "The All-Star trips allowed me to make connections in the US which led to me playing there for a whole summer".

In 1989, two years before receiving the first of his four All-Stars, Gary Kirby was picked as a replacement for Ciarán Barr. "The trip was eight days long; we went to New York and Florida. We had two great games against the champions, Galway. The trips brought me out of myself. I got to meet fellas you wouldn't meet only for those trips. Fellas like Ultan McFetridge, Bobby Ryan, Pete Finnerty and Pat Fox. When I meet those guys now, the connection is still there".

END OF AN ERA

In 1987 the Kerry team travelled for the last time as All-Ireland champions. "We were nearing the end of the road by then", recalls Pat Spillane. "We played the All-Stars in San Francisco, and the mileage was catching up on us. We were realising this could be our last trip. So, the day before the second match, we decided to go out early. We were in the Buena Vista Bar in Fisherman's Wharf drinking Irish coffees and Jesus, we had the mother of all sessions. So much so that we never made it to the official All-Star function that night".

Pat recalls a headline written by Michael Ellard in *The Irish Examiner* (then called *The Cork Examiner*) back home, "something about the Kerry players snubbing the All-Star function.

"But we didn't snub it; we were comatose back in the hotel! We had to line out the next day, we got the shit kicked out of us, we were in the horrors. It was the only time it ever happened".

The All-Stars hammered Kerry and Mikey Sheehy recalled, "the heat was unbearable, almost 100 degrees. The All-Stars had been training and Kerry hadn't so we died in the match the next day".

Dear Barney,
    Our Executive Committee request that you would accept the captaincy of the Bank of Ireland Allstar Football team on the forthcoming visit to the United States.
    As you may have read in the newspapers Arthur Nolan, Dublin's Central Council representative, has been named as manager of the team and we trust you will have a very successful co-operation with him on the tour.
    On behalf of our committee I take this opportunity of wishing you and all the players a very enjoyable trip.
                    Yours sincerely,
                    MICK DUNNE
                    Hon. Secretary.

Also to
Pat Fleury
Hurling

Barney Rock is invited to captain the All-Star football team

50 Years of the GAA All-Stars

The Kerry team after the infamous beach run in San Francisco in 1987.
Front L to R: Páidí Ó Sé, Eoin Liston, Timmy Dowd, Mick O'Dwyer, Seán Walsh, Seán Kelly, John Kennedy, Mick Spillane
Back L to R: Tom Spillane, Domo Lyne, Pat Spillane, Ogie Moran, Mikey Sheehy, Willie Maher, Mick Galway, John Higgins, Ambrose O'Donovan, Ger Lynch, Stephen Stack

Right - Michael Ellard's article in *The Cork Examiner*

Pat laughed, "the following morning Dwyer was really angry that we let the county down. He brought us for a run on the beach in San Francisco. Imagine the state of us? He made us run a race 30 minutes out and 30 minutes back on soft sand. The race was won by Seán Kelly, who was the vice-chairman of the Kerry County Board at the time. He ran the entire race in a pair of sandals, and he still beat the lot of us. The Bomber hid on the way out and finished second in the race!".

Tom Spillane produces the photographic evidence and says, "we were hockeyed by the All-Stars and Mick O'Dwyer was like a bear. If you look at me in the photo of the beach run, I am still wearing my shirt from the night before. Micko made a speech at the Irish Centre that night and put our defeat down to age".

Liam Irwin and Colm Browne returned early from that All-Star tour in May 1987 to play for Laois against Carlow in the Championship. "We were very jetlagged lining out that Sunday after returning from the trip, but we managed to win".

MEATH VS THE ALL-STARS

In May 1988, when the National League Final between Meath and Dublin ended in a draw, the replay was scheduled for two weeks later. The All-Star tour to America took place between the two matches. The touring party included Meath as reigning All-Ireland champions and Kieran Duff – the sole Dub on the All-Star team.

"At the time Dublin had a good rivalry with Meath", said Kieran. "I knew the Meath players well as I used to travel with them to Railway Cup training sessions in Portlaoise. Those matches were played together over a weekend, so we often went on the tear together afterwards. On that All-Star trip there was probably a bit of ongoing tension from the drawn League Final. We went to Boston first,

The All-Star team in Gaelic Park in 1985, captained by Barney Rock
Back L to R: Jimmy Grey, Mickey Quinn, Larry Tompkins, Colm O'Rourke, John O'Leary, Eamon McEneaney, Mick Lyons, John Crofton, Brian O'Donnell, Jim Reilly, Séamus McHugh
Front L to R: Tommy Smyth, PJ Buckley, Liam Tierney, Joe Kernan, Plunkett Donaghy, Barney Rock, Eddie Mahon, Noel Roche

All-Star Gazing

Kerry and the All-Stars parade in 1987. All-Stars Colm Brown and Liam Irwin line out at number seven and nine, replacement Charlie Redmond is at number 11

then on to San Francisco. In the match in San Francisco, I remember getting three clips in the first half. Then in the second half I went for a high ball, and I got a box".

He continued, "that night it got a bit heated between me and some of the Meath players. There were some 'verbals', but that was it. Back home there were reports that it was more than that. Word even got back to our manager Gerry McCaul. I remember that the journalists were out looking for an interview in Dublin Airport when we returned home".

Football referee Mickey Kearins remembered, "there was a bit of tension at the All-Star function that night, so I just left early". Kieran concluded, "It was just the journalists trying to blow it out of proportion. We all got friendly on those All-Star trips. I remember being downtown with David Beggy, who had his guitar with him, and we were all singing along together".
For Tom Spillane, the All-Star trip of 1988 is the one that stands out most for him. He travelled with teammate Ger Lynch to play on the All-Star team. "We reckoned that it might be our last trip, so we made the most of it".

As soon as they touched down in San Francisco, they booked flights to LA and went to Disney. "We missed the training session and I remember that the manager of the All-Stars, Fr. Seán Hegarty, was not impressed with us at all".

NEW YORK ANNIVERSARY

In 1989 the All-Star hurlers and champions Galway travelled to New York to take part in a double bill that included the National Football League Final. New York GAA had affiliated with the GAA Central Council the previous year and as a result the League match was played in Gaelic Park for the first time since the suspension of league activities in 1970.

The Cork footballers played a New York team in the National League Final. The double-bill also marked the 75th anniversary of the establishment of the GAA in New York and the football final was broadcast live on RTÉ back home.

Mick Dunne wrote in the programme notes about the significance of Gaelic Park to the Irish Community in New York. He quoted one emigrant who described it as "a corner of Ireland in the middle of the Bronx that enabled any young Irish man or woman to get through homesickness on their arrival from Ireland".

In 1989 the football All-Stars travelled to San Francisco and New York with champions Cork. Kevin O'Brien was invited on tour as a replacement. "Guys from other counties weren't available so you would get called in. Being a replacement was big here because it was Wicklow and there hadn't been too many. Coming from Wicklow you want to do well and when you are playing with the best players, they make it easy. The All-Star trips were brilliant. Lads were allowed to let off a bit of steam".

50 Years of the GAA All-Stars

| The Meath players leave the field after a training session on the All-Star tour in 1988.
Inset - Hugh Duggan, Fr. Seán Hegarty and Mick Dunne at an All-Star function in the San Francisco Cultural Centre in 1988.

| Top - The hurling All-Stars line up in Gaelic Park in 1989.
Above - Galway line up in Gaelic Park in 1989
Left - Programme for the hurling matches in Gaelic Park in 1989

All-Star Gazing

> Dear Paddy,
> Congratulations on your selection as manager to the Bank of Ireland Allstar Football team for the trip to the U.S.
> On behalf of our Steering Committee I would like to point out that the selection and placing of the players will be the sole responsibility of yourself and the coach. Should any of the sports journalists who are Allstar selectors be on the tour they will be there solely in their professional capacities and, consequently, have no say at this stage in the selection of the Allstar team.
> I have enclosed a list of the squad you will have on the tour. As I have already indicated placing is your responsibility, but we do ask that you and Mick O'Dwyer ensure that the players adhere to the squad numbers listed as these have been communicated to the organising committees in New York and San Francisco. We would suggest also that you would make the individual players responsible for their jerseys and kit from one Sunday to the next.
> We wish you a very successful and enjoyable trip,
> Yours sincerely,
> MICK DUNNE
> Hon. Secretary.

> Dear Mick,
> Congratulations on your selection as coach to the Bank of Ireland Allstar Football team for the trip to the U.S.
> On behalf of our Steering Committee I would like to point out that the selection and placing of the players will be the sole responsibility of yourself and the manager. Should any of the sports journalists who are Allstar selectors be on the tour they will be there solely in their professional capacities and, consequently, have no say at this stage in the selection of the Allstar team.
> I have enclosed a list of the squad you will have on the tour. As I have already indicated placing is your responsibility, but we would ask that you ensure that the players adhere to the squad numbers listed as these have been communicated to the organising committees in New York and San Francisco. We would suggest also that you would make the individual players responsible for their jerseys and kit from one Sunday to the next.
> We wish you a very successful and enjoyable trip,
> Yours sincerely,
> MICK DUNNE
> Hon. Secretary.

Kevin continued, "meeting the journalists too was very important. Mick Dunne always had a kind word for the lads from the smaller counties, he never went past us. And Paddy Downey was a gentleman. I had huge respect for them. They were very good at their jobs and if either of them rang you for an interview you never let them down".

Paddy Cullen was appointed manager and Mick O'Dwyer coach of the All-Star team that year. Mick laughed, "I was there as a coach because the GAA were afraid I would be giving them big bills if I was a manager".

ALL-STAR MATCHES IN IRELAND

In contrast to all the matches played overseas, the All-Stars have only lined out twice at home. The first occasion was in October 1984 when the 1983 All-Star hurlers played against centenary champions Cork in a curtain-raiser before the International Rules match between Ireland and Australia in Cork.

The following April both All-Star teams played against 'Rest of Ireland' selections in the Matt Connor Benefit Games in O'Connor Park, Tullamore. The Offaly star's playing career had been cut short when he was seriously injured in a car accident the previous Christmas. Fifteen thousand people turned out to see the two matches.

Martin Furlong remembers an emotional event. "It was more than an ordinary exhibition match; it had a great purpose. When you think of Matt, he was only 25, the top scorer in

1989 All-Star Footballers in San Francisco 1990
Back L to R: Mick O'Dwyer, Donal Reid, Tony McManus, Ambrose O'Donovan, Mickey Linden, Gabriel Irwin, Willie Joe Padden, Tommy Carr, Gerry Hargan, Liam McHale, Paddy Muldoon
Front L to R: Pat Doorey, Connie Murphy, Val Daly, Martin McHugh, Jimmy Browne, Kevin O'Brien, Jim McConville, Dermot Flanagan, Dessie Barry, Noel Durkin

50 Years of the GAA All-Stars

Leinster for the previous six years. He was a class act, and he hadn't peaked yet. It was a terrible blow to Matt and his family and a big setback for Offaly football. I remember that it was a nice day for the game and there was a huge turnout. Fair play to all the All-Stars that showed up from the other counties".

John O'Leary who played in goals for the All-Stars that day wrote in his book Back to the Hill, "the esteem Matt was held in was perfectly illustrated in Tullamore in April 1985 when two games were held in support of his Trust Fund. It really was a great occasion. It was an honour to be involved, and I think all players felt the same".

Connor's career may have ended prematurely but he still inspires the players of today. 2020 Footballer of the Year Brian Fenton says Matt Connor stands out when he watches the old Kerry matches with his dad on GAA Gold. "I would be slagging Dad who is from Kerry, saying 'they are no good at all, they wouldn't get to play for Dublin now the way the game has changed'. But you watch a player like Matt Connor, and he was so talented. He would be a modern-day star. To hear his story…you would love to sit down with him and have a pint".

| Match programme for the Ireland vs Australia match in 1984. Below - The hurling All-Stars lineout against Cork

| The match programme and All Star lineouts for the Matt Connor benefit games in 1985

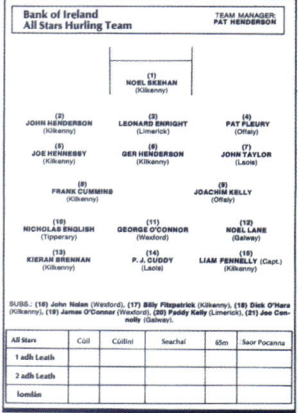

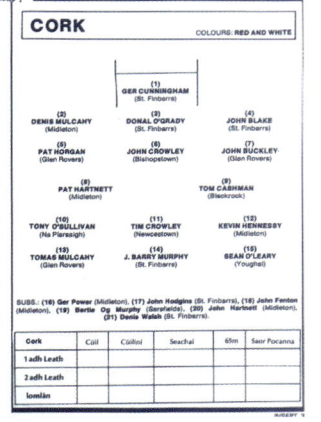

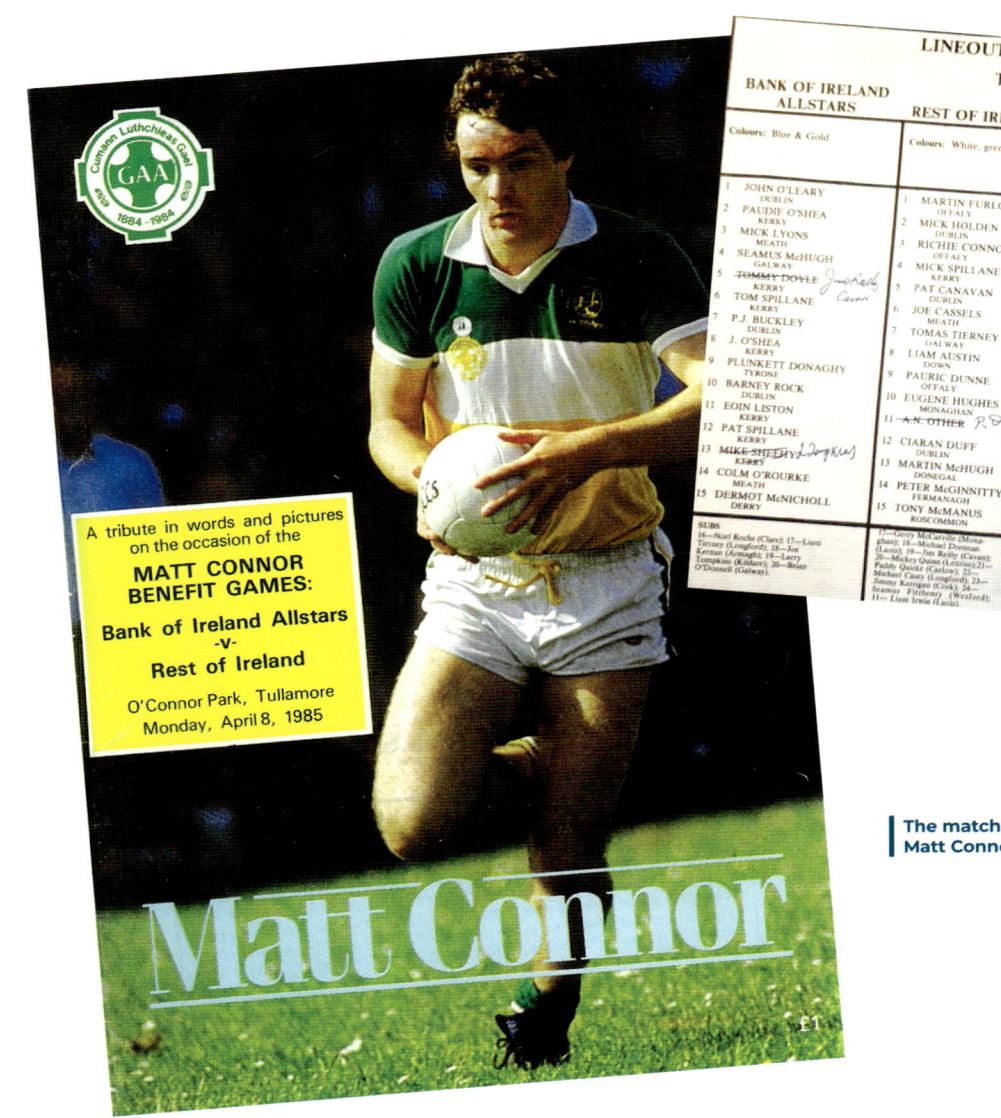

All-Star Gazing

Pastures New in the Nineties

In early 1990, the GAA accepted an invitation from Brian Farmer, the President of the Canadian GAA to stage hurling and football exhibition matches in Toronto during the city's St Patrick's Day Festival. The GAA and Bank of Ireland sponsored the trip with additional support from Powerscreen, a Tyrone based recycling company. Further financial backing was provided by John Dunne, a Canadian businessman who was originally from Tipperary. He owned a large chain of supermarkets across Canada called 'A & P Dominion'. With overall sponsorship for the trip estimated to be C$1 million, the visit to Toronto brought the All-Star trips up to a new level.

For the first time ever, the All-Star matches would be broadcast live both locally on Canadian TV and back home on RTÉ.

The 1989 hurling All-Stars were invited to Toronto to play All-Ireland champions Tipperary. As the football All-Stars were already scheduled to travel to the US in May 1990, the beaten All-Ireland semi-finalists from the previous year, Dublin and Tyrone, were chosen for the football match. Powerscreen who had strong connections in Tyrone were keen to include their county and as the request from the GAA in Canada was that "the matches would be keenly contested and competitive", the Dublin team was chosen as opposition.

The match venue was the brand new SkyDome stadium, home to the Toronto Blue Jays baseball team. With a capacity of 50,000, it cost C$570 million to build and was the first stadium in the world to have a fully retractable motorised roof. The scoreboard, a giant Sony JumboTron, was three stories high and nine stories wide. The press suites had accommodation for 100 journalists and a hotel surrounded the stadium with restaurants and bedrooms that overlooked the pitch. Nothing like it had ever been seen in Ireland!

| The Jumbotron scoreboard surrounded by hotel bedrooms in the Skydome show the teams parading before the match and, inset, anticipation in the *Toronto Irish News* headlines and the brochure for the Exhibition Matches in Toronto

ADVANCE PROMOTION

The 'Irish games' in Toronto were marketed in advance to generate interest. Slogans like 'you think ice-hockey is macho? See just how tough the Irish are' were used to build the hype among locals.

Bobby Ryan and Barney Rock were flown out on a promotional trip in February. Bobby recalled a press conference in the SkyDome. "The local journalists were firing lots of questions at me about hurling. When I got home, Babs Keating, asked me 'what's the story with the SkyDome?' When I replied, 'it makes Croke Park look like a henhouse, Babs was horrified. He said to me 'don't ever say that about Croke Park. And don't put that in your report to the county board'", laughed Bobby.

Barney joked, "we created the new Croke Park on that trip! Myself and Bobby went over to promote the game with Danny Lynch, the GAA Public Relations Officer. It was from that trip that Danny came home with all the ideas, having seen all the restaurants around the stadium. I remember him saying, 'this is the way forward for Croke Park'".

Bobby remembers that Barney's wife was expecting a baby at the time. "Barney kept ringing home every few hours to check on her. Of course, it turned out to be Dean, and I often think of that trip when I see Dean scoring now for Dublin".

All the promotion had an impact because 10 days before the games, the organisers had sold over 15,000 tickets. The four teams, officials and a large group of supporters took an Air Transat flight to Toronto. On arrival, there was a reception at the airport and a police escort into the city.

Everyone stayed together in the Sheraton Centre downtown, which was within walking distance of the SkyDome. In the build-up to the match, The *Toronto Star* newspaper reported that the "Hurling and Gaelic Football stars were here to strut their stuff". They compared Nicky English to their Ice Hockey superstar Wayne Gretzky. Nicky took it all in his stride; the paper quoted him, "I've never seen him (Gretzky) play, I don't think most people back home would know who he is either".

The report went on to explain, "for the sake of comparison hurling is like a hybrid of field hockey and lacrosse while Gaelic Football combines many elements of soccer and rugby. Both games appear violent, but none of the players wear pads".

There were training sessions in the SkyDome the week of the match so that the players could get used to the artificial grass and the floodlights. Conal Bonnar said, "It was a huge thrill to be in the SkyDome. It was fantastic. I remember training every day, changing into the All-Star gear in the hotel and just walking through the city to the SkyDome".

| Team captains Tommy Carr and John Kennedy chat with tour officials before leaving Dublin Airport

PLAYING IN THE SKYDOME

With all the build-up beforehand and a high volume of ticket sales, Canadian GAA President Brian Farmer started to pile on the pressure. "We need five-star performances from all four teams. The managers assure me that the players realise the importance of the occasion and are fully committed".

On St Patrick's Day the four teams travelled by coach to the SkyDome escorted by the police. The players all wore shoulder, knee and elbow pads for protection on the artificial surface and had 'eye black' under their eyes to reduce the floodlight glare. The anthems of both countries were played before throw-in. The only glitch – instead of Amhrán na bhFiann, 'God Save the Queen' rang out across the stadium!

In the centre of the pitch the GAA crest was marked out along with the sponsor's logo, prompting Mick Dunne to speculate, "perhaps a new idea for the centre of Croke Park next September?". While the temperatures outside the SkyDome dropped below zero, it was hot and humid inside the covered stadium during the matches. Paddy Downey reported, "the games were played in four quarters to give the players a chance to deal with the humidity".

Raymond Munroe who played on the Tyrone team, wrote an article on his return for local magazine 'An Tearmann'. "The heat was stifling at first, but the air conditioning helped to make the whole thing bearable. The heat, the tension and the excitement all around speeded everything up and the players remarked that even their own performances speeded up under these conditions. It still was not as hot as the 1989 Ulster Final in Clones!".

He continued, "the whole presentation was very professional, and everything had to fit in exactly with the TV ads. The big screens caused us some worry but once the game started, we never looked up once…even though we were aware that the repeats were shown immediately after the scores or controversial decisions".

| Barney Rock training in the Skydome

| The programme for the matches in the SkyDome in 1990

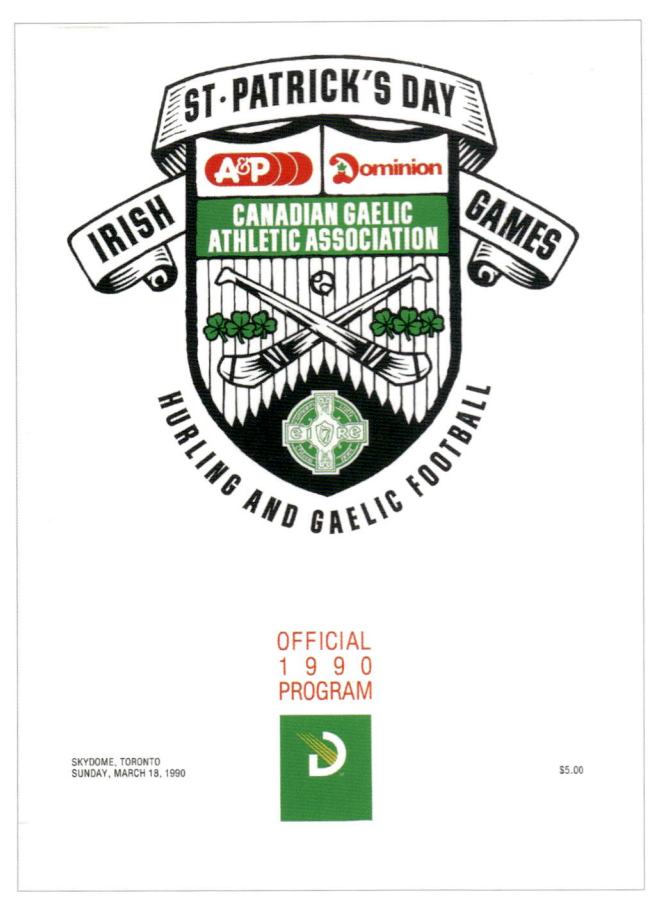

Jim Nelson, the Antrim manager, had been invited by Canadian TV TSN to explain the game of hurling to viewers and "supply analysis of the play" during intervals in the commentary. Mick O'Dwyer co-commentated on the football match for RTÉ.

The organisers were delighted when a crowd of 25,952 turned up. The hurling match provided a great exhibition of skills although Tipperary were clear winners. Nicky English lived up to the pre-match hype and was top scorer as Tipperary beat the All-Stars, 5-15 to 3-11. Cormac Bonnar scored two of the goals and his brother Conal recalled, "the Canadian cameramen couldn't keep up with the speed of the ball even though they were used to ice hockey matches". Tipperary captain Declan Carr gave his view of the contest, "the teams felt they needed to put on a show, so we played a tough match".

Most of the interest before the games was in the hurling, because of the anticipated intensity of the game. As it transpired, it was the football match between Dublin and Tyrone that proved the more competitive. Dublin beat Tyrone by just a single point (1-8 to 10 points) despite being reduced to 14 men when referee Michael Greenan sent Mick Deegan off for a foul on Peter Canavan. Vinnie Murphy scored a controversial goal, David Foran had to retire, and Seán McNally was taken to hospital with an eye injury.

It was described by Seán Kilfeather in The Irish Times as

Tommy Carr, Joe McNally and Paul Curran training in the Skydome

"a turbulent clash". Paddy Downey went further, "if the Canadians in the SkyDome yesterday were disappointed that the hurling game did not produce the crunching clashes and eruptions of temper which are a regular feature of ice hockey, they got more than enough rough and tough stuff in the Gaelic football clash that followed".

"Perhaps the players may have too literally taken the exhortation of the Canadian GAA Officials that they should not treat the game as a mere friendly", reported Mick Dunne. "The match inexplicably turned into a hostile contest despite the comradeship and rapport that had developed between the Tyrone and Dublin players as they socialised during the five days prior to the game".

Dublin captain Tommy Carr reflected, "the organisers wanted a football match that mattered so they picked two teams that would be competitive, Dublin and Tyrone. We kicked lumps out of each other! Looking back now, I don't actually know why the game was tough because there was no real rivalry between us at that time. But there is always an edge with Tyrone".

Kieran Duff told us, "There was a sponsor from Tyrone, so the Tyrone footballers took it very seriously and they wanted to win. We trained well but we socialised well too. I remember Peter Canavan was there, he was only 18".

And the Tyrone perspective? Raymond Munroe wrote, "we admired the commitment and dedication of the Dublin players, and it was no shame to be beaten by such a wonderful bunch of athletes. Next time it might be different!". He added, "on a personal level, it was great for me to be marking Barney Rock, a legend in his own time".

All-Star Hurlers Seán Treacy, Joe Cooney, Liam Walsh, Michael Coleman, Mark Corrigan, Éanna Ryan with Jim Nelson on the way to the Skydome. Inset, police ready to escort the players.

All-Star Gazing

The captains and officials line up on the GAA logo in the Skydome

Nicky English giving an exhibition of hurling in the Skydome

STRANGE ATMOSPHERE

The players enjoyed playing in the SkyDome as it was such a new experience for them, long before the redevelopment of Croke Park into the 82,300-seater stadium it is today.

"Toronto was a different trip, and the stadium was amazing", said Declan Carr, "There was no such thing as a SkyDome in Ireland at the time. We couldn't get our heads around it; it was so huge. It was the first time we had ever seen floodlights. And there was a roof which was so high we couldn't hit it with the sliotar. We couldn't even see the ball! We had black paint under our eyes and had to wear padding to avoid getting cuts, it was mad stuff".

His brother Tommy continued, "The stadium was more than half full, with a crowd of 25,000 but the atmosphere seemed strange. It felt like it was empty as you could hear everyone talking to each other on the pitch".

Joe Cooney who played on the All-Star hurling team recalled, "there was no noise from the crowd as they were all in these Corporate boxes which we had never seen before. We didn't think there was anyone there at the start". Joe's brother Jimmy travelled to Toronto as a supporter.

Barney Rock recalled, "a great trip, one we all remember. To actually play on a full-size pitch indoors was fabulous".

Afterwards each winning captain was presented with an impressive trophy called 'The Canada Cup'.

At the post-match banquet that evening all the winners received a gold ring, a unique memento of the occasion.

The Dublin and Tyrone teams ahead of the football game

The 14-carat rings with garnet stones had been specially commissioned for the occasion.

Declan Carr recalled, "we all got these huge rings, like the ones given to Pro Footballers in the US. They were gold and had rubies in them. We were told at the time that they were worth C$5,000!".

Tommy added, "we all thought these rings were great, but of course once you got back home, they looked ridiculous, nobody ever wore them". Keith Barr laughed about the rings and joked, "Vinnie Murphy was the only one who ever wore the ring back home!".

The next day all three Toronto newspapers had extensive coverage of the games. "Irish goalie denies that he is insane",

50 Years of the GAA All-Stars

Captains Tommy Carr and John Kennedy each receive a 'Canada Cup' and, inset, Gold rings for the Winners

read the headline in *The Toronto Star,* referring to Tipperary's Ken Hogan. Wendall Clark, an Ice Hockey star with the Maple Leafs, who had attended the matches, was quoted, "these guys sure are brave, it was tough out there".

GUESTS OF HONOUR

There was a busy social schedule for the visitors off the pitch. They went to see the Toronto Maple Leafs play ice hockey and attended a concert in the Roy Thomson Concert Hall. "We saw Phil Coulter there", recalled Keith Barr. "It was a huge venue like Carnegie Hall. I remember that the GAA players were the guests of honour".

The sponsors hosted a lunch in a revolving restaurant overlooking Niagara Falls. "We went on a trip to Niagara Falls", said James McCartan, "and I remember a great sing-song on the bus on the way back. Tom Dempsey from Wexford was singing rebel songs that I never heard before". Brendan Grace was flown over for a Canadian Irish business breakfast which was "the funniest hour ever", according to journalist Donal Keenan.

And there was plenty of informal socialising too. Kieran Duff recalled the night of the match. "I was with Terence McNaughton from Antrim. The bar closed quite early in Canada, about 12 o'clock at night. The Tyrone lads had a bath full of beer in their room and they invited us to join them. They had been slagging me all night, so Terence didn't want to go up to the room. But we did and it was fine. That was it when you were all away together; you were just interested in having a good time".

SUCCESSFUL TRIP

For 19-year-old student Conal Bonnar, playing his first championship year with Tipperary, the trip was an incredible experience. "I got my first passport to go on that trip. My club gave me £100 before I went, then Bank of Ireland gave everyone £100 for expenses, the County Board gave me £200, and the Munster council gave me a few bob too. So, I ended up with around £1,000 and at the time my student grant for the full year in college was only £1,500! Then we needed special boots to play on the AstroTurf which the bank had provided. But they didn't have any in my size, so Dermot Power bought me a pair of Nike Air Max that cost about £100. I couldn't believe it! Imagine going back into UCD in 1990 and walking around with £100 on my feet".

The three Bonnar brothers, Conal, Colm and Cormac, were all on the trip. Another brother, Kieran, lived in Calgary at the time and he was flown to Toronto by the Tipperary Supporters association to surprise the lads at a function the night before the match. Aidan Ryan's brother lived in Canada too. "He came to Toronto and took me and Declan Carr out on the town. He knew all the best places to go, and as the Tipperary hurlers, we were treated like VIPs".

Journalist Paddy Downey at lunch overlooking Niagara Falls

Sponsor John Dunne's welcome message in the matchday programme

Dermot Power, GAA President John Dowling, Liam Mulvihill and Oliver Kelly walk the pitch in the Skydome

Journalists Donal Keenan, Roy Curtis and Peadar O'Brien with GAA PRO Danny Lynch (second left) in the SkyDome on match day

Raymond Munroe wrote, "everything about the trip was so different to the lifestyle that most of us live in this country. We were received at the airport like celebrities and the last thing we expected was for a big city like Toronto to have its streets cordoned off for our benefit! Seán Harte of Canadian GAA, originally from Tyrone, made a major contribution to the success of our trip".

Indeed, the trip was deemed a success by all involved. John Dunne of A&P Dominion said, "when I was first approached about doing something of this magnitude with Gaelic games, I knew there was a risk. Especially with most people in Canada not knowing what hurling is, never mind Gaelic football. But the Canadian GAA did a superb job in organising the trip and were committed to a first-rate show".

Brian Farmer was equally enthusiastic. "The whole thing has been such a success; we'll go ahead with more vigour next year. We see this becoming an annual event around St Patrick's Day, and we'll be looking for the two All-Ireland Champions and the All-Stars in both hurling and football".

Liam Mulvihill expressed his satisfaction and concluded, "it shows what can be done for our games when they are promoted professionally. We are at the start of something big, not just in Toronto but in many places abroad".

On his return home Mick Dunne wrote, "because the Canadian GAA, backed by a professional organisation, brought sports PR experts on board, the two matches got more coverage and promotion in newspapers, television and radio than ever before". He added, "as for the SkyDome it almost defies description. In sporting terms, it is a thing of beauty. The facts and figures make the head dizzy and despite our Minister for Sport Frank Fahy being in attendance, we will never have anything like that here".

Happily, his prediction was wrong and when the GAA redeveloped Croke Park into one of the finest stadia in Europe, he was delighted. He would also have enjoyed the appearance many years later of the GAA logo in the centre of the pitch on All-Ireland final day.

RETURN TO TORONTO

Coca Cola came on board as an additional sponsor for the return trip to Toronto in March 1991. Again, the matches coincided with the St Patrick's Day festival. This time both All-Star teams travelled and, as it happened, both teams played against Cork who had won the double in 1990.

The trip was taken even more seriously this time with players preparing in advance for the artificial surface in the SkyDome. As Bank of Ireland's Dermot Power explained at the time, "a side simply can't come together and perform without any preparation. Last year showed that the pitch is difficult for hurling, being narrow and very fast. In football, players coped well with the extra bounce", adding, "players will be expected to prove that they are match fit, you can take it that the All-Star matches will be competitive this year".

Jim Nelson was appointed manager of the All-Star hurling team while Brian McEniff took charge of the footballers. The two managers organised training sessions on an artificial surface in Dublin before the trip. Declan Carr, returning as a hurling All-Star, remembers those training sessions, "Jim Nelson was taking it very seriously; he specified no drinking in advance of the first match".

The plan nearly came unstuck before the party left Dublin Airport. Declan explained, "we all gathered in the Dublin Airport Hotel before we flew out. Everyone was in their All-Star jackets, shirts and ties. When some of the players arrived out of the bar, the manager wanted to leave them at home".

However, Dermot Power intervened and made sure that nobody was left behind. "We had asked the managers to be competitive, but these trips were a reward for the players too, for all their efforts throughout the season. It was important that fellas could relax and enjoy themselves".

Ciarán Barr recalled, "someone said it was because they were nervous about flying that they went into the bar! But we did take the ban seriously that year. It was important as we really wanted to win. I didn't drink until the banquet after the match in Toronto. But then I made up for it", he said with a laugh.

Understandably the managers wanted to win as the matches had a high profile. A large crowd was anticipated, and the matches were again being televised in Ireland and in Canada.

A young DJ Carey was also a replacement on that tour, having received his first All-Star nomination in 1990. He recalled early morning training sessions in the SkyDome. "The manager had us up at seven in the morning. The footballers and hurlers trained at the same time at different ends of the pitch. It was a big thing for me. I grew up a fan of Kerry football, so I was in awe, being there with those football stars, the likes of Jack O'Shea. I remember the goalkeeper kicking the ball out to O'Shea. I jumped in behind him, jumped up and caught the high ball. The footballers couldn't believe that a hurler had made the catch".

O'Shea was an All-Star replacement on the trip. Conal Bonnar remembers, "I was in awe of O'Shea. I asked him for his jersey which he signed for me. It turned out to be Jack's last All-Star jersey".

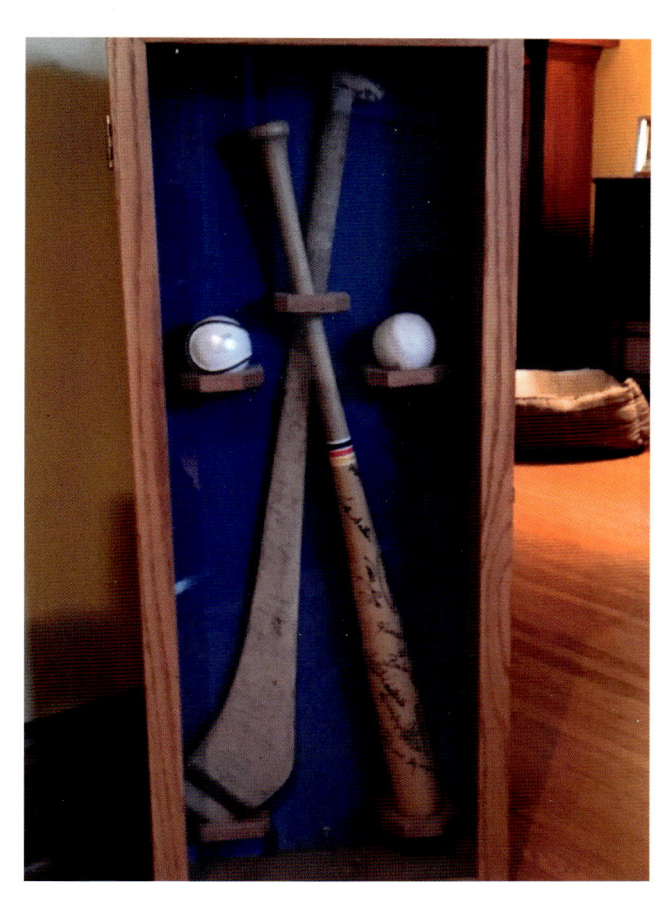

A special display of mementoes from Toronto: Joe Carter's baseball bat from 1991 and Cormac Bonnar's hurl from 1990

CORK VS THE BLUE JAYS

The day before the All-Star matches, the teams were invited to the SkyDome to watch the Blue Jays play the New York Mets in a pre-season exhibition game. The Blue Jays were a top baseball team at that time and went on to win the World Series in 1993 and 1994. "We were given seats behind the first base and the place was hopping. But I remember after about an hour we all got bored", said Brian Whelahan.

To promote the GAA games the next day, a competition took place at half-time between the Cork goalkeeper Ger Cunningham and Joe Carter, the Blue Jays ball-hitting superstar. The plan was for Ger to exhibit his hurling skills, followed by Carter showing the talent that earned him an estimated C$23 million a year. Using their own sticks initially, Ger hit the ball the furthest. Then the two players swapped sticks and balls and Ger hit the ball even further. The Irish crowd went crazy. Ger hit it again, even further this time. The Blue Jays star tried three times to hit the sliotar using the hurl but couldn't master it.

Brian said, "We were all going mad cheering for Ger. The Blue Jays guy threw the hurl down in disgust and wouldn't shake hands with Ger after the competition".

James McCartan recalled, "the Blue Jays star was trying to hit the ball, but he couldn't get it off the ground. I suppose

All-Star Gazing

he was used to another player throwing it to him in baseball. Ger looked at the baseball bat in disdain, then lifted the ball and whacked it out of the stadium. All the Irish in the crowd went wild".

Conal Bonnar who had returned to Toronto as an All-Star in 1991, also remembered the shoot-out. "After half-time I spotted Carter's bat just lying there and the game was about to resume. Nobody seemed interested in it. So, I took it".

The baseball bat had been signed by all the Blue Jay players. Conal's nephew, Devin, who lived in Toronto, was a huge Blue Jays fan so the opportunistic Tipperary man knew that his nephew would love to have the bat.

This piece of All-Star memorabilia is still on display in the Bonnar home in Toronto along with the hurl that Cormac Bonnar used the previous year in the SkyDome. "My brother Cormac scored the winning goal in the match the previous year, and afterwards we got all the Tipperary players to sign it", said Conal.

Billy Morgan, the manager of the Cork football team, remembers the baseball game. "We were all sitting there wondering how we would be able to play on the baseball pitch the following day. When we arrived, it had been completely re-marked. Within 24 hours, it had been transformed into a full-size GAA pitch".

ALL-STAR MATCHES

The two matches took place on Saturday, March 18th. The All-Star hurlers beat All-Ireland champions Cork comfortably by 5-13 to 0-6 points. The football match was more competitive with Cork winning a tight match by 1-12 to 1-09.

Brian Whelahan said he was conscious of the needle between the Cork footballers and the Meath players on that trip to Toronto, after the previous year's All-Ireland final. As Kevin O'Brien recalled, "the carry forward from the All-Ireland final made our match a bit more intense. Brian McEniff the manager, he certainly didn't want to lose. They always said, 'there is a great chance to put down a marker and that is on an All-Star trip'".

Tomás Mulcahy captained the Cork hurlers and recalled their pre-match preparation. "The night before the match we were all up late in the bar. The All-Star hurlers were under this curfew set by Jim Nelson. The goalie Jim Troy was the only All-Star who stayed up with us. Of course, we were encouraging him hoping he wouldn't perform the next day". The plan didn't work however, Troy put in a great performance and was voted Man of the Match.

LIKE-MINDED PEOPLE

Nineteen-year-old Brian Whelahan loved the experience of that trip to Toronto. "It was my first time to travel to the US

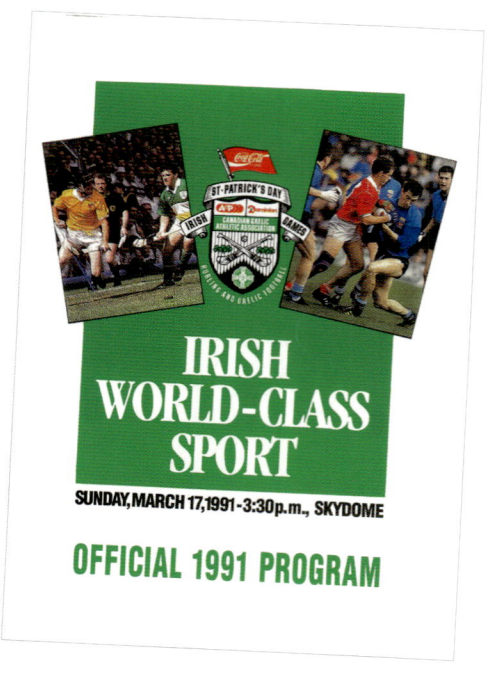

The programme for the matches in the SkyDome in 1991

or Canada and it was a fantastic trip to get. I still remember the girl from the bank ringing to tell me that I was picked. Johnny Pilkington was called up too. Going on a trip with the guys I had been watching growing up like Pete Finnerty was huge. I remember stopping in Shannon Airport, and we saw the US soldiers on their way to fight in the Gulf War. That kind of added to the excitement". Brian added, "It was the last All-Star trip, and it was a big disappointment not to get any more".

Pete Finnerty has great memories of Toronto too even though initially he was not going to travel. "I had just opened Supermac's in Tuam, and I had already been on four or five trips in the 1980s. But the bank insisted that I go. I travelled over later than the rest of the group, arriving on Friday night. I go up to the hotel room, which I was sharing with Conal Bonnar, and there is a half-eaten pizza in the middle of my bed. I wasn't impressed at the time but looking back, I know the bank did it on purpose because of the huge rivalry between Galway and Tipperary!".

Pete continued, "I went out with Joe Cooney and Danny Lynch (the GAA Public Relations Officer) that night. We weren't supposed to be drinking before the match, so we said, 'we'll take it easy, we'll have a quiet day'. We ended up drinking Tequila and playing darts. On the way to the SkyDome the next day, lots of people were out waving Tricolours as it was Paddy's Day. I will always remember Jim Troy saying, 'Offaly must have won the minor'", he said laughing at the memory.

Pete, who captained the All-Star hurlers, said it was important to win against Cork. "They were the All-Ireland Champions and we wanted to put them down". He added, "it was great to be mixing with the footballers as well. I remember meeting James McCartan and he said, 'My father loves you!'".

For Tomás Mulcahy being away with his Cork teammates was fantastic. "It really helped the team spirit. It brought

Kevin O'Brien's pennant from the match in Toronto in 1991 signed by the football All-Stars

the whole team together". The team continued to Miami afterwards for a holiday.

James McCartan said, "I got to know Kevin O'Brien in Toronto and I am still friendly with him. I have been to visit his house in Wicklow. On the All-Stars trips you get on with the other players like a house on fire. It doesn't matter what battles you had on the pitch. Once you meet at the airport, you get on straight away. You don't have to wait. You are with like-minded people. The medals and trophies are great, but for me, it is all about the friendships you make".

"James is a great friend of mine, he was at my wedding", said Kevin. "We knew each other well as we used to play together for Wolfe Tones in New York and tip down to Florida in between the matches. You make friends that you never forget. Then in Toronto it was brilliant to meet the hurlers because you never got the opportunity. The Offaly hurlers! I remember one night Brian Whelahan and Johnny Pilkington held the whole place in raptures doing a rap song. Good job there wasn't any phones at the time!", he joked. "I met Mickey Quinn in Toronto too, he is a lovely fella, and his All-Star award was well deserved".

Conal Bonnar was in college with Johnny Pilkington and Brian Whelahan at the time. "It was great that they were on that trip too". His brother Cormac said, "the All-Star trips were an opportunity to let your hair down and meet other people. You also got to do something that you could never afford to do yourself. Most people had never been on a foreign holiday in those days".

"The organisers of the All-Star trips were ahead of their time", said Tommy Carr. "It was all paid for, and we were transported everywhere. Team holidays were only starting then, and you had to do fundraising for those yourself. The hotels on team trips might be average, whereas with the Bank of Ireland we stayed in superb hotels".

He added, "there was never a chance to meet players from other counties at the time. You mightn't see each other from one end of the year to the next. It was great to mix with the other members of your own team too".

There was huge interest in the trip back home and the events in the SkyDome inspired some future GAA stars. Seán Óg Ó hAilpín remembers watching as a young teenager in Cork. "It was under lights which nobody knew anything about back then".

Brendan Cummins watched the matches as a young kid too. "I was inspired by Ger Cunningham hitting the top of the SkyDome. I had heard all the stories of the All-Stars over the years, that legacy and the history, looking at the posters in bars. I wanted to be part of all that".

TOURS DISCONTINUED

By 1993 the Canadian sponsor had withdrawn support for the All-Star matches, so the trips to Toronto did not continue. "After the success and glamour of those Canadian trips, it was hard to return to the previous format in the US", said Bank of Ireland's Dermot Power. "By that stage, team holidays had started, so the novelty of a trip to the US had faded. The timing had become an issue too. It became harder to find a slot in the calendar when players could travel. Also, the pitch in New York was so bad in those days and that often led to injuries".

As pre-season preparations for the Championship became more serious, inter-county managers were not happy to release players in April or May so close to the start of the championship. Dermot left Bank of Ireland in 1993 to take up a role with the GAA. The bank's focus was now on its sponsorship of the Football Championship and by 1995 they had withdrawn as sponsors of the All-Star scheme. Powerscreen took over sponsorship for the next two years, but there were no tours during that time. In fact, it was to be another 10 years before the annual All-Star tours were revived.

Though the All-Star scheme continued throughout the 1990s, the sponsorship changed three times and there were no tours from 1992 to 1997. Having heard so many stories about previous trips, some of the All-Stars chosen in those years feel they missed out.

Among them nine-time All-Star DJ Carey. "When I went to Toronto in 1991, I never thought that would be my only All-Star trip. I never actually travelled as an All-Star, as I was only a replacement that first year".

"A great bunch of players", said Kevin O'Neill of the All-Star team in 1993. "It was a pity there was no tour that year. We only really had the one night together at the All-Star banquet. I felt I missed out not going on a trip". Charlie Redmond, also on that team agrees, "you just met the players on your All-Star team at the Banquet for one night. It would have been nice to spend more time together".

James McCartan regrets that Down missed two All-Star trips when they were champions in 1991 and 1994. "By then the trips had stopped. It doesn't sit well with us that we missed out". His teammate Greg Blaney was asked to be a replacement in 1982 but had to turn it down as he was doing exams at the time. "So, I never went on any All-Star trips during my career". Maurice Fitzgerald also missed out on an All-Star tour when he was selected three times during that period.

The campaign to send the All-Stars of the 1990s on a retrospective tour starts here!

All-Star Gazing

ALL-STAR TOURS FROM 1999 TO 2019

1999 BOSTON
(H) 1998 All-Stars vs 1999 All-Ireland Champions Cork
(F) 1999 Football Finalists Meath vs Cork

2001 DUBAI
(F) 1999 All-Stars vs 2000 All-Stars

2002 BUENOS AIRES
(H) 2000 All-Stars vs 2001 All-Stars

2003 SAN DIEGO
(F) 2001 All-Stars vs 2002 All-Stars

2004 PHOENIX ARIZONA, LAS VEGAS
(H) 2002 All-Stars vs 2003 All-Stars

2005 HONG KONG
(F) 2003 All-Stars vs 2004 All-Stars

2006 SINGAPORE
(H) 2004 All-Stars vs 2005 All-Stars

2007 DUBAI (JAN)
(F) 2005 All-Stars vs 2006 Allstars

2007 NEW YORK (DEC)
(H) 2006 All-Stars vs 2007 All-Stars

2008 SAN FRANCISCO
(F) 2007 All-Stars vs 2008 Allstars

2009 BUENOS AIRES
(H) 2008 All-Stars vs 2009 All-Stars

2010 KUALA LUMPUR
(F) 2009 All-Stars vs 2010 All-Stars

2011 SAN FRANCISCO
(H) 2010 All-Stars vs 2011 All-Stars

2012 NEW YORK
(F) 2011 All-Stars vs 2012 All-Stars

2013 SHANGHAI
(H) 2012 All-Stars vs 2013 All-Stars

2014 BOSTON
(F) 2013 All-Stars vs 2014 All-Stars

2015 AUSTIN (TEXAS)
(H) 2014 All-Stars vs 2015 All-Stars

2016 ABU DHABI, DUBAI
(F) 2015 All-Stars vs 2016 All-Stars

2017 SINGAPORE
(H) 2016 All-Stars vs 2017 All-Stars

2018 PHILADELPHIA
(F) 2017 All-Stars vs 2018 All-Stars

2019 ABU DHABI, DUBAI (H)
2018 All-Stars vs 2019 All-Stars

2020 NO TOUR

A Golden Spell in the Noughties

T he GAA was keen to reinstate the All-Star tours and when Eircell took over sponsorship in 1997, they provided the financial support. In October 1999 four teams travelled to Boston: the 1999 football finalists Cork and Meath and the 1998 hurling All-Stars and reigning All-Ireland champions, Cork. Seán Kilfeather wrote, "the purpose of the trip is to support the opening of a spectacular new permanent home for the Boston GAA in Canton, South Boston".

Dual player Seán Óg Ó hAilpín travelled with Cork and split his time equally, playing in one half of the football match and one half of the hurling match. Brian Whelahan, who was on the All-Star hurling team, laughed as he remembered, "Cork wore ESAT on their jerseys. I remember the Eircell guy really wanted us to beat them because of that! He said to us, 'get out there and beat them and I'll look after you'. The incentive worked as the All-Stars won the game. He hired a bar for the night so that we could celebrate".

That trip was a success, but it was a few more years before the All-Star trips were to become an annual event.

HEADING EAST

In January 2001, the GAA community in Dubai invited the All-Stars to visit. This marked the start of "a golden spell for the All-Star tours", according to selector Jim O'Sullivan. The touring party, which included the football All-Stars of 1999 and 2000, plus officials and journalists, made history as the first official GAA group to visit Asia.

Although the trip only lasted five days, the exotic destination in the depths of the Irish winter was welcomed by players and journalists alike. Martin Breheny wrote from Dubai, "it was a change from last Sunday in Aughrim where the winter chills seeped through the bone marrow as the O'Byrne Cup cranked the new GAA season into life".

The two All-Star football teams, managed by John O'Mahony and Páidí Ó Sé, played each other in an exhibition match in

All-Star managers Páidí Ó Sé and John O'Mahony on the sideline in Dubai

Anthony Tohill and Kieran McKeever in the Dubai desert

the Dubai Exiles rugby ground which attracted a crowd of several thousand.

Work and personal commitments ruled out some of the All-Star players, so the tradition of bringing replacements continued into the new era.

The hosts arranged some novel events for the touring party, including a cultural evening in the Dubai desert. Stories and photos soon emerged of GAA players as never seen before. Anthony Tohill recalled, "my abiding memory of that trip was, they put on a night in the desert for us, and we were treated to local cuisine. So, you had 30 or 40 footballers who could eat really well and the local cuisine wasn't agreeing too well with the palette. Thankfully, there was alcohol and we managed to get stuck into that. I think I had enough of it to convince me to get up on a camel with Kieran McKeever. I was encouraged by the desert and the hot climate and the alcohol!".

"It was a great trip", said Pádraic Joyce with a smile. "Liam Hassett was like a madman, on a camel, rolling down the sand dunes".

There were no pubs in Dubai back then, so a lot of socialising took place around the hotel swimming pool. Joyce recalled, "we got £400 spending money at the start, and it was gone in two days".

"There were a lot of Kerry lads on the trip who I had got to know the previous year in Australia", said Ciarán Whelan. "We had great craic and the match was really only an exhibition. I remember all the lads were acting the maggot around the pool, pushing people in. Next thing they pushed in Brian Carthy. But Brian couldn't swim, and he was actually drowning. Jim O'Sullivan had to jump in and save him".

Paddy Reynolds remembered Brian being pushed in the pool. "We didn't realise that he couldn't swim!".

"The good thing about the match was that a lot of people

All-Star Ciarán Whelan and replacement Ian Robertson in the Dubai dessert

Reporter Marty Morrissey with Graham Geraghty, Trevor Giles, Paddy Reynolds and Mark O'Reilly in Dubai

from back home were able to see GAA players live and there were also people who had never seen Gaelic football before", said Anthony Tohill. "The game itself was free flowing and high scoring, nobody was putting their body on the line. I remember when it came to it Páidí Ó Sé said, 'lads, go out and don't get injured. Enjoy yourself but don't be doing anything stupid'".

ANNUAL EVENT

The successful trip to Dubai generated a lot of interest among other GAA communities abroad. When the organisation received invitations from South America, the Middle East and China, it recognised the opportunity to promote Gaelic games in new parts of the world. Also, when the tours returned to the US a few years later, new destinations were chosen, such as Austin, Phoenix and San Diego, along with the traditional cities like Boston, New York and San Francisco.

Once again, the All-Star tour became an annual event. As the All-Ireland champions no longer travelled, the All-Star teams from the preceding two years travelled to play each other so the annual tour alternated between hurling and football.

All-Star Gazing

Journalist Brian Carthy outside The Hurling Club in Buenos Aires

In 2001 Donal Keenan became the liaison between the GAA and sponsors Vodafone, who had by then acquired Eircell. He believes that the sponsor's generous approach at that time cemented the success of the tours. "Like the Bank of Ireland and Carrolls before them, Vodafone insisted that no expense be spared", he explained. "The Director of Marketing in Vodafone at the time was Tara Delaney and if you approached her with any proposal to make the experience better for the players and their partners, she would approve instantly. That meant that when you reached a destination you could alter the itinerary to suit your location. In Singapore we arranged a day at the races which was hugely enjoyed by everyone. Golf outings, shopping trips, sight-seeing trips were all arranged as required. People like Enda Lynch and Olga Mulvany from Vodafone were really enthusiastic too".

Donal continued, "The players responded to the generosity. If either the sponsors or the GAA wanted the players to do a coaching clinic, a photo shoot or a press conference for the journalists, they would do it. It meant tours got the valuable publicity back home that pleased both the sponsor and the GAA". Martin Breheny felt that the resumption of the All-Star trips on an annual basis at that stage was vital. "It gave a big impetus to the All-Star scheme because at the time it was close to fading out".

ARGENTINA IN 2002

In January 2002 the All-Star hurling teams of 2000 and 2001 travelled to Buenos Aires in Argentina. They played an exhibition match in the aptly named Hurling Club, located in the quiet suburbs of the city.

Journalist Keith Duggan wrote, "Saturday night's exhibition at the sedate social club was mostly about tribute, a remembrance of the Argentine hurling games that were silenced by distance and war. How the founders of the game, in these most unlikely settings, would have relished the sight of the best players in the modern game thrilling their descendants on a balmy evening".

Hurling was no longer played at the club but there was still an active hurling community in Buenos Aires. The All-Star match produced plenty of goals for both teams, but goalkeeper Brendan Cummins was still voted the star man. "I was thrilled to meet Damien Fitzhenry on that tour. He was a hero of mine and I just followed him around the whole time we were there! I roomed with Diarmuid O'Sullivan, and we had great fun, drinking in the Kilkenny Bar".

'King' Henry Shefflin was on that trip too. "The club gave me expenses for the All-Star trips which was great, especially when I was younger. I went to Argentina in 2002 and there had been a political coup before we arrived. It was great fun interacting with players from other counties. Some of the best days of fun I ever had were on those trips. Randomly talking to Tipperary and Galway lads and a few months previous you would have been belting the heads off each other. It is crazy to think that hurling would bring you to those places".

"My main memory of that match", recalled Michael Lyster, "was of Mícheál Ó Muircheartaigh taking the mickey out of

Diarmuid O'Sullivan, Brendan Cummins and Damien Fitzhenry check the local news

Eoin Kelly, Denis Byrne and Jim O'Sullivan in downtown Buenos Aires

everyone in his match commentary over a loudspeaker". Ollie Canning enjoyed meeting the legendary commentator. "Having the opportunity to meet legends within the game, especially people like Mícheál Ó Muircheartaigh, where we could enjoy personal conversations outside of hurling talk, is something I will always remember and appreciate".

He continued, "the All-Star Trips away were generally to some country you'd never been to before, so we got to explore new parts of the world which was a great experience. Meeting players from other counties in a social, relaxed environment, you soon realised we were all the same. This social time together outside the competitive environment of league or championship games was a really nice aspect to the All-Star Trips".

A few days later the All-Star party visited the La Bombonera, the home of Boca Juniors soccer team. During the stadium tour, the hurlers asked if they could get a photo on the famous pitch. The club initially refused as people are not allowed to step onto the sacred surface. "Eventually after much persuasion they agreed", explains Lyster. "After the photo, Charlie Carter and Diarmuid O'Sullivan started pucking around and of course, they ended up taking up lumps of grass. The groundsmen were going nuts!".

The hurling All-Star team of 2001 pose for a team photo in the Hurling Club, Buenos Aires
Back (L-R): Liam Hodgins, Eoin Kelly, Eddie Enright, Damien Fitzhenry, Brian Begley, Philip Maher, Ollie Moran, Mark O'Leary
Front (L-R): Kevin Broderick, Ollie Canning, Darragh Ryan, Éamonn Corcoran, Thomas Dunne and Jamesie O'Connor

The hurling All-Star team of 2000 pose for a team photo in the Hurling Club, Buenos Aires
Back (L-R): Diarmuid O'Sullivan, Andy Comerford, Henry Shefflin, Brendan Cummins, Cathal Moore, Joe Rabbitte, Peter Barry, Frank Lohan and Seán McMahon.
Front (L-R): Joe Deane, Noel Hickey, Johnny Dooley, Denis Byrne, Ken McGrath, John Carroll and Charlie Carter.

All-Star Gazing

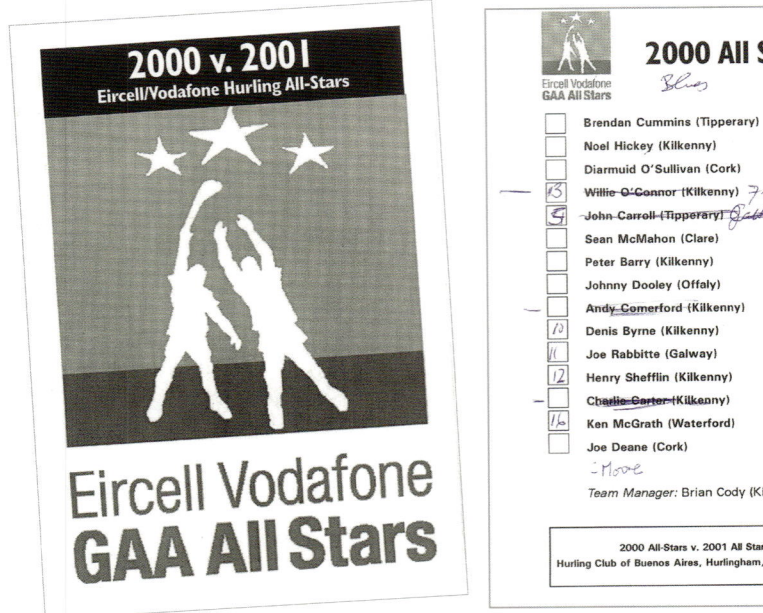

Match programme for the hurling All-Star trip to Argentina in 2002 and lineups for the two teams managed by Brian Cody and Nicky English

Eoin Kelly recalled the stadium tour too. "I remember the Kilkenny lads in the dressing room, up at the soccer display board picking a hurling team! I loved getting to know players from the other counties. You build up a respect for guys when you get to know them on tour. I went drinking with all the Kilkenny lads in a place called the Kilkenny Bar".

For Frank Lohan, the trip to Argentina was the trip of a lifetime. "There were a few Clare lads on it with me. I remember that it was the time of the economic collapse in Buenos Aires". The collapse had led to civil unrest and rioting. When 16 people were killed just weeks before the scheduled tour departure date, there was a doubt about the tour going ahead, but the Irish Ambassador to Argentina soon confirmed that the political and social situation had stabilised.

The All-Star's visit, helped reignite interest in hurling within the Irish community and a summer GAA coaching camp was held at the Hurling Club for a few years after the trip.

RETURN TO THE US IN 2003

The football All-Stars of 2001 and 2002 travelled to San Diego in early 2003. Kieran McGeeney captained the 2002 team that won the exhibition game by an unusual football score-line of 19-19 to 13-18. Martin Breheny reported, "in a surreal game where tackling was an optional extra, both sets of forwards prospered in the intense heat leaving defenders in a beaten haze".

McGeeney reflected on his All-Star tour experience. "When you play on tour you notice the best players and some of them are often not from the top counties. Some top stars are lost when they don't have their team structure around them. There is very little difference between players. Really talented players or those with the right attitude can excel on their own. Players like Declan Browne and Dessie Dolan".

Kieran McGeeney, Peter Canavan and Benny Tierney at a training session in San Diego. Kieran described Peter as "the best I have ever seen"

Kieran McGeeney's medallion from San Diego

It was Declan Browne's first All-Star trip. "I remember I was nervous heading off on the trip on my own. I didn't drink so I hung around with Dessie Dolan and the other pioneers. We did our own thing. I roomed with Benny Tierney, and he made me feel welcome. It was fantastic to have the chance to form friendships and bonds and play with players from other counties".

In 2004 the All-Star hurlers of 2003 and 2002 visited Phoenix and Las Vegas. Cyril Lyons and Brian Cody managed the two teams. The exhibition match, played in heavy rain on a short pitch with soccer goals, was not the tour's highlight. "The social side was great in Phoenix", said Brendan Cummins. "I was on Cody's team, I played well for him but not too well!".

Eoin Kelly's highlight was a road trip to the Grand Canyon with Tommy Walsh, Benny Dunne and their partners. "Tommy was only about 20 years old at that time. It took four hours to get there and back and we had a great time along the way".

Henry Shefflin has some great memories too. "I went shopping in Arizona with the Waterford lads, John Mullane and Dan Shanahan. It was just a spontaneous thing that happened, and we had such a laugh. I made friends that I am still in contact with to this day. The trips helped to build those bonds".

HONG KONG IN 2005

The All-Star tour returned to Asia in 2005 at the invitation of the Hong Kong GAA club, which had been founded in 1995. This trip had an added dimension as it coincided with an Enterprise Ireland trade mission. An Taoiseach Bertie Ahern attended the All-Star exhibition match between the football All-Stars of 2003 and 2004.

Seán Cavanagh recalled, "the pitch in Hong Kong had the city skyline as a backdrop. All our wives and girlfriends were there, and the pictures were amazing. I have a great photo of a line-up of all the Tyrone girls which includes Michaela Harte. As time passes and people are gone, a picture like that is a special memory". Seán added, "The tours were amazing because you found yourself on a pitch with players who were your heroes, guys like Declan Browne".

Pádraic Joyce was also in Hong Kong in 2005. "Guinness sponsored the event the night of the match. They flew in the best bar staff from each county back home. We were on the 50th floor in the Hyatt Hotel, and there was a table full of Guinness. I just remember Peter Canavan, the Gooch and Adrian Logan doing a 'choo-choo' train around the place. There were a lot of guys from Tyrone and Armagh, and I remember Michaela Harte was there too".

Declan Browne and Matty Forde were appointed captains for the exhibition match. "My team won so I was presented with the trophy", recalls Declan.

Bertie Ahern greets Ciarán McDonald before the All-Star match in Hong Kong

The 'Tyrone Girls' are photographed by the All-Stars against the backdrop of the city skyline

Captains Matty Forde and Declan Browne in Hong Kong and, right, The match programme for the All-Star exhibition match in Hong Kong in 2005

All-Star Gazing

"Peter Canavan insisted afterwards that I bring it home and keep it. I was delighted". The trophy had extra significance for Declan because it was made by fellow Tipperary man Jarlath Daly, the All-Star sculptor.

Matty Forde enjoyed the experience. "Playing with guys you wouldn't know coming from Wexford and meeting guys you have only ever seen on television, you found out what other teams were doing".

Brian McGuigan concurs, "the trips were good, a chance to meet up with the boys you never knew. I spoke to the Armagh guys, who I would have had good battles with. And I saw them in a different light on the trip". Brian's brother Tommy was in Hong Kong too as a replacement. When the rest of the touring party returned home, Brian continued to Australia, where he lived for a year. "My girlfriend and I had been talking about going for a while but when Cormac (McAnallen) died in 2004, we decided to do it. When my Tyrone teammates left for home, I was heading in the opposite direction for Sydney. It was hard to see them go".

Regarding the All-Star match, Brian said, "It wasn't much of a match. I remember the two managers had a bet between them to try to introduce a bit of competitiveness". The All-Star match programme carried a tribute to McAnallen who had been selected on the 2003 All-Star team and may have been on the trip to Hong Kong, if not for his untimely death in March 2004.

There were five Kerry players on that trip, including a young Colm Cooper. "I remember the mad names for the island nearby and the Kerry lads trying to pronounce it". For Colm even getting to know the other Kerry players was amazing. "I was still in awe of them in my first few years. I roomed with Paul Galvin, and I remember him saying, 'Colm, they are big into their fashion here in Hong Kong'".

Colm added, "it was enriching to get to know fellas and find out what was going on in their lives. It opened up our minds. Seeing fellas who used to kill each other on the pitch, you realised how much fun you could have together".

Declaring the visit to Hong Kong a success, GAA President Seán Kelly said, "it was a wonderful experience to witness the enthusiasm and the drive of the Irish community and indeed the local community in Hong Kong for Gaelic games. Many Irish people are doing their best to spread the Gaelic games gospel all over the world, so it's nice to be able to reward them by presenting them with an opportunity to see our best hurlers and footballers". He continued, "the players love the idea too, so we'll try to ensure that the January tours continue".

| The All-Star match programme in 2005

SINGAPORE IN 2006

The All-Star hurlers visited Asia for the first time in 2006 when the tour destination was Singapore. The teams from 2004 and 2005 played an exhibition match in the Singapore Polo Club and also held a coaching session at a local school.

Four-time All-Star, Brian Lohan, had missed previous tours due to work commitments. He made the trip to Singapore. "When I went on tour towards the end of my career, I remember wishing I had gone on more trips. It was good to meet other hurlers: the Kilkenny lads and the likes of Waterford's Paul Flynn. I had only ever met him on the field and was surprised, realising, jeez he's not a bad fella after all".

He enjoyed playing alongside an up-and-coming hurling star. "I was playing full back alongside Tommy Walsh in the All-Star match. I just remember every ball I went for Walsh jumped in ahead of me. I would be thinking 'here's an easy catch', but every time he caught the ball, he would have it gone. He played the whole match on his toes. I couldn't believe it. He was at a different level. He probably didn't even realise it. He was so good. Just that bit different, he could play anywhere".

Programme of events the day the All-Star hurlers played at the Polo Grounds in Singapore.

Adrian Fenlon trains pupils at the Overseas Family School in Singapore

DUBAI IN 2007

The All-Star footballers returned to Dubai in January 2007 at the invitation of the Dubai Celts. The club had grown since the first All-Star visit in 2001 to become one of the largest GAA clubs overseas. There was criticism from some intercounty managers at home due to the timing of the trip. GAA President Nickey Brennan defended the purpose and value of the All-Star trip at the time. "Clearly there is the issue of counties going on holidays of their own at this time of year, but we still feel it's an opportunity to bring our players away. Vodafone are very keen too, so the trip is still an important element to the overall awards scheme".

The trip to Dubai was Alan Brogan's first All-Star trip. "There weren't many Dubs on that tour, so I was knocking around with the Kerry lads. I would have known Marc Ó Sé from college. To get to know those lads was brilliant. I remember we went horse-racing one night. There is no official betting in Dubai. All the Irish guys wanted to be betting so it was all done under the table so that the Sheikhs wouldn't find out.

"There were a good few of the Tyrone lads on that trip too. It was great to meet lads like that who we had a fierce enough rivalry with at the time. There would have been no friendships with the lads from Northern counties because we just wouldn't come across them, as they would be in college in Jordanstown or Belfast. I remember some local politics and security meant we had to stay in one city and fly to the other for matches and back again".

The scoreboard is updated during the All-Star exhibition match at the Singapore Polo Club

Waterford contingent in Singapore - Séamus Prendergast, Eoin Kelly, John Mullane, Ken McGrath and Paul Flynn

Nickey Brennan presents the All-Star commemorative medallion to Alan Brogan in Dubai

Conor Mortimer and Alan Dillon after the All-Star exhibition match in Dubai in 2007

Conor Mortimer was also there. "Dubai was unbelievable, somewhere you would never ever go yourself", he recalled. "I remember the Tyrone and Kerry lads. It was great to see them. You never meet these guys as you are usually travelling back to Mayo after matches. At the start, you are thinking, 'oh no, I have to see these guys for two weeks'. But it was fabulous, everyone getting on, everyone having the craic. There was lots of diversity on that trip. It was great seeing how those guys lived, what they ate. Players wouldn't want to give others the edge either though".

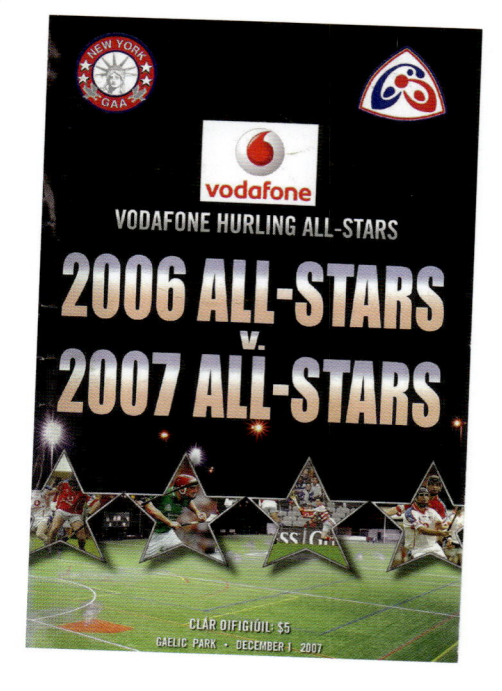

NEW YORK IN 2007

The All-Star hurlers of 2005 and 2006 also travelled in 2007, returning to the familiar destination of New York. The trip coincided with the reopening of

The match day programme for the visit of the All-Stars to Dubai in 2007

John Mullane keeping warm in the snow in Gaelic Park

the upgraded Gaelic Park. Officiating, the GAA President Nickey Brennan said, "it is a source of much celebration for those who work so hard to promote Gaelic games in the city. I have never seen Gaelic Park looking so well. It has a special place in the hearts and minds of Irish people who have come to this city over many years".

In stark contrast to the recent All-Star trips in warmer climes, the match in New York was played during an arctic snowstorm under the new floodlights. Michael Lyster remembers John Mullane wearing a woolly hat while playing. John takes up the story, "it was pre-helmet days! We were so cold we were drinking 'hot toddies' at half-time".

RETURN TO SAN FRANCISCO IN 2008

There was a sense of nostalgia when the All-Stars returned to San Francisco in 2008, the city that hosted the first tour in 1972. The visit coincided with the official opening of the San Francisco GAA headquarters on Treasure Island. Fourteen replacements were required to make up the 2007 and 2008 All-Star teams, reflecting the increasing difficulty for players to fit the tour into the busy off-season period.

Shane Ryan was on that trip which had a special significance for his family. Both his parents, Jack and Orla Ryan and his two grandfathers, Séamus Ó Riain and Seán Ó Síocháin, were on the first trip to San Francisco in 1972. "As kids, we knew Dad had been to San Francisco, but it wasn't until this year, that I realised it was the All-Star trip he was on. He thought it would be a great idea to come back".

Jack who had played for the Tipperary hurlers in 1972 said, "I loved San Francisco so much and I have great memories of my time there".

The All-Star tours often gave players the experience of playing for a manager from a rival county. That year the teams were managed by Pat O'Shea and Mickey Harte. The Ó Sé brothers Darragh and Marc were both on Mickey Harte's team along with Shane. "I remember the matches were taken very seriously. Even the training sessions – I was five minutes late down to a team meeting one day, and Mickey was ringing the room looking for me", laughed Ryan.

Jack Ryan returns to San Francisco with his son Shane 36 years after his first trip in 1972

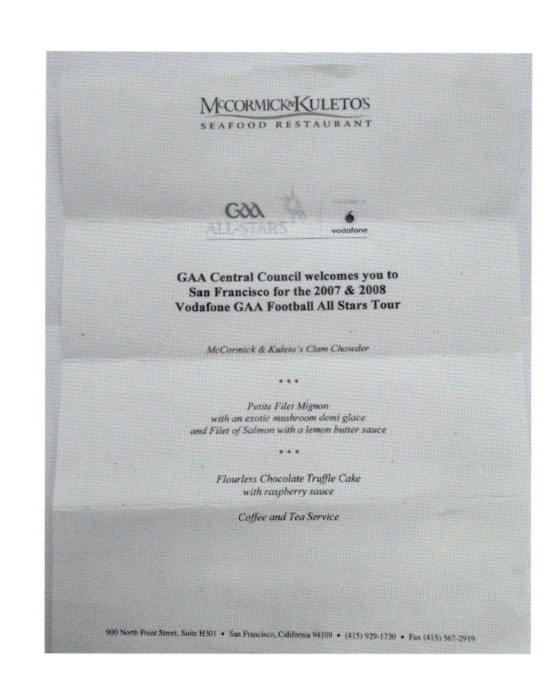

Welcome Dinner for the travelling party in San Francisco in 2008

Kerry contingent, Pat O'Shea, Marc Ó Sé, Colm Cooper, Seamus Scanlon and Darragh Ó Sé at the All-Star match in San Francisco

All-Star Gazing

RETURN TO BUENOS AIRES IN 2009

Following the success of the first trip to Argentina, the hurling All-Stars of 2008 and 2009 returned in 2009. After a long journey from Dublin via Madrid, the players arrived at the hotel in Buenos Aires tired and weary. John Mullane recalls this gem, "all anyone wanted was a shower and change of clothes. But Cha Fitzpatrick discovered his suitcase was full of newspapers. He had been out the night before he left, and his flat-mates took out all his clothes and stuffed the case with papers and magazines!".

Seán Óg Ó hAilpín was the only Cork man in a touring party dominated by Tipperary and Kilkenny players. "I was fascinated watching the interaction between the two sets of rivals and I remember the tension between them".

| The programme of matches for the day in Kuala Lumpur

The Boca Juniors soccer stadium was again on the itinerary and this time the players went to see a soccer match. "I couldn't believe the conditions around the stadium", recalls John Mullane. "It was a slum, a shanty town. I was wearing my De la Salle jersey, which is white with a red stripe. It is not unlike the River Plate jersey (the Boca Juniors arch-rivals.) On the way out in the taxi, the driver advised me to take it off".

Joe Canning, who was on this trip, said, "the All-Star trips were great to meet other players from different counties. You got to see their personalities differently than when they were on the field in opposition. I remember staying with Martin Comerford from Kilkenny in Argentina. It was great craic along with the likes of Tony Browne and John Mullane and these guys. They were players I looked up to when I was

| Paddy Keenan, Michael Shields and Andy Moran, prior to departure for Kuala Lumpur

| The All-Stars run towards local player Nguyen Ngoc Quynh to celebrate his winning penalty in 2010

growing up and then to be in their company on a trip like that was great. Good characters off the field and we just had a good laugh together".

KUALA LUMPUR IN 2010

The football All-Stars of 2009 and 2010 travelled to Malaysia in late 2010 for an exhibition match in the Royal Selangor Club in Kuala Lumpur. The event was organised by the Orang Éire GAA Club which had been formed just three years previously to represent Malaysia at the 2007 Asian Gaelic Games. James McCartan was the manager of the 2010 All-Stars. "Jack O'Connor was supposed to go, and he couldn't, so I got to go instead. I remember when I got the call from GAA President Christy Cooney I was thrilled. It was great to see how popular the GAA was out in Asia. It's the skill, speed and the amount of scores that makes it an attractive game for Asian kids to play".

The All-Stars were top of a bill that included the Men's Asian All-Stars and the Ladies Asian All-Stars. One of the Asian stars, Nguyen Ngoc Quynh, was invited to play on the 2009 All-Star team and ended up scoring the winning penalty in the exhibition match.

Paddy Keenan travelled to Kuala Lumpur after a memorable season for Louth. "The All-Star trip in 2010 was a great experience. I had used up my time off at work with all the matches that year, but they looked after me so I could go. There were lots of Down and Cork lads there. And Kildare lads that I had played college football with. It was a chance to make friends with people you played against but hadn't met. The party started on the way out because we had a five-hour lay-over in Abu Dhabi. People were still in their own factions to start with. But after a few hours, everyone was singing. We had all mixed before we even got to Kuala Lumpur".

James McCartan recalled, "there were lots of Cork lads there. They were the champions, having beaten us in the final that year. When we arrived at the airport, the Cork lads were all in a corner together. The Down lads were looking over, and I said, 'right lads, start mingling'. Everyone got on great for the rest of the trip. Great friendships were formed. As the manager, I was 20 years older than the rest of them, so I wasn't up all night, even though I might have wanted to".

NEW YORK IN 2012

The football All-Stars travelled to New York in 2012. Pat Gilroy and Jim McGuinness were the managers of the 2011 and 2012 teams. Dublin's Paul Flynn loved those trips. "They were fantastic. On an All-Star trip you get a chance to let your hair down with the guys you are playing against. We are all so similar; we have such a common purpose for so long that you have so much to talk about. To go on the All-Star trips was just a lovely icing on the cake".

Dónal Óg Cusack, Michael Darragh Macauley, Paul Flynn and Bernard Brogan visit Breezy Point in Queens during the All-Star trip of 2012

"The trips were always a good week away to get to know each other", agreed Bernard Brogan. "I remember palling around with David Moran. I think he was the only Kerry lad on that New York trip. Mick Macauley and myself out on the beers several nights with him. He's a gas character. Dónal Óg Cusack too, a character going around New York, with that Cork accent, arguing about cricket!".

The trip came just weeks after Hurricane Sandy had swept the East Coast of America, causing devastation to hundreds of coastal towns. During the tour, the All-Stars visited Breezy Point, an Irish community on the Rockaway Peninsula in Queens, to help with the clean-up of the area.

Donal Óg, who had travelled in his capacity as Chairman of the GPA, recalled, "we went out to Breezy Point, but we were a bit embarrassed to be honest. These people have been hit with a disaster and we were there on a bit of a tour in our nice tracksuits posing for pictures. I remember saying to Pat Gilroy, 'what we are going to do is come back with a proper crew to help'. Within a couple of months, we brought back 20 people, and we did proper work in the community. We stayed in the Fire Station and helped rebuild the Community Centre which housed the youth sports facilities. Aer Lingus sponsored us, and I got some volunteers from Johnson & Johnson, where I work, to come too".

The return visit to Breezy Point was reported locally on NBC Nightly News, in a segment called 'Making a Difference'. The group included Brian McGuigan, Ollie Canning and Lar Corbett, as well as Dónal and Pat. Their work was commended by President Barack Obama the following March at the St Patrick's Day reception in the White House. "Gaelic rock stars pitched in and raised money", he said. "Athletes from Gaelic games did construction work and brought the Sam Maguire chalice with them to lift spirits". Dónal laughed, "even Obama gave us a call out. It was a great experience that built a really strong connection with the Irish community there. And it all came from that All-Star trip".

All-Star Gazing

Galway's David Collins with students at the Shanghai University

The Donegal players depart for the All-Star tour to Boston

SHANGHAI IN 2013

In 2013 the first official GAA game was played in China. Following an invitation from the Shanghai GAA Club, the All-Star hurlers of 2012 and 2013 played an exhibition match in the Shanghai Rugby Football Club in Waigaoqiao.

Brian Murphy, Chairman of the Shanghai Gaelic Football Club, welcomed the party. "It is a privilege to welcome the All-Stars to the wonderful and dynamic city of Shanghai and to witness a game that will have the cream of Ireland's hurling talent".

Seán Moran reported, "the end of term feeling was in evidence at the Shanghai Rugby Club. As is traditional on All-Star tours, goals flashed in at either end. It all made for a pleasantly diverting spectacle on a crisp but beautifully sunny afternoon before a respectable crowd of a few hundred mostly ex-patriots, including the Irish Ambassador Paul Kavanagh and Consul General Austin Gormley". The game was preceded by a reception at Shanghai University where the hurlers demonstrated their skills to some of the students.

The All-Star match signalled the final game in John Mullane's long inter-county career. He finished on a high with two goals as the 2012 All-Stars won the match. "It is probably the end of an era for me. This is my sixth All-Star tour and it's great to be out here with some of the cream of the crop", he said at the time. John was accompanied by his wife Stephanie. "We were always well looked after on the All-Star trips; long may they continue".

BOSTON IN 2014

The All-Star tour returned to Boston in 2014. An Irish GAA celebration was held in Boston before an exhibition match between the football All-Stars of 2013 and 2014. Aidan O'Shea was on the trip to Boston. "There were about 12 Mayo players there as replacements. Lots of players from Kerry, Donegal and Dublin too. I think the tours should always go to places like Boston where there is such a big interest locally".

AUSTIN IN 2015

The GAA's decision to visit Austin, Texas in 2015 was in recognition of the growth in popularity of Gaelic games in that part of the United States. It was a big occasion for the Celtic Cowboys GAA club, which had only been founded in 2004. Anthony Daly and Anthony Cunningham were the managers of the 2014 and 2015 All-Star hurling teams. GAA President Aogán Ó Fearghail said, "While the United States has always been a popular location for visiting GAA teams, we, as an organisation, have never visited this part of the world with an All-Star tour. Our overseas network has never been as buoyant, and the general awareness about our games continues to rise. I sincerely hope that this visit enthuses all of those involved in the promotion of our games here".

The founder of the Celtic Cowboys Pat Doab, who hails from Limerick, was particularly delighted that it was the turn of the hurling All-Stars that year. "We applied for the All-Star trip in 2014, and when we heard that we got it the next year we were like kids at Christmas", said Pat. "We got the US GAA Convention the same year, and it really helped us grow the awareness of the sport here in Austin". The Mayor of Austin, Steve Adler, was invited to throw in the ball at the start of the match. Pat described the scene. "He dropped the ball on the ground instead of throwing it up. There was mayhem, and when a hurley broke in the clash that ensued, he got the fright of his life! He still talks about it".

"The tour helped us generate interest for the club. We now have a lot of American kids playing as well as Irish kids. Our ladies were National Gaelic Football champions a few years ago with only two Irish girls on the team, the rest were local kids".

50 Years of the GAA All-Stars

Pat Doab and Mayor Adler, left, and the programme and teams for the All-Stars games in Austin

Three-year old Eoin Moriarty, a member of the Celtic Cowboys club, is inspired by hurlers David O'Callaghan and Kieran Bergin and right, the Mayor of Austin declares "Irish Hurling in Austin Day"

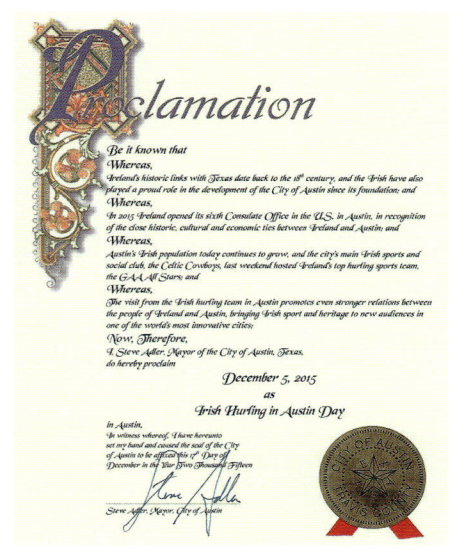

ABU DHABI AND DUBAI IN 2016

In 2016, the All-Stars of 2015 and 2016 returned to Abu Dhabi for a football exhibition match in the Sheikh Zayed Sports City Stadium. The teams were managed by Mickey Harte and Liam Kearns. Irish ex-patriots and locals were treated to an All-Star goal-rush as the 13-a-side teams hit the back of the net 24 times.

Aogán Ó Fearghail said after the match, "it is lovely to see that the original concept (of the All-Stars), devised many years ago by Mick Dunne and his journalist colleagues, is still there. It's about reward and recognition. This trip is a thank-you to the players. We're in the Arabian desert, and the Irish are driving things forward here. They have the same passion for the GAA as we do in Ireland".

Dean Rock follows in his father's footsteps in Abu Dhabi as he captains the All-Stars of 2016. Barney was the captain of the All-Star footballers in 1985

All-Star Gazing

SINGAPORE IN 2017

The hurling All-Stars of 2016 and 2017 travelled to Singapore in 2017. The tour included a coaching session for local kids and the exhibition match took place in the Singapore Recreation ground.

Séamus Callanan has fond memories of that trip. "The local GAA club in Singapore did an amazing job organising everything. You could see the Marina Bay Sands Hotel from the pitch. We all went up to the top at night and got amazing pictures. We trained kids in the local GAA club, and the organisers said our going out there helped them promote the games. The matches were 11-a-side. Everyone mixed so well. I had a good time with a few of the Wexford lads".

The trip gives you a chance to go to places that you wouldn't go yourself", adds Pádraic Maher. "I really enjoyed coaching the kids in Singapore. There was fantastic interest out there. It was great to spend time coaching with players from other counties too. A chance to get to know them in a different way".

PHILADELPHIA IN 2018

For the first time in All-Star tour history, no All-Star match was played in 2018 when the 2017 and 2018 All-Stars visited Philadelphia. GAA Director of Communications Alan Milton explained, "we just took a different direction, we put the focus on coaching the local kids this year. We decided there was more merit in it, as the score lines from previous years had suggested that whatever competitive streak that was in it previously was no longer there".

| Lee Chin teaches his skills to a group of local children in Singapore

| All-Ireland champions Con O'Callaghan, James McCarthy, Brian Howard take Sam Maguire on tour to Philadelphia

| The All-Star party with local kids after a training session in Philadelphia

The All-Star match takes place below the impressive Marina Bay Sands Hotel

Colm Cavanagh was in the travelling party to Philadelphia and said, "it was nice to give something back and not just play matches. We did a coaching session with local kids. The players were in teams of four, and we worked with different groups of kids throughout the day. There were lots of American kids and Irish people. The Irish over there love seeing you".

DUBAI AND ABU DHABI IN 2019

In 2019 the hurling All-Stars of 2018 and 2019 travelled to Dubai and Abu Dhabi. Séamus Callanan spoke excitedly in advance of the trip, "Off to Dubai this year. It will be a great gathering of Irish people. Lots of Tipp fellas are living out in the Far East and they all travel down to be at the matches".

The touring party included numerous replacements, an opportunity reported on with pride in the smaller counties. Online publication 'laoistoday.ie' reported, "two Laois players will jet off to the Middle East this week to take part in this year's All-Star hurling game. As Joe McDonagh Cup Player of the Year, Paddy Purcell gets a place on the trip. Abbeyleix's Enda Rowland has also been called in". Goalkeeper Rowland was an All-Star nominee in 2019 but lost out when Brian Hogan was selected.

The performance of replacement Declan Coulter was the highlight of the All-Star match. "The well-received policy of inviting players from outside the top tier of the game was vindicated in the case of Donegal's (and formerly Armagh's) Declan Coulter, who scored 1-6 and won the Man of the Match award chosen by the travelling media", reported Seán Moran.

Declan Coulter receives the Man of the Match award from GAA President John Horan.

All-Star Gazing

GLOBAL PANDEMIC

Due to the global Covid-19 pandemic in 2020, which stopped all non-essential travel, there was no trip for the 2019 and 2020 football All-Stars. Brian Fenton said, "yeah we have missed one now due to Covid. I'm gonna push the new president Larry McCarthy, to see if there is any chance of rescheduling it! They are great trips; I would love to go again. It is a nice touch that the GAA bring the partners because of the sacrifice they make and what they put up with. It is very much appreciated by them too".

While it may be hard for a full complement of All-Stars to travel each year, the players still value the opportunity to spend time together. Due to time restraints as a schoolteacher, Tomás Ó Sé never went on the All-Star trips in the years he was selected. "I had to give time to team holidays in the same year as the final appearances". In 2013 he went to New York as a replacement so that he could experience at least one All-Star trip. "It was great to mix with the other players".

Seán Cavanagh told us, "It was special to mix with Kerry guys who, at the time, I had a real rivalry with". His brother Colm added, "yes, as much as you are thinking, 'I should hate him' you see a different side to him in the bar and think he's dead on. You are almost disappointed! On the tours, there were organised nights that forced you to mix together. You mix and have the craic and find out all about them in general life. Sometimes you are in the exact same scenario as them. You can relate to everyone".

Colm Cooper enjoyed getting to know the journalists on tour. "As an inter-county player, you are taught to be wary of them and what they might print about you. The tour helped you understand the journalists and the pressures they were under".

Seán Cavanagh agreed, "I enjoyed getting to know the journalists like Paul Collins, Damian Lawlor and Marty Morrissey. Drinking shots in a bar with Damian in Hong Kong, we made a lifelong friendship, and he ended up writing my book with me. With the journalists, you got to understand the other side of things. I got to know the circuit; it put me at ease. I made amazing friendships and got opportunities from it".

Pádraic Maher also valued the opportunity, "having a chance to get to know the journalists was great as nowadays we don't get to talk to them much".

Regarding the All-Star matches, Michael Lyster had this to say. "The seriousness of games depended on the year, whether it was the hurlers or the footballers. The hurlers were more intense on the field but mixed well off the pitch. It is probably because hurling is a smaller community, so they have got to know each other better over the years. The footballers are more disciplined off the field, so maybe there was not as much mixing".

Dónal Óg Cusack was never much of a fan of the All-Star matches abroad as he thought they did a disservice to the games. "It is an ambassadorial kind of trip. But as it was

| Rory O'Connell's All-Star jersey takes pride of place in the Athlone GAA clubhouse

also a holiday for the players, they wouldn't take the game seriously. People would often be brought along to see these matches and I felt it was a pity because they often didn't reflect the beauty of our game. I always felt there was more that could be done".

"The reality is that nowadays the matches are a non-event", said Martin Breheny. "There are tiny crowds at them. You get crazy scores that don't mean anything. So, for parents, there is no point bringing their kids along. It is hard to know how you could make it more competitive. Also, it is harder to get players to go on the trips. I can see them stopping".

Ever the competitor, Brendan Cummins did his best over the years to introduce a bit of competition. "We always made sure that the two teams would leave on separate buses on the morning of the match to get into the zone. That was important – to have a bit of edge in the game".

Aidan O'Shea shared an idea. "I often thought there should be a prize for the All-Star matches on tour to make them competitive. Each team could play for a different charity. One charity versus another, that would put weight on it and give it a bit of meaning".

On the last day on the tour, all the All-Star jerseys are signed by each player as a memento. Rory O'Connell told us, "A few years ago, my club Athlone GAA was having a fundraiser for the local hospice. My mum had died eight years earlier and Dave Allen, a huge figure at the club had passed away too. They both got great care from the local hospice so, I gave the club my All-Star jersey with all the signatures to be auctioned. It raised €5,000. That shows the value of the All-Stars". Rory was delighted when the club bought back the jersey and it now hangs in the clubhouse.

GAA GROWTH ABROAD

The All-Star visits to GAA clubs in the Far East, China, South America as well as the less traditional GAA cities in America have helped Irish ex-patriots promote the games abroad. In 2017 Gaelic games was added to the school curriculum in Hong Kong and many countries run an annual youth championship. This, in turn, has led to overseas entries to the annual Féile Peil na nÓg finals in Ireland. In 2019 both the boys and girls U14 teams from New York celebrated victory at the tournament.

Also in 2019, students from Shanghai University who were studying in Ireland, played at half time during a quarter-final round-robin football match in Croke Park. The short game against St John's Club from County Down took place to mark 40 years of diplomatic relationships between Ireland and China. The link with the University stems from the All-Star trip to China in 2013 when an exhibition of skills by the All-Star hurlers sparked a lot of interest. Soon afterwards Gaelic games was offered on the academic curriculum. The option gives students a chance to come to Ireland to study the games here.

Vice-chair of the Asian Board Paraic McGrath told Seán Moran about the students' preparation for the match in Croke Park. "Jack Meng from Athlone IT has played in our club in Shanghai, so he trained the students in Ireland. Seán Cunningham, another officer of the Asian Board, is from St John's so he pulled the match together".

Former GPA CEO Paul Flynn said, "these GAA clubs abroad are so important to Irish people when they leave home. The first place they go to find a bit of common ground is the GAA club. And people come back as very strong GAA people. That is the strength of the GAA globally, no matter where you go in the world there is a GAA club. All-Star trips are important for the volunteers, mainly ex-pats, who are investing so much time to promote the game. So, if you can bring guys abroad to congratulate them on winning an All-Star but also continue to build the overall GAA community, that's fantastic".

When asked about the increasing challenge for players finding time for the trips, Paul replied, "I think there is still a window for it. You just need to carve it out. The feedback from players is that they love it. I would be very disappointed if it discontinued".

Aidan O'Shea hopes they don't get rid of the All-Star trips. "It is the only opportunity for Gaelic footballers to mix. If you look at the Kerry and Dublin guys from the 1970s, they are all still very friendly. We have no other opportunity to get to know each other now".

And John Mullane's thoughts? "It is sad to think that the trips are fading. I feel they should continue".

The under 14 Girls from New York win at Féile Peile na nÓg finals in 2019

All-Star Gazing

Selecting the All-Stars

Each year, soon after the GAA championship concludes, a shortlist of All-Star nominees is drawn up by the All-Star selectors. While the nominations generally cause little surprise, the final team line-up can cause great debate. Everyone has an opinion on which players should make the team so most years the selectors come in for criticism about their final selections. In the past, newspapers ran competitions inviting readers to select their teams and in 2019, sponsors PwC asked fans to submit their teams via the All-Star app.

Tomás Ó Sé remembers picking the team with his mates in school every year. "It is still a popular pastime. If you want a lot of hits on social media, pick your All-Star team and post it". Brendan Cummins gets a call from the newspapers every year asking for his All-Star team based on the nominees. "It builds the hype at a time of year when there is a GAA media vacuum", he said.

"It causes a lot of debate, and that's good for the GAA because it keeps the GAA on the back pages and keeps people talking about it", observed Dónal Óg Cusack. When Colm Cooper was selected, his parents chose not to accompany him to the All-Star banquets. "They preferred to watch it at home, then Dad would go across to the pub and discuss the selections with the old lads. That's what he wanted to do".

First All-Star Selection Committee in 1971

STEERING COMMITTEE
Paddy Downey (*Irish Times*)
Mick Dunne (*RTÉ*)
John D. Hickey (*Irish Independent*)
Pádraig Puirséal (*Irish Press*)
Pat Heneghan (*Carrolls*)

SELECTION COMMITTEE – BOTH CODES
Donal Carroll (*Evening Herald*)
John Comyn (*Sunday Independent*)
Paddy Downey (*Irish Times*)
Mick Dunne (*RTÉ*)
John D. Hickey (*Irish Independent*)
Eugene McGee (*Sunday Press*)
Eoin McQuillan (*Newsletter*)
Seán Óg Ó Ceallacháin (*Irish Press*)
Michael O'Hehir (*RTÉ*)
Pádraig Puirséal (*Irish Press*)
Jim O'Sullivan (*Cork Examiner*)

Selecting the best 15 hurlers and footballers each year is bound to be controversial. There is often dissatisfaction

Campaign poster in New York for the selection of Charlie Nelligan

about players omitted or included. More recently, the controversy has centred around players being picked out of position. The debate has not always been confined to Ireland either. In 1979 the All-Star selectors were greeted with a sign in the bar of Gaelic Park, New York asking, "What must Charlie Nelligan do to get an All-Star award?".

WHO SELECTS THE ALL-STARS?

For all but two of the 50 years since 1971, the All-Star teams have been selected by a panel of journalists. In 1995 and 1996, when Powerscreen sponsored the scheme, the inter-county players voted for the top 15 players in each code. The journalists were reinstated in 1998 and they have picked the All-Star teams ever since.

The selection panel includes Gaelic games correspondents from print, radio, TV and nowadays digital media. The journalists' selections are ratified by the All-Star Steering Committee, a smaller group of experienced All-Star selectors. Either the GAA President or the Ard Stiúrthóir chairs the selection meetings.

Reflecting on his time as an All-Star selector, Jim O'Sullivan said, "in terms of my journalistic career, the best thing that ever happened to me was to be invited to be an All-Star selector in the inaugural year of the scheme. It coincided with my appointment as GAA Correspondent with the then *Cork Examiner* and I was further honoured to be named as a member of what came to be known as the Steering Committee".

Paddy Hickey joined the selection panel in 1981. "I was delighted, privileged to be part of it". Paddy is the son of the late John D Hickey, one of the founders of the scheme in 1971.

In the early years, one panel of selectors chose both All-Star teams but in recent years two separate groups have been established to pick the hurling and the football teams. The members of the Steering Committee sit on both panels, to provide continuity.

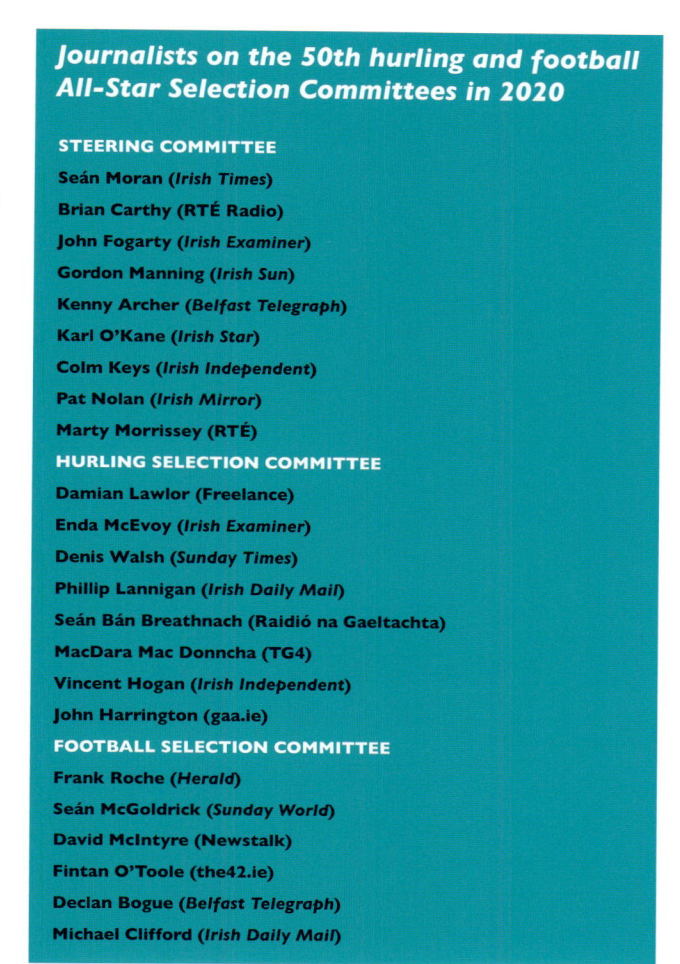

Journalists on the 50th hurling and football All-Star Selection Committees in 2020

STEERING COMMITTEE
Seán Moran (*Irish Times*)
Brian Carthy (*RTÉ Radio*)
John Fogarty (*Irish Examiner*)
Gordon Manning (*Irish Sun*)
Kenny Archer (*Belfast Telegraph*)
Karl O'Kane (*Irish Star*)
Colm Keys (*Irish Independent*)
Pat Nolan (*Irish Mirror*)
Marty Morrissey (*RTÉ*)

HURLING SELECTION COMMITTEE
Damian Lawlor (*Freelance*)
Enda McEvoy (*Irish Examiner*)
Denis Walsh (*Sunday Times*)
Phillip Lannigan (*Irish Daily Mail*)
Seán Bán Breathnach (*Raidió na Gaeltachta*)
MacDara Mac Donncha (*TG4*)
Vincent Hogan (*Irish Independent*)
John Harrington (*gaa.ie*)

FOOTBALL SELECTION COMMITTEE
Frank Roche (*Herald*)
Seán McGoldrick (*Sunday World*)
David McIntyre (*Newstalk*)
Fintan O'Toole (*the42.ie*)
Declan Bogue (*Belfast Telegraph*)
Michael Clifford (*Irish Daily Mail*)

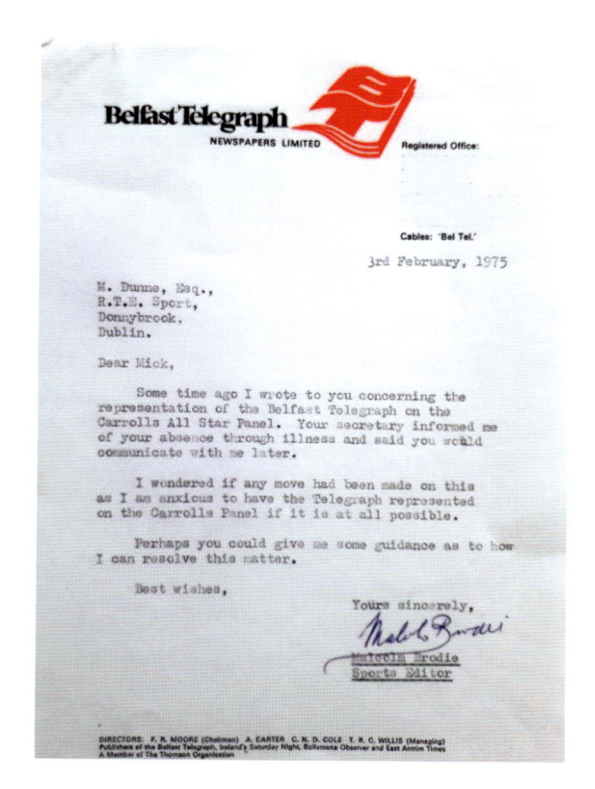

NOMINATING PLAYERS

In the 1970s very few matches were shown on TV so there was a need for a larger group of journalists to submit nominations for the All-Star teams. Called the Nomination Panel, this group consisted of about 27 national Gaelic games journalists.

This helped bring attention to players who excelled locally but were in danger of being overlooked at a national level. Inevitably it led to accusations of county and provincial bias, usually from other local journalists!

It also resulted in long lists of nominees; in 1972, 120 players were nominated for the All-Star hurling team. In 1985, the number of nominees for each team was capped at 45, three per position.

By the time the journalists were reinstated as selectors in 1997, there was no need for a nomination panel. The same group of journalists now perform both roles, nominating and selecting the All-Stars each year.

| Request from the Belfast Telegraph

First Nomination Panel in 1971

John D. Hickey (*Independent Newspapers*)
Con Kenealy (*Independent Newspapers*)
Tom O'Riordan (*Independent Newspapers*)
Mitchel Cogley (*Independent Newspapers*)
Bob Hyland (*Independent Newspapers*)
Donal Carroll (*Independent Newspapers*)
Tommy Kelly (*Independent Newspapers*)
John Comyn (*Independent Newspapers*)
Pádraig Puirséal (*Irish Press Group*)
Gerry McCarty (*Irish Press Group*)
Peadar O'Brien (*Irish Press Group*)
Seán Óg Ó Ceallacháin (*Irish Press Group*)
Eugene McGee (*Irish Press Group*)
Paddy Downey (*Irish Press Group*)
Ned Van Esbeck (*Irish Press Group*)
Peter Byrne (*Irish Press Group*)
Jim O'Sullivan (*Cork Examiner*)
Val Dorgan (*Cork Examiner*)
Michael Ellard (*Cork Examiner*)
Gerry McGuigan (*Belfast Telegraph*)
Eoin McQuillan (*Newsletter*)
Denis O'Hara (*Irish News*)
Michael O'Hehir (*RTÉ*)
Mick Dunne (*RTÉ*)
Maurice Reidy (*RTÉ*)
Liam McDowell (*BBC*)

All-Star Gazing

LONG NIGHTS SELECTING THE ALL-STARS

The challenge for the selectors is to ensure that the list of players nominated and selected reflects the season as a whole and not just the recent Championship matches, freshest in the selector's minds. To prevent this, each selector submits their nominations three times during the season: after the Leagues, the provincial championships and the All-Ireland series. They nominate 45 players in each code: three goalkeepers, 18 defenders, six midfielders and 18 forwards.

Michael Lyster, a member of the All-Star selection committee from 1986 to 2018, explained, "there was a nomination process in the past, but then everyone arrived on the day, and it was like a battlefield. Now it is a bit less fun but more ordered. By the time we get to the nominations stage, it is pretty much decided. If somebody gets a rake of nominations for a position, there is no point discussing it. Out of the 45 players nominated, there might be a debate about three or four places, but in terms of the overall picture you could go in pretty much knowing who most of them are".

Selection meetings in the 1970s could be a little more fraught. Mick Dunne said at the time, "it is well known that wide and vehement differences of opinions arise". Jim O'Sullivan expanded. "By and large, debates on the merits and demerits of players were concluded in a gentlemanly fashion, but it wasn't unknown for them to become heated on occasions. Not out of disrespect for people's opinions, but because of a passionate belief in a candidate's skills and consistency".

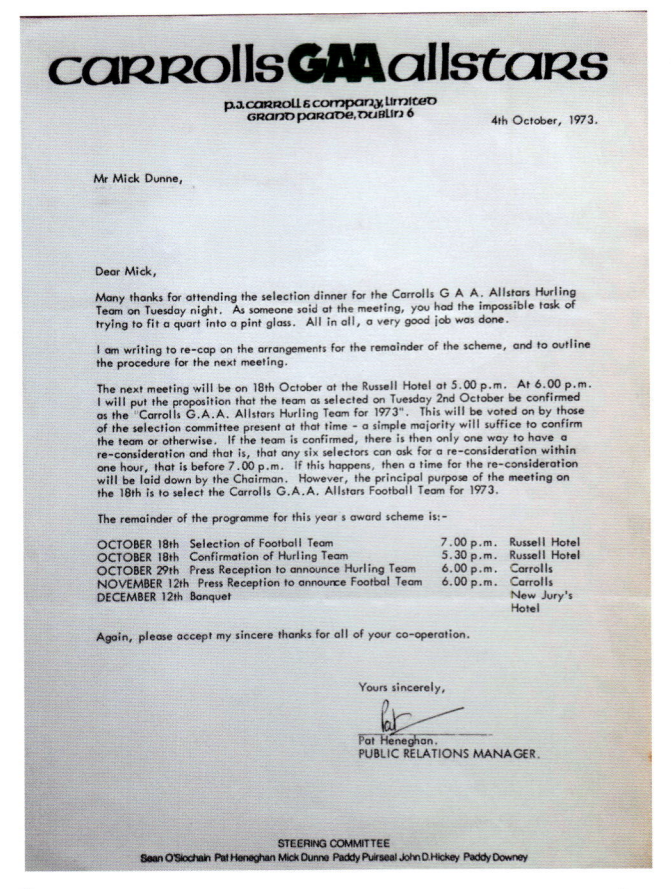

Pat Heneghan from Carroll's comments after the All-Star Selection Meeting in 1973

Pat Heneghan from Carrolls, an observer at many of the early selection meetings, congratulated Mick Dunne after a long night in 1973. "You had the impossible task of fitting a quart into a pint glass".

An All-Star Selection Meeting in the early 1980s
L to R standing: Donal Carroll, Mick Ellard, Paddy Hickey, Liam Kelly, Liam McDowell, Eugene McGee
L to R seated: Tony McGee, Michael McGeary, Jim O'Sullivan, Mick Dunne, Michael O'Hehir, Mícheál Ó Sé, Seán Óg Ó Ceallacháin, Liam Mulvihill, John Neiland, Paddy McFlynn, Paddy Buggy

Liam Mulvihill reflected. "There would be cliques among the selectors – the Northern lobby, the Dublin lobby. These journalists would meet beforehand and decide among themselves who they wanted to get on the team. Then they would lobby for those players. They ganged up". Paddy Hickey disputes this and claims, "most were impartial!".

CRITERIA FOR SELECTION

In the 1970s, players were put forward for any position they played in during the season. In 1994 the Steering Committee amended the rules so that, "selectors will be allowed the flexibility to pick a player in any position in which they feel he has credibility".

The rules continue to evolve to keep pace with the games, particularly in recent years as team positions have become more fluid. In 2018 a new rule said that "the selection of an outfield player in an area other than the one for which they were nominated" was possible.

Recent selections of players out of position have led to criticism. However, it is interesting to note that the selectors used a positional switch on the very first football team to accommodate two players nominated at full forward. Seán O'Neill was named at full forward on the All-Star team with Ray Cummins at centre half forward, even though Ray had played most of the season at full forward.

Michael Lyster makes a case for picking players out of position. "You may have two or three players worthy of an All-Star, but they play in the same position. You want the best 15 players in the country on the All-Star team. So, you work the system to achieve that. We primarily asked the question, 'does he deserve an All-Star?' regardless of position".

The goalkeeper remains the purest selection on each All-Star team as it obviously can't be affected by positional switches. There have been many great goalkeeping rivalries down the years, particularly among the hurlers. On the All-Star positional debate, Brendan Cummins said, "the scheme has to go back to three per position. Let there be controversy. It has to mean something. The only reason I was happy to win was because someone else lost. You are saying 'thank God that's not me'. There has to be real losers".

Colm Cooper agrees that being picked in position added to the achievement. "It was a pretty special feeling, to be chosen as the best player in that position in all of Ireland". Gay O'Driscoll said, "it meant a lot to be picked as the best in your position in the country".

"In today's games players are playing roles rather than in position. The All-Stars needs to reflect that", according to Kieran McGeeney.

Charlie Redmond appreciates the recent changes but reflected, "the All-Stars had to change with the modern game. But maybe it has changed a bit too much".

ELIGIBILITY FOR SELECTION

At the start of the scheme, two criteria for All-Star selection were outlined: 1) excellence and 2) sportsmanship on the field of play. In his speech to announce the inaugural scheme, GAA President Pat Fanning emphasised the importance of the latter to the Association. "I expect that the quality of sportsmanship and bearing on, and off, the field will be an important factor in determining any man's right to become an All-Star".

In practical terms, the sportsmanship rule meant that the selectors could not pick any player serving a suspension following dismissal in a match. The rule was far-reaching as it included club, inter-company, provincial, league and championship matches. Many players missed out on an All-Star as a result. This was particularly tough on players who might have only one chance in their career to get an award. Even players who had won multiple awards already, found it hard if they missed out due to the rule.

"One year I was sent off in a club match versus Castleisland, so I wasn't selected and I was raging", said six-time All-Star Ger Power. "I think 'Nudie' [Eugene] Hughes got it instead". Having already been selected on the All-Star hurling teams in 1971 and 1972, Éamonn Cregan was upset when he wasn't eligible in 1973. "I missed out because I was sent off unfairly!". He added, "but I felt the sportsmanship rule was right if the play that led to the dismissal was dangerous".

Joe Connolly was disappointed in 1981 when he was sent off in the All-Ireland semi-final following a tussle with Jimmy Carroll from Limerick. "I would have loved a second All-Star, but that ruled me out".

Michael Lyster, Brian Carthy, Alan Milton and Seán Moran casting their votes at an All-Star selection meeting in 2017

All-Star Gazing

As the players became aware of the rule's stringency, it began to have the desired effect. "It had a big impact", said Seán O'Neill. "Players behaved themselves so that they could get an All-Star". Mikey Sheehy remembered a county final in 1986. "There was an incident in the game, and I ended up in a tussle with another payer. I was sure I would be sent off, but the referee booked us both instead. Afterwards he said to me 'I saved your All-Star'".

Inevitably some teams began to use the rule to their advantage. John Quigley recalled, "it would be on your mind all right. I remember a league match in the late 1980s. I was told to 'do a job on Tony Keady' because he was nominated for an All-Star at the time so he wouldn't be able to retaliate".

BANNED FROM THE TOUR

The GAA enforced the rule so strictly that a player could be penalised even after his selection as an All-Star. This resulted in some high-profile omissions from All-Star banquets and tours.

Dermot Earley received the first of his two All-Star awards in 1974. The following Spring, he was sent off in a League match between Dublin and Roscommon and received a two-month suspension. As the All-Star trip took place during the suspension period, the GAA Activities Committee banned him from travelling. Dermot was widely known as one of the game's gentlemen and many felt the decision was harsh. In fact, this was the only time he received a sanction during a long successful career.

The All-Star Steering Committee issued a statement to explain their position in relation to the decision. "It is the function of the All-Star selection committee to choose the 15 outstanding hurlers and footballers for the Carrolls GAA All-Star awards. The jurisdiction.....does not extend to the American tour".

Before the tour departed, Dermot received an invitation from John Kerry O'Donnell to travel to New York during the All-Star trip. O'Donnell, who enjoyed being at loggerheads with the GAA Administrators, audaciously sent the invitation by telegram directly to the GAA addressed 'Dermot Earley, Croke Park, Dublin'.

Dermot travelled out to New York but was not included in the official All-Star party. Many years later in an interview with Martin Breheny, he said he regretted his decision to go. Breheny wrote, "it was a shabby way to treat one of the game's great ambassadors, but it didn't change Dermot's view that the All-Star scheme had added greatly to the GAA scene".

His son Dermot confirmed his father's regard for the scheme. "When I was younger, we would watch the All-Stars

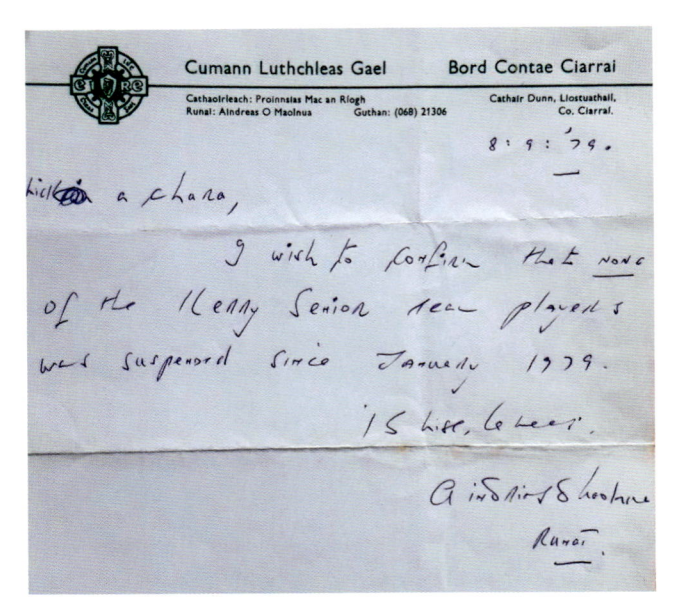

Letter from the Kerry County Board in 1979

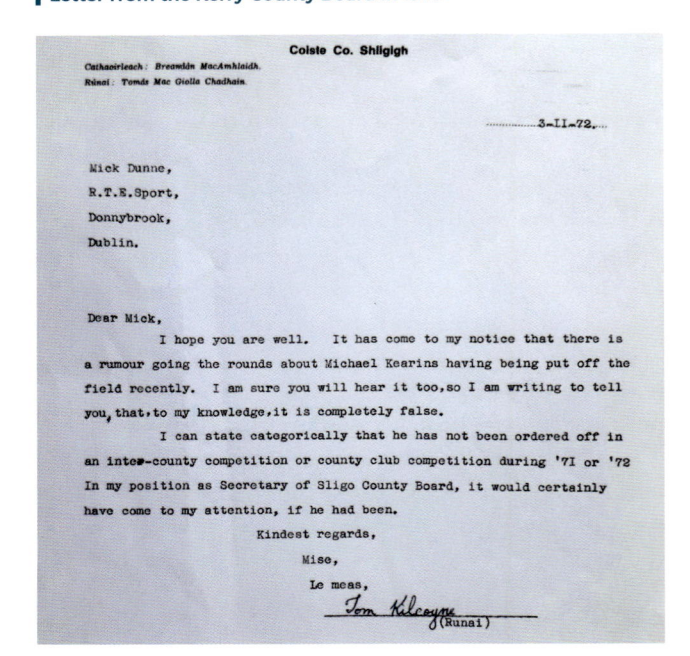

Letter from the Sligo County Board pleading Mickey Kearins innocence in 1972

Letter from players' representative Robbie Kelleher

50 Years of the GAA All-Stars

No hard feelings– Dermot Earley takes RTÉ's Mick Dunne and Dermot Kelly on a tour of the United Nations Headquarters in New York in 1988, where he was working at the time

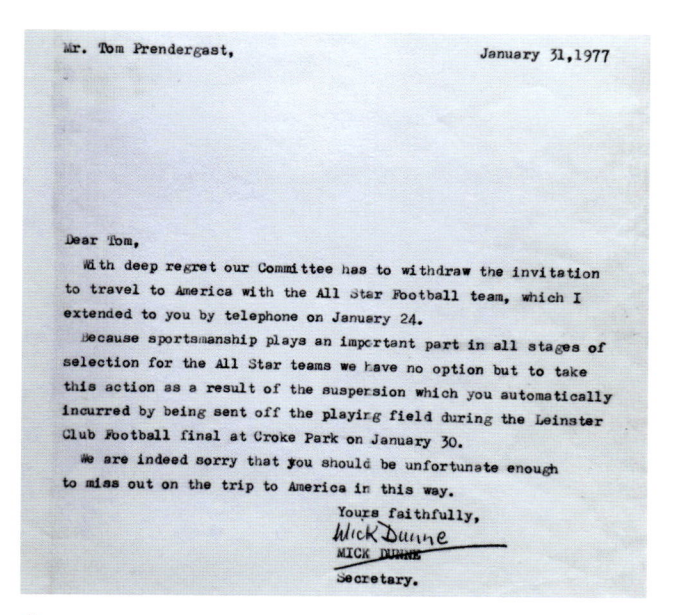

Letter to Tom Prendergast confirming his withdrawn invitation for the All-Star trip

on TV at home. I remember Dad jumping up and down when Uncle Paul won his All-Star in 1985". Dermot Snr travelled officially on All-Star trips many times before and after 1975, both as an All-Star and a replacement.

A similar situation arose two years later when Tom Prendergast was suspended after the Leinster Club Final. His invitation to travel on the All-Star trip in the spring of 1978 was withdrawn.

BANNED FROM THE BANQUET

In 1982 Pat Fleury was selected on the All-Star hurling team in mid-October but was sent off soon afterwards playing for Offaly in an Oireachtas hurling semi-final against Clare. He did not receive an invitation to the banquet to collect his award.

At the time Seán Kilfeather wrote, "the decision that Pat Fleury is not to be invited to the All-Star banquet is scandalous. Pat was sent off for a foul when his hurley accidentally caught an opponent over the eye. The people who made the decision should be collectively ashamed and the Bank of Ireland are guilty of bad manners and social ineptitude". He continued, "this rule gives referees a say in the selection of the All-Stars. Referees in the hurly burly of a match can make mistakes".

The Offaly County Board sent a letter to GAA Ard Stiúrthóir Liam Mulvihill to plead Pat's case, but the decision stood, and Pat missed the banquet.

Rather than dwell on that incident in 1982, Pat prefers to talk about the good times he had on five All-Star trips. His first trip came just months after the All-Star banquet. "Losing that opportunity would have been much worse than missing 'the dance' in the Burlington", he reflected. He was

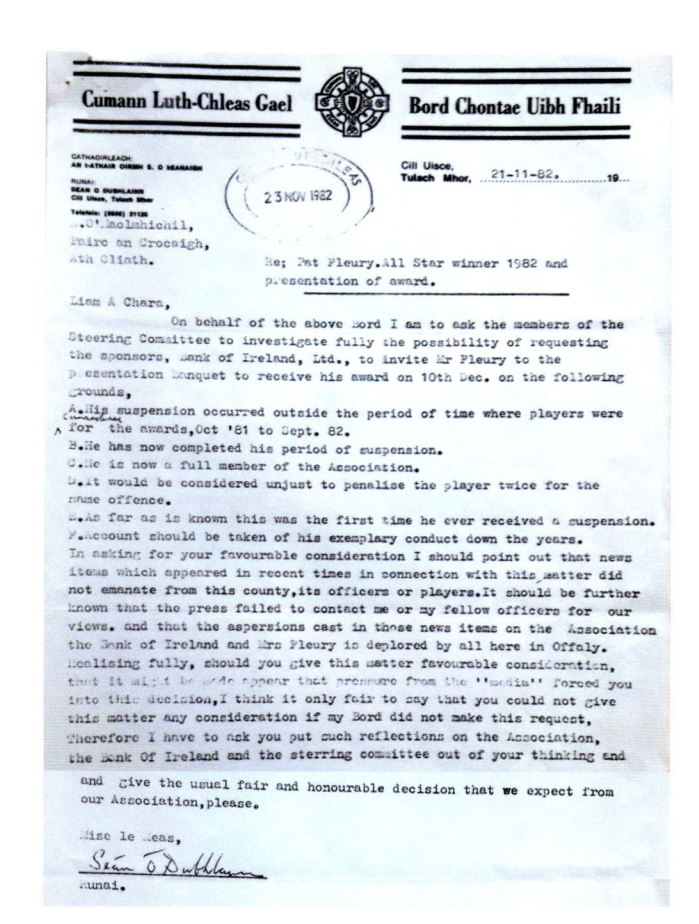

John Dowling, secretary of the Offaly County Board in 1982 makes a case for Pat Fleury

asked to captain the All-Star hurlers in San Francisco and New York in 1985. "I made great friends on those trips".

"I was lucky to win that All-Star in 1982 because we weren't All-Ireland champions. There is no point in being bitter. I was sent off; there was a set of rules. It was a wonderful scheme and to get an All-Star back then was a dream come true. When I was sent off in the match in Ennis, I remember John

Dowling saying, 'I wonder how will that affect your All-Star?' He promised he would do his best for me".

A couple of months later, Pat was invited to lunch in Limerick by the Bank of Ireland manager. Afterwards, he took Pat into the branch. "One of the regional managers walked over to a desk, pulled out a black refuse sack and said, 'there you go'. I just said, 'thanks very much' but I could have said more. I still have the trophy, and I have another one to go with it", said Pat. "But in Offaly, we did wonder would it have happened if I was from Tipperary or Cork, a county with more clout?".

Clout didn't save Kilkenny's Mick 'Cloney' Brennan, however, when he was excluded from the All-Star banquet in 1979. The All-Star tour that year took place in October, so Mick had already travelled before the banquet in December. Mick threatened to retire from inter-county hurling over the incident, but he went on to play until 1982.

RESIGNATIONS

The strict application of the Sportsmanship rule caused arguments among the selectors and even led to some resignations. When Eamon McEneaney missed out on selection in 1985, Martin Breheny felt it was a massive injustice. Monaghan had won the National League and brought Kerry to an All-Ireland semi-final replay. "That year Eamon was, by a distance, the leading centre forward candidate for the All-Star team, only to lose out on a daft technicality", wrote Breheny at the time. The "daft technicality" resulted from a sending off for McEneaney in a seven-a-side competition.

Martin explained, "after the incident at the seven-a-side the referee said, 'you are grand Eamon, you can play on'. But the sending off was treated officially through the disciplinary channels and Eamon was later deemed ineligible for All-Star selection. It was probably his only chance, and it was taken away from him. Bureaucracy won out in a flawed system". Martin resigned from the Steering Committee in protest.

He still thinks it is a shame that McEneaney never received an All-Star but looking back at his resignation letter, he laughed and said, "wasn't I a right pup back then?".

The pressure to relax the sportsmanship rule came mainly from younger journalists who joined the Selection Committee in the 1980s. In 1985 the Steering Committee modified the rule to include, "where mistakes are made in a two-week suspension, we will accept the nomination of the player if the controlling body puts in writing that the referee had made a mistake".

Mick Brennan is banned from the banquet in 1979

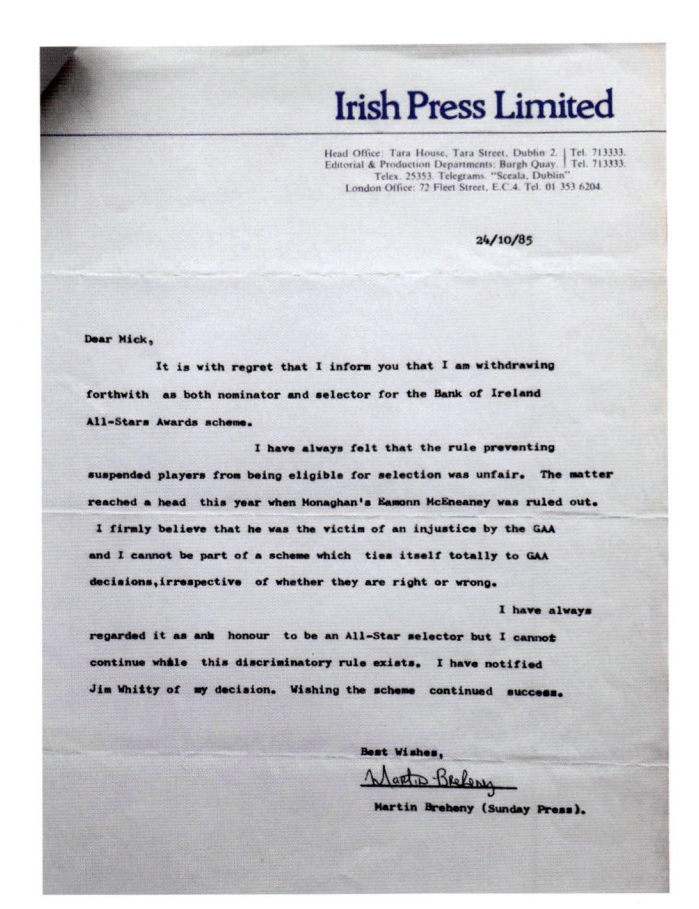

Martin Breheny's resignation letter from 1985

In 1986 a motion to drop the rule, proposed by Donal Keenan, was defeated. Only two journalists voted for change. "It wasn't so much the Steering Committee who enforced the rule so strictly, it was the GAA themselves who were keen to ensure that players who were sent off were penalised", Breheny told us.

PLAYERS' VIEWS

Opinion varies among the All-Stars from that era. Eddie Keher valued the rule but felt that the inclusion of the club games made it a bit unfair. Mick Jacob said, "sportsmanship was a good idea. It was part of the honour".

Seán O'Neill was in no doubt about the importance of the rule. "It was a privilege to be picked on the top team because it rewarded sportsmanship. When this rule was changed, I feel that it diminished the value of the All-Star award". Pat Reynolds disagrees, "it was rubbish".

John Fenton thought it was a good thing. "I would like if it was still in place today. It added to the honour as it rewarded good behaviour as well as excellence. Fellas knew they had to go out and play in the spirit of the game".

Pat Henderson said, "I agreed with the rule on principle until you would hear a tough story about a player losing out". Mickey Kearins had concerns about the refereeing decisions, "I didn't agree with the rule as you could easily be sent off in the wrong".

DJ Carey, who was never sent off during his career, really valued the rule. "I agree that if you were sent off, you should get no All-Star".

On the other hand, Billy Morgan said, "the sportsmanship rule was unfair on a player like Charlie Nelligan who got sent off in an All-Ireland Final and then couldn't be selected for an All-Star. He wasn't a dirty player. And for someone like Martin Furlong, it prevented him from winning for years because of his reputation. He eventually got his second in 1982 when Offaly beat Kerry".

Pat Hartigan said, "I agreed with it particularly for dangerous play, but it needed to have more flexibility". Richie Connor concurs, "because back then if you were sent off, you must have deserved it".

Paul Earley, Dermot's younger brother, felt that the sportsmanship rule helped his selection in 1985. "Eoin Liston had been sent off so he couldn't be picked. I was nominated with Ambrose Rodgers and Éamonn Murphy but as we didn't even win Connacht that year, I wasn't expecting to win".

Pete Finnerty thought the rule was harsh. "One little infringement could cost you. It might have been better if they had a rule that two offences were needed to make someone ineligible. Sometimes you would be watching or playing a game, and if someone was sent off you would think, 'ah Jaysus, that's his All-Star gone'. But it was part of why you got the All-Star, how you represented yourself on and off the field as well. Mind you; it was much more difficult to get sent off back then", he laughed.

Greg Blaney agreed, "In those days it was much harder to get sent off so if you did, you probably deserved it". "It was a silly rule", said Colm O'Rourke, who lost out himself one year when he was sent off.

In 1990 the rule was still in place. James McCartan remembers playing club football in London for Tír Chonaill Gaels after Down had been knocked out of the Championship. "In one match there was a player on the other team called 'Basher Hughes'. I think he was a bare-knuckle fighter or something; he was definitely bashing me all through the game! Anyway, I got sent off. I had already been nominated for an All-Star, so we buried the story, and it never got reported. The referees didn't have to lodge a report of the match over there".

CHANGES IN THE 1990S

In 1990 the rule was changed to state, "in the event of a player being suspended subsequent to being selected, he would be eligible to receive his award provided he served his term of suspension prior to the night of the banquet".

Later that year, when Kevin O'Brien was the first Wicklow man to be selected on an All-Star team, he created history as the first player to be honoured after serving a suspension. "I got sent off for something trivial and got two weeks. An All-Star was the furthest thing from my mind during a normal league match in Blessington. It was down to the referee – he could either give me two weeks or four weeks", said Kevin. "Colm O'Neill was having a sensational season that year, he was one of the best forwards in the country. But he got sent off in the All-Ireland final against Meath and got a month's suspension. I must fix up Mick Lyons what I owe him for that!", he joked.

The following year further flexibility was shown when Cormac Bonnar became the first player to receive an All-Star while technically still under suspension. A two-week ban for a sending off was due to expire at midnight the night of the presentation banquet. When the hurling team was announced earlier that week, Jim O'Sullivan wrote in *The Irish Examiner,* "Bonnar can only wait and hope. His prospect of being presented with his award depends on two things – the length of his suspension and the attitude of the GAA leadership". The GAA showed leniency this time and Bonnar collected his award. He was lucky because that year the All-Star banquet was held on the Saturday night for the first time. The extra 24 hours made all the difference.

By 1993 the rules changed to allow selectors make a case for suspended players. Donal Keenan wrote to the All-Star Steering Committee about Anthony Tohill and Charlie Redmond's suspensions. Keenan's pleas were convincing as both footballers were picked on the All-Star team later that year.

Tohill recalled, "I was really lucky in 1993. I was playing for Queens in a Ryan Cup game, which I normally avoided. I went to shoulder one of the UCC players. I thought I caught him in the shoulder, but he went down holding his face and I got sent off. I got a four-week suspension. We went on to win the All-Ireland that year. Some really decent journalists made the case on my behalf and got my suspension overturned so that I was able to win the award. If it wasn't for them, I wouldn't have won that second All-Star in 1993. It would have just left a bad taste if you missed out because of something that had happened back in January after going on to win the All-Ireland".

In 1995 when the GAA disbanded the selection committees, nobody was surprised that the sportsmanship rule was dropped. Charlie Redmond recalled, "1995 was the first year that the journalists were not the selectors. I got an All-Star even though I had been sent off in the All-Ireland final". By then Charlie didn't even have to appeal his case, his eligibility for an All-Star was never in question.

The spirit of sportsmanship behind the rule continued however and still had an impact on players in the 2000s. Brendan Cummins recalled a club match in 2003. "I was playing for Arravale Rovers, and I was getting abuse from the side-line when I was taking the frees. Comments like, 'you think you are a great fella, you are only playing to get an All-Star'".

Towards the end of a tight match, Brendan hit a free which landed short and dropped into the goal. "We won by a point and then it got a bit heated. I reacted but immediately after the match, I started thinking about the All-Star. I was thinking, 'I have to kill the story'. I knew Davy Fitz had lost out one year for a similar incident, so it was on my mind. There was that fear factor about losing an All-Star. So, I went into the opposition dressing room afterwards and said, 'sorry my behaviour was out of order. I hope there are no hard feelings. Anything I can do for the club, under-age training or anything, I will do it'".

Brendan feels that sportsmanship is a fair consideration for selection. "If you have an All-Star, you are the torchbearer of the standard. Standards off the field and how you handle yourself are important".

SELECTION LEAKS

Another controversial issue that dogged the All-Star scheme was the leaking of the team before the official announcement. In 1982 the entire football team was known in advance. In 1986 Seán Óg Ó Ceallacháin was told by Eddie Rogers, a reporter with the *Offaly Tribune*, that he knew the All-Star hurling selection a week before it was published.

The problem often stemmed from accurate speculation by

Journalist Donal Keenan makes the case for Redmond and Tohill

GAA journalists who were not on the selection committee. "Martin Breheny saw it as a challenge and was determined to crack it every year", said Liam Mulvihill. "He would ring different journalists asking each one if a particular player was on the team. Then he would piece it all together and work it out".

The GAA later invited Martin back onto the All-Star selection committee when they reinstated the journalists in 1998. He went on to play a vital role on the Steering Committee until his retirement in 2019. Liam laughed, "It was a case of poacher turned gamekeeper".

In 1988 a secret ballot was introduced to deal with the problem. The selectors voted in secret just two days before the banquet and only the Steering Committee saw the full makeup of the team before its announcement. While this may have helped stop the leaks, it led to a new problem. In a letter to the Steering Committee in 1989 Donal Keenan said, "the secret ballot does not allow us the opportunity to review our selection, and that to me is extremely dangerous. Is it not ridiculous that a group of people select two teams and at the end of their deliberations do not know who they have selected?".

Roy Curtis and Tom O'Riordan report on Brian Whelahan's omission from the 1994 All-Star Hurling Team

SELECTION CONTROVERSIES

Like an accident waiting to happen, the secret ballot led to a selection issue in 1994 that is generally accepted as the most significant controversy in All-Star history. Brian Whelahan was hotly tipped for an award that year having delivered some spectacular performances throughout Offaly's championship-winning season. He had already picked up numerous Player of the Year awards and went on to win the Texaco Hurler of the Year a few weeks later. When he was not named on the All-Star hurling team at the banquet, many people were outraged.

The next day, the newspaper headlines screamed, "That All-Star Shambles" and a "Grotesque Scandal". Tom O'Riordan wrote that, "a puzzled look fell across the faces of invited guests at last night's presentation banquet at the Burlington Hotel when it became known that Whelahan had not won a place in the team". Other headlines read, "Selectors under a cloud as Offaly ace omitted".

What caused the controversial decision that year? "It was simple", explained Jim O'Sullivan. "Whelahan and Limerick defender David Clarke were viewed as the leading candidates for the two wing back positions and that was the way it was meant to work out. However, because of a glitch in the process, Whelahan wasn't picked. Clarke was named right half back and Offaly's Kevin Martin gained the left half back position. The selectors were unaware of what half back line had been chosen".

Twenty years later, selector Seán Moran devoted his *Irish Times* column to the omission and did a full analysis of what happened in 1994. "I'd often intended to set down a perspective on how this came about, and the 20th anniversary seems as good a time as any. Problems arose because one of the candidates for Whelahan's position at right wing back was Limerick's Dave Clarke, who was a consensus choice as one of the best half backs that year. A plan was hatched to nominate both of them (Whelahan and Clarke) for each of the wing back positions. GAA President Jack Boothman, present as an observer, expressed surprise that none of the other wing backs were receiving any consideration. At this point, long-standing issues began to surface. Among some of the older and founder-selectors was a firmly held view that players shouldn't be allowed to change positions".

Moran continued, "the upshot was that Clarke and Whelahan were nominated for both positions but an additional two candidates, Offaly's Kevin Martin and Wexford's Larry O'Gorman, were put forward at left wing back so there were two nominations at right wing back and four on the left. Voting instructions were clear for the latter selection: a form of PR was used, requiring the candidates to be voted one to four in order of preference with a first preference worth four points, a second worth three and so on. We were specifically asked to vote down the list. It turned out Clarke had beaten Whelahan on the right and on the left Martin had won. It later emerged some of those who had disagreed with the concept of putting Clarke or Whelahan on the left wing hadn't voted for either of them at all, in clear contravention of the voting instructions".

All-Star Gazing

Brian Whelahan with Eddie Keher, Jimmy Doyle, Ray Cummins, John Doyle and Tony Reddan at the launch of a commemorative set of stamps to mark the 2000 team of the millennium

Well, that clears it up then! Essentially it seems that the reason for Brian's omission was a combination of the secret ballot and differing views among the selectors on positional switches. Whelahan's vote was split across two positions, and two other players gained more votes than him in both of those positions.

Donal Keenan explained why the steering committee didn't change the team when they realised Whelahan had lost out. "Consideration was given to calling a special meeting to review what had happened, but this avenue was not pursued by Croke Park and the sponsors. At that stage, they felt it would be worse if it became known that Kevin Martin had been selected and subsequently dropped from the All-Star team".

The selectors were embarrassed and annoyed. Denis Walsh resigned straight away. "Many of us wanted a meeting as soon as possible after Christmas to seek full accountability for what had happened", said Moran. However, that meeting never took place as Bank of Ireland withdrew from the All-Stars to concentrate on their sponsorship of the football championship. Powerscreen took over and the selection committees were disbanded.

Not everyone at the banquet was aware that Brian didn't make the team as the players named were deemed to be deserving recipients. Brian Lohan said, "we weren't surprised on the night because Dave Clarke was outstanding that year, so I didn't even notice".

How does the man himself feel about the omission? Like his county man Pat Fleury, Brian was more interested in talking about the four All-Star awards he received and the fantastic experiences he had on All-Star tours to New York and Toronto. "In 1994 we won the All-Ireland. If you had asked me what mattered most, it was winning the All-Ireland. It was great to get an All-Star in 1995, but I was bitterly disappointed to have lost the All-Ireland final that year to Clare. So that's my only regret that I never won both an All-Ireland medal and an All-Star in the same year".

Of the night itself, Brian reminisced, "the three nominees for the same positions were all sitting together at the table. I remember the half back line was called out, then the midfielders, but it wasn't until the forwards were named that I realised I wasn't going to win. I was sorta stunned. It was tough because Kevin Martin, who won his first award, felt really bad about it. He said to me that he felt he had won my award. I said to him, 'listen, enjoy your night, I'm certainly going to'. Afterwards, my dad rang me and said, 'why didn't you tell me?' I said, 'I didn't know'.

"I was told afterwards that I got more votes than David or Kevin, but they were split over two positions. And when the error was realised, Jack Boothman made the call and said, 'no that's the team'".

Every cloud has a silver lining, and for Brian, the incident turned out to be a great boost for his new business. "As it happened, I had just opened my pub in Birr that December and because of the huge controversy over the All-Stars, I got loads of publicity out of it". He concluded, "In 1994 it was all about the All-Ireland – that was the big achievement for me".

Other All-Star omissions have caused surprise, but when Brian McGuigan was left off the football team in 2005, his father Frank was so upset he sold the All-Star trophy that he had received himself in 1984.

Brian was still living in Australia in 2005 but had been flown home by Mickey Harte that summer to help Tyrone win their second All-Ireland title. He was voted Man of the Match for his performance in the final against Kerry. Brian was nominated for an All-Star and had returned to Australia by the time the team was announced.

"My two brothers went down to the banquet to represent me. I was in work in Australia, and it was early in the morning over there. My brother heard beforehand that I hadn't won. He texted me, so I knew before the show. It certainly helped that I was out in the sunshine in Australia".

Brian went on to say, "Peter Canavan was picked in my position, but he hadn't played at centre half forward. Peter is a good friend of mine. He told me that he was embarrassed going up to collect the award".

Brian's father Frank still feels very strongly about his son's omission that year. "Peter Canavan was picked out of position in 2005 to deprive Brian of an All-Star. Brian should have got one. He was the Man of the Match in the All-Ireland final". Referring to the selectors Frank asked, "Who are these guys? There have been some ridiculous decisions. You can't judge a game on an iPad. How many fellas should have All-Stars that didn't get one over the years? I know you can only pick 15. But you can avoid controversy by not picking men out of position. I don't agree with the current system. In 2019 they could have named 10 Dubs, and they would have all deserved it. But there would have been an outcry. How did Ciarán Kilkenny not win one?".

What would Frank do differently? "It would be better to get five or six managers picking the All-Stars. Straight guys, who would pick the best in their positions. No bias, no politics".

PLAYERS AS SELECTORS

Managers have never been asked to select the All-Stars to date but the inter-county players were given the job in the mid-1990s. "The GAA decided to go with something new in 1995. The new sponsors Powerscreen were big on players", explained Dermot Power. Asked whether the decision to move away from the journalists was influenced by the Whelahan affair the previous year, Dermot replied, "yes absolutely".

Liam Mulvihill reflected on how the journalists reacted. "To be honest, they were happy to withdraw at that stage. They were relieved not to have to pick the All-Stars, and they were glad that they couldn't be blamed".

Every inter-county player had a chance to vote and 70% returned their voting papers. "The players' response clearly demonstrates that they appreciate being involved in the process", said Mulvihill at the time. Powerscreen held a press conference in the Europa Hotel in Belfast to announce the nominations. "I remember all the journalists boycotted it, so it got no press coverage", recalled Dermot.

A new Steering Committee made the decision on the final positions of players for both teams. Journalists Jim O'Sullivan, Brian Carthy (RTÉ), Adrian Logan (UTV) and Mártan Ó Ciardha (RnaG) sat on that committee.

Seán Kilfeather wrote, "the critics seem to believe that the selection process should be limited to players of the games. Players, by the very nature of what they do, seldom see matches and could scarcely be expected to be open-minded about matches in which they or their friends and colleagues and indeed their opponents are involved".

Martin Breheny concurred, "players can't be let loose on it because they have tunnel vision. It is and was a journalists' scheme, and that's important. Back in 1971, those four founding journalists, what they said counted. Their match reports told the story".

Frank Lohan wasn't a fan of the players as selectors either. "We all got a card to vote. At the banquet in 1995, I remember that Jason Sherlock didn't win POTY. I don't think he even won an All-Star. That was a big surprise as he was the difference for Dublin that year. I think the players shouldn't be let near the selection of the teams. It's better that the journalists are the selectors. You feel you have been chosen as the best".

In 1996, the second year of player-led selections, there was some embarrassment within the GAA, when five suspended players were named on the All-Star football team. The situation arose as many of the top players had been suspended following the controversial All-Ireland final that year between Meath and Mayo.

Selection of suspended players embarrasses officials

| Reaction to the 1996 All-Star selection in *The Cork Examiner*

All-Star Gazing

In 1997 the player experiment ended, and the journalists were reinstated as selectors. Dermot Power said, "at that stage it was a chance to put a structure in place to avoid any future selection issues".

The journalists continue to select the All-Stars as the scheme reaches its 50th anniversary in 2021. Due to the Covid-19 global pandemic in 2020, meetings to select the 2020 All-Stars were forced to shift online.

All-Star Selectors on tour in Arizona in 2004
Back L to R: Brian Carthy, Michael Lyster, Martin Breheny, Cian Murphy, Donal Keenan, Fergal McGill
Front L to R: Jim O'Sullivan, Alan Milton, Jackie Cahill, Eamon O'Hara

Cameras on, cameras off - a virtual All-Star Selection meeting during the Covid-19 pandemic in 2020

Gazing into the Future

As he sat watching the All-Star awards on TV, six-time All-Star Jack O'Shea sent a text to Brian Fenton congratulating him on his All-Star and Player of the Year awards. "It hit me that there was no banquet, so no-one there for him to share it with", explained 'Jacko'. "I just said 'Congratulations, it's a great achievement. I admire you and I love watching you play'. Brian mentioned it the following day in the papers, and it went viral!".

We know it meant a lot to Brian, but the gesture was typical of the man Jim Whitty believes to be the greatest All-Star of them all. "If I was to pick one who epitomised the All-Star, it would be him", says Jim, "the way he went about the game". There is no doubt O'Shea is held in high esteem by hurlers and footballers alike – whether it was mentoring and rooming with a young James McCartan, signing an All-Star jersey for the Bonnar brothers, or having a kick around with a young DJ Carey in the SkyDome, they all speak warmly of him.

Jack, in turn, speaks of mixing with other players and of friendships forged on tour, the likes of Mickey Quinn. The first player from St Mary's in Caherciveen to bring home an All-Star in 1980, he remembers taking it to the club's annual function. Knockmore, in Co. Mayo, made a special presentation to Kevin O'Neill when he became an All-Star in 1993, while Aghyaran, in Tyrone, invited the whole parish to a celebration when Ronan McNamee was honoured in 2019. Bobby Ryan was the first player from Borrisoleigh to get an All-Star. He told us that as the awards were being televised, two of his dad's clubmates drove in around the farmyard, honking their horns. "Dad giving out, all part of the celebrations!".

This is what Kieran McGeeney calls the 'ripple effect' – an All-Star award coming to a club or parish affects more than the player who gets it. It's a source of pride for families and clubs, and an inspiration for those coming behind.

Of course, great rivalries have built up over time among the All-Stars. Seán Óg Ó hAilpín says, "my paltry three are due to intense competition from Tommy Walsh and JJ Delaney", while Joe Cooney blames Ciarán Barr for interrupting a potential six in-a-row for him! Andy McCallin says his All-Star was even more special because he knew Mick O'Dwyer was a fellow nominee, while Larry Tompkins was up against the great Matt Connor who, he thought, was one the best players ever.

Though many feel some of the early 'lustre' may have worn off the All-Star scheme, today's players don't see it like that. Pádraig Faulkner was one of three Cavan footballers named on the 2020 All-Star team following their historic Ulster Championship victory after 23 years. Because of Covid-19, he missed out on the razzmatazz of the annual banquet but still felt it was a "massive honour" to have received the All-star.

"It was a privilege to bring the award home to my family and club. Myself, Raymond (Galligan) and Thomas (Galligan) were the lucky ones this year, but these individual awards wouldn't be possible without the backing of the entire team and management". He too is proud to join the All-Star Roll of Honour and says, "hopefully this will encourage young players all around Cavan and Kingscourt to believe anything is achievable".

Eleven-time All-Star Henry Shefflin has no doubts about the future of the scheme. "I saw my own boys and girls looking at the programme last week, dreaming of it. That picture at the start of the RTÉ All-Star programme of the young fella looking up saying, 'when I grow up, I want to be an All-Star' – that was me. That's what I felt when I won it. The other day I was talking to a little fella from Galway, who had written to me, and we were talking about the All-Stars. Kids talking about an All-Star. That's the magic moment".

He continues, "it'll get stronger ... it still means so much, particularly to the weaker counties". Will his record ever be equalled? "Why not ... look at Dublin, playing so far ahead of everyone else. And there's nothing to stop a team like Limerick going on and winning all around them – they're very young". Who might catch Henry? A young gun from Limerick or maybe even his own nephew and godson Eoin Cody, the 2020 young hurler of the year.

Gary Kirby talked about his 'young gun' from Limerick.

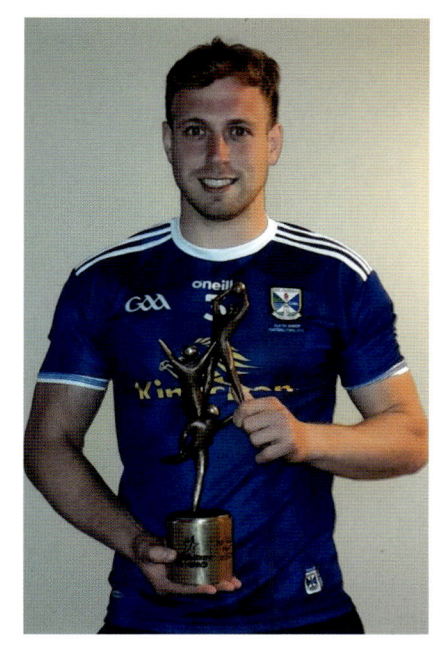

| Cavan's Pádraig Faulkner with his 2020 All-Star trophy

"When my young fella Patrick says that he wants to win an All-Star someday, I tell him, 'You have to be consistent all year round to win one'". Patrick is well on his way having won a minor All-Star on the 2019 Electric Ireland Hurling Team of the Year.

So how might the scheme evolve in the future? For the past 50 years the format of the All-Stars has remained virtually unchanged but if the Sportsmanship rule caused controversy in the early days, positional issues are making selections difficult now. Tommy Carr reckons there has always been a bit of confusion. "Is it the best 15 players in Ireland or the best player in each of the 15 positions?" he asks. "Which is it? It was never clear".

When Offaly's Brian Whelahan was chosen at wing back and full forward and Ger Power impressed six times at half back, half forward and full forward in the 1970s, they had played in those positions. The controversy now surrounds players being picked out of position.

Martin Breheny fears backs are losing out the most. "It is getting problematic", he says, while Brendan Cummins goes further "Selectors need balls, to sit in a room and pick the best corner back or full back. Players might not be so keen on rotation if they thought they would be picked in their position".

Kieran McGeeney speaks of the current player's 'role rather than position', but that can see players lose out too. Bryan Cullen was one of the few members of the Dublin team not nominated in 2011. "It was tough on Bryan", recalls Alan Brogan. "In the team we very much valued Bryan's role, and he was the captain. That was the role Bryan played; he did the work that probably others didn't do".

Another aspect of today's All-Star selections is the dominance of the counties who reach the latter stages of the championship. Liam Sammon and Tomás Ó Sé allude to the fact that players from nine counties featured on the first All-Star football team. "You'd never get nine counties represented now", says Tomás, and he's right, just four counties featured on the 2020 team while in hurling, there were five, compared to seven in 1971. Mick Bermingham, who was on that team, feels the scheme should honour players from the lesser counties more, saying "The Railway Cups had a big impact on selection way back then". Anthony Tohill was honoured in 1992 on the back of Derry's success in the League, but believes that since the introduction of the qualifiers, its influence has waned.

Referring to the fact that two counties, Carlow and Longford, have no All-Star in either code, Martin Breheny says, "I think it's terrible really. You would think that in 50 years they could have got one each, but every year it's looked at in isolation, not across the whole period". He feels a player from each county should be nominated every year and go into the mix. "It would mean so much to the smaller counties". Larry Tompkins wonders will there need to be a second tier All-Stars in the future?

Many players think more could be made of the current scheme. McGeeney believes there could be a celebration built around the All-Ireland weekend. "All the past players go up to Dublin anyway that weekend". He refers to Australia where a whole week of events takes place in the run-up to their Grand Final, including the presentation of the Brownlow medal, awarded to the "best and fairest" player in the AFL.

Tadhg Kennelly shared his experience of that Grand Final week. "Throughout the season players are competing for the Brownlow medal and the award is presented at a banquet in Melbourne the Monday before the final. In 2005, when Sydney Swans won, I had to travel to Melbourne on the Monday, and back again the following weekend".

How would today's inter-county managers react to that?

Colm Cooper laments the fact the Irish don't get to see the All-Stars play at home. "For the 50th anniversary have them play an exhibition match under lights", he suggests, "nobody gets to see them here".

There is no doubt that the All-Stars still mean a lot after 50 years, and most players are glad that the scheme merged with the GPA awards as part of a wider agreement in 2011.

"They should never let the All-Stars die", says Jimmy Cooney.

"Even if the trips made it for us, the honour is still the same". says Pat Henderson.

"The players love it", says Brian Fenton, adding, "they will go crazy if it's not there".

"Long may it continue!", says Dónal Óg.

It is also clear that the Roll of Honour is becoming more significant with the passage of time. "That's what's important now", says Colm Cooper.

"You don't think much about it", says Pete Finnerty, "yet when you see your name at the top of the list, you realise what you've achieved".

Whenever All-Stars meet, tales are told of the Hotel Richelieu and Harrington's Bar in San Francisco, the Kilkenny Bar in Buenos Aires, Tony Keady's white suit and John 'Schillaci' Fitzgibbon's exploits, not to mention the many great nights in the Burlington Hotel.

Let us salute the All-Stars to date, and all those who helped to get them there, starting with four journalists on a wet day in Belfield.....

1) the GAA All-Star Posters from 1971 to 2016 and
2) newspaper archives from 2017 to 2020.

List of Hurling All-Stars

#	Year	Name	County	Position
1	1971	Damien Martin	Offaly	Goalkeeper
2	1971	Tony Maher	Cork	Right Full-Back
3	1971	Pat Hartigan	Limerick	Full-Back
4	1971	Jim Treacy	Kilkenny	Left Full-Back
5	1971	Tadhg O'Connor	Tipperary	Right Half-Back
6	1971	Mick Roche	Tipperary	Centre Half-Back
7	1971	Martin Coogan	Kilkenny	Left Half-Back
8	1971	John Connolly	Galway	Centrefield
9	1971	Frank Cummins	Kilkenny	Centrefield
10	1971	Francis Loughnane	Tipperary	Right Half-Forward
11	1971	Michael "Babs" Keating	Tipperary	Centre Half-Forward
12	1971	Eddie Keher	Kilkenny	Left Half-Forward
13	1971	Mick Bermingham	Dublin	Right Full-Forward
14	1971	Ray Cummins	Cork	Full-Forward
15	1971	Éamonn Cregan	Limerick	Left Full-Forward
16	1972	Noel Skehan	Kilkenny	Goalkeeper
17	1972	Tony Maher	Cork	Right Full-Back
18	1972	Pat Hartigan	Limerick	Full-Back
19	1972	Jim Treacy	Kilkenny	Left Full-Back
20	1972	Pat Lawlor	Kilkenny	Right Half-Back
21	1972	Mick Jacob	Wexford	Centre Half-Back
22	1972	Con Roche	Cork	Left Half-Back
23	1972	Frank Cummins	Kilkenny	Centrefield
24	1972	Denis Coughlan	Cork	Centrefield
25	1972	Francis Loughnane	Tipperary	Right Half-Forward
26	1972	Pat Delaney (K)	Kilkenny	Centre Half-Forward
27	1972	Eddie Keher	Kilkenny	Left Half-Forward
28	1972	Charlie McCarthy	Cork	Right Full-Forward
29	1972	Ray Cummins	Cork	Full-Forward
30	1972	Éamonn Cregan	Limerick	Left Full-Forward
31	1973	Noel Skehan	Kilkenny	Goalkeeper
32	1973	Phil "Fan" Larkin	Kilkenny	Right Full-Back
33	1973	Pat Hartigan	Limerick	Full-Back
34	1973	Jim O'Brien	Limerick	Left Full-Back
35	1973	Colm Doran	Wexford	Right Half-Back
36	1973	Pat Henderson	Kilkenny	Centre Half-Back
37	1973	Seán Foley	Limerick	Left Half-Back
38	1973	Liam "Chunky" O'Brien	Kilkenny	Centrefield
39	1973	Richie Bennis	Limerick	Centrefield
40	1973	Francis Loughnane	Tipperary	Right Half-Forward
41	1973	Pat Delaney (K)	Kilkenny	Centre Half-Forward
42	1973	Éamonn Grimes	Limerick	Left Half-Forward
43	1973	Martin Quigley	Wexford	Right Full-Forward
44	1973	Kieran Purcell	Kilkenny	Full-Forward
45	1973	Eddie Keher	Kilkenny	Left Full-Forward
46	1974	Noel Skehan	Kilkenny	Goalkeeper
47	1974	Phil "Fan" Larkin	Kilkenny	Right Full-Back
48	1974	Pat Hartigan	Limerick	Full-Back
49	1974	John Horgan	Cork	Left Full-Back
50	1974	Ger Loughnane	Clare	Right Half-Back
51	1974	Pat Henderson	Kilkenny	Centre Half-Back
52	1974	Con Roche	Cork	Left Half-Back
53	1974	Liam "Chunky" O'Brien	Kilkenny	Centrefield
54	1974	John Galvin	Waterford	Centrefield
55	1974	Joe McKenna	Limerick	Right Half-Forward
56	1974	Martin Quigley	Wexford	Centre Half-Forward
57	1974	Mick Crotty	Kilkenny	Left Half-Forward
58	1974	John Quigley	Wexford	Right Full-Forward
59	1974	Kieran Purcell	Kilkenny	Full-Forward
60	1974	Eddie Keher	Kilkenny	Left Full-Forward

List of Hurling All-Stars

#	Year	Name	County	Position
61	1975	Noel Skehan	Kilkenny	Goalkeeper
62	1975	Niall McInerney	Galway	Right Full-Back
63	1975	Pat Hartigan	Limerick	Full-Back
64	1975	Brian Cody	Kilkenny	Left Full-Back
65	1975	Tadhg O'Connor	Tipperary	Right Half-Back
66	1975	Seán Silke	Galway	Centre Half-Back
67	1975	Iggy Clarke	Galway	Left Half-Back
68	1975	Liam "Chunky" O'Brien	Kilkenny	Centrefield
69	1975	Gerald McCarthy	Cork	Centrefield
70	1975	Martin Quigley	Wexford	Right Half-Forward
71	1975	Joe McKenna	Limerick	Centre Half-Forward
72	1975	Éamonn Grimes	Limerick	Left Half-Forward
73	1975	Mick Brennan	Kilkenny	Right Full-Forward
74	1975	Kieran Purcell	Kilkenny	Full-Forward
75	1975	Eddie Keher	Kilkenny	Left Full-Forward
76	1976	Noel Skehan	Kilkenny	Goalkeeper
77	1976	Phil "Fan" Larkin	Kilkenny	Right Full-Back
78	1976	Willie Murphy	Wexford	Full-Back
79	1976	Johnny McMahon	Clare	Left Full-Back
80	1976	Joe McDonagh	Galway	Right Half-Back
81	1976	Mick Jacob	Wexford	Centre Half-Back
82	1976	Denis Coughlan	Cork	Left Half-Back
83	1976	Frank Burke	Galway	Centrefield
84	1976	Pat Moylan	Cork	Centrefield
85	1976	Mick Malone	Cork	Right Half-Forward
86	1976	Martin Quigley	Wexford	Centre Half-Forward
87	1976	Jimmy Barry Murphy	Cork	Left Half-Forward
88	1976	Mick Brennan	Kilkenny	Right Full-Forward
89	1976	Tony Doran	Wexford	Full-Forward
90	1976	Seánie O'Leary	Cork	Left Full-Forward
91	1977	Séamus Durack	Clare	Goalkeeper
92	1977	Johnny McMahon	Clare	Right Full-Back
93	1977	Martin O'Doherty	Cork	Full-Back
94	1977	John Horgan	Cork	Left Full-Back
95	1977	Ger Loughnane	Clare	Right Half-Back
96	1977	Mick Jacob	Wexford	Centre Half-Back
97	1977	Denis Coughlan	Cork	Left Half-Back
98	1977	Tom Cashman	Cork	Centrefield
99	1977	Michael Moroney	Clare	Centrefield
100	1977	Christy Keogh	Wexford	Right Half-Forward
101	1977	Jimmy Barry Murphy	Cork	Centre Half-Forward
102	1977	PJ Molloy	Galway	Left Half-Forward
103	1977	Charlie McCarthy	Cork	Right Full-Forward
104	1977	Ray Cummins	Cork	Full-Forward
105	1977	Seánie O'Leary	Cork	Left Full-Forward
106	1978	Séamus Durack	Clare	Goalkeeper
107	1978	Phil "Fan" Larkin	Kilkenny	Right Full-Back
108	1978	Martin O'Doherty	Cork	Full-Back
109	1978	John Horgan	Cork	Left Full-Back
110	1978	Joe Hennessy	Kilkenny	Right Half-Back
111	1978	Ger Henderson	Kilkenny	Centre Half-Back
112	1978	Denis Coughlan	Cork	Left Half-Back
113	1978	Tom Cashman	Cork	Centrefield
114	1978	Iggy Clarke	Galway	Centrefield
115	1978	Jimmy Barry Murphy	Cork	Right Half-Forward
116	1978	Noel Casey	Clare	Centre Half-Forward
117	1978	Colm Honan	Clare	Left Half-Forward
118	1978	Charlie McCarthy	Cork	Right Full-Forward
119	1978	Joe McKenna	Limerick	Full-Forward
120	1978	Tommy Butler	Tipperary	Left Full-Forward
121	1979	Pat McLoughney	Tipperary	Goalkeeper
122	1979	Brian Murphy	Cork	Right Full-Back
123	1979	Martin O'Doherty	Cork	Full-Back
124	1979	Tadhg O'Connor	Tipperary	Left Full-Back
125	1979	Dermot McCurtain	Cork	Right Half-Back
126	1979	Ger Henderson	Kilkenny	Centre Half-Back
127	1979	Iggy Clarke	Galway	Left Half-Back
128	1979	John Connolly	Galway	Centrefield
129	1979	Joe Hennessy	Kilkenny	Centrefield
130	1979	John Callinan	Clare	Right Half-Forward
131	1979	Frank Burke	Galway	Centre Half-Forward
132	1979	Liam "Chunky" O'Brien	Kilkenny	Left Half-Forward
133	1979	Mick Brennan	Kilkenny	Right Full-Forward
134	1979	Joe McKenna	Limerick	Full-Forward
135	1979	Ned Buggy	Wexford	Left Full-Forward
136	1980	Pat McLoughney	Tipperary	Goalkeeper
137	1980	Niall McInerney	Galway	Right Full-Back
138	1980	Leonard Enright	Limerick	Full-Back
139	1980	Jimmy Cooney	Galway	Left Full-Back
140	1980	Dermot McCurtain	Cork	Right Half-Back
141	1980	Seán Silke	Galway	Centre Half-Back
142	1980	Iggy Clarke	Galway	Left Half-Back
143	1980	Joachim Kelly	Offaly	Centrefield
144	1980	Mossie Walsh	Waterford	Centrefield
145	1980	Joe Connolly	Galway	Right Half-Forward
146	1980	Pat Horgan	Cork	Centre Half-Forward
147	1980	Pat Carroll	Offaly	Left Half-Forward
148	1980	Bernie Forde	Galway	Right Full-Forward
149	1980	Joe McKenna	Limerick	Full-Forward
150	1980	Éamonn Cregan	Limerick	Left Full-Forward
151	1981	Séamus Durack	Clare	Goalkeeper
152	1981	Brian Murphy	Cork	Right Full-Back
153	1981	Leonard Enright	Limerick	Full-Back
154	1981	Jimmy Cooney	Galway	Left Full-Back
155	1981	Liam O'Donoghue	Limerick	Right Half-Back
156	1981	Seán Stack	Clare	Centre Half-Back
157	1981	Ger Coughlan	Offaly	Left Half-Back
158	1981	Steve Mahon	Galway	Centrefield
159	1981	Liam Currams	Offaly	Centrefield
160	1981	John Callinan	Clare	Right Half-Forward
161	1981	George O'Connor	Wexford	Centre Half-Forward
162	1981	Mark Corrigan	Offaly	Left Half-Forward
163	1981	Pat Carroll	Offaly	Right Full-Forward
164	1981	Joe McKenna	Limerick	Full-Forward
165	1981	Johnny Flaherty	Offaly	Left Full-Forward
166	1982	Noel Skehan	Kilkenny	Goalkeeper
167	1982	John Galvin	Waterford	Right Full-Back
168	1982	Brian Cody	Kilkenny	Full-Back
169	1982	Pat Fleury	Offaly	Left Full-Back
170	1982	Aidan Fogarty	Offaly	Right Half-Back
171	1982	Ger Henderson	Kilkenny	Centre Half-Back
172	1982	Paddy Prendergast	Kilkenny	Left Half-Back
173	1982	Tim Crowley	Cork	Centrefield
174	1982	Frank Cummins	Kilkenny	Centrefield
175	1982	Tony O'Sullivan	Cork	Right Half-Forward
176	1982	Pat Horgan	Cork	Centre Half-Forward
177	1982	Richie Power Snr	Kilkenny	Left Half-Forward
178	1982	Billy Fitzpatrick	Kilkenny	Right Full-Forward
179	1982	Christy Heffernan	Kilkenny	Full-Forward
180	1982	Jim Greene	Waterford	Left Full-Forward

#	Year	Name	County	Position
181	1983	Noel Skehan	Kilkenny	Goalkeeper
182	1983	John Henderson	Kilkenny	Right Full-Back
183	1983	Leonard Enright	Limerick	Full-Back
184	1983	Dick O'Hara	Kilkenny	Left Full-Back
185	1983	Joe Hennessy	Kilkenny	Right Half-Back
186	1983	Ger Henderson	Kilkenny	Centre Half-Back
187	1983	Tom Cashman	Cork	Left Half-Back
188	1983	John Fenton	Cork	Centrefield
189	1983	Frank Cummins	Kilkenny	Centrefield
190	1983	Nicholas English	Tipperary	Right Half-Forward
191	1983	Ger Fennelly	Kilkenny	Centre Half-Forward
192	1983	Noel Lane	Galway	Left Half-Forward
193	1983	Billy Fitzpatrick	Kilkenny	Right Full-Forward
194	1983	Jimmy Barry Murphy	Cork	Full-Forward
195	1983	Liam Fennelly	Kilkenny	Left Full-Forward
196	1984	Ger Cunningham	Cork	Goalkeeper
197	1984	Paudie Fitzmaurice	Limerick	Right Full-Back
198	1984	Eugene Coughlan	Offaly	Full-Back
199	1984	Pat Fleury	Offaly	Left Full-Back
200	1984	Joe Hennessy	Kilkenny	Right Half-Back
201	1984	Johnny Crowley	Cork	Centre Half-Back
202	1984	Dermot McCurtain	Cork	Left Half-Back
203	1984	John Fenton	Cork	Centrefield
204	1984	Joachim Kelly	Offaly	Centrefield
205	1984	Nicholas English	Tipperary	Right Half-Forward
206	1984	Kieran Brennan	Kilkenny	Centre Half-Forward
207	1984	Paddy Kelly	Limerick	Left Half-Forward
208	1984	Tomás Mulcahy	Cork	Right Full-Forward
209	1984	Noel Lane	Galway	Full-Forward
210	1984	Seánie O'Leary	Cork	Left Full-Forward
211	1985	Ger Cunningham	Cork	Goalkeeper
212	1985	Séamus Coen	Galway	Right Full-Back
213	1985	Eugene Coughlan	Offaly	Full-Back
214	1985	Sylvie Linnane	Galway	Left Full-Back
215	1985	Peter Finnerty	Galway	Right Half-Back
216	1985	Pat Delaney (O)	Offaly	Centre Half-Back
217	1985	Ger Coughlan	Offaly	Left Half-Back
218	1985	John Fenton	Cork	Centrefield
219	1985	Pat Critchley	Laois	Centrefield
220	1985	Nicholas English	Tipperary	Right Half-Forward
221	1985	Brendan Lynskey	Galway	Centre Half-Forward
222	1985	Joe Cooney	Galway	Left Half-Forward
223	1985	Pat Cleary	Offaly	Right Full-Forward
224	1985	Pádraig Horan	Offaly	Full-Forward
225	1985	Liam Fennelly	Kilkenny	Left Full-Forward
226	1986	Ger Cunningham	Cork	Goalkeeper
227	1986	Denis Mulcahy	Cork	Right Full-Back
228	1986	Conor Hayes	Galway	Full-Back
229	1986	Sylvie Linnane	Galway	Left Full-Back
230	1986	Peter Finnerty	Galway	Right Half-Back
231	1986	Tony Keady	Galway	Centre Half-Back
232	1986	Bobby Ryan	Tipperary	Left Half-Back
233	1986	John Fenton	Cork	Centrefield
234	1986	Richie Power Snr	Kilkenny	Centrefield
235	1986	Tony O'Sullivan	Cork	Right Half-Forward
236	1986	Tomás Mulcahy	Cork	Centre Half-Forward
237	1986	Joe Cooney	Galway	Left Half-Forward
238	1986	David Kilcoyne	Westmeath	Right Full-Forward
239	1986	Jimmy Barry Murphy	Cork	Full-Forward
240	1986	Kevin Hennessy	Cork	Left Full-Forward
241	1987	Ken Hogan	Tipperary	Goalkeeper
242	1987	Joe Hennessy	Kilkenny	Right Full-Back
243	1987	Conor Hayes	Galway	Full-Back
244	1987	Ollie Kilkenny	Galway	Left Full-Back
245	1987	Peter Finnerty	Galway	Right Half-Back
246	1987	Ger Henderson	Kilkenny	Centre Half-Back
247	1987	John Conran	Wexford	Left Half-Back
248	1987	Steve Mahon	Galway	Centrefield
249	1987	John Fenton	Cork	Centrefield
250	1987	Michael McGrath	Galway	Right Half-Forward
251	1987	Joe Cooney	Galway	Centre Half-Forward
252	1987	Aidan Ryan	Tipperary	Left Half-Forward
253	1987	Pat Fox	Tipperary	Right Full-Forward
254	1987	Nicholas English	Tipperary	Full-Forward
255	1987	Liam Fennelly	Kilkenny	Left Full-Forward
256	1988	John Commins	Galway	Goalkeeper
257	1988	Sylvie Linnane	Galway	Right Full-Back
258	1988	Conor Hayes	Galway	Full-Back
259	1988	Martin Hanamay	Offaly	Left Full-Back
260	1988	Peter Finnerty	Galway	Right Half-Back
261	1988	Tony Keady	Galway	Centre Half-Back
262	1988	Bobby Ryan	Tipperary	Left Half-Back
263	1988	Colm Bonnar	Tipperary	Centrefield
264	1988	George O'Connor	Wexford	Centrefield
265	1988	Declan Ryan	Tipperary	Right Half-Forward
266	1988	Ciarán Barr	Antrim	Centre Half-Forward
267	1988	Martin Naughton	Galway	Left Half-Forward
268	1988	Michael McGrath	Galway	Right Full-Forward
269	1988	Nicholas English	Tipperary	Full-Forward
270	1988	Tony O'Sullivan	Cork	Left Full-Forward
271	1989	John Commins	Galway	Goalkeeper
272	1989	Aidan Fogarty	Offaly	Right Full-Back
273	1989	Eamon Cleary	Wexford	Full-Back
274	1989	Dessie Donnelly	Antrim	Left Full-Back
275	1989	Conal Bonnar	Tipperary	Right Half-Back
276	1989	Bobby Ryan	Tipperary	Centre Half-Back
277	1989	Seán Treacy	Galway	Left Half-Back
278	1989	Michael Coleman	Galway	Centrefield
279	1989	Declan Carr	Tipperary	Centrefield
280	1989	Eanna Ryan	Galway	Right Half-Forward
281	1989	Joe Cooney	Galway	Centre Half-Forward
282	1989	Olcan McFetridge	Antrim	Left Half-Forward
283	1989	Pat Fox	Tipperary	Right Full-Forward
284	1989	Cormac Bonnar	Tipperary	Full-Forward
285	1989	Nicholas English	Tipperary	Left Full-Forward
286	1990	Ger Cunningham	Cork	Goalkeeper
287	1990	John Considine	Cork	Right Full-Back
288	1990	Noel Sheehy	Tipperary	Full-Back
289	1990	Seán O'Gorman	Cork	Left Full-Back
290	1990	Peter Finnerty	Galway	Right Half-Back
291	1990	Jim Cashman	Cork	Centre Half-Back
292	1990	Liam Dunne	Wexford	Left Half-Back
293	1990	Michael Coleman	Galway	Centrefield
294	1990	Johnny Pilkington	Offaly	Centrefield
295	1990	Michael Cleary	Tipperary	Right Half-Forward
296	1990	Joe Cooney	Galway	Centre Half-Forward
297	1990	Tony O'Sullivan	Cork	Left Half-Forward
298	1990	Éamonn Morrissey	Kilkenny	Right Full-Forward
299	1990	Brian McMahon	Dublin	Full-Forward
300	1990	John Fitzgibbon	Cork	Left Full-Forward

List of Hurling All-Stars

#	Year	Name	County	Position
301	1991	Michael Walsh	Kilkenny	Goalkeeper
302	1991	Paul Delaney	Tipperary	Right Full-Back
303	1991	Noel Sheehy	Tipperary	Full-Back
304	1991	Seán Treacy	Galway	Left Full-Back
305	1991	Conal Bonnar	Tipperary	Right Half-Back
306	1991	Jim Cashman	Cork	Centre Half-Back
307	1991	Cathal Casey	Cork	Left Half-Back
308	1991	Terence McNaughton	Antrim	Centrefield
309	1991	John Leahy	Tipperary	Centrefield
310	1991	Michael Cleary	Tipperary	Right Half-Forward
311	1991	Gary Kirby	Limerick	Centre Half-Forward
312	1991	DJ Carey	Kilkenny	Left Half-Forward
313	1991	Pat Fox	Tipperary	Right Full-Forward
314	1991	Cormac Bonnar	Tipperary	Full-Forward
315	1991	John Fitzgibbon	Cork	Left Full-Forward
316	1992	Tommy Quaid	Limerick	Goalkeeper
317	1992	Brian Corcoran	Cork	Right Full-Back
318	1992	Pat Dwyer	Kilkenny	Full-Back
319	1992	Liam Simpson	Kilkenny	Left Full-Back
320	1992	Brian Whelahan	Offaly	Right Half-Back
321	1992	Ciarán Carey	Limerick	Centre Half-Back
322	1992	Willie O'Connor	Kilkenny	Left Half-Back
323	1992	Michael Phelan	Kilkenny	Centrefield
324	1992	Seánie McCarthy	Cork	Centrefield
325	1992	Gerard McGrattan	Down	Right Half-Forward
326	1992	John Power	Kilkenny	Centre Half-Forward
327	1992	Tony O'Sullivan	Cork	Left Half-Forward
328	1992	Michael Cleary	Tipperary	Right Full-Forward
329	1992	Liam Fennelly	Kilkenny	Full-Forward
330	1992	DJ Carey	Kilkenny	Left Full-Forward
331	1993	Michael Walsh (K)	Kilkenny	Goalkeeper
332	1993	Eddie O'Connor	Kilkenny	Right Full-Back
333	1993	Seán O'Gorman	Cork	Full-Back
334	1993	Liam Simpson	Kilkenny	Left Full-Back
335	1993	Liam Dunne	Wexford	Right Half-Back
336	1993	Pat O'Neill	Kilkenny	Centre Half-Back
337	1993	Pádraig Kelly	Galway	Left Half-Back
338	1993	Pat Malone	Galway	Centrefield
339	1993	Paul McKillen	Antrim	Centrefield
340	1993	Martin Storey	Wexford	Right Half-Forward
341	1993	John Power	Kilkenny	Centre Half-Forward
342	1993	DJ Carey	Kilkenny	Left Half-Forward
343	1993	Michael Cleary	Tipperary	Right Full-Forward
344	1993	Joe Rabbitte	Galway	Full-Forward
345	1993	Barry Egan	Cork	Left Full-Forward
346	1994	Joe Quaid	Limerick	Goalkeeper
347	1994	Anthony Daly	Clare	Right Full-Back
348	1994	Kevin Kinahan	Offaly	Full-Back
349	1994	Martin Hanamay	Offaly	Left Full-Back
350	1994	Dave Clarke	Limerick	Right Half-Back
351	1994	Hubert Rigney	Offaly	Centre Half-Back
352	1994	Kevin Martin	Offaly	Left Half-Back
353	1994	Mike Houlihan	Limerick	Centrefield
354	1994	Ciarán Carey	Limerick	Centrefield
355	1994	Johnny Dooley	Offaly	Right Half-Forward
356	1994	Gary Kirby	Limerick	Centre Half-Forward
357	1994	John Leahy	Tipperary	Left Half-Forward
358	1994	Billy Dooley	Offaly	Right Full-Forward
359	1994	DJ Carey	Kilkenny	Full-Forward
360	1994	Damien Quigley	Limerick	Left Full-Forward
361	1995	Davy Fitzgerald	Clare	Goalkeeper
362	1995	Kevin Kinahan	Offaly	Right Full-Back
363	1995	Brian Lohan	Clare	Full-Back
364	1995	Liam Doyle	Clare	Left Full-Back
365	1995	Brian Whelahan	Offaly	Right Half-Back
366	1995	Seánie McMahon	Clare	Centre Half-Back
367	1995	Anthony Daly	Clare	Left Half-Back
368	1995	Michael Coleman	Galway	Centrefield
369	1995	Ollie Baker	Clare	Centrefield
370	1995	Johnny Dooley	Offaly	Right Half-Forward
371	1995	Gary Kirby	Limerick	Centre Half-Forward
372	1995	Jamesie O'Connor	Clare	Left Half-Forward
373	1995	Billy Dooley	Offaly	Right Full-Forward
374	1995	DJ Carey	Kilkenny	Full-Forward
375	1995	Ger O'Loughlin	Clare	Left Full-Forward
376	1996	Joe Quaid	Limerick	Goalkeeper
377	1996	Tom Helebert	Galway	Right Full-Back
378	1996	Brian Lohan	Clare	Full-Back
379	1996	Larry O'Gorman	Wexford	Left Full-Back
380	1996	Liam Dunne	Wexford	Right Half-Back
381	1996	Ciarán Carey	Limerick	Centre Half-Back
382	1996	Mark Foley	Limerick	Left Half-Back
383	1996	Adrian Fenlon	Wexford	Centrefield
384	1996	Mike Houlihan	Limerick	Centrefield
385	1996	Rory McCarthy	Wexford	Right Half-Forward
386	1996	Martin Storey	Wexford	Centre Half-Forward
387	1996	Larry Murphy	Wexford	Left Half-Forward
388	1996	Liam Cahill	Tipperary	Right Full-Forward
389	1996	Gary Kirby	Limerick	Full-Forward
390	1996	Tom Dempsey	Wexford	Left Full-Forward
391	1997	Damien Fitzhenry	Wexford	Goalkeeper
392	1997	Paul Shelly	Tipperary	Right Full-Back
393	1997	Brian Lohan	Clare	Full-Back
394	1997	Willie O'Connor	Kilkenny	Left Full-Back
395	1997	Liam Doyle	Clare	Right Half-Back
396	1997	Seánie McMahon	Clare	Centre Half-Back
397	1997	Liam Keoghan	Kilkenny	Left Half-Back
398	1997	Colin Lynch	Clare	Centrefield
399	1997	Tommy Dunne	Tipperary	Centrefield
400	1997	Jamesie O'Connor	Clare	Right Half-Forward
401	1997	Declan Ryan	Tipperary	Centre Half-Forward
402	1997	John Leahy	Tipperary	Left Half-Forward
403	1997	Kevin Broderick	Galway	Right Full-Forward
404	1997	Ger O'Loughlin	Clare	Full-Forward
405	1997	DJ Carey	Kilkenny	Left Full-Forward
406	1998	Stephen Byrne	Offaly	Goalkeeper
407	1998	Willie O'Connor	Kilkenny	Right Full-Back
408	1998	Kevin Kinahan	Offaly	Full-Back
409	1998	Martin Hanamay	Offaly	Left Full-Back
410	1998	Anthony Daly	Clare	Right Half-Back
411	1998	Seánie McMahon	Clare	Centre Half-Back
412	1998	Kevin Martin	Offaly	Left Half-Back
413	1998	Tony Browne	Waterford	Centrefield
414	1998	Ollie Baker	Clare	Centrefield
415	1998	Michael Duignan	Offaly	Right Half-Forward
416	1998	Martin Storey	Wexford	Centre Half-Forward
417	1998	Jamesie O'Connor	Clare	Left Half-Forward
418	1998	Joe Dooley	Offaly	Right Full-Forward
419	1998	Brian Whelahan	Offaly	Full-Forward
420	1998	Charlie Carter	Kilkenny	Left Full-Forward

#	Year	Player	County	Position
421	1999	Dónal Óg Cusack	Cork	Goalkeeper
422	1999	Fergal Ryan	Cork	Right Full-Back
423	1999	Diarmuid O'Sullivan	Cork	Full-Back
424	1999	Frank Lohan	Clare	Left Full-Back
425	1999	Brian Whelahan	Offaly	Right Half-Back
426	1999	Brian Corcoran	Cork	Centre Half-Back
427	1999	Peter Barry	Kilkenny	Left Half-Back
428	1999	Andy Comerford	Kilkenny	Centrefield
429	1999	Tommy Dunne	Tipperary	Centrefield
430	1999	DJ Carey	Kilkenny	Right Half-Forward
431	1999	John Troy	Offaly	Centre Half-Forward
432	1999	Brian McEvoy	Kilkenny	Left Half-Forward
433	1999	Seánie McGrath	Cork	Right Full-Forward
434	1999	Joe Deane	Cork	Full-Forward
435	1999	Niall Gilligan	Clare	Left Full-Forward
436	2000	Brendan Cummins	Tipperary	Goalkeeper
437	2000	Noel Hickey	Kilkenny	Right Full-Back
438	2000	Diarmuid O'Sullivan	Cork	Full-Back
439	2000	Willie O'Connor	Kilkenny	Left Full-Back
440	2000	John Carroll	Tipperary	Right Half-Back
441	2000	Eamon Kennedy	Kilkenny	Centre Half-Back
442	2000	Peter Barry	Kilkenny	Left Half-Back
443	2000	Johnny Dooley	Offaly	Centrefield
444	2000	Andy Comerford	Kilkenny	Centrefield
445	2000	Denis Byrne	Kilkenny	Right Half-Forward
446	2000	Joe Rabbitte	Galway	Centre Half-Forward
447	2000	Henry Shefflin	Kilkenny	Left Half-Forward
448	2000	Charlie Carter	Kilkenny	Right Full-Forward
449	2000	DJ Carey	Kilkenny	Full-Forward
450	2000	Joe Deane	Cork	Left Full-Forward
451	2001	Brendan Cummins	Tipperary	Goalkeeper
452	2001	Darragh Ryan	Wexford	Right Full-Back
453	2001	Philip Maher	Tipperary	Full-Back
454	2001	Ollie Canning	Galway	Left Full-Back
455	2001	Éamonn Corcoran	Tipperary	Right Half-Back
456	2001	Liam Hodgens	Galway	Centre Half-Back
457	2001	Mark Foley	Limerick	Left Half-Back
458	2001	Tommy Dunne	Tipperary	Centrefield
459	2001	Eddie Enright	Tipperary	Centrefield
460	2001	Mark O'Leary	Tipperary	Right Half-Forward
461	2001	Jamesie O'Connor	Clare	Centre Half-Forward
462	2001	Kevin Broderick	Galway	Left Half-Forward
463	2001	Charlie Carter	Kilkenny	Right Full-Forward
464	2001	Eugene Cloonan	Galway	Full-Forward
465	2001	Eoin Kelly	Tipperary	Left Full-Forward
466	2002	Davy Fitzgerald	Clare	Goalkeeper
467	2002	Michael Kavanagh	Kilkenny	Right Full-Back
468	2002	Brian Lohan	Clare	Full-Back
469	2002	Philly Larkin Jnr	Kilkenny	Left Full-Back
470	2002	Fergal Hartley	Waterford	Right Half-Back
471	2002	Peter Barry	Kilkenny	Centre Half-Back
472	2002	Paul Kelly	Tipperary	Left Half-Back
473	2002	Colin Lynch	Clare	Centrefield
474	2002	Derek Lyng	Kilkenny	Centrefield
475	2002	Eoin Kelly	Waterford	Right Half-Forward
476	2002	Henry Shefflin	Kilkenny	Centre Half-Forward
477	2002	Ken McGrath	Waterford	Left Half-Forward
478	2002	Eoin Kelly	Tipperary	Right Full-Forward
479	2002	Martin Comerford	Kilkenny	Full-Forward
480	2002	DJ Carey	Kilkenny	Left Full-Forward
481	2003	Brendan Cummins	Tipperary	Goalkeeper
482	2003	Michael Kavanagh	Kilkenny	Right Full-Back
483	2003	Noel Hickey	Kilkenny	Full-Back
484	2003	Ollie Canning	Galway	Left Full-Back
485	2003	Seán Óg Ó hAilpín	Cork	Right Half-Back
486	2003	Ronan Curran	Cork	Centre Half-Back
487	2003	JJ Delaney	Kilkenny	Left Half-Back
488	2003	Derek Lyng	Kilkenny	Centrefield
489	2003	Tommy Walsh	Kilkenny	Centrefield
490	2003	John Mullane	Waterford	Right Half-Forward
491	2003	Henry Shefflin	Kilkenny	Centre Half-Forward
492	2003	Eddie Brennan	Kilkenny	Left Half-Forward
493	2003	Setanta Ó hAilpín	Cork	Right Full-Forward
494	2003	Martin Comerford	Kilkenny	Full-Forward
495	2003	Joe Deane	Cork	Left Full-Forward
496	2004	Damien Fitzhenry	Wexford	Goalkeeper
497	2004	Wayne Sherlock	Cork	Right Full-Back
498	2004	Diarmuid O'Sullivan	Cork	Full-Back
499	2004	Tommy Walsh	Kilkenny	Left Full-Back
500	2004	JJ Delaney	Kilkenny	Right Half-Back
501	2004	Ronan Curran	Cork	Centre Half-Back
502	2004	Seán Óg Ó hAilpín	Cork	Left Half-Back
503	2004	Ken McGrath	Waterford	Centrefield
504	2004	Jerry O'Connor	Cork	Centrefield
505	2004	Dan Shanahan	Waterford	Right Half-Forward
506	2004	Niall McCarthy	Cork	Centre Half-Forward
507	2004	Henry Shefflin	Kilkenny	Left Half-Forward
508	2004	Eoin Kelly	Tipperary	Right Full-Forward
509	2004	Brian Corcoran	Cork	Full-Forward
510	2004	Paul Flynn	Waterford	Left Full-Forward
511	2005	Davy Fitzgerald	Clare	Goalkeeper
512	2005	Pat Mulcahy	Cork	Right Full-Back
513	2005	Diarmuid O'Sullivan	Cork	Full-Back
514	2005	Ollie Canning	Galway	Left Full-Back
515	2005	Derick Hardiman	Galway	Right Half-Back
516	2005	John Gardiner	Cork	Centre Half-Back
517	2005	Seán Óg Ó hAilpín	Cork	Left Half-Back
518	2005	Jerry O'Connor	Cork	Centrefield
519	2005	Paul Kelly	Tipperary	Centrefield
520	2005	Ben O'Connor	Cork	Right Half-Forward
521	2005	Henry Shefflin	Kilkenny	Centre Half-Forward
522	2005	Tommy Walsh	Kilkenny	Left Half-Forward
523	2005	Ger Farragher	Galway	Right Full-Forward
524	2005	Eoin Kelly	Tipperary	Full-Forward
525	2005	Damien Hayes	Galway	Left Full-Forward
526	2006	Dónal Óg Cusack	Cork	Goalkeeper
527	2006	Eoin Murphy	Waterford	Right Full-Back
528	2006	JJ Delaney	Kilkenny	Full-Back
529	2006	Brian Murphy	Cork	Left Full-Back
530	2006	Tony Browne	Waterford	Right Half-Back
531	2006	Ronan Curran	Cork	Centre Half-Back
532	2006	Tommy Walsh	Kilkenny	Left Half-Back
533	2006	Jerry O'Connor	Cork	Centrefield
534	2006	James "Cha" Fitzpatrick	Kilkenny	Centrefield
535	2006	Dan Shanahan	Waterford	Right Half-Forward
536	2006	Henry Shefflin	Kilkenny	Centre Half-Forward
537	2006	Eddie Brennan	Kilkenny	Left Half-Forward
538	2006	Eoin Kelly	Tipperary	Right Full-Forward
539	2006	Martin Comerford	Kilkenny	Full-Forward
540	2006	Tony Griffin	Clare	Left Full-Forward

List of Hurling All-Stars

#	Year	Name	County	Position
541	2007	Brian Murray	Limerick	Goalkeeper
542	2007	Michael Kavanagh	Kilkenny	Right Full-Back
543	2007	Declan Fanning	Tipperary	Full-Back
544	2007	Jackie Tyrell	Kilkenny	Left Full-Back
545	2007	Tommy Walsh	Kilkenny	Right Half-Back
546	2007	Ken McGrath	Waterford	Centre Half-Back
547	2007	Tony Browne	Waterford	Left Half-Back
548	2007	Michael Walsh	Waterford	Centrefield
549	2007	James "Cha" Fitzpatrick	Kilkenny	Centrefield
550	2007	Dan Shanahan	Waterford	Right Half-Forward
551	2007	Ollie Moran	Limerick	Centre Half-Forward
552	2007	Stephen Molumphy	Waterford	Left Half-Forward
553	2007	Andrew O'Shaughnessy	Limerick	Right Full-Forward
554	2007	Henry Shefflin	Kilkenny	Full-Forward
555	2007	Eddie Brennan	Kilkenny	Left Full-Forward
556	2008	Brendan Cummins	Tipperary	Goalkeeper
557	2008	Michael Kavanagh	Kilkenny	Right Full-Back
558	2008	Noel Hickey	Kilkenny	Full-Back
559	2008	Jackie Tyrell	Kilkenny	Left Full-Back
560	2008	Tommy Walsh	Kilkenny	Right Half-Back
561	2008	Conor O'Mahoney	Tipperary	Centre Half-Back
562	2008	JJ Delaney	Kilkenny	Left Half-Back
563	2008	James "Cha" Fitzpatrick	Kilkenny	Centrefield
564	2008	Shane McGrath	Tipperary	Centrefield
565	2008	Ben O'Connor	Cork	Right Half-Forward
566	2008	Henry Shefflin	Kilkenny	Centre Half-Forward
567	2008	Eoin Larkin	Kilkenny	Left Half-Forward
568	2008	Eddie Brennan	Kilkenny	Right Full-Forward
569	2008	Eoin Kelly	Waterford	Full-Forward
570	2008	Joe Canning	Galway	Left Full-Forward
571	2009	PJ Ryan	Kilkenny	Goalkeeper
572	2009	Ollie Canning	Galway	Right Full-Back
573	2009	Pádraic Maher	Tipperary	Full-Back
574	2009	Jackie Tyrell	Kilkenny	Left Full-Back
575	2009	Tommy Walsh	Kilkenny	Right Half-Back
576	2009	Michael Walsh	Waterford	Centre Half-Back
577	2009	Conor O'Mahoney	Tipperary	Left Half-Back
578	2009	Michael Rice	Kilkenny	Centrefield
579	2009	Alan McCrabbe	Dublin	Centrefield
580	2009	Lar Corbett	Tipperary	Right Half-Forward
581	2009	Henry Shefflin	Kilkenny	Centre Half-Forward
582	2009	Eoin Larkin	Kilkenny	Left Half-Forward
583	2009	Noel McGrath	Tipperary	Right Full-Forward
584	2009	Joe Canning	Galway	Full-Forward
585	2009	John Mullane	Waterford	Left Full-Forward
586	2010	Brendan Cummins	Tipperary	Goalkeeper
587	2010	Noel Connors	Waterford	Right Full-Back
588	2010	Paul Curran	Tipperary	Full-Back
589	2010	Jackie Tyrell	Kilkenny	Left Full-Back
590	2010	Tommy Walsh	Kilkenny	Right Half-Back
591	2010	Michael Walsh	Waterford	Centre Half-Back
592	2010	JJ Delaney	Kilkenny	Left Half-Back
593	2010	Michael Fennelly	Kilkenny	Centrefield
594	2010	Brendan Maher	Tipperary	Centrefield
595	2010	Damien Hayes	Galway	Right Half-Forward
596	2010	Noel McGrath	Tipperary	Centre Half-Forward
597	2010	Lar Corbett	Tipperary	Left Half-Forward
598	2010	John Mullane	Waterford	Right Full-Forward
599	2010	Richie Power Jnr	Kilkenny	Full-Forward
600	2010	Eoin Kelly	Tipperary	Left Full-Forward
601	2011	Gary Maguire	Dublin	Goalkeeper
602	2011	Paul Murphy	Kilkenny	Right Full-Back
603	2011	Paul Curran	Tipperary	Full-Back
604	2011	Michael Cahill	Tipperary	Left Full-Back
605	2011	Tommy Walsh	Kilkenny	Right Half-Back
606	2011	Brian Hogan	Kilkenny	Centre Half-Back
607	2011	Pádraic Maher	Tipperary	Left Half-Back
608	2011	Liam Rushe	Dublin	Centrefield
609	2011	Michael Fennelly	Kilkenny	Centrefield
610	2011	Michael Rice	Kilkenny	Right Half-Forward
611	2011	Richie Power Jnr	Kilkenny	Centre Half-Forward
612	2011	Henry Shefflin	Kilkenny	Left Half-Forward
613	2011	John Mullane	Waterford	Right Full-Forward
614	2011	Lar Corbett	Tipperary	Full-Forward
615	2011	Richie Hogan	Kilkenny	Left Full-Forward
616	2012	Anthony Nash	Cork	Goalkeeper
617	2012	Paul Murphy	Kilkenny	Right Full-Back
618	2012	JJ Delaney	Kilkenny	Full-Back
619	2012	Fergal Moore	Galway	Left Full-Back
620	2012	Brendan Bugler	Clare	Right Half-Back
621	2012	Brian Hogan	Kilkenny	Centre Half-Back
622	2012	David Collins	Galway	Left Half-Back
623	2012	Iarla Tannian	Galway	Centrefield
624	2012	Kevin Moran	Waterford	Centrefield
625	2012	TJ Reid	Kilkenny	Right Half-Forward
626	2012	Henry Shefflin	Kilkenny	Centre Half-Forward
627	2012	Damien Hayes	Galway	Left Half-Forward
628	2012	John Mullane	Waterford	Right Full-Forward
629	2012	Joe Canning	Galway	Full-Forward
630	2012	David Burke	Galway	Left Full-Forward
631	2013	Anthony Nash	Cork	Goalkeeper
632	2013	Richie McCarthy	Limerick	Right Full-Back
633	2013	Peter Kelly	Dublin	Full-Back
634	2013	David McInerney	Clare	Left Full-Back
635	2013	Brendan Bugler	Clare	Right Half-Back
636	2013	Liam Rushe	Dublin	Centre Half-Back
637	2013	Patrick Donnellan	Clare	Left Half-Back
638	2013	Colm Galvin	Clare	Centrefield
639	2013	Conor Ryan	Clare	Centrefield
640	2013	Séamus Harnedy	Cork	Right Half-Forward
641	2013	Tony Kelly	Clare	Centre Half-Forward
642	2013	Danny Sutcliffe	Dublin	Left Half-Forward
643	2013	Pádraic Collins	Clare	Right Full-Forward
644	2013	Patrick Horgan	Cork	Full-Forward
645	2013	Conor McGrath	Clare	Left Full-Forward
646	2014	Darren Gleeson	Tipperary	Goalkeeper
647	2014	Paul Murphy	Kilkenny	Right Full-Back
648	2014	JJ Delaney	Kilkenny	Full-Back
649	2014	Séamus Hickey	Limerick	Left Full-Back
650	2014	Brendan Maher	Tipperary	Right Half-Back
651	2014	Pádraic Maher	Tipperary	Centre Half-Back
652	2014	Cillian Buckley	Kilkenny	Left Half-Back
653	2014	Richie Hogan	Kilkenny	Centrefield
654	2014	Shane McGrath	Tipperary	Centrefield
655	2014	John O'Dwyer	Tipperary	Right Half-Forward
656	2014	Patrick "Bonnar" Maher	Tipperary	Centre Half-Forward
657	2014	TJ Reid	Kilkenny	Left Half-Forward
658	2014	Colin Fennelly	Kilkenny	Right Full-Forward
659	2014	Séamus Callanan	Tipperary	Full-Forward
660	2014	Shane Dowling	Limerick	Left Full-Forward

#	Year	Name	County	Position
661	2015	Colm Callanan	Galway	Goalkeeper
662	2015	Paul Murphy	Kilkenny	Right Full-Back
663	2015	Joey Holden	Kilkenny	Full-Back
664	2015	Noel Connors	Waterford	Left Full-Back
665	2015	Daithí Burke	Galway	Right Half-Back
666	2015	Tadhg de Búrca	Waterford	Centre Half-Back
667	2015	Cillian Buckley	Kilkenny	Left Half-Back
668	2015	Michael Fennelly	Kilkenny	Centrefield
669	2015	David Burke	Galway	Centrefield
670	2015	Cathal Mannion	Galway	Right Half-Forward
671	2015	Richie Hogan	Kilkenny	Centre Half-Forward
672	2015	TJ Reid	Kilkenny	Left Half-Forward
673	2015	Ger Aylward	Kilkenny	Right Full-Forward
674	2015	Séamus Callanan	Tipperary	Full-Forward
675	2015	Maurice Shanahan	Waterford	Left Full-Forward
676	2016	Eoin Murphy	Kilkenny	Goalkeeper
677	2016	Cathal Barrett	Tipperary	Right Full-Back
678	2016	James Barry	Tipperary	Full-Back
679	2016	Daithí Burke	Galway	Left Full-Back
680	2016	Pádraig Walsh	Kilkenny	Right Half-Back
681	2016	Ronan Maher	Tipperary	Centre Half-Back
682	2016	Pádraic Maher	Tipperary	Left Half-Back
683	2016	Jamie Barron	Waterford	Centrefield
684	2016	David Burke	Galway	Centrefield
685	2016	Walter Walsh	Kilkenny	Right Half-Forward
686	2016	Austin Gleeson	Waterford	Centre Half-Forward
687	2016	Patrick "Bonnar" Maher	Tipperary	Left Half-Forward
688	2016	Richie Hogan	Kilkenny	Right Full-Forward
689	2016	Séamus Callanan	Tipperary	Full-Forward
690	2016	John McGrath	Tipperary	Left Full-Forward
691	2017	Stephen O'Keeffe	Waterford	Goalkeeper
692	2017	Pádraic Mannion	Galway	Right Full-Back
693	2017	Daithí Burke	Galway	Full-Back
694	2017	Noel Connors	Waterford	Left Full-Back
695	2017	Pádraic Maher	Tipperary	Right Half-Back
696	2017	Gearóid McInerney	Galway	Centre Half-Back
697	2017	Mark Coleman	Cork	Left Half-Back
698	2017	Jamie Barron	Waterford	Centrefield
699	2017	David Burke	Galway	Centrefield
700	2017	Kevin Moran	Waterford	Right Half-Forward
701	2017	Joe Canning	Galway	Centre Half-Forward
702	2017	Michael Walsh	Waterford	Left Half-Forward
703	2017	Conor Whelan	Galway	Right Full-Forward
704	2017	Conor Cooney	Galway	Full-Forward
705	2017	Patrick Horgan	Cork	Left Full-Forward
706	2018	Eoin Murphy	Kilkenny	Goalkeeper
707	2018	Seán Finn	Limerick	Right Full-Back
708	2018	Daithí Burke	Galway	Full-Back
709	2018	Richie English	Limerick	Left Full-Back
710	2018	Pádraic Mannion	Galway	Right Half-Back
711	2018	Declan Hannon	Limerick	Centre Half-Back
712	2018	Dan Morrissey	Limerick	Left Half-Back
713	2018	Cian Lynch	Limerick	Centrefield
714	2018	Darragh Fitzgibbon	Cork	Centrefield
715	2018	Peter Duggan	Clare	Right Half-Forward
716	2018	Joe Canning	Galway	Centre Half-Forward
717	2018	Séamus Harnedy	Cork	Left Half-Forward
718	2018	Patrick Horgan	Cork	Right Full-Forward
719	2018	John Conlon	Clare	Full-Forward
720	2018	Graeme Mulcahy	Limerick	Left Full-Forward
721	2019	Brian Hogan	Tipperary	Goalkeeper
722	2019	Seán Finn	Limerick	Right Full-Back
723	2019	Ronan Maher	Tipperary	Full-Back
724	2019	Cathal Barrett	Tipperary	Left Full-Back
725	2019	Brendan Maher	Tipperary	Right Half-Back
726	2019	Pádraig Walsh	Kilkenny	Centre Half-Back
727	2019	Pádraic Maher	Tipperary	Left Half-Back
728	2019	Noel McGrath	Tipperary	Centrefield
729	2019	Diarmuid O'Keeffe	Wexford	Centrefield
730	2019	Lee Chin	Wexford	Right Half-Forward
731	2019	TJ Reid	Kilkenny	Centre Half-Forward
732	2019	Colin Fennelly	Kilkenny	Left Half-Forward
733	2019	Aaron Gillane	Limerick	Right Full-Forward
734	2019	Séamus Callanan	Tipperary	Full-Forward
735	2019	Patrick Horgan	Cork	Left Full-Forward
736	2020	Nickie Quaid	Limerick	Goalkeeper
737	2020	Seán Finn	Limerick	Right Full-Back
738	2020	Dan Morrissey	Limerick	Full-Back
739	2020	Daithí Burke	Galway	Left Full-Back
740	2020	Diarmaid Byrnes	Limerick	Right Half-Back
741	2020	Tadhg de Búrca	Waterford	Centre Half-Back
742	2020	Kyle Hayes	Limerick	Left Half-Back
743	2020	Jamie Barron	Waterford	Centrefield
744	2020	Tony Kelly	Clare	Centrefield
745	2020	Gearóid Hegarty	Limerick	Right Half-Forward
746	2020	Cian Lynch	Limerick	Centre Half-Forward
747	2020	Tom Morrissey	Limerick	Left Half-Forward
748	2020	Aaron Gillane	Limerick	Right Full-Forward
749	2020	TJ Reid	Kilkenny	Full-Forward
750	2020	Stephen Bennett	Waterford	Left Full-Forward

All-Star Gazing

| Henry Shefflin

Hurling All-Stars Roll of Honour

| DJ Carey | Tommy Walsh | Noel Skehan | JJ Delaney |

| Pádraic Maher | Eoin Kelly | Nicky English | Joe McKenna |

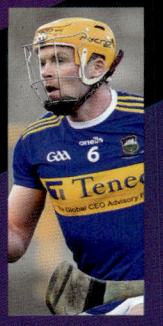

Shefflin, Henry	11	O'Connor, Jerry	3
Carey, DJ	9	Hickey, Noel	3
Walsh, Tommy	9	Ó hAilpín, Seán Óg	3
Skehan, Noel	7	Purcell, Kieran	3
Delaney, JJ	7	Barry, Peter	3
Maher, Pádraic	6	Shanahan, Dan	3
Kelly, Eoin	6	Carter, Charlie	3
English, Nicholas	6	Fitzpatrick, James	3
McKenna, Joe	6	Cummins, Ray	3
Cummins, Brendan	5	McGrath, Ken	3
Keher, Eddie	5	Jacob, Mick	3
Hennessy, Joe	5	Dunne, Liam	3
Mullane, John	5	Cashman, Tom	3
Cooney, Joe	5	Dunne, Tommy	3
Barry Murphy, Jimmy	5	Curran, Ronan	3
Canning, Joe	5	Durack, Séamus	3
Fenton, John	5	Daly, Anthony	3
O'Sullivan, Tony	5	Kinahan, Kevin	3
Finnerty, Peter	5	O'Connor, Tadhg	3
Hartigan, Pat	5	Deane, Joe	3
Henderson, Ger	5	O'Doherty, Martin	3
Reid, TJ	5	Browne, Tony	3
Burke, Daithí	5	O'Leary, Seánie	3
Cleary, Michael	4	Leahy, John	3
Walsh, Michael 'Brick'	4	Fennelly, Michael	3
O'Sullivan, Diarmuid	4	Linnane, Sylvie	3
Tyrrell, Jackie	4	Comerford, Martin	3
Clarke, Iggy	4	Ryan, Bobby	3
Burke, David	4	Loughnane, Francis	3
O'Connor, Jamesie	4	Connors, Noel	3
Cummins, Frank	4	Maher, Brendan	3
Quigley, Martin	4	Storey, Martin	3
O'Brien, Liam	4	Dooley, Johnny	3
Hogan, Richie	4	McCarthy, Charlie	3
Lohan, Brian	4	Hayes, Damien	3
Whelahan, Brian	4	Hayes, Conor	3
Fennelly, Liam	4	Horgan, John	3
Horgan, Patrick	4	Finn, Seán	3
Murphy, Paul	4	Barron, Jamie	3
Kavanagh, Michael	4	Delaney, Pat (KK)	2
O'Connor, Willie	4	Rushe, Liam	2
Cunningham, Ger	4	Callinan, John	2
Callanan, Séamus	4	Kelly, Paul	2
Canning, Ollie	4	Carroll, Pat	2
Coughlan, Denis	4	Power, John	2
Kirby, Gary	4	Lane, Noel	2
Larkin, Phil 'Fan'	4	Barrett, Cathal	2
Brennan, Eddie	4	Larkin, Eoin	2
McMahon, Seánie	3	Coughlan, Ger	2
Enright, Leonard	3	Dooley, Billy	2
Fox, Pat	3	Bugler, Brendan	2
McCurtain, Dermot	3	Rabbitte, Joe	2
Hanamy, Martin	3	Sheehy, Noel	2
Brennan, Mick	3	Cashman, Jim	2
Coleman, Michael	3	Buckley, Cillian	2
Corbett, Lar	3	Bonnar, Conal	2
Fitzgerald, Davy	3	Cody, Brian	2
Corcoran, Brian	3	Loughnane, Ger	2
McGrath, Noel	3	Henderson, Pat	2
Carey, Ciarán	3	Lynch, Colin	2
Murphy, Eoin (KK)	2	O'Loughlin, Ger	2
Cregan, Eamonn	3	Lyng, Derek	2

Hogan, Brian (KK)	2	Burke, Daithí	2	Hardiman, Derek	1	Bennis, Richie	1
Power Jnr, Richie	2	Morrissey, Dan	2	Barr, Ciarán	1	Pilkington, Johnny	1
Fitzgibbon, John	2	de Búrca, Tadgh	2	Quaid, Tommy	1	Brennan, Kieran	1
Quaid, Joe	2	Griffin, Tony	1	Barry, James	1	Hannon, Declan	1
Fitzhenry, Damien	2	Murphy, Larry	1	Crowley, Johnny	1	McGrath, Seánie	1
Rice, Michael	2	Chin, Lee	1	Lynskey, Brendan	1	Prendergast, Paddy	1
Maher, Patrick	2	Cloonan, Eugene	1	Rigney, Hubert	1	Conran, John	1
Ryan, Declan	2	Gardiner, John	1	Maguire, Gary	1	Crotty, Mick	1
Maher, Ronan	2	Cahill, Michael	1	Ryan, Aidan	1	Delaney, Pat (OY)	1
Silke, Seán	2	Keating, Michael	1	Dwyer, Pat	1	McGratten, Gerard	1
Maher, Tony	2	Cleary, Eamonn	1	Byrne, Denis	1	Quigley, Damien	1
Treacy, Jim	2	Coen, Seamus	1	Egan, Barry	1	McInerney, David	1
Mahon, Steve	2	Delaney, Paul	1	Hennessey, Kevin	1	Hartley, Fergal	1
Walsh, Michael	2	O'Keeffe, Diarmuid	1	Buggy, Ned	1	McInerney, Gearóid	1
Mannion, Pádraic	2	Dempsey, Tom	1	Shelly, Paul	1	Crowley, Tim	1
O'Connor, George	2	Critchley, Pat	1	Maher, Philip	1	Considine, John	1
Martin, Kevin	2	Donnellan, Patrick	1	Currams, Liam	1	Heffernan, Christy	1
Cusack, Donal Óg	2	Ryan, Conor	1	English, Richie	1	Coogan, Martin	1
Fitzpatrick, Billy	2	Kelly, Paddy	1	Tannian, Iarla	1	Helebert, Tom	1
Comerford, Andy	2	Hogan, Ken	1	Enright, Eddie	1	McKillen, Paul	1
Bonnar, Cormac	2	Kelly, Pádraig	1	Honan, Colm	1	Butler, Tommy	1
O'Gorman, Seán	2	Carroll, John	1	Conlon, John	1	Cooney, Conor	1
Fleury, Pat	2	Donnelly, Dessie	1	Cahill, Liam	1	Henderson, John	1
Commins, John	2	Flynn, Paul	1	Malone, Mick	1	McMahon, Brian	1
Coughlan, Eugene	2	Kelly, Peter	1	Whelan, Conor	1	Ryan, Darragh	1
McGrath, Michael	2	Forde, Bernie	1	Malone, Pat	1	Fitzgibbon, Darragh	1
O'Mahony, Conor	2	Kennedy, Eamonn	1	Murphy, Brian (Bride Rvrs)	1	Ryan, Éanna	1
Fogarty, Aidan	2	Gleeson, Darren	1	Mannion, Cathal	1	Ryan, PJ	1
Connolly, John	2	Keogh, Christy	1	Flaherty, Johnny	1	McNaughton, Terence	1
McGrath, Shane	2	Casey, Noel	1	Fanning, Declan	1	Shanahan, Maurice	1
Power Snr, Richie	2	Keoghan, Liam	1	Corcoran, Eamonn	1	Molloy, PJ	1
McInerney, Niall	2	Quigley, John	1	Martin, Damien	1	Clarke, Dave	1
Doyle, Liam	2	Kilcoyne, David	1	Murray, Brian	1	Molumphy, Stephen	1
Foley, Mark	2	Roche, Mick	1	Farragher, Ger	1	Sherlock, Wayne	1
Horgan, Pat	2	Kilkenny, Ollie	1	Naughton, Martin	1	Moore, Fergal	1
McLoughney, Pat	2	Ryan, Fergal	1	Fenlon, Adrian	1	Hodgins, Liam	1
Baker, Ollie	2	Coleman, Mark	1	Corrigan, Mark	1	Carr, Declan	1
McMahon, Johnny	2	Hickey, Séamus	1	McCarthy, Gerard	1	Stack, Seán	1
Roche, Con	2	Dooley, Joe	1	Bonnar, Colm	1	Moran, Ollie	1
Burke, Frank	2	Holden, Joey	1	McCarthy, Niall	1	Sutcliffe, Danny	1
Cooney, Jimmy	2	Callanan, Colm	1	Foley, Seán	1	Moroney, Michael	1
Moran, Kevin	2	Walsh, Walter	1	McCarthy, Richie	1	Byrne, Stephen	1
Broderick, Kevin	2	Larkin Jnr, Philly	1	McCarthy, Rory	1	Troy, John	1
Mulcahy, Tomás	2	Bermingham, Mick	1	McCarthy, Seánie	1	Morrissey, Eamonn	1
Keady, Tony	2	Doran, Colm	1	O'Donoghue, Liam	1	Horan, Pádraig	1
Galvin, John	2	Murphy, Willie	1	McCrabbe, Alan	1	Moylan, Pat	1
Simpson, Liam	2	Doran, Tony	1	O'Gorman, Larry	1	Walsh, Mossie	1
Murphy, Brian (Nemo Rgrs)	2	O'Brien, Jim	1	Connolly, Joe	1	Mulcahy, Denis	1
Kelly, Eoin	2	Lawlor, Pat	1	Gilligan, Niall	1	Cleary, Pat	1
Grimes, Éamonn	2	O'Connor, Eddie	1	McDonagh, Joe	1	Mulcahy, Graeme	1
Treacy, Seán	2	Dowling, Shane	1	O'Hara, Dick	1	Aylward, Ger	1
Curran, Paul	2	Galvin, Colm	1	McEvoy, Brian	1	Mulcahy, Pat	1
Kelly, Joachim	2	Collins, David	1	O'Keeffe, Stephen	1	Fitzmaurice, Paudie	1
Nash, Anthony	2	O'Dwyer, John	1	McFetridge, Olcan	1	Hogan, Brian (TIPP)	1
Walsh, Pádraig	2	Duggan, Peter	1	Murphy, Eoin (WD)	1	Quaid, Nickie	1
Harnedy, Séamus	2	Ó hAilpín, Setanta	1	Gleeson, Austin	1	Byrnes, Diarmaid	1
Fennelly, Colin	2	Lohan, Frank	1	McGrath, Conor	1	Hayes, Kyle	1
O'Connor, Ben	2	O'Leary, Mark	1	Greene, Jim	1	Hegarty, Gearóid	1
Houlihan, Mike	2	Duignan, Michael	1	McGrath, John	1	Morrissey, Tom	1
Kelly, Tony	2	O'Neill, Pat	1	O'Shaughnessy, Andrew	1	Bennett, Stephen	1
Gillane, Aaron	2	Collins, Pádraic	1	Fennelly, Ger	1		
Lynch, Cian	2	Phelan, Michael	1	Casey, Cathal	1	**TOTAL PLAYERS**	**369**

Hurling All-Stars County Roll of Honour

ANTRIM
McKillen, Paul	1
Barr, Ciarán	1
McNaughton, Terence	1
Donnelly, Dessie	1
McFetridge, Olcan	1
Total	**5**

CLARE
Lohan, Brian	4
O'Connor, Jamesie	4
McMahon, Seánie	3
Daly, Anthony	3
Durack, Séamus	3
Fitzgerald, Davy	3
O'Loughlin, Ger	2
Doyle, Liam	2
McMahon, Johnny	2
Bugler, Brendan	2
Callinan, John	2
Loughnane, Ger	2
Lynch, Colin	2
Baker, Ollie	2
Kelly, Tony	2
Stack, Seán	1
Moroney, Michael	1
Conlon, John	1
Honan, Colm	1
Gilligan, Niall	1
McInerney, David	1
Donnellan, Patrick	1
Casey, Noel	1
Lohan, Frank	1
Galvin, Colm	1
Collins, Pádraic	1
Ryan, Conor	1
Duggan, Peter	1
McGrath, Conor	1
Griffin, Tony	1
Total	**53**

DOWN
McGrattan, Gerard	1
Total	**1**

DUBLIN
Rushe, Liam	2
Bermingham, Mick	1
McMahon, Brian	1
Kelly, Peter	1
Sutcliffe, Danny	1
Maguire, Gary	1
McCrabbe, Alan	1
Total	**8**

CORK
O'Sullivan, Tony	5
Barry Murphy, Jimmy	5
Fenton, John	5
Horgan, Patrick	4
Coughlan, Denis	4
Cunningham, Ger	4
O'Sullivan, Diarmuid	4
McCurtain, Dermot	3
Corcoran, Brian	3
O'Doherty, Martin	3
O'Leary, Seánie	3
McCarthy, Charlie	3
Ó hAilpín, Seán Óg	3
O'Connor, Jerry	3
Cummins, Ray	3
Deane, Joe	3
Curran, Ronan	3
Cashman, Tom	3
Horgan, John	3
Cashman, Jim	2
Harnedy, Séamus	2
Mulcahy, Tomás	2
Murphy, Brian (Nemo Rgs)	2
O'Gorman, Seán	2
Nash, Anthony	2
Cusack, Donal Óg	2
O'Connor, Ben	2
Fitzgibbon, John	2
Roche, Con	2
Horgan, Pat	2
Maher, Tony	2
McCarthy, Gerard	1
Considine, John	1
Sherlock, Wayne	1
McGrath, Seánie	1
Ó hAilpín, Setanta	1
Moylan, Pat	1
McCarthy, Seánie	1
Mulcahy, Denis	1
Egan, Barry	1
Mulcahy, Pat	1
Malone, Mick	1
Gardiner, John	1
Fitzgibbon, Darragh	1
Coleman, Mark	1
McCarthy, Niall	1
Hennessey, Kevin	1
Ryan, Fergal	1
Crowley, Johnny	1
Casey, Cathal	1
Crowley, Tim	1
Murphy, Brian (Bride Rvrs)	1
Total	**112**

GALWAY
Finnerty, Peter	5
Cooney, Joe	5
Canning, Joe	5
Burke, Daithí	5
Burke, David	4
Clarke, Iggy	4
Canning, Ollie	4
Hayes, Conor	3
Coleman, Michael	3
Linnane, Sylvie	3
Hayes, Damien	3
Mahon, Steve	2
Rabbitte, Joe	2
McGrath, Michael	2
Commins, John	2
Treacy, Seán	2
Connolly, John	2
Mannion, Padraic	2
Cooney, Jimmy	2
McInerney, Niall	2
Burke, Frank	2
Silke, Seán	2
Broderick, Kevin	2
Keady, Tony	2
Lane, Noel	2
Forde, Bernie	1
Cooney, Conor	1
Hardiman, Derek	1
Hodgins, Liam	1
Callanan, Colm	1
Connolly, Joe	1
Moore, Fergal	1
Kelly, Pádraig	1
Cloonan, Eugene	1
Kilkenny, Ollie	1
Helebert, Tom	1
McInerney, Gearóid	1
Coen, Séamus	1
Molloy, P. J.	1
Lynskey, Brendan	1
Naughton, Martin	1
Collins, David	1
Ryan, Éanna	1
Malone, Pat	1
Tannian, Iarla	1
Mannion, Cathal	1
Whelan, Conor	1
Farragher, Ger	1
McDonagh, Joe	1
Total	**96**

KILKENNY
Shefflin, Henry	11
Walsh, Tommy	9
Carey, DJ	9
Skehan, Noel	7
Delaney, JJ	7
Hennessy, Joe	5
Henderson, Ger	5
Keher, Eddie	5
Reid, TJ	5
O'Connor, Willie	4
Larkin, Phil "Fan"	4
Hogan, Richie	4
Cummins, Frank	4
Murphy, Paul	4
Brennan, Eddie	4
Tyrrell, Jackie	4
Fennelly, Liam	4
Kavanagh, Michael	4
O'Brien, Liam	4
Fennelly, Michael	3
Purcell, Kieran	3
Fitzpatrick, James	3
Comerford, Martin	3
Brennan, Mick	3
Hickey, Noel	3
Barry, Peter	3
Carter, Charlie	3
Power Snr, Richie	2
Fennelly, Colin	2
Henderson, Pat	2
Simpson, Liam	2
Power Jnr, Richie	2
Hogan, Brian	2
Power, John	2
Cody, Brian	2
Rice, Michael	2
Fitzpatrick, Billy	2
Buckley, Cillian	2
Comerford, Andy	2
Treacy, Jim	2
Lyng, Derek	2
Walsh, Pádraig	2
Murphy, Eoin	2
Delaney, Pat	2
Larkin, Eoin	2
Walsh, Michael	2
Henderson, John	1
Crotty, Mick	1
Byrne, Denis	1
Heffernan, Christy	1
Larkin Jnr, Philly	1
Coogan, Martin	1
O'Connor, Eddie	1
McEvoy, Brian	1
Holden, Joey	1
Fennelly, Ger	1
O'Hara, Dick	1
O'Neill, Pat	1
Ryan, PJ	1
Phelan, Michael	1
Lawlor, Pat	1
Brennan, Kieran	1
Dwyer, Pat	1
Aylward, Ger	1
Morrissey, Eamonn	1
Kennedy, Eamonn	1
Walsh, Walter	1
Prendergast, Paddy	1
Keoghan, Liam	1
Total	**188**

LAOIS
Critchley, Pat	1
Total	**1**

LIMERICK
McKenna, Joe	6
Hartigan, Pat	5
Kirby, Gary	4
Enright, Leonard	3
Cregan, Éamonn	3
Carey, Ciarán	3
Finn, Seán	3
Foley, Mark	2
Houlihan, Mike	2
Quaid, Joe	2
Grimes, Éamonn	2
Gillane, Aaron	2
Lynch, Cian	2
Morrissey, Dan	2
Dowling, Shane	1
Moran, Ollie	1
McCarthy, Richie	1
Mulcahy, Graeme	1
Murray, Brian	1
O'Donoghue, Liam	1
Foley, Seán	1
English, Richie	1
Fitzmaurice, Paudie	1
Kelly, Paddy	1
O'Brien, Jim	1
Hannon, Declan	1
O'Shaughnessy, Andrew	1
Quaid, Tommy	1
Clarke, Dave	1
Quigley, Damien	1
Bennis, Richie	1
Hickey, Seamus	1
Quaid, Nickie	1
Byrnes, Diarmaid	1
Hayes, Kyle	1
Hegarty, Gearóid	1
Morrissey, Tom	1
Total	**64**

TIPPERARY
Kelly, Eoin	6
Maher, Pádraic	6
English, Nicholas	6
Cummins, Brendan	5
Callanan, Séamus	4
Cleary, Michael	4
Dunne, Tommy	3
Loughnane, Francis	3
Leahy, John	3
Maher, Brendan	3
McGrath, Noel	3
Corbett, Lar	3
Fox, Pat	3
O'Connor, Tadhg	3
Ryan, Bobby	3
Bonnar, Cormac	2
Maher, Patrick	2
Kelly, Paul	2
Curran, Paul	2
Maher, Ronan	2
McLoughney, Pat	2
McGrath, Shane	2
Bonnar, Conal	2
Barrett, Cathal	2
O'Mahony, Conor	2
Sheehy, Noel	2
Ryan, Declan	2
Cahill, Liam	1
Corcoran, Eamonn	1
Bonnar, Colm	1
Delaney, Paul	1
O'Dwyer, John	1
Barry, James	1
Ryan, Aidan	1
Carr, Declan	1
Butler, Tommy	1
Enright, Eddie	1
Keating, Michael	1
Fanning, Declan	1
O'Leary, Mark	1
Maher, Phillip	1
Roche, Mick	1
Carroll, John	1
Cahill, Michael	1
McGrath, John	1
Gleeson, Darren	1
Shelly, Paul	1
Hogan, Brian	1
Hogan, Ken	1
Total	**104**

WATERFORD
Mullane, John	5
Walsh, Michael	4
McGrath, Ken	3
Browne, Tony	3
Connors, Noel	3
Shanahan, Dan	3
Barron, Jamie	3
Moran, Kevin	2
Galvin, John	2
Kelly, Eoin	2
de Búrca, Tadgh	2
Shanahan, Maurice	1
O'Keeffe, Stephen	1
Walsh, Mossie	1
Molumphy, Stephen	1
Hartley, Fergal	1
Gleeson, Austin	1
Flynn, Paul	1
Greene, Jim	1
Murphy, Eoin	1
Bennett, Stephen	1
Total	**42**

WESTMEATH
Kilcoyne, David	1
Total	**1**

OFFALY
Whelahan, Brian	4
Hanamy, Martin	3
Kinahan, Kevin	3
Dooley, Johnny	3
Fleury, Pat	2
Kelly, Joachim	2
Fogarty, Aidan	2
Coughlan, Ger	2
Martin, Kevin	2
Dooley, Billy	2
Carroll, Pat	2
Coughlan, Eugene	2
Troy, John	1
Martin, Damien	1
Pilkington, Johnny	1
Horan, Pádraig	1
Rigney, Hubert	1
Corrigan, Mark	1
Currams, Liam	1
Dooley, Joe	1
Delaney, Pat	1
Cleary, Pat	1
Flaherty, Johnny	1
Byrne, Stephen	1
Duignan, Michael	1
Total	**42**

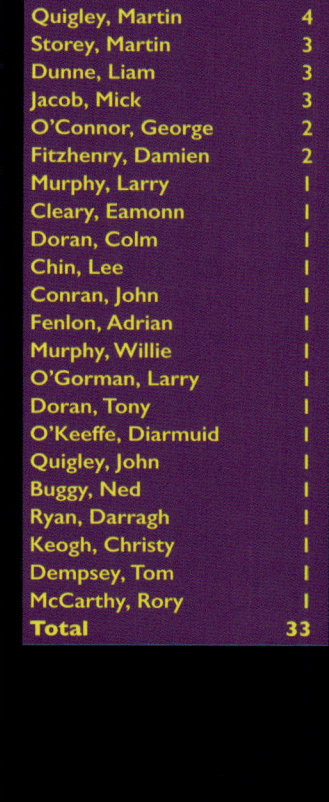

WEXFORD
Quigley, Martin	4
Storey, Martin	3
Dunne, Liam	3
Jacob, Mick	3
O'Connor, George	2
Fitzhenry, Damien	2
Murphy, Larry	1
Cleary, Eamonn	1
Doran, Colm	1
Chin, Lee	1
Conran, John	1
Fenlon, Adrian	1
Murphy, Willie	1
O'Gorman, Larry	1
Doran, Tony	1
O'Keeffe, Diarmuid	1
Quigley, John	1
Buggy, Ned	1
Ryan, Darragh	1
Keogh, Christy	1
Dempsey, Tom	1
McCarthy, Rory	1
Total	**33**

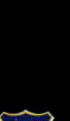

Hurling All-Star Nominees

The statistics included in this book have been cross-checked to the best of our ability. Our data sources for the Nominations data were Mick Dunne's files, Jim O'Sullivan's files, Donal Keenan's files, the Irish Press, the Irish Independent and the Irish Times Newspaper Archives

Data has been confirmed where possible, but the 1971 list of nominees could not be fully verified as, in those days, the names of the All-Star nominees were not published in advance of team selection. The names listed for 1971 are based on files belonging to Mick Dunne and Jim O'Sullivan. Should any inaccuracies come to light, we will be delighted to update these lists.

1971

GOALKEEPERS
Damien Martin, Offaly
Jim Hogan, Limerick
Mick Butler, London
Noel Skehan, Kilkenny
Ollie Walsh, Kilkenny
Paddy Barry, Cork
Pat Nolan, Wexford
Peter O'Sullivan, Tipperary

RIGHT FULL-BACK
Dan Quigley, Wexford
Fan Larkin, Kilkenny
Jim O'Donnell, Limerick
Noel Lane, Tipperary
Pat Hartigan, Limerick
Pat McDonnell, Cork
Tony Maher, Cork
Tony O'Brien, Limerick

FULL-BACK
Dan Quigley, Wexford
John Faul, Galway
John Kelly, Tipperary
Pa Dillon, Kilkenny
Pat Hartigan, Limerick
Pat McDonnell, Cork

LEFT FULL-BACK
Jim O'Brien, Limerick
Jim Treacy, Kilkenny
John Gleeson, Tipperary
John Horgan, Cork
John Quigley, Wexford

RIGHT HALF-BACK
Christy Campbell, Limerick
Con Roche, Cork
Gerald McCarthy, Cork
Justin McCarthy, Cork
Matt Browne, Wexford
Niall Wheeler, Antrim
Pat Lawlor, Kilkenny
Tadgh O'Connor, Tipperary

CENTRE HALF-BACK
Jim O'Donnell, Limerick
Mick Roche, Tipperary
Pat Henderson, Kilkenny
Tadgh O'Connor, Tipperary
Teddy Murphy, Galway

LEFT HALF-BACK
Con Roche, Cork
Gerald McCarthy, Cork
John Horgan, Cork
John Quigley, Wexford
Len Gaynor, Tipperary
Martin Coogan, Kilkenny
Phil Bennis, Limerick

CENTREFIELD
Bernie Hartigan, Limerick
David Bernie, Wexford
Frank Cummins, Kilkenny
John Connolly, Galway
Justin McCarthy, Cork
Mick Roche, Tipperary
PJ Ryan, Tipperary
Willie Murphy, Wexford

RIGHT HALF-FORWARD
Éamonn Cregan, Limerick
Eddie Keher, Kilkenny
Francis Loughnane, Tipperary
Paddy Fahy, Galway
Richie Bennis, Limerick

CENTRE HALF-FORWARD
Éamonn Cregan, Limerick
Francis Loughnane, Tipperary
John Flanagan, Tipperary
Michael Keating, Tipperary
Mick Graham, Limerick
Moss Murphy, Kilkenny
Noel O'Dwyer, Tipperary
Pat Delaney, Kilkenny
Richie Bennis, Limerick
Tony Doran, Wexford

LEFT HALF-FORWARD
Éamonn Cregan, Limerick
Éamonn Grimes, Limerick
Eddie Keher, Kilkenny
Pat Hegarty, Cork
Richie Bennis, Limerick

RIGHT FULL-FORWARD
Charlie McCarthy, Cork
Dónal Flynn, Limerick
Éamonn Cregan, Limerick
Jimmy McNamara, Clare
John Flanagan, Tipperary
Michael Keating, Tipperary
Mick Bermingham, Dublin
Mick Brennan, Kilkenny
Moss Murphy, Kilkenny
Richie Bennis, Limerick

FULL-FORWARD
Kieran Purcell, Kilkenny
Michael Keating, Tipperary
Ray Cummins, Cork

LEFT FULL-FORWARD
Éamonn Cregan, Limerick
Éamonn Grimes, Limerick
Michael Keating, Tipperary
Mick Bermingham, Dublin

1972

GOALKEEPERS
Damien Martin, Offaly
Jim Corr, Antrim
Jim Hogan, Limerick
Noel Skehan, Kilkenny
Ollie Gallagher, Westmeath
Pat Barry, Cork
Pat Nolan, Wexford
Peter O'Sullivan, Tipperary
Séamus Durack, Clare

RIGHT FULL-BACK
Fan Larkin, Kilkenny
Nicky Orr, Kilkenny
Pat Hartigan, Limerick
Pat McDonnell, Cork
Tom Neville, Wexford
Tony Maher, Cork

FULL-BACK
Pa Dillon, Kilkenny
Pat Hartigan, Limerick
Pat McDonnell, Cork
Brian Murphy, Cork
Jim Treacy, Kilkenny
John Walsh, Galway
Pat Jackson, Westmeath
Teddie O'Connor, Wexford

RIGHT HALF-BACK
Colm Doran, Wexford
Con Roche, Cork
Dave Duggan, Wexford
Eugene Moore, Laois
Frank Norberg, Cork
Gus Lohan, Clare
Jackie O'Gorman, Clare
Justin McCarthy, Cork
Len Gaynor, Tipperary
Mick Jacob, Wexford
Mick Roche, Tipperary
Niall Wheeler, Antrim
Pat Lawlor, Kilkenny
Phil Bennis, Limerick
Séamus Looney, Cork
Tadgh O'Connor, Tipperary

CENTRE HALF-BACK
John Kirwan, Waterford
Mick Jacob, Wexford
Mick Roche, Tipperary
Pat Dunny Kildare
Pat Hartigan, Limerick
Pat Henderson, Kilkenny
Ted Murphy, Galway

LEFT HALF-BACK
Aidan McCamphill, Antrim
Con Roche, Cork
Iggy Clarke, Galway
Jackie O'Gorman, Clare
John Quigley, Wexford
John Walsh, Galway
Len Gaynor, Tipperary
Mick Graham, Limerick
Ted Murphy, Galway

1973

GOALKEEPERS
Jack Carroll, Laois
Noel Skehan, Kilkenny
Pat Nolan, Wexford
Séamus Durack, Clare
Séamus Horgan, Limerick

RIGHT FULL-BACK
Fan Larkin, Kilkenny
Jim Fogarty, Tipperary
Jim O'Brien, Limerick
John Quigley, Wexford
Tony Maher, Cork
Vincent Loftus, Clare
Willie Moore, Limerick

FULL-BACK
Pat Hartigan, Limerick

LEFT FULL-BACK
Fan Larkin, Kilkenny
Jim O'Brien, Limerick
Jim Treacy, Kilkenny
Seán Foley, Limerick

RIGHT HALF-BACK
Colm Doran, Wexford
Con Roche, Cork
Davy Duggan, Waterford
Éamonn Cregan, Limerick
Len Gaynor, Tipperary
Mick Roche, Tipperary
Pat Lawlor, Kilkenny
Tadgh O'Connor, Tipperary

CENTRE HALF-BACK
Éamonn Cregan, Limerick
Mick Jacob, Wexford
Pádraig Horan, Offaly
Pat Henderson, Kilkenny
Tadgh O'Connor, Tipperary

LEFT HALF-BACK
Colm Doran, Wexford
Éamonn Cregan, Limerick
Mick Mahon, Laois
Pádraig Horan, Offaly
Pat Lawlor, Kilkenny
Seán Foley, Limerick
Tadgh O'Connor, Tipperary
Willie Moore, Limerick
Willie Murphy, Wexford

CENTREFIELD
Denis Coughlan, Cork
Éamonn Grimes, Limerick
Frank Cummins, Kilkenny
Liam O'Brien, Kilkenny
Martin Quigley, Wexford
Richie Bennis, Limerick
Séamus Hogan, Tipperary
Tadgh O'Connor, Tipperary

RIGHT HALF-FORWARD
Éamonn Cregan, Limerick
Éamonn Grimes, Limerick
Eddie Keher, Kilkenny
Francis Loughnane, Tipperary
Martin Quigley, Wexford
Mick Roche, Tipperary
Richie Bennis, Limerick

CENTRE HALF-FORWARD
Éamonn Cregan, Limerick
Martin Quigley, Wexford
Pat Delaney, Kilkenny
Ray Cummins, Cork
Richie Bennis, Limerick

LEFT HALF-FORWARD
Bernie Hartigan, Limerick
Éamonn Cregan, Limerick
Éamonn Grimes, Limerick
Eddie Keher, Kilkenny
Gerald McCarthy, Cork
John Flanagan, Tipperary
Liam O'Donoghue, Limerick
Martin Quigley, Wexford
Richie Bennis, Limerick
Tom Byrne, Wexford

RIGHT FULL-FORWARD
Colm Doran, Wexford
Éamonn Cregan, Limerick
Éamonn Grimes, Limerick
Eddie Keher, Kilkenny
Joe McKenna, Limerick
John Flanagan, Tipperary
Kieran Purcell, Kilkenny
Martin Quigley, Wexford
Mick Crotty, Kilkenny
Ray Cummins, Cork
Roger Ryan, Tipperary
Stephen Greene, Waterford
Tom Byrne, Wexford

FULL-FORWARD
Colm Doran, Wexford
Kieran Purcell, Kilkenny
Ned Rea, Limerick
Pat Delaney, Kilkenny
Ray Cummins, Cork

LEFT FULL-FORWARD
Colm Doran, Wexford
Éamonn Cregan, Limerick
Eddie Keher, Kilkenny
John Quigley, Wexford
Kieran Purcell, Kilkenny
Ray Cummins, Cork
Richie Bennis, Limerick
Roger Ryan, Tipperary

1974

GOALKEEPERS
Noel Skehan, Kilkenny
Séamus Durack, Clare
Séamus Horgan, Limerick

RIGHT FULL-BACK
Fan Larkin, Kilkenny
Martin Kirwan, Waterford
Tony Maher, Cork

FULL-BACK
Nicky Orr, Kilkenny
Pat Hartigan, Limerick

LEFT FULL-BACK
Jim O'Brien, Limerick
John Horgan, Cork
John Kelly, Tipperary
Séamus Hannon, Waterford

RIGHT HALF-BACK
Colm Doran, Wexford
Ger Loughnane, Clare
Martin Hickey, Waterford
Pat Lawlor, Kilkenny
Paul Kelly, Waterford
Tadgh O'Connor, Tipperary

CENTRE HALF-BACK
Éamonn Cregan, Limerick
Jim Greene, Waterford
John Horgan, Cork
Mick Jacob, Wexford
Pat Henderson, Kilkenny
Seán Hehir, Clare

LEFT HALF-BACK
Colm Doran, Wexford
Con Roche, Cork
Iggy Clarke, Galway
Jackie O'Gorman, Clare
Len Gaynor, Tipperary
Pat McGrath, Waterford
Seán Foley, Limerick

CENTREFIELD
Bernie Hartigan, Limerick
Éamonn Grimes, Limerick
Frank Cummins, Kilkenny
John Connolly, Galway
John Galvin, Waterford
Liam O'Brien, Kilkenny
Martin Quigley, Wexford
Mick Moroney, Clare
Pat Hegarty, Cork
Pat O'Grady, Waterford
Séamus Hogan, Tipperary

RIGHT HALF-FORWARD
Francis Loughnane, Tipperary
Joe McKenna, Limerick
Johnny Walsh, Kildare
Liam O'Brien, Kilkenny
Liam O'Donoghue, Limerick
Martin Quigley, Wexford

CENTRE HALF-FORWARD
Declan Hanniffy, Offaly
Eddie Donnelly, Antrim
Francis Loughnane, Tipperary
John Connolly, Galway
Kieran Purcell, Kilkenny
Martin Quigley, Wexford
Pat Delaney, Kilkenny

LEFT HALF-FORWARD
Éamonn Grimes, Limerick
Gerald McCarthy, Cork
Liam O'Brien, Kilkenny
Mick Crotty, Kilkenny
Pat O'Grady, Waterford
Pat Quigley, Dublin
PJ Molloy, Galway

RIGHT FULL-FORWARD
Charlie McCarthy, Cork
John Quigley, Wexford
Liam O'Donoghue, Limerick
Martin Quigley, Wexford
Mick Brennan, Kilkenny

FULL-FORWARD
Eamonn Rea, Limerick
John Kirwan, Waterford
Kieran Purcell, Kilkenny
Mick Malone, Cork
Pat Delaney, Kilkenny
Tony Doran, Wexford

LEFT FULL-FORWARD
Eddie Keher, Kilkenny
Frank Nolan, Limerick
Tom Byrne, Wexford

1975

GOALKEEPERS
Martin Coleman, Cork
Michael Conneely, Galway
Noel Skehan, Kilkenny
Patsy Cunningham, Dublin
Séamus Durack, Clare
Séamus Shinnors, Tipperary

RIGHT FULL-BACK
Fan Larkin, Kilkenny
Liam King, Tipperary
Niall McInerney, Galway

FULL-BACK
Jim Keogh, Tipperary
Joe Clarke, Galway
Nicky Orr, Kilkenny
Pat Hartigan, Limerick
Pat McDonnell, Cork

LEFT FULL-BACK
Brian Cody, Kilkenny
Brian Murphy, Cork
Jim O'Brien, Limerick
John Horgan, Cork
Pat Dunny, Kildare
Séamus Hannon, Waterford
Teddie O'Connor, Wexford

RIGHT HALF-BACK
Colm Doran, Wexford
Ger Loughnane, Clare
Joe McDonagh, Galway
Pat Hegarty, Cork
Pat Lawlor, Kilkenny
Paudie Fitzmaurice, Limerick
Tadgh O'Connor, Tipperary
Vinny Holden, Dublin

CENTRE HALF-BACK
Éamonn Cregan, Limerick
Noel O'Dwyer, Tipperary
Pat Henderson, Kilkenny
Seán Silke, Galway

LEFT HALF-BACK
Con Roche, Cork
Iggy Clarke, Galway
Jackie O'Gorman, Clare
Ned Buggy, Wexford

CENTREFIELD
Frank Cummins, Kilkenny
Gerald McCarthy, Cork
Jim Kehoe, Tipperary
Joe McKenna, Limerick
John Connolly, Galway
Liam O'Brien, Kilkenny
Séamus Hogan, Tipperary
Seán Foley, Limerick
Seán Murphy, Galway

RIGHT HALF-FORWARD
Francis Loughnane, Tipperary
Gerry Coone, Galway
Jimmy Barry Murphy, Cork
Liam O'Donoghue, Limerick
Martin Quigley, Wexford
Mick Crotty, Kilkenny

CENTRE HALF-FORWARD
Frank Burke, Galway
Ger Moloney, Limerick
Joe McKenna, Limerick
Kieran Purcell, Kilkenny
Martin Quigley, Wexford
Pat Delaney, Kilkenny
Willie Walsh, Cork

LEFT HALF-FORWARD
Denis Allen, Cork
Éamonn Grimes, Limerick
Pádraig Fahy, Galway
PJ Molloy, Galway

Hurling All-Star Nominees

RIGHT FULL-FORWARD
Charlie McCarthy, Cork
Eddie Donnelly, Antrim
Frankie Nolan, Limerick
John Flanagan, Tipperary
John Quigley, Wexford
Mick Brennan, Kilkenny
FULL-FORWARD
Kieran Purcell, Kilkenny
PJ Qualter, Galway
Ray Cummins, Cork
Tony Doran, Wexford
LEFT FULL-FORWARD
Eddie Keher, Kilkenny
Michael Keating, Tipperary
Pádraig Fahy, Galway
Richie Bennis, Limerick
Seán O'Leary, Cork

1976

GOALKEEPERS
Jim Corr, Antrim
John Nolan, Wexford
Martin Coleman, Cork
Noel Skehan, Kilkenny
Séamus Durack, Clare
Séamus Shinnors, Tipperary
Brian Murphy, Cork
RIGHT FULL-BACK
Fan Larkin, Kilkenny
Niall McInerney, Galway
Teddie O'Connor, Wexford
Jim Keogh, Tipperary
FULL-BACK
Jim Power, Clare
Pat Hartigan, Limerick
Pat McDonnell, Cork
Vinny Holden, Dublin
Willie Murphy, Wexford
Brian Cody, Kilkenny
LEFT FULL-BACK
Jackie O'Gorman, Clare
Jim Prendergast, Wexford
John McMahon, Clare
Martin O'Doherty, Cork
Pat Dunny Kildare
Teddie O'Connor, Wexford
Colm Doran, Wexford
RIGHT HALF-BACK
Ger Loughnane, Clare
Joe McDonagh, Galway
Pat Lawlor, Kilkenny
Tadgh O'Connor, Tipperary
Mick Jacob, Wexford
CENTRE HALF-BACK
Pat Henderson, Kilkenny
Seán Silke, Galway
Denis Coughlan, Cork
LEFT HALF-BACK
Ger Henderson, Kilkenny
Iggy Clarke, Galway
Noel O'Dwyer, Tipperary
CENTREFIELD
Frank Burke, Galway
Frank Cummins, Kilkenny
Gerald McCarthy, Cork
Jim Kehoe, Tipperary
John Connolly, Galway
Liam O'Brien, Kilkenny
Michael Connolly, Galway

Ned Buggy, Wexford
Pat Moylan, Cork
RIGHT HALF-FORWARD
Jimmy McNamara, Clare
Martin Quigley, Wexford
Mick Malone, Cork
CENTRE HALF-FORWARD
Jimmy Barry Murphy, Cork
John Connolly, Galway
Martin Quigley, Wexford
Ray Cummins, Cork
Tony Doran, Wexford
LEFT HALF-FORWARD
Colm Honan, Clare
Éamonn Grimes, Limerick
Jimmy Barry Murphy, Cork
John Quigley, Wexford
PJ Molloy, Galway
RIGHT FULL-FORWARD
Charlie McCarthy, Cork
Mick Brennan, Kilkenny
Mick Butler, Wexford
Pat Moriarty Kerry
FULL-FORWARD
Éamonn Cregan, Limerick
John Grogan, Tipperary
Ray Cummins, Cork
Tony Doran, Wexford
LEFT FULL-FORWARD
Eddie Donnelly, Antrim
Eddie Keher, Kilkenny
Seán O'Leary, Cork

1977

GOALKEEPERS
Damien Martin, Offaly
Jim Corr, Antrim
John Carroll, Laois
John Nolan, Wexford
Martin Coleman, Cork
Noel Skehan, Kilkenny
Pat McLoughney, Tipperary
Séamus Durack, Clare
RIGHT FULL-BACK
Brian Murphy, Cork
Fan Larkin, Kilkenny
Jackie O'Gorman, Clare
John McMahon, Clare
Niall McInerney, Galway
Pat Fitzelle, Tipperary
Teddie O'Connor, Wexford
FULL-BACK
Jim Keogh, Tipperary
Joe Clarke, Galway
Martin O'Doherty, Cork
Pat Fleury, Offaly
Willie Murphy, Wexford
LEFT FULL-BACK
Andy Fenton, Galway
Dick O'Hara, Kilkenny
Jackie O'Gorman, Clare
Jim Prendergast, Wexford
John Horgan, Cork
John McMahon, Clare
RIGHT HALF-BACK
Colm Doran, Wexford
Ger Loughnane, Clare
Joe McDonagh, Galway
Pat Lawlor, Kilkenny

CENTRE HALF-BACK
Colm Doran, Wexford
Gus Lohan, Clare
John Crowley, Cork
Mick Jacob, Wexford
Noel O'Dwyer, Tipperary
Pat Hartigan, Limerick
Pat McGrath, Waterford
Seán Silke, Galway
Tadgh O'Connor, Tipperary
Vinny Holden, Dublin
LEFT HALF-BACK
Colm Doran, Wexford
Denis Coughlan, Cork
Ger Henderson, Kilkenny
Iggy Clarke, Galway
Seán Hehir, Clare
CENTREFIELD
Colm Honan, Clare
Frank Cummins, Kilkenny
John Connolly, Galway
Michael Connolly, Galway
Mick Jacob, Wexford
Mick Moroney, Clare
Mossy Carroll, Limerick
Mossy Whelan, Waterford
Ned Buggy, Wexford
Tim Crowley, Cork
Tom Cashman, Cork
RIGHT HALF-FORWARD
Christy Keogh, Wexford
Colm Honan, Clare
Jimmy McNamara, Clare
John Callinan, Clare
Johnny Walsh Kildare
Liam O'Brien, Kilkenny
Matt Ruth, Kilkenny
Mick Brennan, Kilkenny
Mick Malone, Cork
CENTRE HALF-FORWARD
Enda O'Connor, Clare
Jimmy Barry Murphy, Cork
Liam O'Brien, Kilkenny
Martin Quigley, Wexford
Tim Crowley, Cork
Tommy Butler, Tipperary
LEFT HALF-FORWARD
Jimmy Barry Murphy, Cork
Mick Butler, Wexford
PJ Molloy, Galway
RIGHT FULL-FORWARD
Charlie McCarthy, Cork
John Quigley, Wexford
Mick Brennan, Kilkenny
Mick Butler, Wexford
FULL-FORWARD
Éamonn Cregan, Limerick
Noel Casey, Clare
Paddy Moriarty Kerry
Ray Cummins, Cork
Tony Doran, Wexford
LEFT FULL-FORWARD
Eddie Keher, Kilkenny
Seán O'Leary, Cork

1978

GOALKEEPERS
Martin Coleman, Cork
Noel Skehan, Kilkenny
Séamus Durack, Clare

Mick Crotty, Kilkenny
Noel Casey, Clare
Tommy Butler, Tipperary
Vinny Holden, Dublin
LEFT HALF-FORWARD
Billy Fitzpatrick, Kilkenny
Colm Honan, Clare
Éamonn Grimes, Limerick
Jimmy Barry Murphy, Cork
John Callinan, Clare
Ned Buggy, Wexford
Pat Moylan, Cork
PJ Molloy, Galway
Tim Crowley, Cork
RIGHT FULL-FORWARD
Charlie McCarthy, Cork
Mick Brennan, Kilkenny
Pat O'Connor, Clare
FULL-FORWARD
Joe McKenna, Limerick
John Connolly, Galway
Noel Casey, Clare
Tony Doran, Wexford
LEFT FULL-FORWARD
Billy Fitzpatrick, Kilkenny
Christy Keogh, Wexford
Enda O'Connor, Clare
Finbarr Gantley, Galway
Liam Donoghue, Limerick
Matt Ruth, Kilkenny
Mick Butler, Wexford
Noel Casey, Clare
Seán O'Leary, Cork
Tony Doran, Wexford
Willie Fitzmaurice, Limerick

1979
GOALKEEPERS
Noel Skehan, Kilkenny
Pat McLoughney, Tipperary
Séamus Durack, Clare
Séamus Shinnors, Galway
Tommy Quaid, Limerick
RIGHT FULL-BACK
Brendan Keeshan, Offaly
Brian Murphy, Cork
Fan Larkin, Kilkenny
Niall McInerney, Galway
Nicky Cashin, Waterford
Paddy Williams, Tipperary
FULL-BACK
Conor Hayes, Galway
Jim Keogh, Tipperary
Martin O'Doherty, Cork
Paddy Prendergast, Kilkenny
Pat Hartigan, Limerick
Willie Murphy, Wexford
LEFT FULL-BACK
Andy Fenton, Galway
John Henderson, Kilkenny
John Horgan, Cork
Paddy Prendergast, Kilkenny
Séamus Hannon, Waterford
Tadgh O'Connor, Tipperary
RIGHT HALF-BACK
Dermot McCurtain, Cork
Eddie Walsh, Wexford
Ger Loughnane, Clare
Joe McDonagh, Galway

CENTRE HALF-BACK
Ger Henderson, Kilkenny
John Crowley, Cork
Mick Jacob, Wexford
Mossy Carroll, Limerick
Noel O'Dwyer, Tipperary
Seán Silke, Galway
LEFT HALF-BACK
Colm Doran, Wexford
Denis Coughlan, Cork
Iggy Clarke, Galway
Nicky Brennan, Kilkenny
Pat Fitzelle, Tipperary
Seán Foley, Limerick
Seán Hehir, Clare
Seán Stack, Clare
CENTREFIELD
Frank Cummins, Kilkenny
Ger Stapleton, Tipperary
Joachim Kelly, Offaly
Joe Hennessy, Kilkenny
John Connolly, Galway
John Fenton, Cork
Leonard Enright, Limerick
Mossy Walsh, Waterford
Paddy Quirke Carlow
Pat Moylan, Cork
Paudie Fitzmaurice, Limerick
Peadar Carton, Dublin
Steve Mahon, Galway
RIGHT HALF-FORWARD
Bernie Forde, Galway
Billy Fitzpatrick, Kilkenny
Eamon O'Shea, Tipperary
John Callinan, Clare
Ned Buggy, Wexford
Paddy Kelly, Limerick
CENTRE HALF-FORWARD
Billy Fitzpatrick, Kilkenny
Frank Burke, Galway
Gerry Moloney, Limerick
Martin Quigley, Wexford
Pat Kirwan, Offaly
LEFT HALF-FORWARD
Colm Honan, Clare
Jimmy Barry Murphy, Cork
Joe Connolly, Galway
Liam O'Brien, Kilkenny
Mick Walsh, Laois
Peadar Queally, Tipperary
PJ Molloy, Galway
Seán Kinsella, Wexford
Tom Cashman, Cork
RIGHT FULL-FORWARD
Charlie McCarthy, Cork
Francis Loughnane, Tipperary
Michael Ormonde, Waterford
Mick Brennan, Kilkenny
Ned Buggy, Wexford
Ollie O'Connor, Limerick
Pat O'Connor, Clare
FULL-FORWARD
Jim Kehoe, Tipperary
Joe McKenna, Limerick
Mick Crotty, Kilkenny
Mick Holden, Dublin
Noel Lane, Galway
Ray Cummins, Cork

LEFT FULL-FORWARD
Enda O'Connor, Clare
Finbarr Gantley, Galway
Joe Henry Mayo
Matt Ruth, Kilkenny
Ned Buggy, Wexford

1980
GOALKEEPERS
Damien Martin, Offaly
Noel Skehan, Kilkenny
Pat McLoughney, Tipperary
Séamus Durack, Clare
Tommy Quaid, Limerick
RIGHT FULL-BACK
Brian Murphy, Cork
Dónal Murray, Limerick
Eugene Coughlan, Offaly
Niall McInerney, Galway
Paddy Williams, Tipperary
FULL-BACK
Conor Hayes, Galway
Leonard Enright, Limerick
Martin O'Doherty, Cork
LEFT FULL-BACK
Dick O'Hara, Kilkenny
Dominic Punch, Limerick
Jimmy Cooney, Galway
John Horgan, Cork
Pat Fleury, Offaly
Tadgh O'Connor, Tipperary
RIGHT HALF-BACK
Denis Coughlan, Cork
Dermot McCurtain, Cork
Pat Fitzelle, Tipperary
CENTRE HALF-BACK
Ger Henderson, Kilkenny
Ger Loughnane, Clare
John Crowley, Cork
Pat Delaney, Offaly
Seán Silke, Galway
LEFT HALF-BACK
Colm Doran, Wexford
Dermot McCurtain, Cork
Iggy Clarke, Galway
Pat McGrath, Waterford
Seán Foley, Limerick
CENTREFIELD
David Punch, Limerick
George O'Connor, Wexford
Jimmy Carroll, Limerick
Joachim Kelly, Offaly
John Connolly, Galway
John Fenton, Cork
Michael Connolly, Galway
Mossy Walsh, Waterford
Paddy Quirke Carlow
Steve Mahon, Galway
Tom Cashman, Cork
RIGHT HALF-FORWARD
Joe Connolly, Galway
John Callinan, Clare
Johnny Walsh Kildare
Mark Corrigan, Offaly
CENTRE HALF-FORWARD
Brendan Bermingham, Offaly
Frank Burke, Galway
Joe Connolly, Galway
John Flanagan, Limerick
Pat Horgan, Cork

LEFT HALF-FORWARD
Declan Fitzpatrick, Waterford
Ger Fennelly, Kilkenny
Jimmy Barry Murphy, Cork
Pat Carroll, Offaly
PJ Molloy, Galway
Tim Crowley, Cork
Tom Cashman, Cork
RIGHT FULL-FORWARD
Bernie Forde, Galway
Ollie O'Connor, Limerick
Pat Kirwan, Offaly
Pat O'Connor, Clare
FULL-FORWARD
Billy Fitzpatrick, Kilkenny
Joe McKenna, Limerick
John Connolly, Galway
Pádraig Horan, Offaly
Ray Cummins, Cork
LEFT FULL-FORWARD
Éamonn Cregan, Limerick
Éamonn O'Donoghue, Cork
Johnny Flaherty, Offaly
Matt Ruth, Kilkenny
Ned Buggy, Wexford
Noel Lane, Galway

1981
GOALKEEPERS
Damien Martin, Offaly
Ger Cunningham, Cork
Michael Conneely, Galway
Noel Skehan, Kilkenny
Pat McLoughney, Tipperary
Séamus Durack, Clare
Tommy Quaid, Limerick
RIGHT FULL-BACK
Barry Smythe, Clare
Brian Murphy, Cork
John Galvin, Waterford
Mick Butler, Wexford
Niall McInerney, Galway
Paddy Williams, Tipperary
Paudie Fitzmaurice, Limerick
Séamus Coen, Galway
FULL-BACK
Conor Hayes, Galway
Eugene Coughlan, Offaly
Jack Russell, Wexford
Joe Murphy, Waterford
John Bohane, Laois
John Ryan, Clare
Leonard Enright, Limerick
Niall McInerney, Galway
LEFT FULL-BACK
Dick O'Hara, Kilkenny
Jimmy Cooney, Galway
John Horgan, Cork
Liam Bennett, Wexford
Pat Fleury, Offaly
Tadgh O'Connor, Tipperary
Tommy Keane, Clare
RIGHT HALF-BACK
Christy Jones, Laois
Dermot McCurtain, Cork
Ger Loughnane, Clare
John Conran, Wexford
Liam O'Donoghue, Limerick
Sylvie Linnane, Galway

All-Star Gazing

Hurling All-Star Nominees

CENTRE HALF-BACK
Mick Jacob, Wexford
Mossy Carroll, Tipperary
Pat Delaney, Offaly
Pat McGrath, Waterford
Seán Silke, Galway
Seán Stack, Clare
LEFT HALF-BACK
Colm Doran, Wexford
Denis Cahill, Tipperary
Dominic Punch, Limerick
Ger Coughlan, Offaly
Ger Henderson, Kilkenny
Iggy Clarke, Galway
Seán Hehir, Clare
Tom Cashman, Cork
CENTREFIELD
Declan Coote, Clare
George O'Connor, Wexford
Ger Fennelly, Kilkenny
Joachim Kelly, Offaly
Joe Hennessy, Kilkenny
John Fenton, Cork
Johnny Murphy, Wexford
Liam Currams, Offaly
Michael Connolly, Galway
Mick Walsh, Laois
Mike Grimes, Limerick
Mossy Walsh, Waterford
Mossy Whelan, Waterford
Pat Fitzelle, Tipperary
Steve Mahon, Galway
Tim Crowley, Cork
Tony Nugent, Clare
RIGHT HALF-FORWARD
Billy Fitzpatrick, Kilkenny
John Callinan, Clare
Martin Brophy, Laois
Ollie O'Connor, Limerick
Tim Crowley, Cork
Tomás Maher, Waterford
Brendan Bermingham, Offaly
George O'Connor, Wexford
Jimmy Barry Murphy, Cork
John Flanagan, Limerick
Martin Cuddy, Laois
Paddy Quirke Carlow
Pat Horgan, Cork
LEFT HALF-FORWARD
Billy Bohane, Laois
Brian Carroll, Limerick
Eamon O'Shea, Tipperary
John Fleming, Wexford
Mark Corrigan, Offaly
Pat Carroll, Offaly
PJ Molloy, Galway
Tom Casey, Waterford
RIGHT FULL-FORWARD
Bernie Forde, Galway
Ollie O'Connor, Limerick
Pádraig Crowley, Cork
Pat Carroll, Offaly
FULL-FORWARD
Jimmy Barry Murphy, Cork
Joe McKenna, Limerick
Pádraig Horan, Offaly
Peadar Queally, Tipperary
Tony Doran, Wexford

LEFT FULL-FORWARD
Éamonn Cregan, Limerick
Éamonn O'Donoghue, Cork
Jim Greene, Waterford
Johnny Flaherty, Offaly
Noel Lane, Galway

1982
GOALKEEPERS
Ger Cunningham, Cork
John Farrell, Tipperary
Noel Skehan, Kilkenny
Séamus Durack, Clare
RIGHT FULL-BACK
Brendan Keeshan, Offaly
Brian Murphy, Cork
John Galvin, Waterford
John Henderson, Kilkenny
FULL-BACK
Brian Cody, Kilkenny
Eugene Coughlan, Offaly
Leonard Enright, Limerick
Martin O'Doherty, Cork
LEFT FULL-BACK
Jimmy Cooney, Galway
John Blake, Cork
Liam Bennett, Wexford
Pat Fleury, Offaly
RIGHT HALF-BACK
Aidan Fogarty, Offaly
Liam O'Donoghue, Limerick
Nicky Brennan, Kilkenny
Sylvie Linnane, Galway
CENTRE HALF-BACK
Ger Henderson, Kilkenny
Pat Delaney, Offaly
Pat McGrath, Waterford
Seán Stack, Clare
LEFT HALF-BACK
Dermot McCurtain, Cork
Ger Coughlan, Offaly
Iggy Clarke, Galway
Paddy Prendergast, Kilkenny
CENTREFIELD
Frank Cummins, Kilkenny
George O'Connor, Wexford
Joachim Kelly, Offaly
Joe Hennessy, Kilkenny
Mossy Walsh, Waterford
Steve Mahon, Galway
Tim Crowley, Cork
Tom Cashman, Cork
RIGHT HALF-FORWARD
John Callinan, Clare
Pat Carroll, Offaly
Richard Power, Kilkenny
Tony O'Sullivan, Cork
CENTRE HALF-FORWARD
Brendan Bermingham, Offaly
Ger Fennelly, Kilkenny
Pat Horgan, Cork
Stephen Breen, Waterford
LEFT HALF-FORWARD
Jimmy Barry Murphy, Cork
Kieran Brennan, Kilkenny
Mark Corrigan, Offaly
Martin Brophy, Laois
RIGHT FULL-FORWARD
Billy Fitzpatrick, Kilkenny
PJ Molloy, Galway

Seán O'Leary, Cork
Tom Casey, Waterford
FULL-FORWARD
Christy Heffernan, Kilkenny
Pádraic Horan, Offaly
Ray Cummins, Cork
Tony Doran, Wexford
LEFT FULL-FORWARD
Jim Greene, Waterford
Johnny Flaherty, Offaly
Liam Fennelly, Kilkenny
Noel Lane, Galway

1983
GOALKEEPERS
Damien Martin, Offaly
Ger Cunningham, Cork
John Nolan, Wexford
Noel Skehan, Kilkenny
RIGHT FULL-BACK
Denis Mulcahy, Cork
Jackie Bergin, Tipperary
John Henderson, Kilkenny
Paudie Fitzmaurice, Limerick
FULL-BACK
Conor Hayes, Galway
Dónal O'Grady, Cork
Eugene Coughlan, Offaly
Leonard Enright, Limerick
LEFT FULL-BACK
Dick O'Hara, Kilkenny
John Hodgins, Cork
Pat Fleury, Offaly
Pat Herbert, Limerick
RIGHT HALF-BACK
Aidan Fogarty, Offaly
Joe Hennessy, Kilkenny
Pat Fitzelle, Tipperary
Tom Cashman, Cork
CENTRE HALF-BACK
Ger Henderson, Kilkenny
John Crowley, Cork
John McIntyre, Tipperary
Seán Stack, Clare
LEFT HALF-BACK
Bobby Ryan, Tipperary
Dermot McCurtain, Cork
Ger Coughlan, Offaly
John Taylor, Laois
CENTREFIELD
Frank Cummins, Kilkenny
George O'Connor, Wexford
Jimmy Carroll, Limerick
Joachim Kelly, Offaly
John Fenton, Cork
Michael Connolly, Galway
Pat Critchley, Laois
Pat Hartnett, Cork
RIGHT HALF-FORWARD
Kieran Brennan, Kilkenny
Mark Corrigan, Offaly
Nicholas English, Tipperary
Paddy Kelly, Limerick
CENTRE HALF-FORWARD
Brian Donnelly, Antrim
Danny Fitzpatrick, Limerick
Kieran Brennan, Kilkenny
Tim Crowley, Cork

LEFT HALF-FORWARD
Kevin Hennessy, Cork
Kieran Brennan, Kilkenny
Paddy Kelly, Limerick
Pat Carroll, Offaly
RIGHT FULL-FORWARD
Billy Fitzpatrick, Kilkenny
Martin Fitzhenry, Wexford
Ollie O'Connor, Limerick
Tomás Mulcahy, Cork
FULL-FORWARD
Christy Heffernan, Kilkenny
Jimmy Barry Murphy, Cork
Noel Lane, Galway
Séamus Power, Tipperary
LEFT FULL-FORWARD
Joe Dooley, Offaly
Liam Fennelly, Kilkenny
Matt Rea, Limerick
Seán O'Leary, Cork

1984
GOALKEEPERS
Damien Martin, Offaly
Ger Cunningham, Cork
John Nolan, Wexford
Noel Skehan, Kilkenny
RIGHT FULL-BACK
Denis Mulcahy, Cork
Jackie Bergin, Tipperary
John Henderson, Kilkenny
Paudie Fitzmaurice, Limerick
FULL-BACK
Conor Hayes, Galway
Dónal O'Grady, Cork
Eugene Coughlan, Offaly
Leonard Enright, Limerick
LEFT FULL-BACK
Dick O'Hara, Kilkenny
John Hodgins, Cork
Pat Fleury, Offaly
Pat Herbert, Limerick
RIGHT HALF-BACK
Aidan Fogarty, Offaly
Joe Hennessy, Kilkenny
Pat Fitzelle, Tipperary
Tom Cashman, Cork
CENTRE HALF-BACK
Ger Henderson, Kilkenny
John Crowley, Cork
John McIntyre, Tipperary
Seán Stack, Clare
LEFT HALF-BACK
Bobby Ryan, Tipperary
Dermot McCurtain, Cork
Ger Coughlan, Offaly
John Taylor, Laois
CENTREFIELD
Frank Cummins, Kilkenny
George O'Connor, Wexford
Jimmy Carroll, Limerick
Joachim Kelly, Offaly
John Fenton, Cork
Michael Connolly, Galway
Pat Critchley, Laois
Pat Hartnett, Cork
RIGHT HALF-FORWARD
Kieran Brennan, Kilkenny
Mark Corrigan, Offaly
Nicholas English, Tipperary
Paddy Kelly, Limerick

CENTRE HALF-FORWARD
Brian Donnelly, Antrim
Danny Fitzgerald, Limerick
Kieran Brennan, Kilkenny
Tim Crowley, Cork
LEFT HALF-FORWARD
Kevin Hennessy, Cork
Kieran Brennan, Kilkenny
Paddy Kelly, Limerick
Pat Carroll, Offaly
RIGHT FULL-FORWARD
Billy Fitzpatrick, Kilkenny
Martin Fitzhenry, Wexford
Ollie O'Connor, Limerick
Tomás Mulcahy, Cork
FULL-FORWARD
Christy Heffernan, Kilkenny
Jimmy Barry Murphy, Cork
Noel Lane, Galway
Séamus Power, Tipperary
LEFT FULL-FORWARD
Joe Dooley, Offaly
Liam Fennelly, Kilkenny
Matt Rea, Limerick
Seán O'Leary, Cork

1985
GOALKEEPERS
Ger Cunningham, Cork
Jim Troy, Offaly
Peter Murphy, Galway
RIGHT FULL-BACK
Aidan Fogarty, Offaly
Paudie Fitzmaurice, Limerick
Séamus Coen, Galway
FULL-BACK
Conor Hayes, Galway
Eugene Coughlan, Offaly
Leonard Enright, Limerick
LEFT FULL-BACK
Pat Fleury, Offaly
Pat Fox, Tipperary
Sylvie Linnane, Galway
RIGHT HALF-BACK
Peter Finnerty, Galway
Tom Cashman, Cork
Tom Conneely, Offaly
CENTRE HALF-BACK
Ger Henderson, Kilkenny
Pat Delaney, Offaly
Tony Keady, Galway
LEFT HALF-BACK
Bobby Ryan, Tipperary
Dermot McCurtain, Cork
Ger Coughlan, Offaly
CENTREFIELD
Jimmy Carroll, Limerick
Joachim Kelly, Offaly
John Fenton, Cork
Pat Critchley, Laois
Pat Hartnett, Cork
Steve Mahon, Galway
RIGHT HALF-FORWARD
Nicholas English, Tipperary
Paddy Corrigan, Offaly
Paddy Kelly, Limerick
CENTRE HALF-FORWARD
Brendan Lynskey, Galway
Donie O'Connell, Tipperary
Pat Carroll, Offaly

LEFT HALF-FORWARD
Joe Cooney, Galway
Kieran Brennan, Kilkenny
Mark Corrigan, Offaly
RIGHT FULL-FORWARD
Bernie Forde, Galway
Harry Ryan, Kilkenny
Pat Cleary, Offaly
FULL-FORWARD
Jimmy Barry Murphy, Cork
PJ Cuddy, Laois
Pádraig Horan, Offaly
LEFT FULL-FORWARD
Joe Dooley, Offaly
Kevin Hennessy, Cork
Liam Fennelly, Kilkenny

1986
GOALKEEPERS
Eoin McMahon, Clare
Ger Cunningham, Cork
John Commins, Galway
RIGHT FULL-BACK
Denis Mulcahy, Cork
John Henderson, Kilkenny
Sylvie Linnane, Galway
FULL-BACK
Conor Hayes, Galway
Eugene Coughlan, Offaly
John Henderson, Kilkenny
LEFT FULL-BACK
John Crowley, Cork
Sylvie Linnane, Galway
Tommy Keane, Clare
RIGHT HALF-BACK
Denis Walsh, Cork
Joe Hennessy, Kilkenny
Peter Finnerty, Galway
CENTRE HALF-BACK
James O'Connor, Wexford
Tom Cashman, Cork
Tony Keady, Galway
LEFT HALF-BACK
Bobby Ryan, Tipperary
Gerry McInerney, Galway
John Taylor, Laois
CENTREFIELD
Ger Fennelly, Kilkenny
Jim Cashman, Cork
John Fenton, Cork
Richie Power, Kilkenny
Steve Mahon, Galway
Tony , Kilkenny, Galway
RIGHT HALF-FORWARD
Martin Naughton, Galway
Nicholas English, Tipperary
Tony O'Sullivan, Cork
CENTRE HALF-FORWARD
Jimmy Holohan, Wexford
Kieran Brennan, Kilkenny
Tomás Mulcahy, Cork
LEFT HALF-FORWARD
Gerry McInerney, Clare
Joe Cooney, Galway
Kieran Brennan, Kilkenny
RIGHT FULL-FORWARD
Anthony Cunningham, Galway
David Kilcoyne, Westmeath
Liam Ryan, Kilkenny

FULL-FORWARD
Dessie Donnelly, Antrim
Jimmy Barry Murphy, Cork
Joe Cooney, Galway
LEFT FULL-FORWARD
Kevin Hennessy, Cork
Liam Fennelly, Kilkenny
Noel Lane, Galway

1987
GOALKEEPERS
Ger Cunningham, Cork
John Commins, Galway
Ken Hogan, Tipperary
RIGHT FULL-BACK
Denis Mulcahy, Cork
Joe Hennessy, Kilkenny
Sylvie Linnane, Galway
FULL-BACK
Conor Hayes, Galway
Conor O'Donovan, Tipperary
Paddy Prendergast, Kilkenny
LEFT FULL-BACK
Denis Walsh, Cork
John Henderson, Kilkenny
Ollie Kilkenny, Galway
RIGHT HALF-BACK
Brendan Keeshan, Offaly
Peter Finnerty, Galway
Richard Stakelum, Tipperary
CENTRE HALF-BACK
Ger Henderson, Kilkenny
John Kennedy, Tipperary
Tony Keady, Galway
LEFT HALF-BACK
Gerry McInerney, Galway
John Conran, Wexford
Seán Fennelly, Kilkenny
CENTREFIELD
Colm Bonnar, Tipperary
Ger Fennelly, Kilkenny
John Fenton, Cork
Paul McKillen, Antrim
Steve Mahon, Galway
Teddy McCarthy, Cork
RIGHT HALF-FORWARD
Michael McGrath, Galway
Nicholas English, Tipperary
Teddy McCarthy, Cork
CENTRE HALF-FORWARD
Donie O'Connell, Tipperary
Jimmy Holohan, Wexford
Joe Cooney, Galway
LEFT HALF-FORWARD
Aidan Ryan, Tipperary
Martin Naughton, Galway
Tony O'Sullivan, Cork
RIGHT FULL-FORWARD
Dessie Donnelly, Antrim
Éanna Ryan, Galway
Pat Fox, Tipperary
FULL-FORWARD
Brendan Lynskey, Galway
Liam Fennelly, Kilkenny
Nicholas English, Tipperary
LEFT FULL-FORWARD
Anthony Cunningham, Galway
Liam Fennelly, Kilkenny
Nicholas English, Tipperary

1988
GOALKEEPERS
Ger Cunningham, Cork
John Commins, Galway
Ken Hogan, Tipperary
RIGHT FULL-BACK
Conor O'Donovan, Tipperary
Joe Hennessy, Kilkenny
Sylvie Linnane, Galway
FULL-BACK
Aidan Fogarty, Offaly
Conor Hayes, Galway
Noel Sheehy, Tipperary
LEFT FULL-BACK
Daithí Foran, Waterford
Martin Hanamy, Offaly
Paul Delaney, Tipperary
RIGHT HALF-BACK
Brendan Keeshan, Offaly
John O'Connor, Wexford
Peter Finnerty, Galway
CENTRE HALF-BACK
George O'Connor, Wexford
Martin Baillie, Down
Tony Keady, Galway
LEFT HALF-BACK
Bobby Ryan, Tipperary
Gerry McInerney, Galway
Paul Delaney, Tipperary
CENTREFIELD
Colm Bonnar, Tipperary
George O'Connor, Wexford
Ger Fennelly, Kilkenny
Joe Hayes, Tipperary
Pat Malone, Galway
Paul McKillen, Antrim
RIGHT HALF-FORWARD
Declan Ryan, Tipperary
Michael McGrath, Galway
Vincent Teehan, Offaly
Brendan Lynskey, Galway
Ciarán Barr, Antrim
Joe Cooney, Galway
LEFT HALF-FORWARD
Aidan Ryan, Tipperary
Mark Corrigan, Offaly
Martin Naughton, Galway
RIGHT FULL-FORWARD
Éanna Ryan, Galway
Michael McGrath, Galway
Pat Fox, Tipperary
FULL-FORWARD
Brendan Lynskey, Galway
Nicholas English, Tipperary
Noel Lane, Galway
LEFT FULL-FORWARD
Éanna Ryan, Galway
Olcan McFetridge, Antrim
Tony O'Sullivan, Cork

1989
GOALKEEPERS
Ger Cunningham, Cork
John Commins, Galway
Ken Hogan, Tipperary
RIGHT FULL-BACK
Aidan Fogarty, Offaly
John Heffernan, Tipperary
John Henderson, Kilkenny

Hurling All-Star Nominees

FULL-BACK
Conor O'Donovan, Tipperary
Eamon Cleary, Wexford
Terence Donnelly, Antrim
LEFT FULL-BACK
Dessie Donnelly, Antrim
John Conran, Wexford
Noel Sheehy, Tipperary
RIGHT HALF-BACK
Conal Bonnar, Tipperary
James McNaughton, Antrim
Peter Finnerty, Galway
CENTRE HALF-BACK
Bobby Ryan, Tipperary
Ger Fitzpatrick, Waterford
Michael Coleman, Galway
LEFT HALF-BACK
Ger Hegarty, Limerick
John Kennedy, Tipperary
Seán Treacy, Galway
CENTREFIELD
Declan Carr, Tipperary
Declan Ryan, Tipperary
Ger Hegarty, Limerick
Michael Coleman, Galway
Paul McKillen, Antrim
Teddy McCarthy, Cork
RIGHT HALF-FORWARD
Declan Ryan, Tipperary
Éanna Ryan, Galway
Michael Cleary, Tipperary
CENTRE HALF-FORWARD
Declan Ryan, Tipperary
Joe Cooney, Galway
Shane Ahearne, Waterford
LEFT HALF-FORWARD
Mark Corrigan, Offaly
Martin Naughton, Galway
Olcan McFetridge, Antrim
RIGHT FULL-FORWARD
Declan Ryan, Tipperary
Gerry Burke, Galway
Pat Fox, Tipperary
Shane Fitzgibbon, Limerick
FULL-FORWARD
Brian McMahon, Dublin
Ciarán Barr, Antrim
Cormac Bonnar, Tipperary
LEFT FULL-FORWARD
Éanna Ryan, Galway
Nicholas English, Tipperary
Terence McNaughton, Antrim

1990
GOALKEEPERS
Ger Cunningham, Cork
John Commins, Galway
Niall Patterson, Antrim
RIGHT FULL-BACK
Aidan Fogarty, Offaly
John Conzsidine, Cork
Pat Carey, Limerick
FULL-BACK
Eugene Coughlan, Offaly
Noel Sheehy, Tipperary
Vinny Holden, Dublin
LEFT FULL-BACK
Dessie Donnelly, Antrim
John Twomey, Dublin
Seán O'Gorman, Cork

RIGHT HALF-BACK
Conal Bonnar, Tipperary
Peter Finnerty, Galway
Seán McCarthy, Cork
CENTRE HALF-BACK
Jim Cashman, Cork
John O'Connell, Clare
Roy Mannion, Offaly
LEFT HALF-BACK
Gerry McInerney, Galway
Kieran McGuckian, Cork
Liam Dunne, Wexford
CENTREFIELD
Declan Carr, Tipperary
Joachim Kelly, Offaly
Johnny Pilkington, Offaly
Michael Coleman, Galway
RIGHT HALF-FORWARD
DJ Carey, Kilkenny
Ger Fitzgerald, Cork
Michael Cleary, Tipperary
CENTRE HALF-FORWARD
Joe Cooney, Galway
Mark Foley, Cork
LEFT HALF-FORWARD
Danny Owens, Offaly
John Leahy, Tipperary
Tony O'Sullivan, Cork
RIGHT FULL-FORWARD
Eamon Morrissey, Kilkenny
Tom Dempsey, Wexford
Tomás Mulcahy, Cork
FULL-FORWARD
Brian McMahon, Dublin
Kevin Hennessy, Cork
Michael Duignan, Offaly
LEFT FULL-FORWARD
Éanna Ryan, Galway
John Fitzgibbon, Cork
Nicholas English, Tipperary

1991
GOALKEEPERS
Jim Troy, Offaly
Ken Hogan, Tipperary
Michael Walsh, Kilkenny
RIGHT FULL-BACK
Bill Hennessy, Kilkenny
Paul Delaney, Tipperary
Seán O'Gorman, Cork
FULL-BACK
Damien Byrne, Waterford
Dominic McKinley, Antrim
Noel Sheehy, Tipperary
LEFT FULL-BACK
Liam Simpson, Kilkenny
Michael Ryan, Tipperary
Seán Treacy, Galway
RIGHT HALF-BACK
Conal Bonnar, Tipperary
Liam Walsh, Kilkenny
Michael Houlihan, Limerick
CENTRE HALF-BACK
Jim Cashman, Cork
Liam Dunne, Wexford
Michael Coleman, Galway
LEFT HALF-BACK
Brian Whelahan, Offaly
Cathal Casey, Cork
Liam Dunne, Wexford

CENTREFIELD
Aidan Ryan, Tipperary
Declan Carr, Tipperary
George O'Connor, Wexford
John Leahy, Tipperary
Michael Coleman, Galway
Terence McNaughton, Antrim
RIGHT HALF-FORWARD
John Power, Kilkenny
Martin Storey, Wexford
Michael Cleary, Tipperary
CENTRE HALF-FORWARD
Ciarán Barr, Antrim
Gary Kirby, Limerick
John Power, Kilkenny
LEFT HALF-FORWARD
DJ Carey, Kilkenny
Kieran Delahunty, Waterford
Tony O'Sullivan, Cork
RIGHT FULL-FORWARD
Eamon Morrissey, Kilkenny
Ger Fitzgerald, Cork
Pat Fox, Tipperary
FULL-FORWARD
Cormac Bonnar, Tipperary
Kevin Hennessy, Cork
Michael Duignan, Offaly
LEFT FULL-FORWARD
Joe Rabbitte, Galway
John Fitzgibbon, Cork
Liam McCarthy, Kilkenny

1992
GOALKEEPERS
Ger Cunningham, Cork
Michael Walsh, Kilkenny
Tommy Quaid, Limerick
DEFENDER
Bobby Ryan, Tipperary
Brian Corcoran, Cork
Brian Whelahan, Offaly
Cathal Casey, Cork
Christy Helebert, Galway
Ciarán Carey, Limerick
Conal Bonnar, Tipperary
Denis Mulcahy, Cork
Jim Cashman, Cork
Liam Simpson, Kilkenny
Liam Walsh, Kilkenny
Noel Sheehy, Tipperary
Pat Dwyer, Kilkenny
Pat O'Neill, Kilkenny
Seán O'Gorman, Cork
Willie O'Connor, Kilkenny
MIDFIELD
Bill Hennessy, Kilkenny
Ger Hegarty, Limerick
Michael Coleman, Galway
Michael Phelan, Kilkenny
Pat Malone, Galway
Seán McCarthy, Cork
FORWARD
DJ Carey, Kilkenny
Eamon Morrissey, Kilkenny
Gary Kirby, Limerick
Gerard McGrattan, Down
Joe Cooney, Galway
John Meaney, Waterford
John Power, Kilkenny
Kevin Hennessy, Cork

Brian Lohan, Clare
Brian Whelahan, Offaly
Christy Helebert, Galway
Dave Clarke, Limerick
George Frend, Tipperary
Ger Hegarty, Limerick
Gerry McInerney, Galway
Hubert Rigney, Offaly
Kevin Kinahan, Offaly
Kevin Martin, Offaly
Larry O'Gorman, Wexford
Liam Dunne, Wexford
Martin Hanamy, Offaly
Noel Sheehy, Tipperary
Seán O'Gorman, Cork
Stephen McDonagh, Limerick
MIDFIELD
Ciarán Carey, Limerick
Daithí Regan, Offaly
Johnny Pilkington, Offaly
Michael Coleman, Galway
Mike Houlihan, Limerick
Pat Malone, Galway
FORWARD
Billy Dooley, Offaly
Damien Quigley, Limerick
DJ Carey, Kilkenny
Frankie Carroll, Limerick
Gary Kirby, Limerick
Ger Manley, Cork
Jamesie O'Connor, Clare
Joe Cooney, Galway
Joe Dooley, Offaly
John Leahy, Tipperary
John Troy, Offaly
Johnny Dooley, Offaly
Martin Storey, Wexford
Michael Cleary, Tipperary
Mike Galligan, Limerick
Noel Sands, Down
Pat Heffernan, Limerick
Paul Flynn, Waterford

1995
GOALKEEPERS
David Fitzgerald, Clare
David Hughes, Offaly
Michael Walsh, Kilkenny
DEFENDER
Anthony Daly, Clare
Brian Corcoran, Cork
Brian Lohan, Clare
Brian Whelahan, Offaly
Dave Clarke, Limerick
Eddie O'Connor, Kilkenny
Frank Lohan, Clare
Hubert Rigney, Offaly
Kevin Coulter, Down
Kevin Kinahan, Offaly
Liam Doyle, Clare
Liam Dunne, Wexford
Martin Hanamy, Offaly
Nigel Shaughnessy, Galway
Pádraig Kelly, Galway
Raymie Ryan, Tipperary
Seánie McMahon, Clare
Willie O'Connor, Kilkenny
MIDFIELD
Aidan Ryan, Tipperary
Ciarán Carey, Limerick
Daithí Regan, Offaly
Johnny Pilkington, Offaly
Michael Coleman, Galway
Ollie Baker, Clare
FORWARD
Barry Egan, Cork
Billy Dooley, Offaly
Damien Quigley, Limerick
Denis Byrne, Kilkenny
DJ Carey, Kilkenny
Eamon Morrissey, Kilkenny
Fergus Tuohy, Clare
Gary Kirby, Limerick
Ger O'Loughlin, Clare
Jamesie O'Connor, Clare
Joe Cooney, Galway
Joe Dooley, Offaly
John Troy, Offaly
Johnny Dooley, Offaly
Martin Storey, Wexford
Michael Cleary, Tipperary
Noel Sands, Down
PJ O'Connell, Clare

1996
GOALKEEPERS
Damien Fitzhenry, Wexford
Joe Quaid, Limerick
Noel Keith, Down
DEFENDER
Brian Lohan, Clare
Brian Whelahan, Offaly
Ciarán Carey, Limerick
Colm Bonnar, Tipperary
Colm Kehoe, Wexford
Dave Clarke, Limerick
Declan Nash, Limerick
Ger Cush, Wexford
Larry O'Gorman, Wexford
Liam Dunne, Wexford
Mark Foley, Limerick
Martin Hanamy, Offaly
Nigel Shaughnessy, Galway
Rod Guiney, Wexford
Seán Flood, Wexford
Stephen McDonagh, Limerick
Terence McNaughton, Antrim
Tom Helebert, Galway
MIDFIELD
Adrian Fenlon, Wexford
George O'Connor, Wexford
Michael Cleary, Tipperary
Michael Coleman, Galway
Mike Houlihan, Limerick
Seán O'Neill, Limerick
FORWARD
Cathal Moore, Galway
Declan Ryan, Tipperary
DJ Carey, Kilkenny
Francis Forde, Galway
Garry Laffan, Wexford
Gary Kirby, Limerick
Jamesie O'Connor, Clare
Joe Cooney, Galway
Joe Rabbitte, Galway
John Troy, Offaly
Johnny Dooley, Offaly
Kevin Broderick, Galway
Larry Murphy, Wexford
Liam Cahill, Tipperary
Martin Storey, Wexford
Oliver Collins, Derry
Rory McCarthy, Wexford
Tom Dempsey, Wexford

1997
GOALKEEPERS
Brendan Cummins, Tipperary
Damien Fitzhenry, Wexford
David Fitzgerald, Clare
DEFENDER
Anthony Daly, Clare
Brian Lohan, Clare
Cathal Moore, Galway
Colm Bonnar, Tipperary
Dave Clarke, Limerick
Frank Lohan, Clare
Ger Cush, Wexford
Liam Doyle, Clare
Liam Dunne, Wexford
Liam Keoghan, Kilkenny
Michael O'Halloran, Clare
Michael Ryan, Tipperary
Mike Nash, Limerick
Paul Shelley, Tipperary
Seánie McMahon, Clare
Seán Óg Ó hAilpín, Cork
Stephen McDonagh, Limerick
DEFENDER
Willie O'Connor, Kilkenny
Adrian Fenlon, Wexford
Colin Lynch, Clare
Liam Burke, Galway
Ollie Baker, Clare
Philip Larkin, Kilkenny
Tommy Dunne, Tipperary
FORWARD
Charlie Carter, Kilkenny
Declan Ryan, Tipperary
DJ Carey, Kilkenny
Eugene O'Neill, Tipperary
Gary Kirby, Limerick
Gary Laffan, Wexford
Ger O'Loughlin, Clare
Jamesie O'Connor, Clare
John Leahy, Tipperary
Johnny Dooley, Offaly
Kevin Broderick, Galway
Martin Storey, Wexford
Niall Gilligan, Clare
Noel Sands, Down
PJ O'Connell, Clare
Rory McCarthy, Wexford
Seánie McGrath, Cork
Tom Dempsey, Wexford

1998
GOALKEEPERS
Brendan Landers, Waterford
David Fitzgerald, Clare
Stephen Byrne, Offaly
DEFENDER
Anthony Daly, Clare
Brian Corcoran, Cork
Brian Quinn, Clare
Canice Brennan, Kilkenny
Fergal Hartley, Waterford
Frank Lohan, Clare
Hubert Rigney, Offaly
Kevin Kinahan, Offaly
Kevin Martin, Offaly
Martin Hanamy, Offaly
Pat O'Neill, Kilkenny
Seán Cullinane, Waterford
Seánie McMahon, Clare
Seán Óg Ó hAilpín, Cork
Simon Whelahan, Offaly
Stephen Frampton, Waterford
Tom Feeney, Waterford
Willie O'Connor, Kilkenny
MIDFIELD
Johnny Dooley, Offaly
Johnny Pilkington, Offaly
Ollie Baker, Clare
Philip Larkin, Kilkenny
Tommy Dunne, Tipperary
Tony Browne, Waterford
FORWARD
Alan Markham, Clare
Anthony Kirwan, Waterford
Brian Whelahan, Offaly
Charlie Carter, Kilkenny
Dan Shanahan, Waterford
Gregory O'Kane, Antrim
Jamesie O'Connor, Clare
Joe Deane, Cork
Joe Dooley, Offaly
Joe Errity, Offaly
John Troy, Offaly
Ken McGrath, Waterford
Martin Storey, Wexford
Michael Duignan, Offaly
Niall Gilligan, Clare
Oliver Collins Derry
Paul Codd, Wexford
Paul Flynn, Waterford

1999
GOALKEEPERS
David Fitzgerald, Clare
Dónal Óg Cusack, Cork
James McGarry, Kilkenny
DEFENDER
Anthony Daly, Clare
Brian Corcoran, Cork
Brian Lohan, Clare
Brian Whelahan, Offaly
Cathal Moore, Galway
Diarmuid O'Sullivan, Cork
Fergal Ryan, Cork
Frank Lohan, Clare
John Browne, Cork
Kevin Kinahan, Offaly
Liam Doyle, Clare
Michael Kavanagh, Kilkenny
Peter Barry, Kilkenny
Seánie McMahon, Clare
Seán Óg Ó hAilpín, Cork
Simon Whelahan, Offaly
Wayne Sherlock, Cork
Willie O'Connor, Kilkenny
MIDFIELD
Andy Comerford, Kilkenny
Colin Lynch, Clare
Denis Byrne, Kilkenny
Johnny Dooley, Offaly
Johnny Pilkington, Offaly
Ollie Baker, Clare

Hurling All-Star Nominees

FORWARD
Alan Browne, Cork
Alan Kerins, Galway
Alan Markham, Clare
Ben O'Connor, Cork
Brian McEvoy, Kilkenny
DJ Carey, Kilkenny
Eugene Cloonan, Galway
Fergal McCormack, Cork
Henry Shefflin, Kilkenny
Jamesie O'Connor, Clare
Joe Deane, Cork
John Power, Kilkenny
John Troy, Offaly
Niall Gilligan, Clare
Niall Rigney, Laois
Seánie McGrath, Cork
Timmy McCarthy, Cork
Tommy Dunne, Tipperary

2000

GOALKEEPERS
Brendan Cummins, Tipperary
James McGarry, Kilkenny
Michael Crimmins, Galway
DEFENDER
Brian Corcoran, Cork
Cathal Moore, Galway
Diarmuid O'Sullivan, Cork
Éamonn Corcoran, Tipperary
Eamonn Kennedy, Kilkenny
Fergal Ryan, Cork
Finbarr Gantley, Galway
John Carroll, Tipperary
Liam Hodgins, Galway
Mark Foley, Limerick
Michael Kavanagh, Kilkenny
Noel Hickey, Kilkenny
Peter Barry, Kilkenny
Philip Larkin, Kilkenny
Philip Maher, Tipperary
Seán Óg Ó hAilpín, Cork
Simon Whelahan, Offaly
Willie O'Connor, Kilkenny
MIDFIELD
Andy Comerford , Kilkenny
Brian McEvoy, Kilkenny
John Leahy, Tipperary
Johnny Dooley, Offaly
Rory Gantley, Galway
Tommy Dunne, Tipperary
FORWARD
Alan Kerins, Galway
Brian O'Meara, Tipperary
Charlie Carter, Kilkenny
Denis Byrne, Kilkenny
DJ Carey, Kilkenny
Eugene Cloonan, Galway
Fergal Healy, Galway
Gary Hannify, Offaly
Henry Shefflin, Kilkenny
Joe Deane, Cork
Joe Rabbitte, Galway
John Power, Kilkenny
Johnny Pilkington, Offaly
Ken McGrath, Waterford
Kieran McKeever Derry
Michael Duignan, Offaly
Ollie Fahy, Galway
Seánie McGrath, Cork

2001

GOALKEEPERS
Brendan Cummins, Tipperary
Damien Fitzhenry, Wexford
James McGarry, Kilkenny
DEFENDER
Brian Geary, Limerick
Brian Lohan, Clare
Cathal Moore, Galway
Darragh Ryan, Wexford
David Kennedy, Tipperary
David O'Connor, Wexford
Eamon Kennedy, Kilkenny
Éamonn Corcoran, Tipperary
Frank Lohan, Clare
Liam Hodgins, Galway
Mark Foley, Limerick
Michael Kavanagh, Kilkenny
Ollie Canning, Galway
Paul Kelly, Tipperary
Paul Ormond, Tipperary
Philip Larkin, Kilkenny
Philip Maher, Tipperary
Seánie McMahon, Clare
MIDFIELD
Adrian Fenlon, Wexford
Eddie Enright, Tipperary
Johnny Dooley, Offaly
Larry O'Gorman, Wexford
Richie Murray , Galway
Tommy Dunne, Tipperary
FORWARD
Alan Kerins, Galway
Brian Begley, Limerick
Brian O'Meara, Tipperary
Charlie Carter, Kilkenny
Declan Ryan, Tipperary
DJ Carey, Kilkenny
Eoin Kelly, Tipperary
Eugene Cloonan, Galway
Henry Shefflin, Kilkenny
Jamesie O'Connor, Clare
John Carroll, Tipperary
John Power, Kilkenny
Ken McGrath, Waterford
Kevin Broderick, Galway
Lar Corbett, Tipperary
Mark Kerins, Galway
Mark O'Leary, Tipperary
Ollie Moran, Limerick

2002

GOALKEEPERS
Damien Fitzhenry, Wexford
David Fitzgerald, Clare
James McGarry, Kilkenny
DEFENDER
Brian Lohan, Clare
Declan Ruth, Wexford
Fergal Hartley, Waterford
Gerry Quinn, Clare
JJ Delaney, Kilkenny
Mark Foley, Limerick
Michael Kavanagh, Kilkenny
Noel Hickey, Kilkenny
Ollie Canning, Galway
Paul Kelly, Tipperary
Peter Barry, Kilkenny
Peter Queally, Waterford
Philip Larkin, Kilkenny
Philip Maher, Tipperary
Seánie McMahon, Clare
Stephen McDonagh, Limerick
Tom Feeney, Waterford
Wayne Sherlock, Cork
MIDFIELD
Andy Comerford, Kilkenny
Colin Lynch, Clare
Derek Lyng, Kilkenny
Noel Morris, Tipperary
Richie Murray, Galway
Tony Browne, Waterford
FORWARD
Ben O'Connor, Cork
Benny Dunne, Tipperary
Brian Begley, Limerick
Brian McFall, Antrim
DJ Carey, Kilkenny
Eoin Kelly , Waterford
Eoin Kelly , Tipperary
Henry Shefflin, Kilkenny
Joe Deane, Cork
John Carroll, Tipperary
John Mullane, Waterford
Ken McGrath, Waterford
Kevin Broderick, Galway
Martin Comerford, Kilkenny
Nicky Horan, Meath
Paul Codd, Wexford
Paul Flynn, Waterford
Tony Griffin, Clare

2003

GOALKEEPERS
Brendan Cummins, Tipperary
Damien Fitzhenry, Wexford
James McGarry, Kilkenny
DEFENDER
Ciarán Herron, Antrim
Colm Cassidy, Offaly
Darragh Ryan, Wexford
David Franks, Offaly
Declan Ruth, Wexford
Diarmuid O'Sullivan, Cork
JJ Delaney, Kilkenny
Liam Dunne, Wexford
Michael Kavanagh, Kilkenny
Noel Hickey, Kilkenny
Ollie Canning, Galway
Paul Kelly, Tipperary
Peter Barry, Kilkenny
Ronan Curran, Cork
Seán Dowling, Kilkenny
Seán Óg Ó hAilpín, Cork
Tom Kenny, Cork
Wayne Sherlock, Cork
MIDFIELD
Benny Dunne, Tipperary
Colin Lynch, Clare
Conal Keaney, Dublin
Derek Lyng, Kilkenny
John Gardiner, Cork
Tommy Walsh, Kilkenny
FORWARD
Ben O'Connor, Cork
Brendan Murphy, Offaly
Conor Gleeson, Tipperary
Eddie Brennan, Kilkenny
Eoin Kelly, Tipperary

DEFENDER
Brian Lohan, Clare
Brian Murphy, Cork
Darragh Ryan, Wexford
David Collins, Galway
Derick Hardiman, Galway
Diarmuid Fitzgerald, Tipperary
Diarmuid O'Sullivan, Cork
Gerry Quinn, Clare
John Gardiner, Cork
Noel Hickey, Kilkenny
Ollie Canning, Galway
Pat Mulcahy, Cork
Peter Lawlor, Limerick
Richie Mullally, Kilkenny
Seánie McMahon, Clare
Seán Óg Ó hAilpín, Cork
Tony Browne, Waterford
Tony Óg Regan, Galway
MIDFIELD
Colin Lynch, Clare
David Tierney, Galway
Fergal Healy, Galway
Jerry O'Connor, Cork
Paul Kelly, Tipperary
Tom Kenny, Cork
FORWARD
Alan Kerins, Galway
Ben O'Connor, Cork
Brian Corcoran, Cork
Damien Hayes, Galway
David Forde, Galway
Des Mythen, Wexford
Diarmuid McMahon, Clare
Eoin Kelly, Tipperary
Eoin Kelly, Waterford
Eoin Larkin, Kilkenny
Ger Farragher, Galway
Henry Shefflin, Kilkenny
Joe Deane, Cork
Micheál Webster, Tipperary
Niall Healy, Galway
Séamus Prendergast, Waterford
Tommy Walsh, Kilkenny
Tony Carmody, Clare

2006
GOALKEEPERS
David Fitzgerald, Clare
Dónal Óg Cusack, Cork
James McGarry, Kilkenny
FULL-BACK
Brian Murphy, Cork
Damien Reale, Limerick
Diarmuid O'Sullivan, Cork
Eoin Murphy, Waterford
Frank Lohan, Clare
JJ Delaney, Kilkenny
Noel Hickey, Kilkenny
Paul Curran, Tipperary
Tom Feeney, Waterford
HALF-BACK
Éamonn Corcoran, Tipperary
James Ryall, Kilkenny
John Gardiner, Cork
John Tennyson, Kilkenny
Ken McGrath, Waterford
Ronan Curran, Cork
Seánie McMahon, Clare
Tommy Walsh, Kilkenny
Tony Browne, Waterford

MIDFIELD
Dave Bennett, Waterford
Derek Lyng, Kilkenny
James "Cha" Fitzpatrick, Kilkenny
Jerry O'Connor, Cork
Shane McGrath, Tipperary
Tom Kenny, Cork
HALF-FORWARD
Ben O'Connor, Cork
Dan Shanahan, Waterford
Eddie Brennan, Kilkenny
Eoin Larkin, Kilkenny
Henry Shefflin, Kilkenny
James Young, Laois
Michael Walsh, Waterford
Niall McCarthy, Cork
Tony Carmody, Clare
FULL-FORWARD
Aidan Fogarty, Kilkenny
Brian Corcoran, Cork
Damien Hayes, Galway
Eoin Kelly, Tipperary
Joe Bergin, Offaly
Joe Deane, Cork
John Mullane, Waterford
Martin Comerford, Kilkenny
Tony Griffin, Clare

2007
GOALKEEPERS
Brian Murray, Limerick
Damien Fitzhenry, Wexford
Dónal Óg Cusack, Cork
FULL-BACK
Aidan Kearney, Waterford
Damien Reale, Limerick
Declan Fanning, Tipperary
Jackie Tyrell, Kilkenny
Keith Rossiter, Wexford
Michael Kavanagh, Kilkenny
Noel Hickey, Kilkenny
Séamus Hickey, Limerick
Stephen Lucey, Limerick
HALF-BACK
Brian Geary, Limerick
Conor O'Mahony, Tipperary
Éamonn Corcoran, Tipperary
John Lee, Galway
Ken McGrath, Waterford
Mark Foley, Limerick
Seán Óg Ó hAilpín, Cork
Tommy Walsh, Kilkenny
Tony Browne, Waterford
MIDFIELD
Derek Lyng, Kilkenny
Dónal O'Grady, Limerick
James "Cha" Fitzpatrick, Kilkenny
Jerry O'Connor, Cork
Michael Walsh, Waterford
Tom Kenny, Cork
HALF-FORWARD
Alan Kerins, Galway
Ben O'Connor, Cork
Dan Shanahan, Waterford
Eoin Larkin, Kilkenny
James Young, Laois
Martin Comerford, Kilkenny
Mike Fitzgerald, Limerick
Ollie Moran, Limerick
Stephen Molumphy, Waterford

FULL-FORWARD
Andrew O'Shaughnessy, Limerick
Eddie Brennan, Kilkenny
Eoin McGrath, Waterford
Henry Shefflin, Kilkenny
John Mullane, Waterford
Kieran Murphy, Cork
Neil Ronan, Cork
Séamus Prendergast, Waterford
Willie O'Dwyer, Kilkenny

2008
GOALKEEPERS
Brendan Cummins, Tipperary
Clinton Hennessy, Waterford
PJ Ryan, Kilkenny
FULL-BACK
Brian Murphy, Cork
Conor O'Brien, Tipperary
David Franks, Offaly
Gerry O'Grady, Clare
Jackie Tyrell, Kilkenny
Michael Kavanagh, Kilkenny
Noel Hickey, Kilkenny
Paul Curran, Tipperary
Shane O'Neill, Cork
HALF-BACK
Brian Hogan, Kilkenny
Conor O'Mahony, Tipperary
JJ Delaney, Kilkenny
John Gardiner, Cork
Ronan Fallon, Dublin
Seán Óg Ó hAilpín, Cork
Shane Maher, Tipperary
Tommy Walsh, Kilkenny
Tony Browne, Waterford
MIDFIELD
Brian O'Connell, Clare
Colin Lynch, Clare
Derek Lyng, Kilkenny
James "Cha" Fitzpatrick, Kilkenny
Shane McGrath, Tipperary
Tom Kenny, Cork
HALF FORWARD
Ben O'Connor, Cork
Brian Carroll, Offaly
Cathal Naughton, Cork
Eoin Larkin, Kilkenny
Henry Shefflin, Kilkenny
Jonathan Clancy, Clare
Lar Corbett, Tipperary
Richie Power, Kilkenny
Séamus Callinan, Tipperary
FULL-FORWARD
Aidan Fogarty, Kilkenny
David O'Callaghan, Dublin
Eddie Brennan, Kilkenny
Eoin Kelly, Waterford
Eoin Kelly, Tipperary
Eoin McGrath, Waterford
Joe Canning, Galway
John Mullane, Waterford
Niall Gilligan, Clare

2009
GOALKEEPERS
Brendan Cummins, Tipperary
Clinton Hennessy, Waterford
PJ Ryan, Kilkenny

FULL-BACK
Fergal Moore, Galway
Jackie Tyrell, Kilkenny
JJ Delaney, Kilkenny
Michael Kavanagh, Kilkenny
Noel Connors, Waterford
Ollie Canning, Galway
Paddy Stapleton, Tipperary
Pádraic Maher, Tipperary
Shane O'Neill, Cork
HALF-BACK
Conor O'Mahony, Tipperary
Declan Fanning, Tipperary
John Lee, Galway
John Tennyson, Kilkenny
Mark Foley, Limerick
Michael Walsh, Waterford
Stephen Hiney, Dublin
Tommy Walsh, Kilkenny
Tony Browne, Waterford
MIDFIELD
Alan McCrabbe, Dublin
Gavin O'Mahony, Limerick
James Woodlock, Tipperary
Michael Rice, Kilkenny
Séamus Hickey, Limerick
Shane McGrath, Tipperary
HALF-FORWARD
Aonghus Callinan, Galway
Ben O'Connor, Cork
Eddie Brennan, Kilkenny
Eoin Larkin, Kilkenny
Henry Shefflin, Kilkenny
John O'Brien, Tipperary
Lar Corbett, Tipperary
Pat Kerwick, Tipperary
Séamus Callinan, Tipperary
FULL-FORWARD
Damien Hayes, Galway
David O'Callaghan, Dublin
David Treacy, Dublin
Eoin Kelly, Tipperary
Joe Canning, Galway
John Mullane, Waterford
Martin Comerford, Kilkenny
Noel McGrath, Tipperary
Richie Power, Kilkenny

2010
GOALKEEPERS
Brendan Cummins, Tipperary
Clinton Hennessy, Waterford
Dónal Óg Cusack, Cork
FULL-BACK
Jackie Tyrell, Kilkenny
John Dalton, Kilkenny
Michael Cahill, Tipperary
Noel Connors, Waterford
Ollie Canning, Galway
Paddy Stapleton, Tipperary
Paul Curran, Tipperary
Shane Kavanagh, Galway
Shane O'Neill, Cork
HALF-BACK
Declan Fanning, Tipperary
JJ Delaney, Kilkenny
John Gardiner, Cork
Michael Walsh, Waterford
Pádraic Maher, Tipperary

Hurling All-Star Nominees

Ronan Curran, Cork
Tommy Walsh, Kilkenny
Tony Browne, Waterford
Tony Óg Regan, Galway
MIDFIELD
Brendan Maher, Tipperary
Ger Farragher, Galway
Michael Fennelly, Kilkenny
Michael Rice, Kilkenny
Shane McGrath, Tipperary
Shane O'Sullivan, Waterford
HALF-FORWARD
Damien Hayes, Galway
Eoin Larkin, Kilkenny
Gearóid Ryan, Tipperary
Henry Shefflin, Kilkenny
Lar Corbett, Tipperary
Niall McCarthy, Cork
Noel McGrath, Tipperary
Patrick Bonnar Maher, Tipperary
TJ Reid, Kilkenny
FULL-FORWARD
Aidan Fogarty, Kilkenny
Eoin Kelly, Tipperary
Joe Canning, Galway
John Mullane, Waterford
John O'Brien, Tipperary
Liam Watson, Antrim
Patrick Horgan, Cork
Richie Power, Kilkenny
Shane Dooley, Offaly

2011
GOALKEEPERS
Brendan Cummins, Tipperary
David Herity, Kilkenny
Gary Maguire, Dublin
FULL-BACK
David Collins, Galway
Jackie Tyrell, Kilkenny
Michael Cahill, Tipperary
Niall Corcoran, Dublin
Noel Hickey, Kilkenny
Paul Curran, Tipperary
Paul Murphy, Kilkenny
Peter Kelly, Dublin
Tom Condon, Limerick
HALF-BACK
Brian Hogan, Kilkenny
Conor O'Mahony, Tipperary
JJ Delaney, Kilkenny
Joey Boland, Dublin
Michael Walsh, Waterford
Pádraic Maher, Tipperary
Shane Durkan, Dublin
Tommy Walsh, Kilkenny
Tony Browne, Waterford
MIDFIELD
Dónal O'Grady, Limerick
Gearóid Ryan, Tipperary
Johnny McCaffrey, Dublin
Kevin Moran, Waterford
Liam Rushe, Dublin
Michael Fennelly, Kilkenny
HALF-FORWARD
Conal Keaney, Dublin
Declan Hannon, Limerick
Henry Shefflin, Kilkenny
Michael Rice, Kilkenny
Noel McGrath, Tipperary

Patrick Bonnar Maher, Tipperary
Pauric Mahony, Waterford
Richie Power, Kilkenny
Ryan O'Dwyer, Dublin
FULL-FORWARD
Colin Fennelly, Kilkenny
Eoin Kelly, Tipperary
Eoin Larkin, Kilkenny
Joe Canning, Galway
John Mullane, Waterford
Lar Corbett, Tipperary
Paul Ryan, Dublin
Richie Hogan, Kilkenny
Shane Walsh, Waterford

2012
GOALKEEPERS
Anthony Nash, Cork
James Skehill, Galway
Nickie Quaid, Limerick
FULL-BACK
Fergal Moore, Galway
Jackie Tyrell, Kilkenny
JJ Delaney, Kilkenny
Johnny Coen, Galway
Kevin Hynes, Galway
Michael Cahill, Tipperary
Paul Murphy, Kilkenny
Richie McCarthy, Limerick
Shane O'Neill, Cork
HALF-BACK
Brendan Bugler, Clare
Brian Hogan, Kilkenny
David Collins, Galway
Kieran Joyce, Kilkenny
Michael Walsh, Waterford
Niall Donoghue, Galway
Pádraic Maher, Tipperary
Tommy Walsh, Kilkenny
Tony Óg Regan, Galway
MIDFIELD
Andy Smith, Galway
Iarla Tannian, Galway
Kevin Moran, Waterford
Michael Fennelly, Kilkenny
Pa Cronin, Cork
Stephen Molumphy, Waterford
HALF-FORWARD
Cyril Donnellan, Galway
Damien Hayes, Galway
Danny Sutcliffe, Dublin
Henry Shefflin, Kilkenny
Niall Burke, Galway
Pa Burke, Tipperary
Patrick Bonnar Maher, Tipperary
Richie Power, Kilkenny
TJ Reid, Kilkenny
FULL-FORWARD
Brian O'Meara, Tipperary
David Burke, Galway
Eoin Larkin, Kilkenny
Joe Canning, Galway
John Conlon, Clare
John Mullane, Waterford
Noel McGrath, Tipperary
Patrick Horgan, Cork
Richie Hogan, Kilkenny

2013
GOALKEEPERS
Anthony Nash, Cork
Gary Maguire, Dublin
Patrick Kelly, Clare
FULL-BACK
Conor O'Sullivan, Cork
David McInerney, Clare
Domhnall O'Donovan, Clare
Paul Murphy, Kilkenny
Peter Kelly, Dublin
Richie McCarthy, Limerick
Shane O'Neill, Cork
Tom Condon, Limerick
Tomás Waters, Wexford
HALF-BACK
Brendan Bugler, Clare
Brian Murphy, Cork
Gavin O'Mahony, Limerick
Kieran Joyce, Kilkenny
Liam Rushe, Dublin
Michael Carton, Dublin
Michael Walsh, Waterford
Patrick Donnellan, Clare
Wayne McNamara, Limerick
MIDFIELD
Colm Galvin, Clare
Conor Ryan, Clare
Daniel Kearney, Cork
Joey Boland, Dublin
Kevin Moran, Waterford
Paul Browne, Limerick
HALF-FORWARD
Colin Ryan, Clare
Conal Keaney, Dublin
Danny Sutcliffe, Dublin
Eoin Larkin, Kilkenny
James Ryan, Limerick
John Conlon, Clare
Patrick Cronin, Cork
Séamus Harnedy, Cork
Tony Kelly, Clare
FULL-FORWARD
Conor Lehane, Cork
Conor McGrath, Clare
David O'Callaghan, Dublin
Graeme Mulcahy, Limerick
Patrick Horgan, Cork
Paul Ryan, Dublin
Podge Collins, Clare
Richie Hogan, Kilkenny
Shane O'Donnell, Clare

2014
GOALKEEPER
Alan Nolan, Dublin
Darren Gleeson, Tipperary
Eoin Murphy, Kilkenny
FULL-BACK
Cathal Barrett, Tipperary
Jackie Tyrell, Kilkenny
JJ Delaney, Kilkenny
Liam Ryan, Wexford
Paddy Stapleton, Tipperary
Paul Murphy, Kilkenny
Richie McCarthy, Limerick
Séamus Hickey, Limerick
Stephen McDonnell, Cork

HALF-BACK
Brendan Maher, Tipperary
Cillian Buckley, Kilkenny
Kieran Bergin, Tipperary
Liam Rushe, Dublin
Lorcan McLoughlin, Cork
Mark Ellis, Cork
Pádraic Maher, Tipperary
Pádraig Walsh, Kilkenny
Wayne McNamara, Limerick
MIDFIELD
Conor Fogarty, Kilkenny
James Ryan, Limerick
Lee Chin, Wexford
Paul Browne, Limerick
Richie Hogan, Kilkenny
Shane McGrath, Tipperary
HALF-FORWARD
Conor Cooney, Galway
Conor Lehane, Cork
Declan Hannon, Limerick
Eoin Larkin, Kilkenny
John O'Dwyer, Tipperary
Michael Fennelly, Kilkenny
Noel McGrath, Tipperary
Patrick Bonnar Maher, Tipperary
TJ Reid, Kilkenny
FULL-FORWARD
Alan Cadogan, Cork
Brian Carroll, Offaly
Colin Fennelly, Kilkenny
Conor McDonald, Wexford
Conor McGrath, Clare
Patrick Horgan, Cork
Richie Power, Kilkenny
Séamus Callinan, Tipperary
Shane Dowling, Limerick

2015
GOALKEEPER
Colm Callanan, Galway
Darren Gleeson, Tipperary
Eoin Murphy, Kilkenny
DEFENDER
Austin Gleeson, Waterford
Barry Coughlan, Waterford
Cathal Barrett, Tipperary
Cillian Buckley, Kilkenny
Daithí Burke, Galway
Iarla Tannian, Galway
James Barry, Tipperary
Joey Holden, Kilkenny
Johnny Coen, Galway
Kieran Joyce, Kilkenny
Noel Connors, Waterford
Pádraic Maher, Tipperary
Pádraig Mannion, Galway
Pádraig Walsh, Kilkenny
Paul Murphy, Kilkenny
Philip Mahony, Waterford
Shane Fives, Waterford
Tadhg De Búrca, Waterford
MIDFIELD
Andrew Smith, Galway
Conor Fogarty, Kilkenny
David Burke, Galway
Jamie Barron, Waterford
Kevin Moran, Waterford
Michael Fennelly, Kilkenny

All-Star Gazing

FORWARD
Brendan Maher, Tipperary
Cathal Mannion, Galway
Colin Dunford, Waterford
Conor Whelan, Galway
Eoin Larkin, Kilkenny
Ger Aylward, Kilkenny
Jason Flynn, Galway
Joe Canning, Galway
John O'Dwyer, Tipperary
Jonathon Glynn, Galway
Mark Schutte, Dublin
Maurice Shanahan, Waterford
Michael Walsh, Waterford
Richie Hogan, Kilkenny
Séamus Callinan, Tipperary
Séamus Harnedy, Cork
TJ Reid, Kilkenny
Tony Kelly, Clare

2016
GOALKEEPER
Colm Callanan, Galway
Darren Gleeson, Tipperary
Eoin Murphy, Kilkenny
DEFENDER
Cathal Barrett, Tipperary
Cian Dillon, Clare
Cillian Buckley, Kilkenny
Daithí Burke, Galway
Diarmuid Byrnes, Limerick
James Barry, Tipperary
Matthew O'Hanlon, Wexford
Michael Cahill, Tipperary
Noel Connors, Waterford
Pádraic Maher, Tipperary
Pádraig Mannion, Galway
Pádraig Walsh, Kilkenny
Paul Murphy, Kilkenny
Philip Mahony, Waterford
Ronan Maher, Tipperary
Séamus Kennedy, Tipperary
Shane Fives, Waterford
Tadhg De Búrca, Waterford
MIDFIELD
Brendan Maher, Tipperary
Conor Fogarty, Kilkenny
David Burke, Galway
Jamie Barron, Waterford
Kevin Moran, Waterford
Michael Breen, Tipperary
FORWARD
Alan Cadogan, Cork
Austin Gleeson, Waterford
Colm Gavin, Clare
Conor Cooney, Galway
Dan McCormack, Tipperary
Joe Canning, Galway
John McGrath, Tipperary
John O'Dwyer, Tipperary
Lee Chin, Wexford
Michael Walsh, Waterford
Noel McGrath, Tipperary
Patrick Bonnar Maher, Tipperary
Pauric Mahony, Waterford
Richie Hogan, Kilkenny
Séamus Callinan, Tipperary
TJ Reid, Kilkenny
Tony Kelly, Clare
Walter Walsh, Kilkenny

2017
GOALKEEPER
Anthony Nash, Cork
Colm Callanan, Galway
Stephen O'Keeffe, Waterford
DEFENDER
Adrian Tuohy, Galway
Aidan Harte, Galway
Cillian Buckley, Kilkenny
Colm Spillane, Cork
Conor Gleeson, Waterford
Daithí Burke, Galway
Damien Cahalane, Cork
Darragh Fives, Waterford
Diarmuid O'Keeffe, Wexford
Gearóid McInerney, Galway
John Hanbury, Galway
Mark Coleman, Cork
Matthew O'Hanlon, Wexford
Noel Connors, Waterford
Pádraic Maher, Tipperary
Pádraig Mannion, Galway
Philip Mahony, Waterford
Tadhg De Búrcá, Waterford
MIDFIELD
Brendan Maher, Tipperary
Darragh Fitzgibbon, Cork
David Burke, Galway
Jamie Barron, Waterford
Johnny Coen, Galway
Lee Chin, Wexford
FORWARD
Alan Cadogan, Cork
Austin Gleeson, Waterford
Cathal Mannion, Galway
Conor Cooney, Galway
Conor Lehane, Cork
Conor McDónald, Wexford
Conor Whelan, Galway
Joe Canning, Galway
John McGrath, Tipperary
Joseph Cooney, Galway
Kevin Moran, Waterford
Michael Walsh, Waterford
Noel McGrath, Tipperary
Patrick Horgan, Cork
Pauric Mahony, Waterford
Séamus Callinan, Tipperary
Shane O'Donnell, Clare
TJ Reid, Kilkenny

2018
GOALKEEPER
Anthony Nash, Cork
Eoin Murphy, Kilkenny
Nickie Quaid, Limerick
DEFENDER
Adrian Tuohy, Galway
Aidan Harte, Galway
Chris Crummey, Dublin
Cillian Buckley, Kilkenny
Colm Spillane, Cork
Daithí Burke, Galway
Dan Morrissey, Limerick
David McInerney, Clare
Declan Hannon, Limerick
Diarmuid Byrnes, Limerick
Liam Ryan, Wexford
Mark Coleman, Cork
Mike Casey, Limerick
Pádraic Mannion, Galway
Pádraig Walsh, Kilkenny
Paudie Foley, Wexford
Richie English, Limerick
Seán Finn, Limerick
MIDFIELD
Cian Lynch, Limerick
Colm Galvin, Clare
Darragh Fitzgibbon, Cork
Darragh O'Donovan, Limerick
David Burke, Galway
James Maher, Kilkenny
FORWARD
Aaron Gillane, Limerick
Cathal Mannion, Galway
Conor Whelan, Galway
Daniel Kearney, Cork
Gearóid Hegarty, Limerick
Graeme Mulcahy, Limerick
Jason Forde, Tipperary
Joe Canning, Galway
John Conlon, Clare
Jonathan Glynn, Galway
Kyle Hayes, Limerick
Patrick Horgan, Cork
Peter Duggan, Clare
Séamus Flanagan, Limerick
Séamus Harnedy, Cork
Shane O'Donnell, Clare
TJ Reid, Kilkenny
Tom Morrissey, Limerick

2019
GOALKEEPER
Brian Hogan, Tipperary
Enda Rowland, Laois
Eoin Murphy, Kilkenny
DEFENDER
Barry Heffernan, Tipperary
Brendan Maher, Tipperary
Cathal Barrett, Tipperary
Chris Crummey, Dublin
Conor Fogarty, Kilkenny
Eoghan O'Donnell, Dublin
Huw Lawlor, Kilkenny
Jack Kelly, Laois
Liam Ryan, Wexford
Matthew O'Hanlon, Wexford
Mike Casey, Limerick
Paddy Deegan, Kilkenny
Pádraic Maher, Tipperary
Pádraig Walsh, Kilkenny
Paudie Foley, Wexford
Richie English, Limerick
Ronan Maher, Tipperary
Seán Finn, Limerick
MIDFIELD
Cathal Mannion, Galway
Cian Lynch, Limerick
Diarmuid O'Keeffe, Wexford
Kevin Foley, Wexford
Noel McGrath, Tipperary
William O'Donoghue, Limerick
FORWARD
Aaron Gillane, Limerick
Adrian Mullen, Kilkenny
Alan Cadogan, Cork
Colin Fennelly, Kilkenny
Conor McDónald, Wexford
Conor Whelan, Galway
Graeme Mulcahy, Limerick
Jason Forde, Tipperary
John Donnelly, Kilkenny
John McGrath, Tipperary
John O'Dwyer, Tipperary
Kyle Hayes, Limerick
Lee Chin, Wexford
Patrick Horgan, Cork
Peter Casey, Limerick
Rory O'Connor, Wexford
Séamus Callinan, Tipperary
TJ Reid, Kilkenny

2020
GOALKEEPER
Eibhear Quilligan, Clare
Nickie Quaid, Limerick
Stephen O'Keeffe, Waterford
DEFENDER
Aidan Harte, Galway
Barry Nash, Limerick
Calum Lyons, Waterford
Conor Delaney, Kilkenny
Conor Prunty, Waterford
Daithí Burke, Galway
Dan Morrissey, Limerick
Declan Hannon, Limerick
Diarmuid Byrnes, Limerick
Kyle Hayes, Limerick
Mark Coleman, Cork
Pádraic Mannion, Galway
Pádraig Walsh, Kilkenny
Ronan Maher, Tipperary
Rory Hayes, Clare
Seán Finn, Limerick
Shane McNulty, Waterford
Tadhg De Búrca, Waterford
MIDFIELD
Cian Lynch, Limerick
Conor Browne, Kilkenny
Jamie Barron, Waterford
Michael Breen, Tipperary
Tony Kelly, Clare
William O'Donoghue, Limerick
FORWARD
Aaron Gillane, Limerick
Austin Gleeson, Waterford
Brian Concannon, Galway
Cathal Malone, Clare
Cathal Mannion, Galway
Conor Whelan, Galway
Dessie Hutchinson, Waterford
Dónal Burke, Dublin
Gearóid Hegarty, Limerick
Graeme Mulcahy, Limerick
Jack Fagan, Waterford
Joe Canning, Galway
John Donnelly, Kilkenny
Séamus Flanagan, Limerick
Shane Kingston, Cork
Stephen Bennett, Waterford
TJ Reid, Kilkenny
Tom Morrissey, Limerick

All-Star Gazing

Football All-Star Lists (1971 to 2020)

The statistics included in this book have been cross-checked to the best of our ability. Our data sources for the All-Star data were:

1) the GAA All-Star Posters from 1971 to 2016 and
2) newspaper archives from 2017 to 2020.

List of Football All-Stars

#	Year	Player	County	Position
1	1971	PJ Smyth	Galway	Goalkeeper
2	1971	Johnny Carey	Mayo	Right Full-Back
3	1971	Jack Cosgrove	Galway	Full-Back
4	1971	Donie O'Sullivan	Kerry	Left Full-Back
5	1971	Eugene Mulligan	Offaly	Right Half-Back
6	1971	Nicholas Clavin	Offaly	Centre Half-Back
7	1971	Pat Reynolds	Meath	Left Half-Back
8	1971	Liam Sammon	Galway	Centrefield
9	1971	Willie Bryan	Offaly	Centrefield
10	1971	Tony McTague	Offaly	Right Half-Forward
11	1971	Ray Cummins	Cork	Centre Half-Forward
12	1971	Mickey Kearins	Sligo	Left Half-Forward
13	1971	Andy McCallin	Antrim	Right Full-Forward
14	1971	Seán O'Neill	Down	Full-Forward
15	1971	Séamus Leydon	Galway	Left Full-Forward
16	1972	Martin Furlong	Offaly	Goalkeeper
17	1972	Mick Ryan	Offaly	Right Full-Back
18	1972	Paddy McCormack	Offaly	Full-Back
19	1972	Donie O'Sullivan	Kerry	Left Full-Back
20	1972	Brian McEniff	Donegal	Right Half-Back
21	1972	Tommy Joe "TJ" Gilmore	Galway	Centre Half-Back
22	1972	Kevin Jer O'Sullivan	Cork	Left Half-Back
23	1972	Willie Bryan	Offaly	Centrefield
24	1972	Mick O'Connell	Kerry	Centrefield
25	1972	Johnny Cooney	Offaly	Right Half-Forward
26	1972	Kevin Kilmurray	Offaly	Centre Half-Forward
27	1972	Tony McTague	Offaly	Left Half-Forward
28	1972	Mickey Freyne	Roscommon	Right Full-Forward
29	1972	Seán O'Neill	Down	Full-Forward
30	1972	Paddy Moriarty	Armagh	Left Full-Forward
31	1973	Billy Morgan	Cork	Goalkeeper
32	1973	Frank Cogan	Cork	Right Full-Back
33	1973	Mick Ryan	Offaly	Full-Back
34	1973	Brian Murphy	Cork	Left Full-Back
35	1973	Liam O'Neill	Galway	Right Half-Back
36	1973	Tommy Joe "TJ" Gilmore	Galway	Centre Half-Back
37	1973	Kevin Jer O'Sullivan	Cork	Left Half-Back
38	1973	John O'Keeffe	Kerry	Centrefield
39	1973	Dinny Long	Cork	Centrefield
40	1973	Johnny Cooney	Offaly	Right Half-Forward
41	1973	Kevin Kilmurray	Offaly	Centre Half-Forward
42	1973	Liam Sammon	Galway	Left Half-Forward
43	1973	Jimmy Barry Murphy	Cork	Right Full-Forward
44	1973	Ray Cummins	Cork	Full-Forward
45	1973	Anthony McGurk	Derry	Left Full-Forward
46	1974	Paddy Cullen	Dublin	Goalkeeper
47	1974	Donal Monaghan	Donegal	Right Full-Back
48	1974	Seán Doherty	Dublin	Full-Back
49	1974	Robbie Kelleher	Dublin	Left Full-Back
50	1974	Paddy Reilly	Dublin	Right Half-Back
51	1974	Barnes Murphy	Sligo	Centre Half-Back
52	1974	Johnny Hughes	Galway	Left Half-Back
53	1974	Dermot Earley Snr	Roscommon	Centrefield
54	1974	Paud Lynch	Kerry	Centrefield
55	1974	Tom Naughton	Galway	Right Half-Forward
56	1974	Declan Barron	Cork	Centre Half-Forward
57	1974	David Hickey	Dublin	Left Half-Forward
58	1974	Jimmy Barry Murphy	Cork	Right Full-Forward
59	1974	Jimmy Keaveney	Dublin	Full-Forward
60	1974	Johnny Tobin	Galway	Left Full-Forward
61	1975	Paud O'Mahony	Kerry	Goalkeeper
62	1975	Gay O'Driscoll	Dublin	Right Full-Back
63	1975	John O'Keeffe	Kerry	Full-Back
64	1975	Robbie Kelleher	Dublin	Left Full-Back
65	1975	Peter Stevenson	Derry	Right Half-Back
66	1975	Anthony McGurk	Derry	Centre Half-Back
67	1975	Ger Power	Kerry	Left Half-Back
68	1975	Dinny Long	Cork	Centrefield
69	1975	Colm McAlarney	Down	Centrefield
70	1975	Gerry McElhinney	Derry	Right Half-Forward
71	1975	Ken Rennicks	Meath	Centre Half-Forward
72	1975	Mickey Ned O'Sullivan	Kerry	Left Half-Forward
73	1975	John Egan	Kerry	Right Full-Forward
74	1975	Matt Kerrigan	Meath	Full-Forward
75	1975	Anton O'Toole	Dublin	Left Full-Forward
76	1976	Paddy Cullen	Dublin	Goalkeeper
77	1976	Ger O'Keeffe	Kerry	Right Full-Back
78	1976	John O'Keeffe	Kerry	Full-Back
79	1976	Brian Murphy	Cork	Left Full-Back
80	1976	Johnny Hughes	Galway	Right Half-Back
81	1976	Kevin Moran	Dublin	Centre Half-Back
82	1976	Ger Power	Kerry	Left Half-Back
83	1976	Brian Mullins	Dublin	Centrefield
84	1976	Dave McCarthy	Cork	Centrefield
85	1976	Anton O'Toole	Dublin	Right Half-Forward
86	1976	Tony Hanahoe	Dublin	Centre Half-Forward
87	1976	David Hickey	Dublin	Left Half-Forward
88	1976	Bobby Doyle	Dublin	Right Full-Forward
89	1976	Mikey Sheehy	Kerry	Full-Forward
90	1976	Pat Spillane	Kerry	Left Full-Forward
91	1977	Paddy Cullen	Dublin	Goalkeeper
92	1977	Gay O'Driscoll	Dublin	Right Full-Back
93	1977	Pat Lindsay	Roscommon	Full-Back
94	1977	Robbie Kelleher	Dublin	Left Full-Back
95	1977	Tommy Drumm	Dublin	Right Half-Back
96	1977	Paddy Moriarty	Armagh	Centre Half-Back
97	1977	Pat O'Neill	Dublin	Left Half-Back
98	1977	Brian Mullins	Dublin	Centrefield
99	1977	Joe Kernan	Armagh	Centrefield
100	1977	Anton O'Toole	Dublin	Right Half-Forward
101	1977	Jimmy Smyth	Armagh	Centre Half-Forward
102	1977	Pat Spillane	Kerry	Left Half-Forward
103	1977	Bobby Doyle	Dublin	Right Full-Forward
104	1977	Jimmy Keaveney	Dublin	Full-Forward
105	1977	John Egan	Kerry	Left Full-Forward
106	1978	Ollie Crinnigan	Kildare	Goalkeeper
107	1978	Harry Keegan	Roscommon	Right Full-Back
108	1978	John O'Keeffe	Kerry	Full-Back
109	1978	Robbie Kelleher	Dublin	Left Full-Back
110	1978	Tommy Drumm	Dublin	Right Half-Back
111	1978	Ollie Brady	Cavan	Centre Half-Back
112	1978	Paud Lynch	Kerry	Left Half-Back
113	1978	Colm McAlarney	Down	Centrefield
114	1978	Tomás Connor	Offaly	Centrefield
115	1978	Ger Power	Kerry	Right Half-Forward
116	1978	Declan Barron	Cork	Centre Half-Forward
117	1978	Pat Spillane	Kerry	Left Half-Forward
118	1978	Mikey Sheehy	Kerry	Right Full-Forward
119	1978	Jimmy Keaveney	Dublin	Full-Forward
120	1978	John Egan	Kerry	Left Full-Forward

List of Football All-Stars

#	Year	Name	County	Position
121	1979	Paddy Cullen	Dublin	Goalkeeper
122	1979	Eugene "Nudie" Hughes	Monaghan	Right Full-Back
123	1979	John O'Keeffe	Kerry	Full-Back
124	1979	Tom Heneghan	Roscommon	Left Full-Back
125	1979	Tommy Drumm	Dublin	Right Half-Back
126	1979	Tim Kennelly	Kerry	Centre Half-Back
127	1979	Danny Murray	Roscommon	Left Half-Back
128	1979	Dermot Earley Snr	Roscommon	Centrefield
129	1979	Bernard Brogan Snr	Dublin	Centrefield
130	1979	Ger Power	Kerry	Right Half-Forward
131	1979	Seán Walsh	Kerry	Centre Half-Forward
132	1979	Pat Spillane	Kerry	Left Half-Forward
133	1979	Mikey Sheehy	Kerry	Right Full-Forward
134	1979	Seán Lowry	Offaly	Full-Forward
135	1979	Joe McGrath	Mayo	Left Full-Forward
136	1980	Charlie Nelligan	Kerry	Goalkeeper
137	1980	Harry Keegan	Roscommon	Right Full-Back
138	1980	Kevin Kehily	Cork	Full-Back
139	1980	Gerry Connellan	Roscommon	Left Full-Back
140	1980	Kevin McCabe	Tyrone	Right Half-Back
141	1980	Tim Kennelly	Kerry	Centre Half-Back
142	1980	Danny Murray	Roscommon	Left Half-Back
143	1980	Jack O'Shea	Kerry	Centrefield
144	1980	Colm McKinstry	Armagh	Centrefield
145	1980	Ger Power	Kerry	Right Half-Forward
146	1980	Denis "Dinny" Allen	Cork	Centre Half-Forward
147	1980	Pat Spillane	Kerry	Left Half-Forward
148	1980	Matt Connor	Offaly	Right Full-Forward
149	1980	Eoin Liston	Kerry	Full-Forward
150	1980	John Egan	Kerry	Left Full-Forward
151	1981	Martin Furlong	Offaly	Goalkeeper
152	1981	Jimmy Deenihan	Kerry	Right Full-Back
153	1981	Paddy Kennedy	Down	Full-Back
154	1981	Paud Lynch	Kerry	Left Full-Back
155	1981	Páidí Ó Sé	Kerry	Right Half-Back
156	1981	Richie Connor	Offaly	Centre Half-Back
157	1981	Séamus McHugh	Galway	Left Half-Back
158	1981	Jack O'Shea	Kerry	Centrefield
159	1981	Seán Walsh	Kerry	Centrefield
160	1981	Barry Brennan	Galway	Right Half-Forward
161	1981	Denis "Ogie" Moran	Kerry	Centre Half-Forward
162	1981	Pat Spillane	Kerry	Left Half-Forward
163	1981	Mikey Sheehy	Kerry	Right Full-Forward
164	1981	Eoin Liston	Kerry	Full-Forward
165	1981	Brendan Lowry	Offaly	Left Full-Forward
166	1982	Martin Furlong	Offaly	Goalkeeper
167	1982	Mick Fitzgerald	Offaly	Right Full-Back
168	1982	Liam Connor	Offaly	Full-Back
169	1982	Kevin Kehily	Cork	Left Full-Back
170	1982	Páidí Ó Sé	Kerry	Right Half-Back
171	1982	Seán Lowry	Offaly	Centre Half-Back
172	1982	Liam Currams	Offaly	Left Half-Back
173	1982	Jack O'Shea	Kerry	Centrefield
174	1982	Pádraig Dunne	Offaly	Centrefield
175	1982	Peter McGinnity	Fermanagh	Right Half-Forward
176	1982	Joe Kernan	Armagh	Centre Half-Forward
177	1982	Matt Connor	Offaly	Left Half-Forward
178	1982	Mikey Sheehy	Kerry	Right Full-Forward
179	1982	Eoin Liston	Kerry	Full-Forward
180	1982	John Egan	Kerry	Left Full-Forward
181	1983	Martin Furlong	Offaly	Goalkeeper
182	1983	Páidí Ó Sé	Kerry	Right Full-Back
183	1983	Stephen Kinneavy	Galway	Full-Back
184	1983	John Evans	Cork	Left Full-Back
185	1983	Pat Canavan	Dublin	Right Half-Back
186	1983	Tommy Drumm	Dublin	Centre Half-Back
187	1983	Jimmy Kerrigan	Cork	Left Half-Back
188	1983	Jack O'Shea	Kerry	Centrefield
189	1983	Liam Austin	Down	Centrefield
190	1983	Barney Rock	Dublin	Right Half-Forward
191	1983	Matt Connor	Offaly	Centre Half-Forward
192	1983	Greg Blaney	Down	Left Half-Forward
193	1983	Martin McHugh	Donegal	Right Full-Forward
194	1983	Colm O'Rourke	Meath	Full-Forward
195	1983	Joe McNally	Dublin	Left Full-Forward
196	1984	John O'Leary	Dublin	Goalkeeper
197	1984	Páidí Ó Sé	Kerry	Right Full-Back
198	1984	Mick Lyons	Meath	Full-Back
199	1984	Séamus McHugh	Galway	Left Full-Back
200	1984	Tommy Doyle	Kerry	Right Half-Back
201	1984	Tom Spillane	Kerry	Centre Half-Back
202	1984	PJ Buckley	Dublin	Left Half-Back
203	1984	Jack O'Shea	Kerry	Centrefield
204	1984	Eugene McKenna	Tyrone	Centrefield
205	1984	Barney Rock	Dublin	Right Half-Forward
206	1984	Eoin Liston	Kerry	Centre Half-Forward
207	1984	Pat Spillane	Kerry	Left Half-Forward
208	1984	Mikey Sheehy	Kerry	Right Full-Forward
209	1984	Frank McGuigan	Tyrone	Full-Forward
210	1984	Dermot McNicholl	Derry	Left Full-Forward
211	1985	John O'Leary	Dublin	Goalkeeper
212	1985	Páidí Ó Sé	Kerry	Right Full-Back
213	1985	Gerry Hargan	Dublin	Full-Back
214	1985	Mick Spillane	Kerry	Left Full-Back
215	1985	Tommy Doyle	Kerry	Right Half-Back
216	1985	Ciarán Murray	Monaghan	Centre Half-Back
217	1985	Dermot Flanagan	Mayo	Left Half-Back
218	1985	Jack O'Shea	Kerry	Centrefield
219	1985	Willie Joe Padden	Mayo	Centrefield
220	1985	Barney Rock	Dublin	Right Half-Forward
221	1985	Tommy Conroy	Dublin	Centre Half-Forward
222	1985	Pat Spillane	Kerry	Left Half-Forward
223	1985	Kevin McStay	Mayo	Right Full-Forward
224	1985	Paul Earley	Roscommon	Full-Forward
225	1985	Eugene "Nudie" Hughes	Monaghan	Left Full-Forward
226	1986	Charlie Nelligan	Kerry	Goalkeeper
227	1986	Harry Keegan	Roscommon	Right Full-Back
228	1986	Mick Lyons	Meath	Full-Back
229	1986	John Lynch	Tyrone	Left Full-Back
230	1986	Tommy Doyle	Kerry	Right Half-Back
231	1986	Tom Spillane	Kerry	Centre Half-Back
232	1986	Colm Browne	Laois	Left Half-Back
233	1986	Plunkett Donaghy	Tyrone	Centrefield
234	1986	Liam Irwin	Laois	Centrefield
235	1986	Ray McCarron	Monaghan	Right Half-Forward
236	1986	Eugene McKenna	Tyrone	Centre Half-Forward
237	1986	Pat Spillane	Kerry	Left Half-Forward
238	1986	Mikey Sheehy	Kerry	Right Full-Forward
239	1986	Damian O'Hagan	Tyrone	Full-Forward
240	1986	Ger Power	Kerry	Left Full-Forward

#	Year	Name	County	Position
241	1987	John Kerins	Cork	Goalkeeper
242	1987	Robbie O'Malley	Meath	Right Full-Back
243	1987	Colman Corrigan	Cork	Full-Back
244	1987	Tony Scullion	Derry	Left Full-Back
245	1987	Niall Cahalane	Cork	Right Half-Back
246	1987	Tom Spillane	Kerry	Centre Half-Back
247	1987	Ger Lynch	Kerry	Left Half-Back
248	1987	Brian McGilligan	Derry	Centrefield
249	1987	Gerry McEntee	Meath	Centrefield
250	1987	David Beggy	Meath	Right Half-Forward
251	1987	Larry Tompkins	Cork	Centre Half-Forward
252	1987	Kieran Duff	Dublin	Left Half-Forward
253	1987	Val Daly	Galway	Right Full-Forward
254	1987	Brian Stafford	Meath	Full-Forward
255	1987	Bernard Flynn	Meath	Left Full-Forward
256	1988	Paddy Linden	Monaghan	Goalkeeper
257	1988	Robbie O'Malley	Meath	Right Full-Back
258	1988	Colman Corrigan	Cork	Full-Back
259	1988	Mick Kennedy	Dublin	Left Full-Back
260	1988	Niall Cahalane	Cork	Right Half-Back
261	1988	Noel McCaffrey	Dublin	Centre Half-Back
262	1988	Martin O'Connell	Meath	Left Half-Back
263	1988	Shea Fahy	Cork	Centrefield
264	1988	Liam Hayes	Meath	Centrefield
265	1988	Maurice Fitzgerald	Kerry	Right Half-Forward
266	1988	Larry Tompkins	Cork	Centre Half-Forward
267	1988	Kieran Duff	Dublin	Left Half-Forward
268	1988	Colm O'Rourke	Meath	Right Full-Forward
269	1988	Brian Stafford	Meath	Full-Forward
270	1988	Eugene "Nudie" Hughes	Monaghan	Left Full-Forward
271	1989	Gabriel Irwin	Mayo	Goalkeeper
272	1989	Jimmy Browne	Mayo	Right Full-Back
273	1989	Gerry Hargan	Dublin	Full-Back
274	1989	Dermot Flanagan	Mayo	Left Full-Back
275	1989	Connie Murphy	Kerry	Right Half-Back
276	1989	Conor Counihan	Cork	Centre Half-Back
277	1989	Tony Davis	Cork	Left Half-Back
278	1989	Teddy McCarthy	Cork	Centrefield
279	1989	Willie Joe Padden	Mayo	Centrefield
280	1989	Dave Barry	Cork	Right Half-Forward
281	1989	Larry Tompkins	Cork	Centre Half-Forward
282	1989	Noel Durkin	Mayo	Left Half-Forward
283	1989	Paul McGrath	Cork	Right Full-Forward
284	1989	Eugene McKenna	Tyrone	Full-Forward
285	1989	Tony McManus	Roscommon	Left Full-Forward
286	1990	John Kerins	Cork	Goalkeeper
287	1990	Robbie O'Malley	Meath	Right Full-Back
288	1990	Stephen O'Brien	Cork	Full-Back
289	1990	Terry Ferguson	Meath	Left Full-Back
290	1990	Michael Slocum	Cork	Right Half-Back
291	1990	Conor Counihan	Cork	Centre Half-Back
292	1990	Martin O'Connell	Meath	Left Half-Back
293	1990	Shea Fahy	Cork	Centrefield
294	1990	Mickey Quinn	Leitrim	Centrefield
295	1990	David Beggy	Meath	Right Half-Forward
296	1990	Val Daly	Galway	Centre Half-Forward
297	1990	Joyce McMullan	Donegal	Left Half-Forward
298	1990	Paul McGrath	Cork	Right Full-Forward
299	1990	Kevin O'Brien	Wicklow	Full-Forward
300	1990	James McCartan Jnr	Down	Left Full-Forward
301	1991	Michael McQuillan	Meath	Goalkeeper
302	1991	Mick Deegan	Dublin	Right Full-Back
303	1991	Conor Deegan	Down	Full-Back
304	1991	Enon Gavin	Roscommon	Left Full-Back
305	1991	Tommy Carr	Dublin	Right Half-Back
306	1991	Keith Barr	Dublin	Centre Half-Back
307	1991	Martin O'Connell	Meath	Left Half-Back
308	1991	Barry Breen	Down	Centrefield
309	1991	Martin Lynch	Kildare	Centrefield
310	1991	Ross Carr	Down	Right Half-Forward
311	1991	Greg Blaney	Down	Centre Half-Forward
312	1991	Tommy Dowd	Meath	Left Half-Forward
313	1991	Colm O'Rourke	Meath	Right Full-Forward
314	1991	Brian Stafford	Meath	Full-Forward
315	1991	Bernard Flynn	Meath	Left Full-Forward
316	1992	Gary Walsh	Donegal	Goalkeeper
317	1992	Séamus Clancy	Clare	Right Full-Back
318	1992	Matt Gallagher	Donegal	Full-Back
319	1992	Tony Scullion	Derry	Left Full-Back
320	1992	Paul Curran	Dublin	Right Half-Back
321	1992	Martin Gavigan	Donegal	Centre Half-Back
322	1992	Eamonn Heery	Dublin	Left Half-Back
323	1992	Anthony Molloy	Donegal	Centrefield
324	1992	TJ Kilgallon	Mayo	Centrefield
325	1992	Anthony Tohill	Derry	Right Half-Forward
326	1992	Martin McHugh	Donegal	Centre Half-Forward
327	1992	James McHugh	Donegal	Left Half-Forward
328	1992	Tony Boyle	Donegal	Right Full-Forward
329	1992	Vinny Murphy	Dublin	Full-Forward
330	1992	Enda Gormley	Derry	Left Full-Forward
331	1993	John O'Leary	Dublin	Goalkeeper
332	1993	John Joe Doherty	Donegal	Right Full-Back
333	1993	Dermot Deasy	Dublin	Full-Back
334	1993	Tony Scullion	Derry	Left Full-Back
335	1993	Johnny McGurk	Derry	Right Half-Back
336	1993	Henry Downey	Derry	Centre Half-Back
337	1993	Gary Coleman	Derry	Left Half-Back
338	1993	Anthony Tohill	Derry	Centrefield
339	1993	Brian McGilligan	Derry	Centrefield
340	1993	Kevin O'Neill	Mayo	Right Half-Forward
341	1993	Joe Kavanagh	Cork	Centre Half-Forward
342	1993	Charlie Redmond	Dublin	Left Half-Forward
343	1993	Colin Corkery	Cork	Right Full-Forward
344	1993	Ger Houlahan	Armagh	Full-Forward
345	1993	Enda Gormley	Derry	Left Full-Forward
346	1994	John O'Leary	Dublin	Goalkeeper
347	1994	Michael Magill	Down	Right Full-Back
348	1994	Séamus Quinn	Leitrim	Full-Back
349	1994	Paul Higgins	Down	Left Full-Back
350	1994	Graham Geraghty	Meath	Right Half-Back
351	1994	Stephen O'Brien	Cork	Centre Half-Back
352	1994	DJ Kane	Down	Left Half-Back
353	1994	Jack Sheedy	Dublin	Centrefield
354	1994	Gregory McCartan	Down	Centrefield
355	1994	Peter Canavan	Tyrone	Right Half-Forward
356	1994	Greg Blaney	Down	Centre Half-Forward
357	1994	James McCartan Jnr	Down	Left Half-Forward
358	1994	Mickey Linden	Down	Right Full-Forward
359	1994	Tommy Dowd	Meath	Full-Forward
360	1994	Charlie Redmond	Dublin	Left Full-Forward

List of Football All-Stars

#	Year	Name	County	Position
361	1995	John O'Leary	Dublin	Goalkeeper
362	1995	Tony Scullion	Derry	Right Full-Back
363	1995	Mark O'Connor	Cork	Full-Back
364	1995	Fay Devlin	Tyrone	Left Full-Back
365	1995	Paul Curran	Dublin	Right Half-Back
366	1995	Keith Barr	Dublin	Centre Half-Back
367	1995	Stephen O'Brien	Cork	Left Half-Back
368	1995	Brian Stynes	Dublin	Centrefield
369	1995	Anthony Tohill	Derry	Centrefield
370	1995	Jarlath Fallon	Galway	Right Half-Forward
371	1995	Dessie Farrell	Dublin	Centre Half-Forward
372	1995	Paul Clarke	Dublin	Left Half-Forward
373	1995	Tommy Dowd	Meath	Right Full-Forward
374	1995	Peter Canavan	Tyrone	Full-Forward
375	1995	Charlie Redmond	Dublin	Left Full-Forward
376	1996	Finbar McConnell	Tyrone	Goalkeeper
377	1996	Kenneth Mortimer	Mayo	Right Full-Back
378	1996	Darren Fay	Meath	Full-Back
379	1996	Martin O'Connell	Meath	Left Full-Back
380	1996	Pat Holmes	Mayo	Right Half-Back
381	1996	James Nallen	Mayo	Centre Half-Back
382	1996	Paul Curran	Dublin	Left Half-Back
383	1996	John McDermott	Meath	Centrefield
384	1996	Liam McHale	Mayo	Centrefield
385	1996	Trevor Giles	Meath	Right Half-Forward
386	1996	Tommy Dowd	Meath	Centre Half-Forward
387	1996	James Horan	Mayo	Left Half-Forward
388	1996	Joe Brolly	Derry	Right Full-Forward
389	1996	Peter Canavan	Tyrone	Full-Forward
390	1996	Maurice Fitzgerald	Kerry	Left Full-Forward
391	1997	Declan O'Keeffe	Kerry	Goalkeeper
392	1997	Kenneth Mortimer	Mayo	Right Full-Back
393	1997	Davy Dalton	Kildare	Full-Back
394	1997	Cathal Daly	Offaly	Left Full-Back
395	1997	Séamus Moynihan	Kerry	Right Half-Back
396	1997	Glenn Ryan	Kildare	Centre Half-Back
397	1997	Eamonn Breen	Kerry	Left Half-Back
398	1997	Pat Fallon	Mayo	Centrefield
399	1997	Niall Buckley	Kildare	Centrefield
400	1997	Pa Laide	Kerry	Right Half-Forward
401	1997	Trevor Giles	Meath	Centre Half-Forward
402	1997	Dermot McCabe	Cavan	Left Half-Forward
403	1997	Joe Brolly	Derry	Right Full-Forward
404	1997	Brendan Reilly	Meath	Full-Forward
405	1997	Maurice Fitzgerald	Kerry	Left Full-Forward
406	1998	Martin McNamara	Galway	Goalkeeper
407	1998	Brian Lacey	Kildare	Right Full-Back
408	1998	Seán Marty Lockhart	Derry	Full-Back
409	1998	Tomás Mannion	Galway	Left Full-Back
410	1998	John Finn	Kildare	Right Half-Back
411	1998	Glenn Ryan	Kildare	Centre Half-Back
412	1998	Seán Óg De Paor	Galway	Left Half-Back
413	1998	John McDermott	Meath	Centrefield
414	1998	Kevin Walsh	Galway	Centrefield
415	1998	Michael Donnellan	Galway	Right Half-Forward
416	1998	Jarlath Fallon	Galway	Centre Half-Forward
417	1998	Dermot Earley Jnr	Kildare	Left Half-Forward
418	1998	Karl O'Dwyer	Kildare	Right Full-Forward
419	1998	Pádraic Joyce	Galway	Full-Forward
420	1998	Declan Browne	Tipperary	Left Full-Forward
421	1999	Kevin O'Dwyer	Cork	Goalkeeper
422	1999	Mark O'Reilly	Meath	Right Full-Back
423	1999	Darren Fay	Meath	Full-Back
424	1999	Anthony Lynch	Cork	Left Full-Back
425	1999	Ciarán O'Sullivan	Cork	Right Half-Back
426	1999	Kieran McGeeney	Armagh	Centre Half-Back
427	1999	Paddy Reynolds	Meath	Left Half-Back
428	1999	John McDermott	Meath	Centrefield
429	1999	Ciarán Whelan	Dublin	Centrefield
430	1999	Diarmuid Marsden	Armagh	Right Half-Forward
431	1999	Trevor Giles	Meath	Centre Half-Forward
432	1999	James Horan	Mayo	Left Half-Forward
433	1999	Philip Clifford	Cork	Right Full-Forward
434	1999	Graham Geraghty	Meath	Full-Forward
435	1999	Ollie Murphy	Meath	Left Full-Forward
436	2000	Declan O'Keeffe	Kerry	Goalkeeper
437	2000	Kieran McKeever	Derry	Right Full-Back
438	2000	Séamus Moynihan	Kerry	Full-Back
439	2000	Michael McCarthy	Kerry	Left Full-Back
440	2000	Declan Meehan	Galway	Right Half-Back
441	2000	Kieran McGeeney	Armagh	Centre Half-Back
442	2000	Anthony Rainbow	Kildare	Left Half-Back
443	2000	Anthony Tohill	Derry	Centrefield
444	2000	Darragh Ó Sé	Kerry	Centrefield
445	2000	Michael Donnellan	Galway	Right Half-Forward
446	2000	Liam Hassett	Kerry	Centre Half-Forward
447	2000	Oisín McConville	Armagh	Left Half-Forward
448	2000	Mike Frank Russell	Kerry	Right Full-Forward
449	2000	Pádraic Joyce	Galway	Full-Forward
450	2000	Derek Savage	Galway	Left Full-Forward
451	2001	Cormac Sullivan	Meath	Goalkeeper
452	2001	Kieran Fitzgerald	Galway	Right Full-Back
453	2001	Darren Fay	Meath	Full-Back
454	2001	Coman Goggins	Dublin	Left Full-Back
455	2001	Declan Meehan	Galway	Right Half-Back
456	2001	Francie Grehan	Roscommon	Centre Half-Back
457	2001	Seán Óg De Paor	Galway	Left Half-Back
458	2001	Kevin Walsh	Galway	Centrefield
459	2001	Rory O'Connell	Westmeath	Centrefield
460	2001	Evan Kelly	Meath	Right Half-Forward
461	2001	Stephen O'Neill	Tyrone	Centre Half-Forward
462	2001	Michael Donnellan	Galway	Left Half-Forward
463	2001	Ollie Murphy	Meath	Right Full-Forward
464	2001	Pádraic Joyce	Galway	Full-Forward
465	2001	Johnny Crowley	Kerry	Left Full-Forward
466	2002	Stephen Cluxton	Dublin	Goalkeeper
467	2002	Enda McNulty	Armagh	Right Full-Back
468	2002	Paddy Christie	Dublin	Full-Back
469	2002	Anthony Lynch	Cork	Left Full-Back
470	2002	Aidan O'Rourke	Armagh	Right Half-Back
471	2002	Kieran McGeeney	Armagh	Centre Half-Back
472	2002	Kevin Cassidy	Donegal	Left Half-Back
473	2002	Darragh Ó Sé	Kerry	Centrefield
474	2002	Paul McGrane	Armagh	Centrefield
475	2002	Stephen McDonnell	Armagh	Right Half-Forward
476	2002	Eamonn O'Hara	Sligo	Centre Half-Forward
477	2002	Oisín McConville	Armagh	Left Half-Forward
478	2002	Peter Canavan	Tyrone	Right Full-Forward
479	2002	Ray Cosgrove	Dublin	Full-Forward
480	2002	Colm Cooper	Kerry	Left Full-Forward

#	Year	Player	County	Position
481	2003	Fergal Byron	Laois	Goalkeeper
482	2003	Francis Bellew	Armagh	Right Full-Back
483	2003	Cormac McAnallen	Tyrone	Full-Back
484	2003	Joe Higgins	Laois	Left Full-Back
485	2003	Conor Gormley	Tyrone	Right Half-Back
486	2003	Tom Kelly	Laois	Centre Half-Back
487	2003	Philip Jordan	Tyrone	Left Half-Back
488	2003	Kevin Walsh	Galway	Centrefield
489	2003	Seán Cavanagh	Tyrone	Centrefield
490	2003	Brian Dooher	Tyrone	Right Half-Forward
491	2003	Brian McGuigan	Tyrone	Centre Half-Forward
492	2003	Declan Browne	Tipperary	Left Half-Forward
493	2003	Stephen McDonnell	Armagh	Right Full-Forward
494	2003	Peter Canavan	Tyrone	Full-Forward
495	2003	Adrian Sweeney	Donegal	Left Full-Forward
496	2004	Diarmuid Murphy	Kerry	Goalkeeper
497	2004	Tom o'Sullivan (Rathmore)	Kerry	Right Full-Back
498	2004	Barry Owens	Fermanagh	Full-Back
499	2004	Michael McCarthy	Kerry	Left Full-Back
500	2004	Tomás Ó Sé	Kerry	Right Half-Back
501	2004	James Nallen	Mayo	Centre Half-Back
502	2004	John Keane	Westmeath	Left Half-Back
503	2004	Martin McGrath	Fermanagh	Centrefield
504	2004	Seán Cavanagh	Tyrone	Centrefield
505	2004	Paul Galvin	Kerry	Right Half-Forward
506	2004	Ciarán McDonald	Mayo	Centre Half-Forward
507	2004	Dessie Dolan	Westmeath	Left Half-Forward
508	2004	Colm Cooper	Kerry	Right Full-Forward
509	2004	Enda Muldoon	Derry	Full-Forward
510	2004	Matty Forde	Wexford	Left Full-Forward
511	2005	Diarmuid Murphy	Kerry	Goalkeeper
512	2005	Ryan McMenamin	Tyrone	Right Full-Back
513	2005	Michael McCarthy	Kerry	Full-Back
514	2005	Andy Mallon	Armagh	Left Full-Back
515	2005	Tomás Ó Sé	Kerry	Right Half-Back
516	2005	Conor Gormley	Tyrone	Centre Half-Back
517	2005	Philip Jordan	Tyrone	Left Half-Back
518	2005	Seán Cavanagh	Tyrone	Centrefield
519	2005	Paul McGrane	Armagh	Centrefield
520	2005	Brian Dooher	Tyrone	Right Half-Forward
521	2005	Peter Canavan	Tyrone	Centre Half-Forward
522	2005	Owen Mulligan	Tyrone	Left Half-Forward
523	2005	Colm Cooper	Kerry	Right Full-Forward
524	2005	Stephen O'Neill	Tyrone	Full-Forward
525	2005	Stephen McDonnell	Armagh	Left Full-Forward
526	2006	Stephen Cluxton	Dublin	Goalkeeper
527	2006	Marc Ó Sé	Kerry	Right Full-Back
528	2006	Barry Owens	Fermanagh	Full-Back
529	2006	Karl Lacey	Donegal	Left Full-Back
530	2006	Séamus Moynihan	Kerry	Right Half-Back
531	2006	Ger Spillane	Cork	Centre Half-Back
532	2006	Aidan O'Mahoney	Kerry	Left Half-Back
533	2006	Nicolas Murphy	Cork	Centrefield
534	2006	Darragh Ó Sé	Kerry	Centrefield
535	2006	Paul Galvin	Kerry	Right Half-Forward
536	2006	Alan Brogan	Dublin	Centre Half-Forward
537	2006	Alan Dillon	Mayo	Left Half-Forward
538	2006	Conor Mortimer	Mayo	Right Full-Forward
539	2006	Kieran Donaghy	Kerry	Full-Forward
540	2006	Ronan Clarke	Armagh	Left Full-Forward
541	2007	Stephen Cluxton	Dublin	Goalkeeper
542	2007	Marc Ó Sé	Kerry	Right Full-Back
543	2007	Kevin McCloy	Derry	Full-Back
544	2007	Graham Canty	Cork	Left Full-Back
545	2007	Tomás Ó Sé	Kerry	Right Half-Back
546	2007	Aidan O'Mahoney	Kerry	Centre Half-Back
547	2007	Barry Cahill	Dublin	Left Half-Back
548	2007	Ciarán Whelan	Dublin	Centrefield
549	2007	Darragh Ó Sé	Kerry	Centrefield
550	2007	Stephen Bray	Meath	Right Half-Forward
551	2007	Declan O'Sullivan	Kerry	Centre Half-Forward
552	2007	Alan Brogan	Dublin	Left Half-Forward
553	2007	Colm Cooper	Kerry	Right Full-Forward
554	2007	Paddy Bradley	Derry	Full-Forward
555	2007	Tomás Freeman	Monaghan	Left Full-Forward
556	2008	Gary Connaughton	Westmeath	Goalkeeper
557	2008	Conor Gormley	Tyrone	Right Full-Back
558	2008	Justin McMahon	Tyrone	Full-Back
559	2008	John Keane	Westmeath	Left Full-Back
560	2008	David Harte	Tyrone	Right Half-Back
561	2008	Tomás Ó Sé	Kerry	Centre Half-Back
562	2008	Philip Jordan	Tyrone	Left Half-Back
563	2008	Enda McGinley	Tyrone	Centrefield
564	2008	Shane Ryan	Dublin	Centrefield
565	2008	Brian Dooher	Tyrone	Right Half-Forward
566	2008	Declan O'Sullivan	Kerry	Centre Half-Forward
567	2008	Seán Cavanagh	Tyrone	Left Half-Forward
568	2008	Colm Cooper	Kerry	Right Full-Forward
569	2008	Kieran Donaghy	Kerry	Full-Forward
570	2008	Ronan Clarke	Armagh	Left Full-Forward
571	2009	Diarmuid Murphy	Kerry	Goalkeeper
572	2009	Karl Lacey	Donegal	Right Full-Back
573	2009	Michael Shields	Cork	Full-Back
574	2009	Tom O'Sullivan (Rathmore)	Kerry	Left Full-Back
575	2009	Tomás Ó Sé	Kerry	Right Half-Back
576	2009	Graham Canty	Cork	Centre Half-Back
577	2009	John Miskella	Cork	Left Half-Back
578	2009	Dermot Earley Jnr	Kildare	Centrefield
579	2009	Séamus Scanlon	Kerry	Centrefield
580	2009	Paul Galvin	Kerry	Right Half-Forward
581	2009	Pearse O'Neill	Cork	Centre Half-Forward
582	2009	Tadhg Kennelly	Kerry	Left Half-Forward
583	2009	Daniel Goulding	Cork	Right Full-Forward
584	2009	Declan O'Sullivan	Kerry	Full-Forward
585	2009	Stephen O'Neill	Tyrone	Left Full-Forward
586	2010	Brendan McVeigh	Down	Goalkeeper
587	2010	Peter Kelly	Kildare	Right Full-Back
588	2010	Michael Shields	Cork	Full-Back
589	2010	Charlie Harrison	Sligo	Left Full-Back
590	2010	Paudie Kissane	Cork	Right Half-Back
591	2010	Graham Canty	Cork	Centre Half-Back
592	2010	Philip Jordan	Tyrone	Left Half-Back
593	2010	Paddy Keenan	Louth	Centrefield
594	2010	Aidan Walsh	Cork	Centrefield
595	2010	Daniel Hughes	Down	Right Half-Forward
596	2010	Martin Clarke	Down	Centre Half-Forward
597	2010	John Doyle	Kildare	Left Half-Forward
598	2010	Colm Cooper	Kerry	Right Full-Forward
599	2010	Bernard Brogan Jnr	Dublin	Full-Forward
600	2010	Benny Coulter	Down	Left Full-Forward

List of Football All-Stars

#	Year	Player	County	Position
601	2011	Stephen Cluxton	Dublin	Goalkeeper
602	2011	Marc Ó Sé	Kerry	Right Full-Back
603	2011	Neil McGee	Donegal	Full-Back
604	2011	Michael Foley	Kildare	Left Full-Back
605	2011	Kevin Cassidy	Donegal	Right Half-Back
606	2011	Karl Lacey	Donegal	Centre Half-Back
607	2011	Kevin Nolan	Dublin	Left Half-Back
608	2011	Bryan Sheehan	Kerry	Centrefield
609	2011	Michael Darragh Macauley	Dublin	Centrefield
610	2011	Darran O'Sullivan	Kerry	Right Half-Forward
611	2011	Alan Brogan	Dublin	Centre Half-Forward
612	2011	Paul Flynn	Dublin	Left Half-Forward
613	2011	Colm Cooper	Kerry	Right Full-Forward
614	2011	Andy Moran	Mayo	Full-Forward
615	2011	Bernard Brogan Jnr	Dublin	Left Full-Forward
616	2012	Paul Durcan	Donegal	Goalkeeper
617	2012	Neil McGee	Donegal	Right Full-Back
618	2012	Ger Cafferkey	Mayo	Full-Back
619	2012	Keith Higgins	Mayo	Left Full-Back
620	2012	Lee Keegan	Mayo	Right Half-Back
621	2012	Karl Lacey	Donegal	Centre Half-Back
622	2012	Frank McGlynn	Donegal	Left Half-Back
623	2012	Neil Gallagher	Donegal	Centrefield
624	2012	Aidan Walsh	Cork	Centrefield
625	2012	Paul Flynn	Dublin	Right Half-Forward
626	2012	Alan Dillon	Mayo	Centre Half-Forward
627	2012	Mark McHugh	Donegal	Left Half-Forward
628	2012	Colm O'Neill	Cork	Right Full-Forward
629	2012	Michael Murphy	Donegal	Full-Forward
630	2012	Colm McFadden	Donegal	Left Full-Forward
631	2013	Stephen Cluxton	Dublin	Goalkeeper
632	2013	Colin Walshe	Monaghan	Right Full-Back
633	2013	Rory O'Carroll	Dublin	Full-Back
634	2013	Keith Higgins	Mayo	Left Full-Back
635	2013	Lee Keegan	Mayo	Right Half-Back
636	2013	Cian O'Sullivan	Dublin	Centre Half-Back
637	2013	Colm Boyle	Mayo	Left Half-Back
638	2013	Michael Darragh Macauley	Dublin	Centrefield
639	2013	Aidan O'Shea	Mayo	Centrefield
640	2013	Paul Flynn	Dublin	Right Half-Forward
641	2013	Colm Cooper	Kerry	Centre Half-Forward
642	2013	Seán Cavanagh	Tyrone	Left Half-Forward
643	2013	James O'Donoghue	Kerry	Right Full-Forward
644	2013	Bernard Brogan Jnr	Dublin	Full-Forward
645	2013	Conor McManus	Monaghan	Left Full-Forward
646	2014	Paul Durcan	Donegal	Goalkeeper
647	2014	Paul Murphy	Kerry	Right Full-Back
648	2014	Neil McGee	Donegal	Full-Back
649	2014	Keith Higgins	Mayo	Left Full-Back
650	2014	James McCarthy	Dublin	Right Half-Back
651	2014	Peter Crowley	Kerry	Centre Half-Back
652	2014	Colm Boyle	Mayo	Left Half-Back
653	2014	Neil Gallagher	Donegal	Centrefield
654	2014	David Moran	Kerry	Centrefield
655	2014	Paul Flynn	Dublin	Right Half-Forward
656	2014	Michael Murphy	Donegal	Centre Half-Forward
657	2014	Diarmuid Connolly	Dublin	Left Half-Forward
658	2014	Cillian O'Connor	Mayo	Right Full-Forward
659	2014	Kieran Donaghy	Kerry	Full-Forward
660	2014	James O'Donoghue	Kerry	Left Full-Forward
661	2015	Brendan Kealy	Kerry	Goalkeeper
662	2015	Shane Enright	Kerry	Right Full-Back
663	2015	Rory O'Carroll	Dublin	Full-Back
664	2015	Philly McMahon	Dublin	Left Full-Back
665	2015	Lee Keegan	Mayo	Right Half-Back
666	2015	Cian O'Sullivan	Dublin	Centre Half-Back
667	2015	Jack McCaffrey	Dublin	Left Half-Back
668	2015	Brian Fenton	Dublin	Centrefield
669	2015	Anthony Maher	Kerry	Centrefield
670	2015	Mattie Donnelly	Tyrone	Right Half-Forward
671	2015	Ciarán Kilkenny	Dublin	Centre Half-Forward
672	2015	Donnchadh Walsh	Kerry	Left Half-Forward
673	2015	Conor McManus	Monaghan	Right Full-Forward
674	2015	Aidan O'Shea	Mayo	Full-Forward
675	2015	Bernard Brogan Jnr	Dublin	Left Full-Forward
676	2016	David Clarke	Mayo	Goalkeeper
677	2016	Brendan Harrison	Mayo	Right Full-Back
678	2016	Jonny Cooper	Dublin	Full-Back
679	2016	Philly McMahon	Dublin	Left Full-Back
680	2016	Lee Keegan	Mayo	Right Half-Back
681	2016	Colm Boyle	Mayo	Centre Half-Back
682	2016	Ryan McHugh	Donegal	Left Half-Back
683	2016	Brian Fenton	Dublin	Centrefield
684	2016	Mattie Donnelly	Tyrone	Centrefield
685	2016	Peter Harte	Tyrone	Right Half-Forward
686	2016	Diarmuid Connolly	Dublin	Centre Half-Forward
687	2016	Ciarán Kilkenny	Dublin	Left Half-Forward
688	2016	Dean Rock	Dublin	Right Full-Forward
689	2016	Michael Quinlivan	Tipperary	Full-Forward
690	2016	Paul Geaney	Kerry	Left Full-Forward
691	2017	David Clarke	Mayo	Goalkeeper
692	2017	Chris Barrett	Mayo	Right Full-Back
693	2017	Michael Fitzsimons	Dublin	Full-Back
694	2017	Keith Higgins	Mayo	Left Full-Back
695	2017	Colm Boyle	Mayo	Right Half-Back
696	2017	Cian O'Sullivan	Dublin	Centre Half-Back
697	2017	Jack McCaffrey	Dublin	Left Half-Back
698	2017	Colm Cavanagh	Tyrone	Centrefield
699	2017	James McCarthy	Dublin	Centrefield
700	2017	Dean Rock	Dublin	Right Half-Forward
701	2017	Aidan O'Shea	Mayo	Centre Half-Forward
702	2017	Con O'Callaghan	Dublin	Left Half-Forward
703	2017	Paul Mannion	Dublin	Right Full-Forward
704	2017	Paul Geaney	Kerry	Full-Forward
705	2017	Andy Moran	Mayo	Left Full-Forward
706	2018	Rory Beggan	Monaghan	Goalkeeper
707	2018	Jonny Cooper	Dublin	Right Full-Back
708	2018	Colm Cavanagh	Tyrone	Full-Back
709	2018	Padraig Hampsey	Tyrone	Left Full-Back
710	2018	Karl O'Connell	Monaghan	Right Half-Back
711	2018	James McCarthy	Dublin	Centre Half-Back
712	2018	Jack McCaffrey	Dublin	Left Half-Back
713	2018	Brian Fenton	Dublin	Centrefield
714	2018	Brian Howard	Dublin	Centrefield
715	2018	Paul Mannion	Dublin	Right Half-Forward
716	2018	Ciarán Kilkenny	Dublin	Centre Half-Forward
717	2018	Ryan McHugh	Donegal	Left Half-Forward
718	2018	David Clifford	Kerry	Right Full-Forward
719	2018	Conor McManus	Monaghan	Full-Forward
720	2018	Ian Burke	Galway	Left Full-Forward

#	Year	Name	County	Position
721	2019	Stephen Cluxton	Dublin	Goalkeeper
722	2019	Michael Fitzsimons	Dublin	Right Full-Back
723	2019	Ronan McNamee	Tyrone	Full-Back
724	2019	Tom O'Sullivan (Dingle)	Kerry	Left Full-Back
725	2019	Paddy Durcan	Mayo	Right Half-Back
726	2019	Brian Howard	Dublin	Centre Half-Back
727	2019	Jack McCaffrey	Dublin	Left Half-Back
728	2019	Brian Fenton	Dublin	Centrefield
729	2019	David Moran	Kerry	Centrefield
730	2019	Paul Mannion	Dublin	Right Half-Forward
731	2019	Seán O'Shea	Kerry	Centre Half-Forward
732	2019	Michael Murphy	Donegal	Left Half-Forward
733	2019	David Clifford	Kerry	Right Full-Forward
734	2019	Cathal McShane	Tyrone	Full-Forward
735	2019	Con O'Callaghan	Dublin	Left Full-Forward
736	2020	Raymond Galligan	Cavan	Goalkeeper
737	2020	Oisín Mullin	Mayo	Right Full-Back
738	2020	Pádraig Faulkner	Cavan	Full-Back
739	2020	Michael Fitzsimons	Dublin	Left Full-Back
740	2020	James McCarthy	Dublin	Right Half-Back
741	2020	John Small	Dublin	Centre Half-Back
742	2020	Eoin Murchan	Dublin	Left Half-Back
743	2020	Brian Fenton	Dublin	Centrefield
744	2020	Thomas Galligan	Cavan	Centrefield
745	2020	Niall Scully	Dublin	Right Half-Forward
746	2020	Ciarán Kilkenny	Dublin	Centre Half-Forward
747	2020	Con O'Callaghan	Dublin	Left Half-Forward
748	2020	Cillian O'Connor	Mayo	Right Full-Forward
749	2020	Conor Sweeney	Tipperary	Full-Forward
750	2020	Dean Rock	Dublin	Left Full-Forward

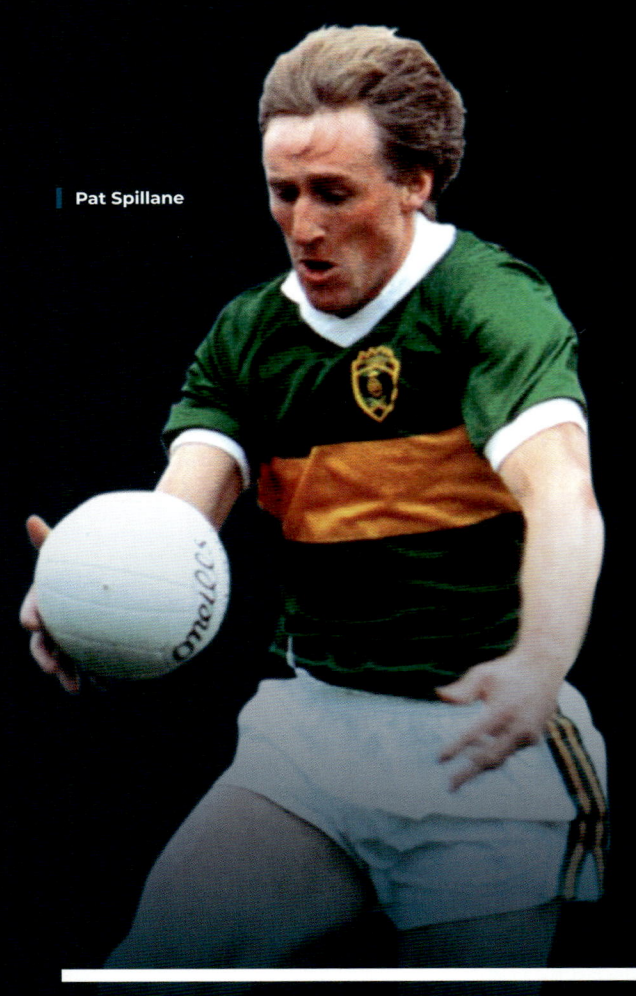

All-Star Gazing

Pat Spillane

Football All-Stars Roll of Honour

Colm Cooper
Mikey Sheehy 
Ger Power 
Stephen Cluxton 
Peter Canavan 
Jack O'Shea  
John O'Keeffe 
Páidí Ó Sé 
Seán Cavanagh 
John Egan  
Tomás Ó Sé 
John O'Leary 

Name	Count
Spillane, Pat	9
Cooper, Colm	8
Sheehy, Mikey	7
Power, Ger	6
Cluxton, Stephen	6
Canavan, Peter	6
O'Shea, Jack	6
O'Keeffe, John	5
Ó Sé, Páidí	5
Cavanagh, Seán	5
Egan, John	5
Ó Sé, Tomás	5
O'Leary, John	5
Fenton, Brian	5
Flynn, Paul	4
Jordan, Phillip	4
Liston, Eoin	4
Keegan, Lee	4
Lacey, Karl	4
O'Connell, Martin	4
Drumm, Tommy	4
Dowd, Tommy	4
Cullen, Paddy	4
Tohill, Anthony	4
Kelleher, Robbie	4
Furlong, Martin	4
Brogan Jnr, Bernard	4
Ó Sé, Darragh	4
Boyle, Colm	4
Scullion, Tony	4
Higgins, Keith	4
McCaffrey, Jack	4
Kilkenny, Ciarán	4
McCarthy, James	4
Ó Sé, Marc	3
Spillane, Tom	3
Hughes, Eugene	3
O'Brien, Stephen	3
Connor, Matt	3
McGee, Neil	3
Keaveney, Jimmy	3
O'Shea, Aidan	3
Curran, Paul	3
Murphy, Diarmuid	3
Lynch, Paud	3
O'Malley, Robbie	3
O'Sullivan, Declan	3
O'Rourke, Colm	3
Murphy, Michael	3
Mannion, Paul	3
O'Sullivan, Cian	3
Moynihan, Seamus	3
Gormley, Conor	3
Donnellan, Michael	3
Galvin, Paul	3
Joyce, Pádraic	3
McKenna, Eugene	3
Walsh, Kevin	3
Brogan, Alan	3
McGeeney, Kieran	3
Donaghy, Kieran	3
McCarthy, Michael	3
Canty, Graham	3
Blaney, Greg	3
Stafford, Brian	3
O'Neill, Stephen	3
Tompkins, Larry	3
Rock, Barney	3
Keegan, Harry	3
McManus, Conor	3
McDonnell, Stephen	3
O'Toole, Anton	3
Doyle, Tommy	3
Fitzgerald, Maurice	3
Dooher, Brian	3
Fay, Darren	3
Giles, Trevor	3
McDermott, John	3
Redmond, Charlie	3
Fitzsimons, Michael	3
Rock, Dean	3
O'Callaghan, Con	3
Owens, Barry	2
Browne, Declan	2
O'Donoghue, James	2
Murray, Danny	2
Hughes, Johnny	2
Kennelly, Tim	2
Shields, Michael	2
O'Sullivan, Tom (Rathmore)	2
Nelligan, Charlie	2
Cooper, Jonny	2
Kehily, Kevin	2
Whelan, Ciarán	2
O'Sullivan, Kevin Ger	2
McAlarney, Colm	2
McHugh, Seamus	2
O'Mahony, Aidan	2
Gilmore, TJ	2
Durcan, Paul	2
Cooney, Johnny	2
Lowry, Sean	2
McHugh, Martin	2
Kilmurray, Kevin	2
de Paor, Sean Óg	2
Lyons, Mick	2
Murphy, Ollie	2
Ryan, Mick	2
Cassidy, Kevin	2
Hargan, Gerry	2
O'Driscoll, Gay	2
Flanagan, Dermot	2
McTague, Tony	2
Padden, Willie Joe	2
Clarke, Ronan	2
McGilligan, Brian	2
Macauley, Michael Darragh	2
Duff, Kieran	2
Kernan, Joe	2
Corrigan, Colman	2
Connolly, Diarmuid	2
Moriarty, Paddy	2
Donnelly, Mattie	2
Kerins, John	2
Clarke, David	2
Daly, Val	2
Cavanagh, Colm	2
Murphy, Brian	2
Barron, Declan	2
Beggy, David	2
Lynch, Anthony	2
Flynn, Bernard	2
Bryan, Willie	2
Cahalane, Niall	2
McConville, Oisín	2
Long, Dinny	2
Meehan, Declan	2
Barry Murphy, Jimmy	2
Earley Snr, Dermot	2
Fahy, Shea	2
McGrane, Paul	2
Counihan, Conor	2
Cummins, Ray	2
McGrath, Paul	2
Keane, John	2
McCartan Jnr, James	2

Doyle, Bobby	2	Doyle, John	1	Connellan, Gerry	1	McHugh, Mark	1
O'Sullivan, Donie	2	Murphy, Vinny	1	Sweeney, Adrian	1	Hassett, Liam	1
Dillon, Alan	2	Nolan, Kevin	1	McConnell, Finbar	1	Linden, Paddy	1
McGurk, Anthony	2	McFadden, Colm	1	Higgins, Joe	1	McCarron, Ray	1
Mullins, Brian	2	Kilgallon, TJ	1	Dalton, Davy	1	McGlynn, Frank	1
Barr, Keith	2	O'Neill, Pat	1	Clavin, Nicholas	1	Naughton, Tom	1
Walsh, Aidan	2	Clancy, Seamus	1	McCabe, Dermot	1	O'Neill, Colm	1
Clifford, David	2	Crinnigan, Ollie	1	McElhinney, Gerry	1	O'Sullivan, Tom (Dingle)	1
Moran, Andy	2	Doherty, John Joe	1	Breen, Eamonn	1	McKeever, Kieran	1
Geraghty, Graham	2	Enright, Shane	1	O'Mahony, Paud	1	Leydon, Seamus	1
Gallagher, Neil	2	Corkery, Colin	1	Freyne, Mickey	1	Donaghy, Plunkett	1
Fallon, Jarlath	2	Quinlivan, Michael	1	McGuigan, Brian	1	Walshe, Colin	1
O'Carroll, Rory	2	Deasy, Dermot	1	Laide, Pa	1	Russell, Mike Frank	1
Hickey, David	2	Barrett, Chris	1	Dolan, Dessie	1	McNally, Joe	1
Moran, David	2	Byron, Fergal	1	Carey, Johnny	1	Savage, Derek	1
Brolly, Joe	2	Houlahan, Ger	1	O'Sullivan, Mickey Ned	1	McCaffrey, Noel	1
Gormley, Enda	2	Kelly, Tom	1	McGuigan, Frank	1	Goggins, Coman	1
O'Neill, Seán	2	Coleman, Gary	1	Stevenson, Peter	1	Brady, Ollie	1
Horan, James	2	McAnallen, Cormac	1	Buckley, Niall	1	Crowley, Johnny	1
McMahon, Philly	2	Heneghan, Tom	1	McGrath, Martin	1	Barry, Dave	1
Mortimer, Kenneth	2	Muldoon, Enda	1	Fallon, Pat	1	Kelly, Evan	1
McHugh, Ryan	2	O'Connell, Karl	1	Rennicks, Ken	1	Crowley, Peter	1
Nallen, James	2	Kerrigan, Matt	1	Daly, Cathal	1	O'Connell, Rory	1
Geaney, Paul	2	Burke, Ian	1	Mallon, Andy	1	Fitzgerald, Kieran	1
Ryan, Glenn	2	McDonald, Ciarán	1	Reilly, Brendan	1	Smyth, PJ	1
O'Keeffe, Declan	2	McNamee, Ronan	1	McMenamin, Ryan	1	Grehan, Francie	1
Walsh, Seán	2	Lynch, Ger	1	Conroy, Tommy	1	Durkin, Noel	1
Howard, Brian	2	O'Shea, Seán	1	Moran, Denis	1	Sullivan, Cormac	1
Sammon, Liam	2	Currams, Liam	1	Murray, Ciarán	1	Kealy, Brendan	1
Earley Jnr, Dermot	2	Sheedy, Jack	1	Hanahoe, Tony	1	Tobin, Johnny	1
O'Connor, Cillian	2	Mortimer, Conor	1	Lacey, Brian	1	Walsh, Donnchadh	1
Lowry, Brendan	1	McCartan, Gregory	1	McCarthy, Dave	1	Lynch, John	1
Kennedy, Mick	1	McCloy, Kevin	1	McCabe, Kevin	1	McGrath, Joe	1
Bray, Stephen	1	McCallin, Andy	1	Dunne, Pádraig	1	Christie, Paddy	1
Evans, John	1	Freeman, Tomás	1	Earley, Paul	1	McCarthy, Teddy	1
Irwin, Gabriel	1	Magill, Michael	1	McGinnity, Peter	1	O'Hagan, Damian	1
Breen, Barry	1	McGinley, Enda	1	Reilly, Paddy	1	Davis, Tony	1
Mulligan, Owen	1	Linden, Mickey	1	Moran, Kevin	1	Cosgrove, Ray	1
Austin, Liam	1	Miskella, John	1	Finn, John	1	Harte, Peter	1
Coulter, Benny	1	Higgins, Paul	1	Fitzgerald, Mick	1	O'Hara, Eamonn	1
Kinneavy, Stephen	1	O'Keeffe, Ger	1	O'Dwyer, Karl	1	Kerrigan, Jimmy	1
Connor, Tomás	1	Quinn, Seamus	1	Bradley, Paddy	1	McKinstry, Colm	1
Carr, Tommy	1	Harrison, Charlie	1	Spillane, Mick	1	O'Brien, Kevin	1
Ferguson, Terry	1	Monaghan, Donal	1	Connaughton, Gary	1	O'Rourke, Aidan	1
Deegan, Mick	1	Keenan, Paddy	1	Lockhart, Seán Marty	1	McNulty, Enda	1
Morgan, Billy	1	Clarke, Paul	1	Harte, David	1	Quinn, Mickey	1
Deegan, Conor	1	Cosgrove, Jack	1	Mannion, Tomás	1	Kennedy, Paddy	1
Murphy, Nicolas	1	Farrell, Dessie	1	McMahon, Justin	1	Brennan, Barry	1
Lynch, Martin	1	Foley, Michael	1	McNamara, Martin	1	Beggan, Rory	1
Kennelly, Tadhg	1	Stynes, Brian	1	Goulding, Daniel	1	Downey, Henry	1
Carr, Ross	1	Canavan, Pat	1	Deenihan, Jimmy	1	Hampsey, Pádraig	1
Kelly, Peter	1	Buckley, PJ	1	Scanlon, Seamus	1	Kavanagh, Joe	1
Gavin, Enon	1	Smyth, Jimmy	1	O'Sullivan, Ciarán	1	Durcan, Paddy	1
Cafferkey, Ger	1	O'Connor, Mark	1	O'Neill, Pearse	1	McGurk, Johnny	1
McQuillan, Michael	1	Hayes, Liam	1	Marsden, Diarmuid	1	McShane, Cathal	1
Murphy, Connie	1	Devlin, Fay	1	Connor, Liam	1	O'Neill, Kevin	1
Boyle, Tony	1	Lindsay, Pat	1	McStay, Kevin	1	Kane, DJ	1
McMullan, Joyce	1	Kearins, Mickey	1	McVeigh, Brendan	1	Galligan, Raymond	1
Gallagher, Matt	1	Reynolds, Pat	1	Allen, Denis	1	Mullin, Oisín	1
Bellew, Francis	1	Doherty, Sean	1	Hughes, Daniel	1	Faulkner, Pádraig	1
Gavigan, Martin	1	Murphy, Paul	1	O'Dwyer, Kevin	1	Small, John	1
Connor, Richie	1	McNicholl, Dermot	1	Clarke, Martin	1	Murchan, Eoin	1
O'Neill, Liam	1	Browne, Jimmy	1	Browne, Colm	1	Galligan, Thomas	1
Forde, Matty	1	McEniff, Brian	1	Kissane, Paudie	1	Scully, Niall	1
McHugh, James	1	Maher, Anthony	1	Clifford, Philip	1	Sweeney, Conor	1
Spillane, Ger	1	Holmes, Pat	1	Mulligan, Eugene	1		
Molloy, Anthony	1	McManus, Tony	1	O'Reilly, Mark	1		
Cahill, Barry	1	McCormack, Paddy	1	Cogan, Frank	1		
Walsh, Gary	1	Harrison, Brendan	1	Reynolds, Paddy	1		
Ryan, Shane	1	McHale, Liam	1	O'Sullivan, Darran	1		
Murphy, Barnes	1	Brogan Snr, Bernard	1	Rainbow, Anthony	1		
McEntee, Gerry	1	O'Connell, Mick	1	Sheehan, Bryan	1		
Heery, Eamon	1	Slocum, Michael	1	Irwin, Liam	1	TOTAL PLAYERS	430

Football All-Star County Roll of Honour

ANTRIM
McCallin, Andy	1
Total	**1**

ARMAGH
McDonnell, Stephen	3
McGeeney, Kieran	3
Kernan, Joe	2
McGrane, Paul	2
Clarke, Ronan	2
Moriarty, Paddy	2
McConville, Oisín	2
Smyth, Jimmy	1
Bellew, Francis	1
Marsden, Diarmuid	1
O'Rourke, Aidan	1
Mallon, Andy	1
McNulty, Enda	1
McKinstry, Colm	1
Houlahan, Ger	1
Total	**24**

CAVAN
McCabe, Dermot	1
Brady, Ollie	1
Galligan, Thomas	1
Faulkner, Pádraig	1
Galligan, Raymond	1
Total	**5**

CLARE
Clancy, Seamus	1
Total	**1**

TYRONE
Canavan, Peter	6
Cavanagh, Seán	5
Jordan, Phillip	4
Dooher, Brian	3
McKenna, Eugene	3
O'Neill, Stephen	3
Gormley, Conor	3
Cavanagh, Colm	2
Donnelly, Mattie	2
Mulligan, Owen	1
Lynch, John	1
Harte, David	1
O'Hagan, Damian	1
McGuigan, Brian	1
McGuigan, Frank	1
McMenamin, Ryan	1
McConnell, Finbar	1
McGinley, Enda	1
McMahon, Justin	1
Harte, Peter	1
Hampsey, Pádraig	1
Devlin, Fay	1
McNamee, Ronan	1
McShane, Cathal	1
McCabe, Kevin	1
Donaghy, Plunkett	1
McAnallen, Cormac	1
Total	**49**

CORK
Tompkins, Larry	3
O'Brien, Stephen	3
Canty, Graham	3
Cahalane, Niall	2
Murphy, Brian	2
Counihan, Conor	2
Barry Murphy, Jimmy	2
O'Sullivan, Kevin Ger	2
Barron, Declan	2
Fahy, Shea	2
Kehily, Kevin	2
Cummins, Ray	2
Lynch, Anthony	2
Long, Dinny	2
Shields, Michael	2
Corrigan, Colman	2
Walsh, Aidan	2
Kerins, John	2
McGrath, Paul	2
Morgan, Billy	1
Barry, Dave	1
O'Neill, Pearse	1
Cogan, Frank	1
Spillane, Ger	1
McCarthy, Teddy	1
Miskella, John	1
Davis, Tony	1
Kissane, Paudie	1
Slocum, Michael	1
Clifford, Philip	1
McCarthy, Dave	1
Murphy, Nicolas	1
Corkery, Colin	1
Goulding, Daniel	1
Kavanagh, Joe	1
Kerrigan, Jimmy	1
O'Connor, Mark	1
Evans, John	1
Allen, Denis	1
O'Neill, Colm	1
O'Sullivan, Ciarán	1
O'Dwyer, Kevin	1
Total	**64**

WESTMEATH
Keane, John	2
Connaughton, Gary	1
O'Connell, Rory	1
Dolan, Dessie	1
Total	**5**

WEXFORD
Forde, Matty	1
Total	**1**

WICKLOW
O'Brien, Kevin	1
Total	**1**

DERRY
Tohill, Anthony	4
Scullion, Tony	4
Brolly, Joe	2
McGilligan, Brian	2
Gormley, Enda	2
McGurk, Anthony	2
McElhinney, Gerry	1
McCloy, Kevin	1
McKeever, Kieran	1
McNicholl, Dermot	1
McGurk, Johnny	1
Lockhart, Seán Marty	1
Bradley, Paddy	1
Muldoon, Enda	1
Coleman, Gary	1
Stevenson, Peter	1
Downey, Henry	1
Total	**27**

DONEGAL
Lacey, Karl	4
McGee, Neil	3
Murphy, Michael	3
Durcan, Paul	2
McHugh, Martin	2
Gallagher, Neil	2
Cassidy, Kevin	2
McHugh, Ryan	2
Gavigan, Martin	1
Molloy, Anthony	1
McFadden, Colm	1
McHugh, Mark	1
Gallagher, Matt	1
McMullan, Joyce	1
McHugh, James	1
Boyle, Tony	1
McGlynn, Frank	1
Sweeney, Adrian	1
Monaghan, Donal	1
Walsh, Gary	1
McEniff, Brian	1
Doherty, John Joe	1
TOTAL	**34**

DOWN
Blaney, Greg	3
McCartan Jnr, James	2
McAlarney, Colm	2
O'Neill, Seán	2
Magill, Michael	1
McVeigh, Brendan	1
Higgins, Paul	1
Kennedy, Paddy	1
Austin, Liam	1
Breen, Barry	1
Linden, Mickey	1
Deegan, Conor	1
Coulter, Benny	1
Clarke, Martin	1
Hughes, Daniel	1
Kane, DJ	1
McCartan, Gregory	1
Carr, Ross	1
Total	**23**

DUBLIN
Cluxton, Stephen	6
O'Leary, John	5
Fenton, Brian	5
Kelleher, Robbie	4
Flynn, Paul	4
Brogan Jnr, Bernard	4
Drumm, Tommy	4
McCaffrey, Jack	4
Cullen, Paddy	4
Kilkenny, Ciarán	4
McCarthy, James	4
Keaveney, Jimmy	3
O'Sullivan, Cian	3
Mannion, Paul	3
Rock, Barney	3
Brogan, Alan	3
O'Toole, Anton	3
Curran, Paul	3
Redmond, Charlie	3
Fitzsimons, Michael	3
Rock, Dean	3
O'Callaghan, Con	3
Whelan, Ciarán	2
O'Driscoll, Gay	2
Hargan, Gerry	2
Cooper, Jonny	2
Duff, Kieran	2
Barr, Keith	2
Hickey, David	2
Macauley, Michael Darragh	2
McMahon, Philly	2
O'Carroll, Rory	2
Mullins, Brian	2
Doyle, Bobby	2
Connolly, Diarmuid	2
Howard, Brian	2
Carr, Tommy	1
Clarke, Paul	1
Canavan, Pat	1
Buckley, PJ	1
McCaffrey, Noel	1
Goggins, Coman	1
Brogan Snr, Bernard	1
Christie, Paddy	1
Hanahoe, Tony	1
Moran, Kevin	1
Stynes, Brian	1
Cosgrove, Ray	1
O'Neill, Pat	1
Conroy, Tommy	1
Deegan, Mick	1
Cahill, Barry	1
Heery, Eamon	1
Ryan, Shane	1
McNally, Joe	1
Reilly, Paddy	1
Sheedy, Jack	1
Doherty, Seán	1
Farrell, Dessie	1
Kennedy, Mick	1
Nolan, Kevin	1
Murphy, Vinny	1
Deasy, Dermot	1
Small, John	1
Murchan, Eoin	1
Scully, Niall	1
Total	**139**

FERMANAGH
Owens, Barry	2
McGrath, Martin	1
McGinnity, Peter	1
Total	**4**

GALWAY
Joyce, Pádraic	3
Donnellan, Michael	3
Walsh, Kevin	3
Hughes, Johnny	2
Fallon, Jarlath	2
Gilmore, TJ	2
de Paor, Seán Óg	2
McHugh, Seamus	2
Meehan, Declan	2
Daly, Val	2
Sammon, Liam	2
Mannion, Tomás	1
Fitzgerald, Kieran	1
Brennan, Barry	1
Cosgrove, Jack	1
Smyth, PJ	1
O'Neill, Liam	1
McNamara, Martin	1
Leydon, Seamus	1
Savage, Derek	1
Naughton, Tom	1
Burke, Ian	1
Tobin, Johnny	1
Kinneavy, Stephen	1
Total	**38**

ROSCOMMON
Keegan, Harry	3
Earley, Dermot	2
Murray, Danny	2
Grehan, Francie	1
McManus, Tony	1
Earley, Paul	1
Heneghan, Tom	1
Gavin, Enon	1
Freyne, Mickey	1
Lindsay, Pat	1
Connellan, Gerry	1
Total	**15**

SLIGO
Harrison, Charlie	1
O'Hara, Eamonn	1
Kearins, Mickey	1
Murphy, Barnes	1
Total	**4**

TIPPERARY
Browne, Declan	2
Quinlivan, Michael	1
Sweeney, Conor	1
Total	**4**

KERRY
Spillane, Pat	9
Cooper, Colm	8
Sheehy, Mikey	7
O'Shea, Jack	6
Power, Ger	6
Egan, John	5
O'Keeffe, John	5
Ó Sé, Tomás	5
Ó Sé, Paidí	5
Liston, Eoin	4
Ó Sé, Darragh	4
Lynch, Paud	3
Galvin, Paul	3
Spillane, Tom	3
Moynihan, Seamus	3
Murphy, Diarmuid	3
McCarthy, Michael	3
Donaghy, Kieran	3
Ó Sé, Marc	3
O'Sullivan, Declan	3
Doyle, Tommy	3
Fitzgerald, Maurice	3
O'Sullivan, Tom (R'more)	2
Moran, David	2
O'Sullivan, Donie	2
Nelligan, Charlie	2
Walsh, Seán	2
O'Donoghue, James	2
Clifford, David	2
Geaney, Paul	2
O'Mahony, Aidan	2
Kennelly, Tim	2
O'Keeffe, Declan	2
Crowley, Peter	1
Russell, Mike Frank	1
Kealy, Brendan	1
O'Sullivan, Mickey Ned	1
Sheehan, Bryan	1
Spillane, Mick	1
Murphy, Paul	1
Lynch, Ger	1
Walsh, Donnchadh	1
O'Connell, Mick	1
Crowley, Johnny	1
Murphy, Connie	1
Hassett, Liam	1
Breen, Eamonn	1
O'Keeffe, Ger	1
Laide, Pa	1
Enright, Shane	1
Deenihan, Jimmy	1
Maher, Anthony	1
Moran, Denis	1
O'Mahony, Paud	1
Kennelly, Tadhg	1
O'Shea, Seán	1
Scanlon, Seamus	1
O'Sullivan, Tom (Dingle)	1
O'Sullivan, Darran	1
Total	**145**

KILDARE
Ryan, Glenn	2
Earley, Dermot	2
Rainbow, Anthony	1
Dalton, Davy	1
Kelly, Peter	1
Lynch, Martin	1
O'Dwyer, Karl	1
Buckley, Niall	1
Doyle, John	1
Lacey, Brian	1
Foley, Michael	1
Crinnigan, Ollie	1
Finn, John	1
Total	**15**

LAOIS
Higgins, Joe	1
Browne, Colm	1
Kelly, Tom	1
Irwin, Liam	1
Byron, Fergal	1
Total	**5**

LEITRIM
Quinn, Seamus	1
Quinn, Mickey	1
Total	**2**

LOUTH
Keenan, Paddy	1
Total	**1**

MAYO
Keegan, Lee	4
Boyle, Colm	4
Higgins, Keith	4
O'Shea, Aidan	3
Padden, Willie Joe	2
Flanagan, Dermot	2
Horan, James	2
Clarke, David	2
Moran, Andy	2
Mortimer, Kenneth	2
Dillon, Alan	2
Nallen, James	2
O'Connor, Cillian	2
Harrison, Brendan	1
O'Neill, Kevin	1
Irwin, Gabriel	1
McGrath, Joe	1
Durcan, Paddy	1
Carey, Johnny	1
Kilgallon, T.J.	1
McDonald, Ciarán	1
Holmes, Pat	1
Browne, Jimmy	1
McStay, Kevin	1
Mortimer, Conor	1
Barrett, Chris	1
Durkin, Noel	1
McHale, Liam	1
Cafferkey, Ger	1
Fallon, Pat	1
Mullin, Oisín	1
Total	**51**

MEATH
Dowd, Tommy	4
O'Connell, Martin	4
McDermott, John	3
Giles, Trevor	3
Fay, Darren	3
O'Rourke, Colm	3
O'Malley, Robbie	3
Stafford, Brian	3
Beggy, David	2
Lyons, Mick	2
Flynn, Bernard	2
Geraghty, Graham	2
Murphy, Ollie	2
Reilly, Brendan	1
Bray, Stephen	1
O'Reilly, Mark	1
McQuillan, Michael	1
Kerrigan, Matt	1
McEntee, Gerry	1
Reynolds, Paddy	1
Rennicks, Ken	1
Kelly, Evan	1
Sullivan, Cormac	1
Hayes, Liam	1
Reynolds, Pat	1
Ferguson, Terry	1
Total	**49**

MONAGHAN
Hughes, Eugene	3
McManus, Conor	3
Walshe, Colin	1
Murray, Ciarán	1
O'Connell, Karl	1
McCarron, Ray	1
Beggan, Rory	1
Linden, Paddy	1
Freeman, Tomás	1
Total	**13**

OFFALY
Furlong, Martin	4
Connor, Matt	3
Bryan, Willie	2
Cooney, Johnny	2
Lowry, Seán	2
McTague, Tony	2
Kilmurray, Kevin	2
Ryan, Mick	2
Dunne, Pádraig	1
Connor, Richie	1
Connor, Liam	1
Mulligan, Eugene	1
Currams, Liam	1
Clavin, Nicholas	1
Fitzgerald, Mick	1
McCormack, Paddy	1
Daly, Cathal	1
Lowry, Brendan	1
Connor, Tomás	1
Total	**30**

Football All-Star Nominees

The statistics included in this book have been cross-checked to the best of our ability. Our data sources for the Nominations data were Mick Dunne's files, Jim O'Sullivan's files, Donal Keenan's files, the Irish Press, the Irish Independent and the Irish Times Newspaper Archives

Data has been confirmed where possible, but the 1971 list of nominees could not be fully verified as, in those days, the names of the All-Star nominees were not published in advance of team selection. The names listed for 1971 are based on files belonging to Mick Dunne and Jim O'Sullivan. Should any inaccuracies come to light, we will be delighted to update these lists.

1971

GOALKEEPER
Billy Morgan, Cork
Eugene Rooney, Mayo
Jimmy "Séamus" Hasson, Derry
Johnny Culloty, Kerry
Martin Furlong, Offaly
Ollie Crinnigan, Kildare
Paddy Cullen, Dublin
Paddy Lyons, Cavan
Paul McCarthy, Monaghan
PJ Smyth, Galway
Seán McCormack, Meath

RIGHT FULL-BACK
Brendan Colleran, Galway
Brendan Sloan, Down
Donie O'Sullivan, Kerry
Johnny Carey, Mayo
Mick Ryan, Offaly
Mick White, Meath

FULL-BACK
Henry Diamond, Derry
Jack Cosgrove, Galway
Jack Quinn, Meath
Jimmy Mulroy, Louth
John Brennan, Sligo
John Conway, Laois
Ray Prendergast, Mayo

LEFT FULL-BACK
Aidan Caffrey, Sligo
Donie O'Sullivan, Kerry
John Morley, Mayo

Mick Scannell, Cork
Noel Colleran, Galway
Séamus Fitzgerald, Kerry
Séamus Killough, Antrim

RIGHT HALF-BACK
Eugene Mulligan, Offaly

CENTRE HALF-BACK
Cathal Cawley, Sligo
John Morley, Mayo
Leslie Toal, Louth
Malachy McAfee, Derry
Mick Carolan, Kildare
Nicholas Clavin, Offaly
Terry Kearns, Meath
Tommy Joe Gilmore, Galway

LEFT HALF-BACK
Brian McEniff, Donegal
Cecil Ward, Down
Coilin McDonagh, Galway
Gerry O'Loughlin, Derry
John Morley, Mayo
Kevin Jer O'Sullivan, Cork
Liam O'Neill, Galway
Martin Heavey, Offaly
Mick O'Shea, Kerry
Pat Reynolds, Meath
Robbie Kelleher, Dublin
Tom Prendergast, Kerry

CENTREFIELD
Bernie O'Neill, Cork
Bobby Millar, Laois
Colm McAlarney, Down
Dermot Earley, Roscommon
Frank Cogan, Cork
Frank Murray, Longford
Larry Diamond, Derry
Liam Sammon, Galway
Mick O'Connell, Kerry
Mick O'Connell, Kerry
Mick Power, Tipperary
Nicholas Clavin, Offaly
Paddy Smith, Armagh
Ray Carolan, Cavan
Willie Bryan, Offaly
Willie Joyce, Galway

RIGHT HALF-FORWARD
Benny Gaughran, Louth
Brendan Lynch, Kerry
Jimmy Barrett, Cork
Jimmy Duggan, Galway
Michael Kearins, Sligo
Seán Cooney, Offaly
Seán O'Connell, Derry
Tony McTague, Offaly

CENTRE HALF-FORWARD
Colm McAlarney, Down
Denis Coughlan, Cork
Jackie Donnelly, Kildare
Jimmy Duggan, Galway
Jimmy Hannify, Longford
Kevin Kilmurray, Offaly
Ray Cummins, Cork
Seán O'Neill, Down

LEFT HALF-FORWARD
Ben Wrynne, Leitrim
Brendan Lynch, Kerry
David Hickey, Dublin

Joe Corcoran, Mayo
Michael Kearins, Sligo
Paddy Moriarty, Armagh
Pat Dunny, Kildare
Tony McTague, Offaly

RIGHT FULL-FORWARD
Andy McCallin, Antrim
Brendan Lynch, Kerry
Denis Coughlan, Cork
Gene Cusack, Cavan
John Lalor, Laois
Michael Keating, Tipperary
Mick O'Dwyer, Kerry
Pat Dunny, Kildare
Ray Cummins, Cork
Séamus Leydon, Galway
Seán O'Neill, Down

FULL-FORWARD
Frank Canavan, Galway
Peter Brennan, Sligo
Ray Cummins, Cork
Seán O'Neill, Down
Willie McGee, Mayo

LEFT FULL-FORWARD
Eamon McPartland, Fermanagh
Joe Corcoran, Mayo
Kevin Teague, Tyrone
Michael Kearins, Sligo
Mick O'Dwyer, Kerry
Ray Cummins, Cork
Séamus Leydon, Galway

1972

GOALKEEPER
Alan Kane, Donegal
Billy Morgan, Cork
Éamonn Fitzgerald, Kerry
JJ Costelloe, Mayo
Martin Furlong, Offaly
Ollie Crinnigan, Kildare
Paddy Cullen, Dublin

RIGHT FULL-BACK
Ciarán Campbell, Fermanagh
Dónal Monaghan, Donegal
Donie O'Sullivan, Kerry
Gerry Mannion, Roscommon
Larry Coughlan, Offaly
Mick Ryan, Offaly

FULL-BACK
Ciarán Campbell, Fermanagh
Jack Cosgrove, Galway
Jim Wall, Waterford
John Brennan, Sligo
Paddy McCormack, Offaly
Paud O'Donoghue, Kerry
Pauric McShea, Donegal
Tom Quinn, Derry

LEFT FULL-BACK
Andy Curran, Donegal
Andy McCabe, Cavan
Dónal Monaghan, Donegal
Donie O'Sullivan, Kerry
Larry Coughlan, Offaly
Mick Begley, Mayo
Mick Carolan, Kildare
Mick O'Rourke, Offaly
Mick Ryan, Offaly

Mick Scannell, Cork
Pauric McShea, Donegal
Séamus Fitzgerald, Kerry
Tom Heneghan, Roscommon

RIGHT HALF-BACK
Brian McEniff, Donegal
Dónal Monaghan, Donegal
Eugene Mulligan, Offaly
Kevin Jer O'Sullivan, Cork
Tom Prendergast, Kerry

CENTRE HALF-BACK
Adrian O'Sullivan, Roscommon
Anthony Gallagher, Donegal
Barnes Murphy, Sligo
Dermot Earley, Roscommon
Eugene Mulligan, Offaly
Gabriel Lalor, Laois
John Morley, Mayo
John O'Keeffe, Kerry
Malachy McAfee, Derry
Nicholas Clavin, Offaly
Tommy Joe Gilmore, Galway

LEFT HALF-BACK
Brian McEniff, Donegal
Brian O'Reilly, Mayo
Eugene Mulligan, Offaly
Gerry Mannion, Roscommon
Gerry O'Loughlin, Derry
Kevin Jer O'Sullivan, Cork
Martin Heavey, Offaly
Mick O'Shea, Kerry
Paudie Lynch, Kerry
Robbie Kelleher, Dublin
Tony Smullen, Kildare

CENTREFIELD
Dermot Earley, Roscommon
Frank Cogan, Cork
Jimmy Duggan, Galway
Jimmy Hannify, Longford
John O'Keeffe, Kerry
Liam Sammon, Galway
Mick O'Connell, Kerry
Nicholas Clavin, Offaly
Pat Mangan, Kildare
Ray Carolan, Cavan
Tom McGuinness, Derry
Willie Bryan, Offaly

RIGHT HALF-FORWARD
Brendan Lynch, Kerry
Martin Carney, Donegal
Seán Cooney, Offaly
Tony McTague, Offaly

CENTRE HALF-FORWARD
Denis Coughlan, Cork
Dermot Earley, Roscommon
Gerry McCann, Antrim
Jim Colleary, Sligo
Kevin Kilmurray, Offaly
Larry Diamond, Derry
Matt Kerrigan, Meath
Mickey Freyne, Roscommon
Ray Cummins, Cork

LEFT HALF-FORWARD
Brendan Lynch, Kerry
Eamon O'Donoghue, Kerry
Martin Carney, Donegal
Michael Kearins, Sligo

Paddy Moriarty, Armagh
Seán Cooney, Offaly
Tony McTague, Offaly
RIGHT FULL-FORWARD
Andy McCallin, Antrim
John Kelly, Roscommon
Kevin Teague, Tyrone
Mickey Freyne, Roscommon
Michael Keating, Tipperary
Paddy Dunny, Kildare
Paddy Fenning, Offaly
Séamus Grannaghan, Donegal
Seán Cooney, Offaly
Seán O'Neill, Down
Tony McTague, Offaly
Willie McGee, Mayo
FULL-FORWARD
Mickey Freyne, Roscommon
Ray Cummins, Cork
Seán Donnelly, Longford
Seán O'Neill, Down
Willie McGee, Mayo
LEFT FULL-FORWARD
Denis Allen, Cork
Gerry McCann, Antrim
Joe O'Reilly, Dublin
Joe Winston, Donegal
Maurice Burke, Galway
Mel Flanagan, Roscommon
Michael Kearins, Sligo
Mick O'Dwyer, Kerry
Paddy Dunny, Kildare
Paddy Fenning, Offaly
Paddy Moriarty, Armagh
Tony McTague, Offaly

1973
GOALKEEPER
Billy Morgan, Cork
RIGHT FULL-BACK
Donie O'Sullivan, Kerry
Frank Cogan, Cork
Joe Waldron, Galway
Mick Ryan, Offaly
FULL-BACK
Humphrey Kelleher, Cork
Jack Cosgrove, Galway
Patsy Kelly, Kildare
Pauric McShea, Donegal
Peter Mulgrew, Tyrone
LEFT FULL-BACK
Brendan Colleran, Galway
Brian Murphy, Cork
Ciarán Campbell, Fermanagh
Denis Dalton, Kildare
Donie O'Sullivan, Kerry
Frank Cogan, Cork
Jimmy Deenihan, Kerry
Matt Trolan, Derry
Mick O'Rourke, Offaly
Mick Ryan, Offaly
Tony Regan, Roscommon
RIGHT HALF-BACK
Con Hartnett, Cork
Danny Nugent, Louth
Eugene Mulligan, Offaly
Jimmy Duggan, Galway

Joe McElroy, Tyrone
Kevin Jer O'Sullivan, Cork
Liam O'Neill, Galway
Mickey Hughes, Tyrone
Nicholas Clavin, Offaly
CENTRE HALF-BACK
Barnes Murphy, Sligo
Malachy McAfee, Derry
Nicholas Clavin, Offaly
Tommy Joe Gilmore, Galway
LEFT HALF-BACK
Con Hartnett, Cork
Frank McGuigan, Tyrone
Gerry O'Loughlin, Derry
Johnny Hughes, Galway
Kevin Jer O'Sullivan, Cork
Liam O'Neill, Galway
Mick Ryan, Offaly
Mickey Hughes, Tyrone
Pat Reynolds, Meath
Paudie Lynch, Kerry
CENTREFIELD
Aidan McMahon, Tyrone
Billy Joyce, Galway
Colm McAlarney, Down
Denis Coughlan, Cork
Denis Long, Cork
Dermot Earley, Roscommon
Frank McGuigan, Tyrone
Jimmy Duggan, Galway
John O'Keeffe, Kerry
Liam Sammon, Galway
Seán Kilbride, Mayo
Willie Bryan, Offaly
RIGHT HALF-FORWARD
Anthony McGurk, Derry
Brendan Lynch, Kerry
Denis Long, Cork
Frank McGuigan, Tyrone
Jimmy Duggan, Galway
Martin Carney, Donegal
Michael Kearins, Sligo
Seán Cooney, Offaly
Seán McElhatton, Tyrone
CENTRE HALF-FORWARD
Brendan Lynch, Kerry
Denis Coughlan, Cork
Dermot Earley, Roscommon
Gerry McCann, Antrim
Jimmy Barrett, Cork
Jimmy Duggan, Galway
John O'Keeffe, Kerry
Kevin Kilmurray, Offaly
Liam Sammon, Galway
Mick O'Sullivan, Kerry
LEFT HALF-FORWARD
Jimmy Barrett, Cork
Jimmy Duggan, Galway
Martin Carney, Donegal
Michael Kearins, Sligo
Packy McGarty, Leitrim
Paddy Moriarty, Armagh
Patsy Hetherington, Tyrone
Tony McTague, Offaly
RIGHT FULL-FORWARD
Anthony McGurk, Derry
Jimmy Barry Murphy, Cork

Seán Cooney, Offaly
Tony McTague, Offaly
FULL-FORWARD
Ray Cummins, Cork
Seán O'Neill, Down
LEFT FULL-FORWARD
Fionn Sherry, Fermanagh
Jimmy Barrett, Cork
Joe Winston, Donegal
Johnny Tobin, Galway
Michael Kearins, Sligo
Mick O'Dwyer, Kerry
Morgan Hughes, Galway
Paddy Moriarty, Armagh
Seán Cooney, Offaly
Seán O'Neill, Down
Tony McTague, Offaly

1974
GOALKEEPER
Billy Morgan, Cork
Gay Mitchell, Galway
John Somers, Derry
Martin Furlong, Offaly
Paddy Cullen, Dublin
Ronan Giles, Meath
RIGHT FULL-BACK
Brian Murphy, Cork
Dónal Monaghan, Donegal
Donie O'Sullivan, Kerry
Harry Keegan, Roscommon
FULL-BACK
Dan McCartan, Down
Humphrey Kelleher, Cork
Jack Cosgrove, Galway
Leslie Toal, Louth
Mick Ryan, Offaly
Pat Lindsay, Roscommon
Pauric McShea, Donegal
Séamus Reilly, Mayo
Seán Doherty, Dublin
LEFT FULL-BACK
Aidan Caffrey, Sligo
Andy Curran, Donegal
Brendan Colleran, Galway
Brian Murphy, Cork
Denis Dalton, Kildare
Derry Crowley, Kerry
Dónal Hunt, Cork
Gerry Mannion, Roscommon
Mick Carolan, Kildare
Robbie Kelleher, Dublin
RIGHT HALF-BACK
Brian McEniff, Donegal
Enda McGowan, Cavan
Eugene Mulligan, Offaly
Ger Feeney, Mayo
Ger Power, Kerry
Kevin Jer O'Sullivan, Cork
Liam O'Neill, Galway
Paddy Reilly, Dublin
Pat Traynor, Meath
CENTRE HALF-BACK
Anthony Gallagher, Donegal
Barnes Murphy, Sligo
Eamonn Tavey, Monaghan
JP O'Kane, Antrim

Paudie Lynch, Kerry
Seán Mulvihill, Longford
Tommy Joe Gilmore, Galway
LEFT HALF-BACK
Con Hartnett, Cork
George Wilson, Dublin
Ger O'Keeffe, Kerry
Johnny Hughes, Galway
John Kerrane, Roscommon
Marty Slevin, Down
Mick Higgins, Mayo
CENTREFIELD
Bobby Miller, Laois
Declan Barron, Cork
Denis Coughlan, Cork
Dermot Earley, Roscommon
Jimmy Duggan, Galway
John O'Keeffe, Kerry
Ken Rennicks, Meath
Martin Carney, Donegal
Mickey Freyne, Roscommon
Mick Carty, Wexford
Pat Mangan, Kildare
Paudie Lynch, Kerry
Peter McGinnity, Fermanagh
Peter Rooney, Down
Steve Rooney, Dublin
Willie Joyce, Galway
RIGHT HALF-FORWARD
Brendan Lynch, Kerry
Colm McAlarney, Down
Frank McGuigan, Tyrone
Michael Laffey, Sligo
Tom Naughton, Galway
Tommy O'Malley, Mayo
CENTRE HALF-FORWARD
Declan Barron, Cork
Dermot Earley, Roscommon
Jimmy Duggan, Galway
Liam Sammon, Galway
Michael Kearins, Sligo
Mick O'Sullivan, Kerry
Mickey Cunningham, Down
Tommy Carew, Kildare
LEFT HALF-FORWARD
Benny Wilkinson, Sligo
Colm McAlarney, Down
Damien Reid, Louth
Dave McCarthy, Cork
David Hickey, Dublin
Gerry O'Loughlin, Derry
Jarleth Burke, Galway
Michael Kearins, Sligo
Neilly Gallagher, Donegal
Tony McTague, Offaly
RIGHT FULL-FORWARD
Anton O'Toole, Dublin
Jimmy Barry Murphy, Cork
John Cooney, Offaly
Johnny Egan, Kerry
Peter Rooney, Down
Séamus Grannaghan, Donegal
FULL-FORWARD
Jimmy Keaveney, Dublin
Liam Sammon, Galway
Ray Cummins, Cork
Séamus Bonner, Donegal
Seán O'Neill, Down

Football All-Star Nominees

LEFT FULL-FORWARD
Anton O'Toole, Dublin
Jimmy Barrett, Cork
John Tobin, Galway
Michael Keating, Tipperary
Mikey Sheehy, Kerry
Neilly Gallagher, Donegal

1975

GOALKEEPER
Billy Morgan, Cork
John Somers, Derry
Paddy Cullen, Dublin
Paudie O'Mahony, Kerry
Ronan Giles, Meath

RIGHT FULL-BACK
Brendan Sloan, Down
Eamon O'Donoghue, Kildare
Eddie Webster, Tipperary
Gay O'Driscoll, Dublin
Ger O'Keeffe, Kerry
Harry Keegan, Roscommon
Paddy Kerr, Monaghan
Robert Lipsett, Sligo

FULL-BACK
Jack Quinn, Meath
John Brennan, Sligo
John O'Keeffe, Kerry
Leslie Toal, Louth
Teddy Murphy, Clare

LEFT FULL-BACK
Brendan Murray, Meath
Gabriel Bradley, Derry
Gerry Mannion, Roscommon
Jimmy Deenihan, Kerry
Robbie Kelleher, Dublin

RIGHT HALF-BACK
Ger Feeney, Mayo
Paddy Reilly, Dublin
Páidi Ó Sé, Kerry
Peter Stevenson, Derry
Phil Smith, Meath

CENTRE HALF-BACK
Alan Larkin, Dublin
Anthony McGurk, Derry
Barnes Murphy, Sligo
Eamon O'Donoghue, Kildare
Eamonn Tavey, Monaghan
Pat Reynolds, Meath
Terry Lennon, Louth
Tim Kennelly, Kerry

LEFT HALF-BACK
George Wilson, Dublin
Ger Power, Kerry
Gerry O'Loughlin, Derry
Johnny Hughes, Galway
Marty Slevin, Down
Mick Higgins, Mayo
Paddy Henry, Sligo
Pat Dunny, Kildare
Peter Lennon, Louth
Seán Leddy, Cavan

CENTREFIELD
Bernard Brogan, Dublin
Bobby Millar, Laois
Brian Mullins, Dublin
Colm McAlarney, Down
Denis Long, Cork
Joe Cassells, Meath
John O'Gara, Roscommon
Mick Ryan, Meath
Pat McCarthy, Kerry
Paudie Lynch, Kerry
Peter McGinnity, Fermanagh
Tom Colleary, Sligo
Tom McGuinness, Derry

RIGHT HALF-FORWARD
Benny Gaughran, Louth
Bobby Doyle, Dublin
Brendan Lynch, Kerry
Gerry McElhinney, Derry
Martin Carney, Donegal
Tommy O'Malley, Mayo

CENTRE HALF-FORWARD
Declan Barron, Cork
John P Kean, Mayo
Ken Rennicks, Meath
Mickey Lynch, Derry
Tony Hanahoe, Dublin

LEFT HALF-FORWARD
David Hickey, Dublin
Denis Allen, Cork
Gerry McElhinney, Derry
Mick O'Sullivan, Kerry
Pat Traynor, Meath
Séamus Darby, Offaly

RIGHT FULL-FORWARD
Des Kerins, Sligo
Jimmy Barry Murphy, Cork
John Egan, Kerry
John O'Leary, Derry
Matt Kerrigan, Meath

FULL-FORWARD
Dermot Earley, Roscommon
Gerry Finlay, Monaghan
Jimmy Keaveney, Dublin
Matt Kerrigan, Meath
Michael Kearins, Sligo
Seán Kilbride, Mayo
Seán O'Connell, Derry

LEFT FULL-FORWARD
Anton O'Toole, Dublin
Ger Farragher, Mayo
Oliver O'Brien, Meath
Pat Spillane, Kerry
Tony McTague, Offaly
Willie Walsh, Down

1976

GOALKEEPER
Gay Mitchell, Galway
Gerry Moore, Antrim
John Somers, Derry
Paddy Cullen, Dublin
Paudie O'Mahony, Kerry

RIGHT FULL-BACK
Eddie Webster, Tipperary
Gay O'Driscoll, Dublin
Ger O'Keeffe, Kerry
Liam Murphy, Derry
Liam O'Neill, Galway
Pat Tinnelly, Cavan

FULL-BACK
Brian Murphy, Cork
John O'Keeffe, Kerry
Seán Doherty, Dublin

LEFT FULL-BACK
Brendan Murray, Meath
Brian Murphy, Cork
Enda McGowan, Cavan
Jimmy Deenihan, Kerry
Michael Judge, Galway
Robbie Kelleher, Dublin
Tom Heneghan, Roscommon

RIGHT HALF-BACK
Ger Feeney, Mayo
John Coleman, Cork
Johnny Hughes, Galway
Mickey Menton, Roscommon
Noel Marley, Armagh
Paddy Reilly, Dublin
Páidi Ó Sé, Kerry
Tommy Drumm, Dublin

CENTRE HALF-BACK
Anthony McGurk, Derry
Kevin Moran, Dublin
Tim Kennelly, Kerry
Tom Creedon, Cork

LEFT HALF-BACK
Ger Power, Kerry
Kevin Kehily, Cork
Kieran Brennan, Laois
Pat Armstrong, Antrim
Séamus McHugh, Galway

CENTREFIELD
Bernard Brogan, Dublin
Brian Mullins, Dublin
Colm McAlarney, Down
Dave McCarthy, Cork
Gerry McElhinney, Derry
Joe Cassells, Meath
Michael Martin, Leitrim
Mick Carty, Wexford
Olly Leddy, Cavan
Tom McGuinness, Derry

RIGHT HALF-FORWARD
Anton O'Toole, Dublin
Bobby Doyle, Dublin
Denis Allen, Cork
Denis 'Ogie' Moran, Kerry
Gerry McElhinney, Derry
John O'Connor, Roscommon
Martin Carney, Donegal
Pat Spillane, Kerry

CENTRE HALF-FORWARD
Denis 'Ogie' Moran, Kerry
Jimmy Duggan, Galway
Mickey Lynch, Derry
Mikey Sheehy, Kerry
Tony Hanahoe, Dublin

LEFT HALF-FORWARD
David Hickey, Dublin
Gerry McElhinney, Derry
Pat Spillane, Kerry
Tom Donnellan, Roscommon

RIGHT FULL-FORWARD
Bobby Doyle, Dublin
Brendan Kelly, Derry
Jimmy Barry Murphy, Cork
John Egan, Kerry

FULL-FORWARD
Jimmy Barry Murphy, Cork
Jimmy Keaveney Dublin
John Egan, Kerry
Mikey Sheehy, Kerry

LEFT FULL-FORWARD
John McCarthy, Dublin
Pat Spillane, Kerry
Steve Duggan, Cavan

1977

GOALKEEPER
Billy Morgan, Cork
Brian McAlinden, Armagh
Gay Mitchell, Galway
Ollie Crinnigan, Kildare
Paddy Cullen, Dublin
Paudie O'Mahony, Kerry
Ronan Giles, Meath

RIGHT FULL-BACK
Denis Stevenson, Armagh
Gay O'Driscoll, Dublin
Ger O'Keeffe, Kerry
Harry Keegan, Roscommon
Jimmy Deenihan, Kerry
Pat Tinnelly, Cavan

FULL-BACK
John Dillon, Galway
John O'Keeffe, Kerry
Kevin McConnell, Meath
Leslie Toal, Louth
Pat Lindsay, Roscommon
Paudie Lynch, Kerry
Seán Doherty, Dublin
Tom Creedon, Cork

LEFT FULL-BACK
Brian Murphy, Cork
Ger O'Keeffe, Kerry
Jim McKerr, Armagh
Robbie Kelleher, Dublin
Tom Heneghan, Roscommon

RIGHT HALF-BACK
Danny Culligan, Louth
Denis 'Ogie' Moran, Kerry
Ger Feeney, Mayo
Páidi Ó Sé, Kerry
Tom Donnellan, Roscommon
Tommy Drumm, Dublin

CENTRE HALF-BACK
Anthony McGurk, Derry
Eamon O'Donoghue, Kildare
John Coleman, Cork
Kevin Moran, Dublin
Paddy Moriarty, Armagh
Tim Kennelly, Kerry

LEFT HALF-BACK
Danny Murray, Roscommon
Dessie McKenna, Tyrone
Ger Power, Kerry
Johnny Hughes, Galway
Kevin Kehily, Cork
Martin Coyne, Meath
Pat O'Neill, Dublin

CENTREFIELD
Bernard Brogan, Dublin
Brian Mullins, Dublin
Denis Long, Cork
Dermot Earley, Roscommon
Gerry McEntee, Meath
Joe Cassells, Meath
Joe Kernan, Armagh
John Geoghegan, Kildare
John O'Gara, Roscommon
Páidí Ó Sé, Kerry
Seán Walsh, Kerry

RIGHT HALF-FORWARD
Anton O'Toole, Dublin
Dermot Earley, Roscommon
John Egan, Kerry
Larry Kearns, Armagh

CENTRE HALF-FORWARD
Brian Talty, Galway
Jimmy Smyth, Armagh
Martin Quigley, Wexford
Mickey Freyne, Roscommon
Mickey Lynch, Derry
Mikey Sheehy, Kerry
Ollie Brady, Cavan
Paudie Lynch, Kerry
Tony Hanahoe, Dublin
Vincent Henry, Offaly

LEFT HALF-FORWARD
Eamonn McManus, Roscommon
Michael Martin, Leitrim
Pat Spillane, Kerry
Willie Brennan, Laois
Bobby Doyle, Dublin
Jimmy Barry Murphy, Cork
Seán Devlin, Armagh
Tony McManus, Roscommon

FULL-FORWARD
Ger Howlin, Wexford
Jimmy Keaveney, Dublin
Matt Kerrigan, Meath
Paddy Moriarty, Armagh
Seán Walsh, Kerry
Tommy Carew, Kildare

LEFT FULL-FORWARD
Damien Reid, Louth
John Egan, Kerry
John McCarthy, Dublin
Mickey Menton, Roscommon
Mikey Sheehy, Kerry
Pat Spillane, Kerry
Peter Loughran, Armagh

1978
GOALKEEPER
Billy Morgan, Cork
Gay Mitchell, Galway
Gay Sheerin, Roscommon
John Somers, Derry
Martin Furlong, Offaly
Martin McCabe, Down
Ollie Crinnigan, Kildare
Paddy Cullen, Dublin

RIGHT FULL-BACK
Brian Murphy, Cork
Denis Dalton, Kildare
Denis Stevenson, Armagh
Gay O'Driscoll, Dublin
Harry Keegan, Roscommon
Jimmy Deenihan, Kerry
Paudie Lynch, Kerry

FULL-BACK
John O'Keeffe, Kerry
Paddy O'Donoghue, Kildare
Seán Doherty, Dublin

LEFT FULL-BACK
Enda McGowan, Cavan
Gerry O'Loughlin, Derry
Jimmy Deenihan, Kerry
Michael Sands, Down
Mick Spillane, Kerry
Ollie Minnock, Offaly
Robbie Kelleher, Dublin
Tom Heneghan, Roscommon

RIGHT HALF-BACK
Colm Browne, Laois
Pat O'Neill, Galway
Tommy Drumm, Dublin

CENTRE HALF-BACK
Brendan Toner, Down
Kevin Moran, Dublin
Mick Wright, Offaly
Ollie Brady, Cavan
Paddy Moriarty, Armagh
Tim Kennelly, Kerry

LEFT HALF-BACK
Danny Murray, Roscommon
Denis 'Ogie' Moran, Kerry
Mickey Moran, Derry
Paudie Lynch, Kerry

CENTREFIELD
Bernard Brogan, Dublin
Brian Mullins, Dublin
Colm McAlarney, Down
Declan Barron, Cork
Dermot Earley, Roscommon
Gerry McElhinney, Derry
Jack O'Shea, Kerry
John O'Gara, Roscommon
John O'Kane, Louth
Liam Austin, Down
Peter McGinnity, Fermanagh
Seán Walsh, Kerry
Tomás Connor, Offaly

RIGHT HALF-FORWARD
Ger Power, Kerry
John O'Connor, Roscommon
Peter McGinnity, Fermanagh

CENTRE HALF-FORWARD
Colm McAlarney, Down
Declan Barron, Cork
Denis 'Ogie' Moran, Kerry
Dermot Earley, Roscommon
Eugene McKenna, Tyrone
Gay McManus, Galway
Jimmy Barry Murphy, Cork
Mikey Sheehy, Kerry
Pat Mangan, Kildare
Pat Spillane, Kerry
Tom Prendergast, Laois
Tony Hanahoe, Dublin

LEFT HALF-FORWARD
Pat Spillane, Kerry

RIGHT FULL-FORWARD
Bobby Doyle, Dublin
Jimmy Barry Murphy, Cork
John Egan, Kerry
John O'Connor, Roscommon
Mikey Sheehy, Kerry
Tony McManus, Roscommon

FULL-FORWARD
Jimmy Barry Murphy, Cork
Jimmy Keaveney, Dublin
Peter Rooney, Down
Seán Walsh, Kerry
Tommy Carew, Kildare

LEFT FULL-FORWARD
Joe Byrne, Down
John Egan, Kerry
Mikey Sheehy, Kerry
Tommy O'Malley, Mayo
Tommy Carew, Kildare

1979
GOALKEEPER
Billy Morgan, Cork
Charlie Nelligan, Kerry
John McDermott, Roscommon
John Somers, Derry
Martin Furlong, Offaly
Paddy Cullen, Dublin
Pat Linden, Monaghan

RIGHT FULL-BACK
Denis Stevenson, Armagh
Eugene Hughes, Monaghan
Eugene Mulligan, Offaly
Harry Keegan, Roscommon
Jimmy Deenihan, Kerry
Mick Kennedy, Dublin
Séamus O'Sullivan, Cork

FULL-BACK
John O'Keeffe, Kerry
Kevin Kehily, Cork
Kevin McConnell, Meath
Mick Holden, Dublin
Pat Lindsay, Roscommon
Richie Connor, Offaly
Tommy McGovern, Down

LEFT FULL-BACK
Kevin Kehily, Cork
Mick Spillane, Kerry
Ollie Minnock, Offaly
Tom Heneghan, Roscommon

RIGHT HALF-BACK
Gerry Fitzmaurice, Roscommon
Johnny Hughes, Galway
Kevin McCabe, Tyrone
Michael Carr, Donegal
Paddy Kerr, Monaghan
Tommy Drumm, Dublin

CENTRE HALF-BACK
Anthony Egan, Mayo
Christy Ryan, Cork
Finian Ward, Donegal
Fran Ryder, Dublin
Paddy Moriarty, Armagh
Pat Brophy, Laois
Seán McCarville, Monaghan
Tim Kennelly, Kerry
Tom Donnellan, Roscommon

LEFT HALF-BACK
Danny Murray, Roscommon
Dermot Reilly, Kildare
Eamonn Tavey, Monaghan
Henry Gavin, Mayo
Pat O'Neill, Dublin
Paudie Lynch, Kerry
Stephen Darby, Offaly

CENTREFIELD
Bernard Brogan, Dublin
Brian Mullins, Dublin
Colm McAlarney, Down
Dermot Earley, Roscommon
Eamon Whelan, Laois
Gerry Carroll, Offaly
Gerry McEntee, Meath
Hugo Clerkin, Monaghan
Jack O'Shea, Kerry
Joe Kernan, Armagh
John Courtney, Cork
John P O'Kane, Louth
Liam Austin, Down
Michael Gallagher, Donegal
Moses Coffey, Wicklow
Peter McGinnity, Fermanagh
Séamus Hayden, Roscommon
Seán Walsh, Kerry
Vincent O'Connor, Kerry
Willie Joe Padden, Mayo
Willie Joyce, Galway

RIGHT HALF-FORWARD
Anton O'Toole, Dublin
Ger Power, Kerry
John O'Connor, Roscommon
Kieran Keeney, Donegal
Pat Baker, Wicklow
Peter McGinnity, Fermanagh
Tommy Doyle, Kerry
Willie Brennan, Laois

CENTRE HALF-FORWARD
Brendan Donnelly, Tyrone
Declan Barron, Cork
Denis 'Ogie' Moran, Kerry
Frank Holohan, Leitrim
Gay McManus, Galway
Jimmy Smyth, Armagh
Joe Kernan, Armagh
John O'Gara, Roscommon
Peter McGinnity, Fermanagh
Seán Walsh, Kerry
Tony Hanahoe, Dublin

LEFT HALF-FORWARD
David Hickey, Dublin
Denis Allen, Cork
John Kent, Sligo
Pat Spillane, Kerry
Seán Kilbride, Roscommon

RIGHT FULL-FORWARD
Dónal Donoghue, Cavan
Jimmy Barry Murphy, Cork
Kieran Finlay, Monaghan
Mick Hickey, Dublin
Mickey Lynch, Derry
Mikey Sheehy, Kerry
Seánie Moloney, Clare
Tony McManus, Roscommon

Football All-Star Nominees

FULL-FORWARD
Bobby Doyle, Dublin
Colm O'Rourke, Meath
Eoin Liston, Kerry
Mickey Freyne, Roscommon
Seán Lowry, Offaly
LEFT FULL-FORWARD
Bobby Doyle, Dublin
Christy Kearney, Cork
Eamonn McManus, Roscommon
Joe McGrath, Mayo
John Egan, Kerry
Johnny Mooney, Offaly
Michael McGee, Wexford

1980

GOALKEEPER
Billy Morgan, Cork
Brian McAlinden, Armagh
Charlie Nelligan, Kerry
Martin Furlong, Offaly
RIGHT FULL-BACK
Denis Stevenson, Armagh
Eugene Hughes, Monaghan
Eugene Mulligan, Offaly
Ger O'Keeffe, Kerry
Harry Keegan, Roscommon
Johnny Hughes, Galway
Mick Kennedy, Dublin
FULL-BACK
John O'Keeffe, Kerry
Kevin Kehily, Cork
Pat Lindsay, Roscommon
LEFT FULL-BACK
Gerry Connellan, Roscommon
Kevin Kehily, Cork
Mick Spillane, Kerry
RIGHT HALF-BACK
Colm Browne, Laois
Kevin McCabe, Tyrone
Paddy Moriarty, Armagh
Páidí Ó Sé, Kerry
Pat Fitzgerald, Offaly
Stephen Darby, Offaly
Tommy Drumm, Dublin
CENTRE HALF-BACK
Christy Ryan, Cork
Fran Ryder, Dublin
Paddy Moriarty, Armagh
Richie Connor, Offaly
Tim Kennelly, Kerry
Tom Creedon, Cork
Tom Donnellan, Roscommon
LEFT HALF-BACK
Danny Murray, Roscommon
Denis 'Ogie' Moran, Kerry
Joey Donnelly, Armagh
Liam Currams, Offaly
PJ Buckley, Dublin
CENTREFIELD
Brian Mullins, Dublin
Colm McKinstry, Armagh
Dermot Earley, Roscommon
Gerry Carroll, Offaly
Jack O'Shea, Kerry
Joe Kernan, Armagh
John Costelloe, Laois

Patsy Kerlin, Tyrone
Seán Walsh, Kerry
Tomás Connor, Offaly
RIGHT HALF-FORWARD
Aidan O'Halloran, Offaly
Anton O'Toole, Dublin
Ger Power, Kerry
John O'Connor, Roscommon
Paddy Moriarty, Armagh
Seán Murphy, Cork
CENTRE HALF-FORWARD
Colm O'Rourke, Meath
Denis Allen, Cork
Eamon Whelan, Laois
Jimmy Smyth, Armagh
John O'Gara, Roscommon
Matt Connor, Offaly
LEFT HALF-FORWARD
Pat Spillane, Kerry
RIGHT FULL-FORWARD
Matt Connor, Offaly
Michael Finneran, Roscommon
Mikey Sheehy, Kerry
FULL-FORWARD
Brian Hughes, Armagh
Eoin Liston, Kerry
Tony McManus, Roscommon
LEFT FULL-FORWARD
John Egan, Kerry

1981

GOALKEEPER
Billy Morgan, Cork
Brian McAlinden, Armagh
Charlie Nelligan, Kerry
John O'Leary, Dublin
Martin Furlong, Offaly
Michael Webb, Mayo
Pat Donnan, Down
Tom Scully, Laois
RIGHT FULL-BACK
Adrian McAufield, Down
Eugene Hughes, Monaghan
Harry Keegan, Roscommon
Jimmy Deenihan, Kerry
Johnny Hughes, Galway
FULL-BACK
Anthony Egan, Mayo
Brian Nerney, Laois
John O'Keeffe, Kerry
Kevin Kehily, Cork
Liam Connor, Offaly
Paddy Kennedy, Down
Paddy O'Donoghue, Kildare
Pat Lindsay, Roscommon
Stephen Kinneavy, Galway
Tommy Drumm, Dublin
LEFT FULL-BACK
Adrian Garvey, Mayo
Charlie Conroy, Offaly
John Evans, Cork
Paudie Lynch, Kerry
Tommy McGovern, Down
RIGHT HALF-BACK
Colm Browne, Laois
Gerry Connellan, Roscommon
Henry Gavin, Mayo

Kevin McCabe, Tyrone
Mick Kennedy, Dublin
Owen Doyle, Wicklow
Páidí Ó Sé, Kerry
Pat O'Neill, Galway
CENTRE HALF-BACK
Christy Ryan, Cork
Fran Ryder, Dublin
Peter Lee, Galway
Richie Connor, Offaly
Seán Walshe, Kerry
Tim Kennelly, Kerry
Tom Kearney, Mayo
LEFT HALF-BACK
Danny Murray, Roscommon
Jimmy Kerrigan, Cork
Liam Currams, Offaly
Mick Spillane, Kerry
Séamus McHugh, Galway
CENTREFIELD
Brian Talty, Galway
Colm McKinstry, Armagh
Eugene Young, Derry
Jack O'Shea, Kerry
John Costelloe, Laois
Johnny Mooney, Offaly
Liam Austin, Down
Martin McCarrick, Sligo
Moses Coffey, Wicklow
Padraig Dunne, Offaly
Peter McGinnity, Fermanagh
Seán Walsh, Kerry
Tomás Connor, Offaly
Willie Joe Padden, Mayo
Willie Lowry, Westmeath
Willie Nally, Mayo
RIGHT HALF-FORWARD
Aidan O'Halloran, Offaly
Barry Brennan, Galway
Damien Morgan, Down
Dave Barry, Cork
Ger Power, Kerry
CENTRE HALF-FORWARD
Ambrose Rogers, Down
Colm O'Rourke, Meath
Declan Barron, Cork
Denis Allen, Cork
Denis 'Ogie' Moran, Kerry
Joe Kernan, Armagh
Matty Hoey, Sligo
Tommy Doyle, Kerry
Willie Brennan, Laois
Willie Joe Padden, Mayo
LEFT HALF-FORWARD
Damien O'Hagan, Tyrone
Kieran Duff, Dublin
Martin Carney, Mayo
Pat Spillane, Kerry
Tom Prendergast, Laois
RIGHT FULL-FORWARD
Dónal Donoghue, Cavan
Matt Connor, Offaly
Mikey Sheehy, Kerry
Tom Naughton, Galway
FULL-FORWARD
Eoin Liston, Kerry
Seán Lowry, Offaly

Tommy Joe Gilmore, Galway
Tony McManus, Roscommon
LEFT FULL-FORWARD
Anthony McCaul, Dublin
Brendan Lowry, Offaly
Finny O'Mahony, Cork
Gay McManus, Galway
Greg Blaney, Down
Joe McGrath, Mayo
John Egan, Kerry

1982

GOALKEEPER
Brian McAlinden, Armagh
Charlie Nelligan, Kerry
Martin Furlong, Offaly
Padraig Coyne, Galway
RIGHT FULL-BACK
Denis Stevenson, Armagh
Ger O'Keeffe, Kerry
Mick Fitzgerald, Offaly
Tom Creedon, Cork
FULL-BACK
John O'Keeffe, Kerry
Kevin Kehily, Cork
Liam Connor, Offaly
Stephen Kinneavy, Galway
LEFT FULL-BACK
John Evans, Cork
Michael Lowry, Offaly
Paudie Lynch, Kerry
Tommy McGovern, Down
RIGHT HALF-BACK
Michael Moloney, Cork
Páidí Ó Sé, Kerry
Pat Fitzgerald, Offaly
Pat O'Neill, Galway
CENTRE HALF-BACK
Richie Connor, Offaly
Seán Lowry, Offaly
Tim Kennelly, Kerry
Tomás Tierney, Galway
LEFT HALF-BACK
Jimmy Kerrigan, Cork
Liam Currams, Offaly
Séamus McHugh, Galway
Tommy Doyle, Kerry
CENTREFIELD
Brian Talty, Galway
Fran McMahon, Armagh
Jack O'Shea, Kerry
John Costelloe, Laois
Padraig Dunne, Offaly
Peter McGinnity, Fermanagh
Seán Walsh, Kerry
Tomás Connor, Offaly
RIGHT HALF-FORWARD
Barry Brennan, Galway
Dave Barry, Cork
Ger Power, Kerry
Martin McHugh, Donegal
CENTRE HALF-FORWARD
Greg Blaney, Down
Joe Kernan, Armagh
Tom Spillane, Kerry
Val Daly, Galway

LEFT HALF-FORWARD
Barney Rock, Dublin
Denis 'Ogie' Moran, Kerry
Gerry Carroll, Offaly
Richie Lee, Galway
RIGHT FULL-FORWARD
Johnny Mooney, Offaly
Matt Connor, Offaly
Mikey Sheehy, Kerry
Tom Naughton, Galway
FULL-FORWARD
Anthony McCaul, Dublin
Brian Hughes, Armagh
Eoin Liston, Kerry
Gay McManus, Galway
LEFT FULL-FORWARD
Brendan Lowry, Offaly
John Egan, Kerry
Séamus Darby, Offaly
Stephen Joyce, Galway

1983
GOALKEEPER
Charlie Nelligan, Kerry
Gerry Farrell, Cork
John O'Leary, Dublin
Martin Furlong, Offaly
RIGHT FULL-BACK
Mick Holden, Dublin
Páidí Ó Sé, Kerry
Phil Smith, Meath
Tommy McDermot, Donegal
FULL-BACK
Martin Griffin, Donegal
Paddy O'Donoghue, Kildare
Stephen Kinneavy, Galway
Tommy McGovern, Down
LEFT FULL-BACK
Des Newton, Donegal
John Evans, Cork
Matty Coleman, Galway
Padraig Lyons, Meath
RIGHT HALF-BACK
Paddy Kennedy, Down
Padraig Finnerty, Meath
Páidí Ó Sé, Kerry
Pat Canavan, Dublin
CENTRE HALF-BACK
Tommy Drumm, Dublin
LEFT HALF-BACK
Jim Reilly, Cavan
Jimmy Kerrigan, Cork
Michael Carr, Donegal
PJ Buckley, Dublin
CENTREFIELD
Brian Talty, Galway
Dominic Creedon, Cork
Jack O'Shea, Kerry
Liam Austin, Down
Liam Hayes, Meath
Mickey Quinn, Leitrim
Padraig Dunne, Offaly
Peter McGinnity, Fermanagh
RIGHT HALF-FORWARD
Barney Rock, Dublin
Barry Brennan, Galway

Dave Barry, Cork
John Guinan, Offaly
CENTRE HALF-FORWARD
Martin McHugh, Donegal
Matt Connor, Offaly
Tommy Conroy, Dublin
Val Daly, Galway
LEFT HALF-FORWARD
Brian O'Donnell, Galway
Gerry Carroll, Offaly
Greg Blaney, Down
Joyce McMullen, Donegal
RIGHT FULL-FORWARD
Denis Allen, Cork
John Corvan, Armagh
Martin McHugh, Donegal
Mikey Sheehy, Kerry
FULL-FORWARD
Anton O'Toole, Dublin
Colm O'Rourke, Meath
Matt Connor, Offaly
Séamus Bonner, Donegal
LEFT FULL-FORWARD
Joe McNally, Dublin
John Cleary, Cork
Mickey McDónald, Armagh
Stephen Joyce, Galway

1984
GOALKEEPER
Aidan Skelton, Tyrone
Charlie Nelligan, Kerry
John O'Leary, Dublin
Martin Furlong, Offaly
RIGHT FULL-BACK
Harry Keegan, Roscommon
Mick Fitzgerald, Offaly
Noel Roche, Clare
Páidí Ó Sé, Kerry
FULL-BACK
Ciarán McGarvey, Tyrone
Mick Lyons, Meath
Seán Walsh, Kerry
LEFT FULL-BACK
Liam Tierney, Longford
Mick Spillane, Kerry
Noel Roche, Clare
Séamus McHugh, Galway
RIGHT HALF-BACK
Kevin McCabe, Tyrone
Pat Canavan, Dublin
Pat O'Neill, Galway
Tommy Doyle, Kerry
CENTRE HALF-BACK
Michael Lafferty, Donegal
Paddy O'Rourke, Down
Tom Spillane, Kerry
Tommy Drumm, Dublin
LEFT HALF-BACK
Jimmy Kerrigan, Cork
Martin O'Connell, Meath
Matty Coleman, Galway
PJ Buckley, Dublin
CENTREFIELD
Eugene McKenna, Tyrone
Gerry McEntee, Meath
Jack O'Shea, Kerry

Liam Austin, Down
Plunkett Donaghy, Tyrone
RIGHT HALF-FORWARD
Barney Rock, Dublin
Brian O'Donnell, Galway
Dermot McNicholl, Derry
John Kennedy, Kerry
CENTRE HALF-FORWARD
Eoin Liston, Kerry
Eugene McKenna, Tyrone
Larry Tompkins, Kildare
Tommy Conroy, Dublin
LEFT HALF-FORWARD
Greg Blaney, Down
John McCormack, Longford
Kieran Duff, Dublin
Pat Spillane, Kerry
RIGHT FULL-FORWARD
Eugene Hughes, Monaghan
Kevin McStay, Mayo
Martin McHugh, Donegal
Mikey Sheehy, Kerry
FULL-FORWARD
Ambrose Rogers, Down
Colm O'Rourke, Meath
Eoin Liston, Kerry
Frank McGuigan, Tyrone
LEFT FULL-FORWARD
Brendan Mason, Down
Dermot McNicholl, Derry
John Egan, Kerry
Stephen Joyce, Galway

1985
GOALKEEPER
Charlie Nelligan, Kerry
John O'Leary, Dublin
RIGHT FULL-BACK
Eugene Sherry, Monaghan
Martin Carney, Mayo
Páidí Ó Sé, Kerry
FULL-BACK
Gerry Hargan, Dublin
Gerry McCarville, Monaghan
Martin Dempsey, Laois
LEFT FULL-BACK
Dermot Flanagan, Mayo
Fergus Caulfield, Monaghan
Mick Spillane, Kerry
RIGHT HALF-BACK
Brendan Murray, Monaghan
Mick Kennedy, Dublin
Tommy Doyle, Kerry
CENTRE HALF-BACK
Ciarán Murray, Monaghan
Noel McCaffrey, Dublin
Tom Spillane, Kerry
LEFT HALF-BACK
Declan Flanagan, Monaghan
Dermot Flanagan, Mayo
Ger Lynch, Kerry
CENTREFIELD
Brian Mullins, Dublin
David Byrne, Monaghan
Jack O'Shea, Kerry
Liam Irwin, Laois

TJ Kilgallon, Mayo
Willie Joe Padden, Mayo
RIGHT HALF-FORWARD
Barney Rock, Dublin
Kevin McStay, Mayo
Ray McCarron, Monaghan
CENTRE HALF-FORWARD
Jimmy Burke, Mayo
Larry Tompkins, Kildare
Tommy Conroy, Dublin
LEFT HALF-FORWARD
John McCormack, Longford
Noel Durkin, Mayo
Pat Spillane, Kerry
RIGHT FULL-FORWARD
Eugene Hughes, Monaghan
John Kearns, Dublin
Kevin McStay, Mayo
FULL-FORWARD
Ambrose Rogers, Down
Eamonn Murphy, Monaghan
Paul Earley, Roscommon
LEFT FULL-FORWARD
Brendan Lowry, Offaly
Brendan Mason, Down
Eugene Hughes, Monaghan

1986
GOALKEEPER
Aidan Skelton, Tyrone
Charlie Nelligan, Kerry
John O'Leary, Dublin
RIGHT FULL-BACK
Harry Keegan, Roscommon
Joe Cassells, Meath
Páidí Ó Sé, Kerry
FULL-BACK
Ciarán McGarvey, Tyrone
Mick Dempsey, Laois
Mick Lyons, Meath
LEFT FULL-BACK
John Lynch, Tyrone
Mick Spillane, Kerry
Séamus McHugh, Galway
RIGHT HALF-BACK
Kevin McCabe, Tyrone
Niall Cahalane, Cork
Tomás Doyle, Kerry
CENTRE HALF-BACK
Ciarán Murray, Monaghan
Tom Spillane, Kerry
Tomás Tierney, Galway
LEFT HALF-BACK
Colm Browne, Laois
Dave Synnott, Dublin
Ger Lynch, Kerry
CENTREFIELD
Gerry McEntee, Meath
Jack O'Shea, Kerry
Liam Hayes, Meath
Liam Irwin, Laois
Plunkett Donaghy, Tyrone
Willie Joe Padden, Mayo

All-Star Gazing

Football All-Star Nominees

RIGHT HALF-FORWARD
Dermot McNicholl, Derry
Greg Blaney, Down
Ray McCarron, Monaghan
CENTRE HALF-FORWARD
Damien O'Hagan, Tyrone
Eugene McKenna, Tyrone
Gay McManus, Galway
LEFT HALF-FORWARD
Pat Spillane, Kerry
RIGHT FULL-FORWARD
Colm O'Rourke, Meath
Dermot McNicholl, Derry
Mikey Sheehy, Kerry
FULL-FORWARD
Damien O'Hagan, Tyrone
Eamonn Murphy, Monaghan
Eoin Liston, Kerry
LEFT FULL-FORWARD
Brendan Mason, Down
Eugene Hughes, Monaghan
Ger Power, Kerry

1987
GOALKEEPER
John Kerins, Cork
John O'Leary, Dublin
Michael McQuillan, Meath
RIGHT FULL-BACK
Hugh Martin McGurk, Derry
John Fallon, Galway
Robbie O'Malley, Meath
FULL-BACK
Colman Corrigan, Cork
Danny Quinn, Derry
Mick Lyons, Meath
LEFT FULL-BACK
Mick Kennedy, Dublin
Terry Ferguson, Meath
Tony Scullion, Derry
RIGHT HALF-BACK
Dave Synnott, Dublin
Niall Cahalane, Cork
Tommy Doyle, Kerry
CENTRE HALF-BACK
Conor Counihan, Cork
Liam Harnan, Meath
Tom Spillane, Kerry
LEFT HALF-BACK
Ger Lynch, Kerry
Martin O'Connell, Meath
Noel McCaffrey, Dublin
CENTREFIELD
Brian McGilligan, Derry
Gerry McEntee, Meath
Jim Reilly, Cavan
Liam Hayes, Meath
Shea Fahy, Cork
Teddy McCarthy, Cork
RIGHT HALF-FORWARD
David Beggy, Meath
Enda Gormley, Derry
Greg Blaney, Down
CENTRE HALF-FORWARD
Dermot McNicholl, Derry
Larry Tompkins, Cork
Val Daly, Galway

LEFT HALF-FORWARD
Dermot McNicholl, Derry
Kieran Duff, Dublin
PJ Gillic, Meath
RIGHT FULL-FORWARD
John O'Driscoll, Cork
Mikey Sheehy, Kerry
Val Daly, Galway
FULL-FORWARD
Brian Stafford, Meath
LEFT FULL-FORWARD
Bernard Flynn, Meath
Brendan Mason, Down
John Cleary, Cork

1988
GOALKEEPER
John Kerins, Cork
Michael McQuillan, Meath
Paddy Linden, Monaghan
RIGHT FULL-BACK
Robbie O'Malley, Meath
FULL-BACK
Colman Corrigan, Cork
Gerry Hargan, Dublin
Mick Lyons, Meath
LEFT FULL-BACK
Dermot Flanagan, Mayo
Mick Kennedy, Dublin
Niall Cahalane, Cork
RIGHT HALF-BACK
Ciarán Murray, Monaghan
Frank Noone, Mayo
Niall Cahalane, Cork
CENTRE HALF-BACK
Liam Harnan, Meath
Noel McCaffrey, Dublin
Tony Scullion, Derry
LEFT HALF-BACK
Ciarán Murray, Monaghan
Martin O'Connell, Meath
Tony Nation, Cork
CENTREFIELD
Dave Kavanagh, Offaly
Jack O'Shea, Kerry
Liam Hayes, Meath
Seán Maher, Mayo
Shea Fahy, Cork
TJ Kilgallon, Mayo
RIGHT HALF-FORWARD
David Beggy, Meath
Maurice Fitzgerald, Kerry
Paul McGrath, Cork
CENTRE HALF-FORWARD
Larry Tompkins, Cork
Liam McHale, Mayo
Vinnie Murphy, Dublin
LEFT HALF-FORWARD
Kieran Duff, Dublin
Maurice Fitzgerald, Kerry
PJ Gillic, Meath
RIGHT FULL-FORWARD
Colm O'Rourke, Meath
Eugene Hughes, Monaghan
Peter Brady, Offaly

FULL-FORWARD
Brian Stafford, Meath
Dave Barry, Cork
Tony McManus, Roscommon
LEFT FULL-FORWARD
Dessie Barry, Longford
Eugene Hughes, Monaghan
Martin Carney, Mayo

1989
GOALKEEPER
Aidan Skelton, Tyrone
Gabriel Irwin, Mayo
John Kerins, Cork
RIGHT FULL-BACK
Jimmy Browne, Mayo
Niall Cahalane, Cork
Robbie O'Malley, Meath
FULL-BACK
Gerry Hargan, Dublin
Peter Forde, Mayo
Stephen O'Brien, Cork
LEFT FULL-BACK
Dermot Flanagan, Mayo
Jimmy Kerrigan, Cork
Mick Kennedy, Dublin
RIGHT HALF-BACK
Connie Murphy, Kerry
Dónal Reid, Donegal
John McGoldrick, Tyrone
CENTRE HALF-BACK
Ambrose O'Donovan, Kerry
Conor Counihan, Cork
Tommy Carr, Dublin
LEFT HALF-BACK
Anthony Davis, Cork
CENTREFIELD
Fergus Daly, Wicklow
Larry Tompkins, Cork
Liam Hayes, Meath
Liam McHale, Mayo
Teddy McCarthy, Cork
Willie Joe Padden, Mayo
RIGHT HALF-FORWARD
Ciarán Corr, Tyrone
Dave Barry, Cork
Maurice Fitzgerald, Kerry
CENTRE HALF-FORWARD
Gay McManus, Galway
Larry Tompkins, Cork
Martin McHugh, Donegal
LEFT HALF-FORWARD
Barry Coffey, Cork
Joyce McMullen, Donegal
Noel Durkin, Mayo
RIGHT FULL-FORWARD
Paul McGrath, Cork
FULL-FORWARD
Eugene McKenna, Tyrone
Joe McNally, Dublin
Liam McHale, Mayo
LEFT FULL-FORWARD
Dessie Barry, Longford
John Cleary, Cork
Tony McManus, Roscommon

1990
GOALKEEPER
John Kerins, Cork
Pat Comer, Galway
Paul Staunton, Roscommon
RIGHT FULL-BACK
JJ Doherty, Donegal
Robbie O'Malley, Meath
Tony Nation, Cork
FULL-BACK
Conor Deegan, Down
Mick Lyons, Meath
Stephen O'Brien, Cork
LEFT FULL-BACK
Des Newton, Roscommon
John Cunningham, Donegal
Terry Ferguson, Meath
RIGHT HALF-BACK
Keith Barr, Dublin
Michael Slocum, Cork
Paul Hickey, Roscommon
CENTRE HALF-BACK
Alan Mulholland, Galway
Conor Counihan, Cork
Declan Darcy, Leitrim
LEFT HALF-BACK
Eamonn Heery, Dublin
Martin O'Connell, Meath
Martin Shovlin, Donegal
CENTREFIELD
Danny Culloty, Cork
John Newton, Roscommon
Liam Hayes, Meath
Mickey Quinn, Leitrim
Paul Clarke, Dublin
Shea Fahy, Cork
RIGHT HALF-FORWARD
Ambrose Rogers, Down
David Beggy, Meath
Jack O'Shea, Kerry
CENTRE HALF-FORWARD
Dave Barry, Cork
Larry Tompkins, Cork
Val Daly, Galway
LEFT HALF-FORWARD
Joyce McMullen, Donegal
Maurice Fitzgerald, Kerry
Paul McGrath, Cork
RIGHT FULL-FORWARD
Dessie Barry, Longford
Paul McGrath, Cork
Robert McHugh, Wicklow
FULL-FORWARD
Brian Stafford, Meath
Kevin O'Brien, Wicklow
Mickey Linden, Down
LEFT FULL-FORWARD
Bernard Flynn, Meath
James McCartan, Down
Michael McCarthy, Cork

1991
GOALKEEPER
John O'Leary, Dublin
Michael McQuillan, Meath
Neil Collins, Down

RIGHT FULL-BACK
Davy Dalton, Kildare
Kieran McKeever, Derry
Mick Deegan, Dublin
FULL-BACK
Conor Deegan, Down
John Crofton, Kildare
Mick Lyons, Meath
LEFT FULL-BACK
Enon Gavin, Roscommon
Matt Gallagher, Donegal
Terry Ferguson, Meath
RIGHT HALF-BACK
Glenn Ryan, Kildare
Michael Slocum, Cork
Tommy Carr, Dublin
CENTRE HALF-BACK
DJ Kane, Down
Keith Barr, Dublin
Pat Roe, Laois
LEFT HALF-BACK
Barry Coffey, Cork
DJ Kane, Down
Martin O'Connell, Meath
CENTREFIELD
Barry Breen, Down
Fergus Daly, Wicklow
Gerry McEntee, Meath
John Newton, Roscommon
Martin Lynch, Kildare
Plunkett Donaghy, Tyrone
RIGHT HALF-FORWARD
David Beggy, Meath
Jack Sheedy, Dublin
Ross Carr, Down
CENTRE HALF-FORWARD
Colm O'Rourke, Meath
Greg Blaney, Down
Jack Sheedy, Dublin
LEFT HALF-FORWARD
Gary Mason, Down
Maurice Fitzgerald, Kerry
Tommy Dowd, Meath
RIGHT FULL-FORWARD
Colm O'Rourke, Meath
Mickey Linden, Down
Paul McLoughlin, Kildare
FULL-FORWARD
Brian Stafford, Meath
Danny Fitzgerald, Limerick
Peter Withnell, Down
LEFT FULL-FORWARD
Bernard Flynn, Meath
Derek Duggan, Roscommon
James McCartan, Down

1992
GOALKEEPER
Gary Walsh, Donegal
Gay Sheerin, Roscommon
John O'Leary, Dublin
DEFENDER
Anthony Rainbow, Kildare
Dónal Reid, Donegal
Eamonn Heery, Dublin
Gerry Hargan, Dublin
Henry Downey, Derry
John Crofton, Kildare
Keith Barr, Dublin
Kieran McKeever, Derry
Martin Gavigan, Donegal
Martin Shovlin, Donegal
Matt Gallagher, Donegal
Mick Deegan, Dublin
Noel Hegarty, Donegal
Paul Curran, Dublin
Séamus Clancy, Clare
Tomás Tierney, Mayo
Tony Scullion, Derry
MIDFIELD
Anthony Molloy, Donegal
Brian McGilligan, Derry
Brian Murray, Donegal
Paul Clarke, Dublin
Seán McGovern, Kildare
TJ Kilgallon, Mayo
FORWARD
Anthony Tohill, Derry
Damien O'Reilly, Cavan
Declan Bonner, Donegal
Dessie Farrell, Dublin
Enda Gormley, Derry
James McHugh, Donegal
Manus Boyle, Donegal
Martin McHugh, Donegal
Maurice Fitzgerald, Kerry
Mickey Linden, Down
Niall Buckley, Kildare
Noel Roche, Clare
Padraic Conway, Clare
Ray Dempsey, Mayo
Tony Boyle, Donegal
Vinnie Murphy, Dublin

1993
GOALKEEPER
Damien McCusker, Derry
John O'Leary, Dublin
Peter O'Leary, Kerry
DEFENDER
Anthony Davis, Cork
Barry McGowan, Donegal
Ciarán O'Sullivan, Cork
Ciarán Walsh, Dublin
Davy Dalton, Kildare
Dermot Deasy, Dublin
Gary Coleman, Derry
Glenn Ryan, Kildare
Graham Geraghty, Meath
Henry Downey, Derry
John Joe Doherty, Donegal
John McGurk, Derry
John Rafferty, Armagh
Mark O'Connor, Cork
Matt Gallagher, Donegal
Mick Deegan, Dublin
Stephen O'Brien, Cork
Tony Scullion, Derry
MIDFIELD
Anthony Tohill, Derry
Brian McGilligan, Derry
Brian Murray, Donegal
Jack Sheedy, Dublin
John Newton, Roscommon
Shea Fahy, Cork
FORWARD
Barry Coffey, Cork
Charlie Redmond, Dublin
Colin Corkery, Cork
Colm O'Rourke, Meath
Dermot Heaney, Derry
Don Davis, Cork
Enda Gormley, Derry
Ger Houlahan, Armagh
James McHugh, Donegal
Joe Brolly, Derry
Joe Kavanagh, Cork
John O'Driscoll, Cork
Kevin O'Neill, Mayo
Martin McHugh, Donegal
Neil Smyth, Armagh
Peter Lambert, Tipperary
Ray McCarron, Monaghan
Vinnie Murphy, Dublin

1994
GOALKEEPER
John O'Leary, Dublin
Neil Collins, Down
Peter O'Leary, Kerry
DEFENDER
Barry Breen, Down
Brian Burns, Down
Ciarán Walsh, Dublin
DJ Kane, Down
Davy Dalton, Kildare
Declan Darcy, Leitrim
Dermot Deasy, Dublin
Fay Devlin, Tyrone
Graham Geraghty, Meath
Keith Barr, Dublin
Martin O'Connell, Meath
Micheál Magill, Down
Mick Deegan, Dublin
Paddy Moran, Dublin
Paul Curran, Dublin
Paul Higgins, Down
Séamus Quinn, Leitrim
Stephen O'Brien, Cork
MIDFIELD
Brian Burke, Tipperary
Brian Stynes, Dublin
Conor Deegan, Down
Gregory McCartan, Down
Jack Sheedy, Dublin
Pat Donohue, Leitrim
FORWARD
Aidan Farrell, Down
Charlie Redmond, Dublin
Colm Hayden, Carlow
Dessie Farrell, Dublin
Diarmuid Marsden, Armagh
Gary Mason, Down
Ger Heavin, Westmeath
Ger Houlahan, Armagh
Greg Blaney, Down
James McCartan, Down
Mick Galvin, Dublin
Mickey Linden, Down
Niall Buckley, Kildare
Padraig Kenny, Leitrim
Peter Canavan, Tyrone
Peter Lambert, Tipperary
Ross Carr, Down
Tommy Dowd, Meath

1995
GOALKEEPER
Emmet Burke, Laois
Finbar McConnell, Tyrone
John O'Leary, Dublin
DEFENDER
Ciarán O'Sullivan, Cork
Damien O'Reilly, Cavan
Dermot Deasy, Dublin
Fay Devlin, Tyrone
Gary Fahey, Galway
Glenn Ryan, Kildare
Graham Geraghty, Meath
Keith Barr, Dublin
Mark O'Connor, Cork
Martin O'Connell, Meath
Mick Deegan, Dublin
Paddy Moran, Dublin
Paul Curran, Dublin
Séamus McCallan, Tyrone
Seán McLaughlin, Tyrone
Seán Óg De Paor, Galway
Stephen O'Brien, Cork
Tony Scullion, Derry
MIDFIELD
Anthony Tohill, Derry
Brian Stynes, Dublin
Danny Culloty, Cork
Fergal Logan, Tyrone
Liam Honohan, Cork
Paul Bealin, Dublin
FORWARD
Charlie Redmond, Dublin
Ciarán Corr, Tyrone
Ciarán McBride, Tyrone
Colin Corkery, Cork
Colm O'Rourke, Meath
Dessie Farrell, Dublin
Jarlath Fallon, Galway
Jason Sherlock, Dublin
Joe Kavanagh, Cork
Mark O'Sullivan, Cork
Maurice Fitzgerald, Kerry
Mickey Linden, Down
Niall Finnegan, Galway
Paul Clarke, Dublin
Peter Canavan, Tyrone
Tommy Dowd, Meath
Tony Boyle, Donegal
Val Daly, Galway

1996
GOALKEEPER
Conor Martin, Meath
Finbar McConnell, Tyrone
John O'Leary, Dublin
DEFENDER
Ciarán O'Sullivan, Cork
Darren Fay, Meath
Fay Devlin, Tyrone
James Nallen, Mayo
Kenneth Mortimer, Mayo
Kevin Cahill, Mayo

Football All-Star Nominees

Kieran McKeever, Derry
Mark O'Connor, Cork
Mark O'Reilly, Meath
Martin O'Connell, Meath
Mike Hassett, Kerry
Noel Connolly, Mayo
Pat Holmes, Mayo
Paul Curran, Dublin
Paul Devlin, Tyrone
Seán Óg De Paor, Galway
Stephen O'Brien, Cork
Tony Scullion, Derry
MIDFIELD
Anthony Tohill, Derry
Gregory McCartan, Down
John McDermott, Meath
Liam McHale, Mayo
Pascal Canavan, Tyrone
Tony Maher, Laois
FORWARD
Brendan Reilly, Meath
Brian Dooher, Tyrone
Colm McManamon, Mayo
Dara Ó Cinnéide, Kerry
Dermot McCabe, Cavan
Gerard Cavlan, Tyrone
Graham Geraghty, Meath
James Horan, Mayo
Jarlath Fallon, Galway
Joe Brolly, Derry
John Casey, Mayo
Maurice Fitzgerald, Kerry
Maurice Sheridan, Mayo
Peter Canavan, Tyrone
Raymond Gallagher, Fermanagh
Tommy Dowd, Meath
Tony Boyle, Donegal
Trevor Giles, Meath

1997
GOALKEEPER
Declan O'Keeffe, Kerry
Paul O'Dowd, Cavan
Peter Burke, Mayo
DEFENDER
Barry O'Shea, Kerry
Cathal Daly, Offaly
Ciarán O'Sullivan, Cork
Davy Dalton, Kildare
Eamonn Breen, Kerry
Fergal Costello, Mayo
Frankie Griffin, Clare
Gary Coleman, Derry
Gerry Sheridan, Cavan
Glenn Ryan, Kildare
James Nallen, Mayo
Kenneth Mortimer, Mayo
Kieran McKeever, Derry
Killian Burns, Kerry
Liam O'Flaherty, Kerry
Séamus Moynihan, Kerry
Seán Óg De Paor, Galway
Stephen Stack, Kerry
MIDFIELD
Anthony Tohill, Derry
Darragh Ó Sé, Kerry
Dermot McCabe, Cavan

Niall Buckley, Kildare
Pat Fallon, Mayo
William Kirby, Kerry
FORWARD
Brendan Reilly, Meath
Damien O'Reilly, Cavan
Declan Darcy, Dublin
Denis O'Dwyer, Kerry
Joe Brolly, Derry
Joe Cassidy, Derry
Martin Daly, Clare
Maurice Fitzgerald, Kerry
Maurice Sheridan, Mayo
Pa Laide, Kerry
Paul Taylor, Sligo
Peter Brady, Offaly
Peter Reilly, Cavan
Raymond Gallagher, Fermanagh
Ronan Carolan, Cavan
Roy Malone, Offaly
Trevor Giles, Meath
Vinny Claffey, Offaly

1998
GOALKEEPER
Christy Byrne, Kildare
Declan O'Keeffe, Kerry
Martin McNamara, Galway
DEFENDER
Anthony Rainbow, Kildare
Barry McGowan, Donegal
Brian Lacey, Kildare
Damien Donlon, Roscommon
Darren Fay, Meath
Finbarr Cullen, Offaly
Gary Fahey, Galway
Glenn Ryan, Kildare
John Divilly, Galway
John Finn, Kildare
John Kenny, Offaly
Kieran McGeeney, Armagh
Ray Silke, Galway
Ronan Quinn, Kildare
Séamus Moynihan, Kerry
Seán Martin Lockhart, Derry
Seán Óg De Paor, Galway
Tomás Mannion, Galway
MIDFIELD
Darragh Ó Sé, Kerry
John McDermott, Meath
Kevin Walsh, Galway
Niall Buckley, Kildare
Seán O'Domhnaill, Galway
Willie McCreery, Kildare
FORWARD
Brendan Devenney, Donegal
Declan Browne, Tipperary
Declan Kerrigan, Kildare
Derek Savage, Galway
Dermot Earley Jnr, Kildare
Eddie Lohan, Roscommon
Eddie McCormack, Kildare
Jarlath Fallon, Galway
John Crowley, Kerry
Karl O'Dwyer, Kildare
Martin Lynch, Kildare
Michael Donnellan, Galway

Niall Finnegan, Galway
Padraic Joyce, Galway
Paul Brewster, Fermanagh
Tommy Dowd, Meath
Trevor Giles, Meath
Vinny Claffey, Offaly

1999
GOALKEEPER
Benny Tierney, Armagh
Cormac Sullivan, Meath
Kevin O'Dwyer, Cork
DEFENDER
Alan Roche, Mayo
Andrew McCann, Armagh
Anthony Lynch, Cork
Ciarán Hughes, Armagh
Ciarán O'Sullivan, Cork
Cormac Murphy, Meath
Darren Fay, Meath
Enda McManus, Meath
Enda McNulty, Armagh
Justin McNulty, Armagh
Kevin Cahill, Mayo
Kieran McGeeney, Armagh
Mark O'Reilly, Meath
Martin Cronin, Cork
Owen Sexton, Cork
Paddy Reynolds, Meath
Ronan McCarthy, Cork
Séamus Moynihan, Kerry
MIDFIELD
Anthony Tohill, Derry
Ciarán Whelan, Dublin
Jarlath Burns, Armagh
John McDermott, Meath
Michael O'Sullivan, Cork
Nicholas Murphy, Cork
FORWARD
Aodhan MacGearailt, Kerry
Dessie Dolan, Westmeath
Diarmuid Marsden, Armagh
Don Davis, Cork
Dónal Curtis, Meath
Evan Kelly, Meath
Graham Geraghty, Meath
Ian Robertson, Dublin
James Horan, Mayo
Joe Kavanagh, Cork
Oisín McConville, Armagh
Ollie Murphy, Meath
Padraic Joyce, Galway
Patrick McKeever, Armagh
Phillip Clifford, Cork
Podsie O'Mahony, Cork
Shane Mulholland, Down
Trevor Giles, Meath

2000
GOALKEEPER
Christy Byrne, Kildare
Declan O'Keeffe, Kerry
Seán McGreevy, Antrim
DEFENDER
Andrew McCann, Armagh
Anthony Rainbow, Kildare
Declan Meehan, Galway

MIDFIELD
Cormac McAnallen, Tyrone
Darragh Ó Sé, Kerry
David Brady, Mayo
Fergal Doherty, Derry
Kevin Walsh, Galway
Rory O'Connell, Westmeath
FORWARD
Brendan Devenney, Donegal
Colin Corkery, Cork
Derek Savage, Galway
Dessie Dolan, Westmeath
Dessie Farrell, Dublin
Eamonn O'Hara, Sligo
Evan Kelly, Meath
Ger Heavin, Westmeath
Graham Geraghty, Meath
Joe Bergin, Galway
John Crowley, Kerry
Michael Donnellan, Galway
Mike Frank Russell, Kerry
Ollie Murphy, Meath
Paddy Bradley, Derry
Padraic Joyce, Galway
Paul Clancy, Galway
Stephen O'Neill, Tyrone

2002
GOALKEEPER
Declan O'Keeffe, Kerry
Kevin O'Dwyer, Cork
Stephen Cluxton, Dublin
DEFENDER
Aidan O'Rourke, Armagh
Anthony Lynch, Cork
Brian Robinson, Tyrone
Chris Lawn, Tyrone
Ciarán O'Sullivan, Cork
Declan Meehan, Galway
Enda McNulty, Armagh
Kevin Cassidy, Donegal
Kieran McGeeney, Armagh
Leigh O'Brien, Wexford
Marc Ó Sé, Kerry
Michael McCarthy, Kerry
Paddy Christie, Dublin
Peadar Andrews, Dublin
Richie Fahey, Galway
Séamus Moynihan, Kerry
Tomás Mannion, Galway
Tomás Ó Sé, Kerry
MIDFIELD
Ciarán Whelan, Dublin
Darragh Ó Sé, Kerry
Dermot Earley Jnr, Kildare
John Gildea, Donegal
John Quane, Limerick
Paul McGrane, Armagh
FORWARD
Adrian Sweeney, Donegal
Alan Brogan, Dublin
Brendan Jer O'Sullivan, Cork
Colin Corkery, Cork
Colm Cooper, Kerry
Declan Browne, Tipperary
Diarmuid Marsden, Armagh
Eamonn O'Hara, Sligo
John McEntee, Armagh
Michael Hegarty, Donegal
Mike Frank Russell, Kerry
Oisín McConville, Armagh
Padraic Joyce, Galway
Peter Canavan, Tyrone
Ray Cosgrove, Dublin
Ronan Clarke, Armagh
Rory Gallagher, Fermanagh
Stephen McDonnell, Armagh

2003
GOALKEEPER
Enda Murphy, Kildare
Fergal Byron, Laois
Shane Curran, Roscommon
DEFENDER
Andrew McCann, Armagh
Barry Owens, Fermanagh
Ciarán Gourley, Tyrone
Conor Gormley, Tyrone
Cormac McAnallen, Tyrone
Declan Meehan, Galway
Enda McNulty, Armagh
Francie Bellew, Armagh
Joe Higgins, Laois
Kevin Cassidy, Donegal
Kieran McGeeney, Armagh
Niall McCready, Donegal
Paddy Christie, Dublin
Philip Jordan, Tyrone
Raymond Sweeney, Donegal
Ryan McMenamin, Tyrone
Tom Kelly, Laois
Tomás Ó Sé, Kerry
MIDFIELD
Kevin Hughes, Tyrone
Kevin Walsh, Galway
Padraic Clancy, Laois
Paul McGrane, Armagh
Philip Loughran, Armagh
Seán Cavanagh, Tyrone
FORWARD
Adrian Sweeney, Donegal
Brian Dooher, Tyrone
Brian McDónald, Laois
Brian McGuigan, Tyrone
Ciarán McManus, Offaly
Declan Browne, Tipperary
Diarmuid Marsden, Armagh
Enda McGinley, Tyrone
Frankie Dolan, Roscommon
Gerard Cavlan, Tyrone
John McEntee, Armagh
Michael Meehan, Galway
Muiris Gavin, Limerick
Owen Mulligan, Tyrone
Peter Canavan, Tyrone
Ross Munnelly, Laois
Stephen McDonnell, Armagh
Stephen O'Neill, Tyrone

2004
GOALKEEPER
Diarmuid Murphy, Kerry
Niall Tinney, Fermanagh
DEFENDER
Barry Owens, Fermanagh
Conor Mullane, Limerick
David Heaney, Mayo
Dónal O'Donoghue, Westmeath
Éamonn Fitzmaurice, Kerry
Francie Bellew, Armagh
Gary Connaughton, Westmeath
James Nallon, Mayo
Joe Higgins, Laois
John Keane, Westmeath
Kieran Hughes, Armagh
Marc Ó Sé, Kerry
Michael McCarthy, Kerry
Niall Bogue, Fermanagh
Ryan McMenamin, Tyrone
Seán McDermott, Fermanagh
Tom Kelly, Laois
Tom O'Sullivan (Rathmore), Kerry
Tomás Ó Sé, Kerry
MIDFIELD
Fergal Doherty, Derry
John Galvin, Limerick
Martin McGrath, Fermanagh
Ronan McGarrity, Mayo
Seán Cavanagh, Tyrone
William Kirby, Kerry
FORWARD
Ciarán McDónald, Mayo
Colm Bradley, Fermanagh
Colm Cooper, Kerry
Dara Ó Cinnéide, Kerry
David Glennon, Westmeath
Declan O'Sullivan, Kerry
Dessie Dolan, Westmeath
Enda Muldoon, Derry
Eoin Brosnan, Kerry
Jason Sherlock, Dublin
Mark Little, Fermanagh
Matty Forde, Wexford
Paddy Bradley, Derry
Padraic Joyce, Galway
Paul Galvin, Kerry
Stephen McDonnell, Armagh
Stephen O'Neill, Tyrone
Trevor Mortimer, Mayo

2005
GOALKEEPER
Diarmuid Murphy, Kerry
James Reilly, Cavan
Paul Hearty, Armagh
DEFENDER
Aaron Kernan, Armagh
Aidan Fennelly, Laois
Aidan O'Mahony, Kerry
Andy Mallon, Armagh
Anthony Lynch, Cork
Conor Gormley, Tyrone
Francie Bellew, Armagh
Graham Canty, Cork
Joe McMahon, Tyrone
Kevin McCloy, Derry
Kieran McGeeney, Armagh
Marc Ó Sé, Kerry
Michael McCarthy, Kerry
Paul Griffin, Dublin
Philip Jordan, Tyrone
Ryan McMenamin, Tyrone
Stephen O'Shaughnessy, Dublin
Tomás Ó Sé, Kerry
MIDFIELD
Ciarán Whelan, Dublin
Darragh Ó Sé, Kerry
Nicholas Murphy, Cork
Noel Garvan, Laois
Paul McGrane, Armagh
Seán Cavanagh, Tyrone
FORWARD
Alan Brogan, Dublin
Brian Dooher, Tyrone
Brian McGuigan, Tyrone
Bryan Cullen, Dublin
Colm Cooper, Kerry
Enda McGinley, Tyrone
Eoin Brosnan, Kerry
Michael Meehan, Galway
Owen Mulligan, Tyrone
Paddy Bradley, Derry
Padraic Joyce, Galway
Peter Canavan, Tyrone
Ronan Clarke, Armagh
Ross Munnelly, Laois
Stephen McDonnell, Armagh
Stephen O'Neill, Tyrone
Thomas Freeman, Monaghan
Tomás Quinn, Dublin

2006
GOALKEEPER
Alan Quirke, Cork
Gary Connaughton, Westmeath
Stephen Cluxton, Dublin
FULL-BACKS
Barry Owens, Fermanagh
Francie Bellew, Armagh
Graham Canty, Cork
Joe Higgins, Laois
Karl Lacey, Donegal
Keith Higgins, Mayo
Marc Ó Sé, Kerry
Paul Griffin, Dublin
Tom O'Sullivan (Rathmore), Kerry
HALF-BACKS
Aaron Kernan, Armagh
Aidan O'Mahony, Kerry
Barry Dunnion, Donegal
Bryan Cullen, Dublin
Diarmuid Blake, Galway
Ger Spillane, Cork
Karol Slattery, Offaly
Peadar Gardinar, Mayo
Séamus Moynihan, Kerry
MIDFIELDERS
Ciarán Whelan, Dublin
Darragh Ó Sé, Kerry
Nicholas Murphy, Cork
Paul McGrane, Armagh
Ronan McGarrity, Mayo
Shane Ryan, Dublin
HALF-FORWARDS
Alan Brogan, Dublin
Alan Dillon, Mayo
Ciarán McDónald, Mayo

50 Years of the GAA All-Stars

Football All-Star Nominees

Conal Keaney, Dublin
Jason Sherlock, Dublin
Paul Barden, Longford
Paul Galvin, Kerry
Ross Munnelly, Laois
Seán O'Sullivan, Kerry
FULL-FORWARDS
Brian Kavanagh, Longford
Colm Cooper, Kerry
Conor Mortimer, Mayo
James Masters, Cork
Kieran Donaghy, Kerry
Niall McNamee, Offaly
Paddy Bradley, Derry
Ronan Clarke, Armagh
Stephen McDonnell, Armagh

2007
GOALKEEPER
Brendan Murphy, Meath
Diarmuid Murphy, Kerry
Stephen Cluxton, Dublin
FULL-BACKS
Conor Gormley, Tyrone
Darren Fay, Meath
David Henry, Dublin
Dessie Mone, Monaghan
Graham Canty, Cork
Karl Lacey, Donegal
Kevin McCloy, Derry
Marc Ó Sé, Kerry
Ross Donovan, Sligo
HALF-BACKS
Aidan O'Mahony, Kerry
Barry Cahill, Dublin
Caoimhin King, Meath
Damien Freeman, Monaghan
Gary McQuaid, Monaghan
Killian Young, Kerry
Michael McNamara, Sligo
Noel O'Leary, Cork
Tomás Ó Sé, Kerry
MIDFIELDERS
Ciarán Whelan, Dublin
Darragh Ó Sé, Kerry
Fergal Doherty, Derry
Nicholas Murphy, Cork
Paddy Keenan, Louth
Seán Cavanagh, Tyrone
HALF-FORWARDS
Alan Brogan, Dublin
Anthony Moyles, Meath
Bernard Brogan Jnr, Dublin
Declan O'Sullivan, Kerry
John Doyle, Kildare
Nicky Joyce, Galway
Paul Galvin, Kerry
Raymond Mulgrew, Tyrone
Stephen Bray, Meath
FULL-FORWARDS
Colm Cooper, Kerry
Donnacha O'Connor, Cork
Graham Geraghty, Meath
James Masters, Cork
Kieran Donaghy, Kerry
Mark Vaughan, Dublin
Michael Cussen, Cork

Paddy Bradley, Derry
Thomas Freeman, Monaghan

2008
GOALKEEPER
Anthony Masterson, Wexford
Gary Connaughton, Westmeath
James Reilly, Cavan
FULL-BACKS
Anthony Lynch, Cork
Conor Gormley, Tyrone
David Henry, Dublin
Dessie Mone, Monaghan
Finian Hanley, Galway
Francie Bellew, Armagh
John Keane, Westmeath
Justin McMahon, Tyrone
Marc Ó Sé, Kerry
HALF-BACKS
Aidan O'Mahony, Kerry
Davy Harte, Tyrone
Graham Canty, Cork
Michael Ennis, Westmeath
Philip Jordan, Tyrone
Ryan McCluskey, Fermanagh
Ryan McMenamin, Tyrone
Thomas McElroy, Fermanagh
Tomás Ó Sé, Kerry
MIDFIELDERS
Darragh Ó Sé, Kerry
Enda McGinley, Tyrone
Fergal Doherty, Derry
Martin McGrath, Fermanagh
Séamus Scanlon, Kerry
Shane Ryan, Dublin
HALF-FORWARDS
Brian Dooher, Tyrone
Colm McCullough, Tyrone
Declan O'Sullivan, Kerry
John Doyle, Kildare
Michael Cussen, Cork
Padraic Joyce, Galway
Pearse O'Neill, Cork
Redmond Barry, Wexford
Seán Cavanagh, Tyrone
FULL-FORWARDS
Alan Brogan, Dublin
Ciarán Lyng, Wexford
Colm Cooper, Kerry
Kieran Donaghy, Kerry
Matty Forde, Wexford
Michael Meehan, Galway
Ronan Clarke, Armagh
Tommy McGuigan, Tyrone
Tommy Walsh, Kerry

2009
GOALKEEPER
Alan Quirke, Cork
Diarmuid Murphy, Kerry
Stephen Cluxton, Dublin
FULL-BACKS
Anthony Lynch, Cork
Ciarán Hyland, Wicklow
Johnny McCarthy, Limerick
Justin McMahon, Tyrone
Karl Lacey, Donegal

Marc Ó Sé, Kerry
Michael Shields, Cork
Tom O'Sullivan (Rathmore), Kerry
Tommy Griffin, Kerry
HALF-BACKS
Andy Moran, Mayo
Barry Cahill, Dublin
Davy Harte, Tyrone
Graham Canty, Cork
John Miskella, Cork
Johnny Davey, Sligo
Michael McCarthy, Kerry
Ryan McMenamin, Tyrone
Tomás Ó Sé, Kerry
MIDFIELDERS
Alan O'Connor, Cork
Dermot Earley Jnr, Kildare
John Galvin, Limerick
Kevin Hughes, Tyrone
Nicholas Murphy, Cork
Séamus Scanlon, Kerry
HALF-FORWARDS
Alan Brogan, Dublin
James Kavanagh, Kildare
Joe Sheridan, Meath
Leighton Glynn, Wicklow
Paddy Kelly, Cork
Paul Galvin, Kerry
Pearse O'Neill, Cork
Tadhg Kennelly, Kerry
Trevor Mortimer, Mayo
FULL-FORWARDS
Alan Smith, Kildare
Bernard Brogan Jnr, Dublin
Colm Cooper, Kerry
Daniel Goulding, Cork
Declan O'Sullivan, Kerry
Michael McCann, Antrim
Michael Murphy, Donegal
Stephen O'Neill, Tyrone
Tommy Walsh, Kerry

2010
GOALKEEPER
Alan Quirke, Cork
Brendan McVeigh, Down
Pascal McConnell, Tyrone
FULL-BACKS
Charlie Harrison, Sligo
Dan Gordon, Down
John O'Brien, Louth
Justin McMahon, Tyrone
Marc Ó Sé, Kerry
Michael Shields, Cork
Peter Kelly, Kildare
Philip McMahon, Dublin
Rory O'Carroll, Dublin
HALF-BACKS
Eamonn Callaghan, Kildare
Emmet Bolton, Kildare
Graham Canty, Cork
Joe McMahon, Tyrone
Kevin McKernan, Down
Noel O'Leary, Cork
Paudie Kissane, Cork
Philip Jordan, Tyrone
Tomás Ó Sé, Kerry

MIDFIELDERS
Aidan Walsh, Cork
John Galvin, Limerick
Kalum King, Down
Michael Darragh Macauley, Dublin
Nicholas Murphy, Cork
Paddy Keenan, Louth
HALF-FORWARDS
Cathal Cregg, Roscommon
Daniel Hughes, Down
Graham Reilly, Meath
Joe Sheridan, Meath
John Doyle, Kildare
Marty Clarke, Down
Paddy Kelly, Cork
Paul Kerrigan, Cork
Séamus Kenny, Meath
FULL-FORWARDS
Benny Coulter, Down
Bernard Brogan Jnr, Dublin
Colm Cooper, Kerry
Daniel Goulding, Cork
David Kelly, Sligo
Donie Shine, Roscommon
Donnacha O'Connor, Cork
James Kavanagh, Kildare
Padraic Joyce, Galway

2011
GOALKEEPER
Brendan Kealy, Kerry
Paul Durkan, Donegal
Stephen Cluxton, Dublin
FULL-BACKS
Cian O'Sullivan, Dublin
Frank McGlynn, Donegal
Hugh McGrillen, Kildare
Joe McMahon, Tyrone
Marc Ó Sé, Kerry
Michael Foley, Kildare
Neil McGee, Donegal
Rory O'Carroll, Dublin
Tom O'Sullivan (Rathmore), Kerry
HALF-BACKS
Dónal Vaughan, Mayo
Emmet Bolton, Kildare
Ger Brennan, Dublin
Karl Lacey, Donegal
Kevin Cassidy, Donegal
Kevin Nolan, Dublin
Killian Young, Kerry
Tomás Ó Sé, Kerry
Trevor Mortimer, Mayo
MIDFIELDERS
Alan O'Connor, Cork
Bryan Sheehan, Kerry
Denis Bastick, Dublin
John Doyle, Kildare
Michael Darragh Macauley, Dublin
Seán Cavanagh, Tyrone
HALF-FORWARDS
Alan Brogan, Dublin
Alan Dillon, Mayo
Ben Brosnan, Wexford
Darren O'Sullivan, Kerry
Declan O'Sullivan, Kerry
Eamonn Callaghan, Kildare

Kevin McManaman, Dublin
Paddy Kelly, Cork
Paul Flynn, Dublin
FULL-FORWARDS
Andy Moran, Mayo
Bernard Brogan Jnr, Dublin
Cillian O'Connor, Mayo
Colm Cooper, Kerry
Colm McFadden, Donegal
Diarmuid Connolly, Dublin
Donnacha O'Connor, Cork
Eoin Bradley, Derry
Michael Murphy, Donegal

2012

GOALKEEPER
David Clarke, Mayo
Paul Durkan, Donegal
Stephen Cluxton, Dublin
FULL-BACKS
Dónal Keogan, Meath
Eamon McGee, Donegal
Eoin Cadogan, Cork
Ger Cafferkey, Mayo
Keith Higgins, Mayo
Michael Shields, Cork
Neil McGee, Donegal
Paddy McGrath, Donegal
Rory O'Carroll, Dublin
HALF-BACKS
Adrian Flynn, Wexford
Anthony Thompson, Donegal
Colm Boyle, Mayo
Emmet Bolton, Kildare
Frank McGlynn, Donegal
Karl Lacey, Donegal
Kevin Nolan, Dublin
Lee Keegan, Mayo
Michael Quinn, Longford
MIDFIELDERS
Aidan O'Shea, Mayo
Aidan Walsh, Cork
Barry Moran, Mayo
Brendan Quigley, Laois
Neil Gallagher, Donegal
Rory Kavanagh, Donegal
HALF-FORWARDS
Alan Dillon, Mayo
Ciarán Sheehan, Cork
Graham Reilly, Meath
Kevin McLoughlin, Mayo
Mark McHugh, Donegal
Michael Darragh Macauley, Dublin
Paul Barden, Longford
Paul Flynn, Dublin
Paul Kerrigan, Cork
FULL-FORWARDS
Andy Moran, Mayo
Bernard Brogan Jnr, Dublin
Colm Cooper, Kerry
Colm McFadden, Donegal
Colm O'Neill, Cork
Conor Laverty, Down
Donnacha O'Connor, Cork
Jamie Clarke, Armagh
Michael Murphy, Donegal

2013

GOALKEEPER
Robbie Hennelly, Mayo
Rory Beggan, Monaghan
Stephen Cluxton, Dublin
FULL-BACKS
Cathal McCarron, Tyrone
Chris Barrett, Mayo
Colin Walshe, Monaghan
Drew Wylie, Monaghan
Ger Cafferkey, Mayo
Keith Higgins, Mayo
Killian Clarke, Cavan
Marc Ó Sé, Kerry
Rory O'Carroll, Dublin
HALF-BACKS
Cian O'Sullivan, Dublin
Colm Boyle, Mayo
Conor Gormley, Tyrone
Dessie Mone, Monaghan
Dónal Vaughan, Mayo
Jack McCaffrey, Dublin
James Loughrey, Cork
James McCarthy, Dublin
Lee Keegan, Mayo
MIDFIELDERS
Aidan O'Shea, Mayo
Anthony Maher, Kerry
Darren Hughes, Monaghan
Michael Darragh Macauley, Dublin
Paul Conroy, Galway
Séamus O'Shea, Mayo
HALF-FORWARDS
Cian Mackey, Cavan
Ciarán Kilkenny, Dublin
Colm Cooper, Kerry
Diarmuid Connolly, Dublin
Donnachadh Walsh, Kerry
Lorcan Mulvey, London
Mattie Donnelly, Tyrone
Paul Flynn, Dublin
Seán Cavanagh, Tyrone
FULL-FORWARDS
Bernard Brogan Jnr, Dublin
Cillian O'Connor, Mayo
Colm McFadden, Donegal
Conor McManus, Monaghan
James O'Donoghue, Kerry
Martin Dunne, Cavan
Mickey Newman, Meath
Paddy Andrews, Dublin
Paul Mannion, Dublin

2014

GOALKEEPER
Paul Durkan, Donegal
Rory Beggan, Monaghan
Stephen Cluxton, Dublin
FULL-BACKS
Andy Mallon, Armagh
Drew Wylie, Monaghan
Eamon McGee, Donegal
Fionn Fitzgerald, Kerry
Keith Higgins, Mayo
Neil McGee, Donegal
Paul Murphy, Kerry
Philip McMahon, Dublin
Rory O'Carroll, Dublin
HALF-BACKS
Aidan O'Mahony, Kerry
Colin O'Riordan, Tipperary
Colm Boyle, Mayo
Dessie Mone, Monaghan
Frank McGlynn, Donegal
James McCarthy, Dublin
Jonny Cooper, Dublin
Lee Keegan, Mayo
Peter Crowley, Kerry
MIDFIELDERS
Anthony Maher, Kerry
David Moran, Kerry
Michael Darragh Macauley, Dublin
Neil Gallagher, Donegal
Odhran MacNiallais, Donegal
Séamus O'Shea, Mayo
HALF-FORWARDS
Aidan O'Shea, Mayo
Diarmuid Connolly, Dublin
Donnachadh Walsh, Kerry
Johnny Buckley, Kerry
Mark Lynch, Derry
Michael Murphy, Donegal
Paul Flynn, Dublin
Ryan McHugh, Donegal
Shane Walsh, Galway
FULL-FORWARDS
Brian Hurley, Cork
Cillian O'Connor, Mayo
Conor McManus, Monaghan
James O'Donoghue, Kerry
Kevin McManaman, Dublin
Kieran Donaghy, Kerry
Paddy McBrearty, Donegal
Paul Geaney, Kerry
Tony Kernan, Armagh

2015

GOALKEEPER
Brendan Kealy, Kerry
Paul Durkan, Donegal
Rory Beggan, Monaghan
DEFENDER
Cathal McCarron, Tyrone
Chris Barrett, Mayo
Cian O'Sullivan, Dublin
Frank McGlynn, Donegal
Jack McCaffrey, Dublin
James McCarthy, Dublin
Jonathan Lyne, Kerry
Jonny Cooper, Dublin
Karl O'Connell, Monaghan
Keith Higgins, Mayo
Lee Keegan, Mayo
Philip McMahon, Dublin
Ronan McNabb, Tyrone
Ronan McNamee, Tyrone
Rory O'Carroll, Dublin
Ryan McHugh, Donegal
Shane Enright, Kerry
Vinny Corey, Monaghan
MIDFIELD
Anthony Maher, Kerry
Brian Fenton, Dublin
Colm Cavanagh, Tyrone
David Moran, Kerry
Neil Gallagher, Donegal
Tom Parsons, Mayo
FORWARD
Aidan O'Shea, Mayo
Bernard Brogan Jnr, Dublin
Ciarán Kilkenny, Dublin
Cillian O'Connor, Mayo
Conor McManus, Monaghan
Diarmuid Connolly, Dublin
Diarmuid O'Connor, Mayo
Donie Kingston, Laois
Donnachadh Walsh, Kerry
James O'Donoghue, Kerry
Kieran Martin, Westmeath
Mattie Donnelly, Tyrone
Michael Murphy, Donegal
Paddy Andrews, Dublin
Paul Geaney, Kerry
Peter Harte, Tyrone
Seán Cavanagh, Tyrone
Seán Quigley, Fermanagh

2016

GOALKEEPER
David Clarke, Mayo
Evan Comerford, Tipperary
Stephen Cluxton, Dublin
DEFENDER
Brendan Harrison, Mayo
Cathal McCarron, Tyrone
Cian O'Sullivan, Dublin
Colm Boyle, Mayo
Declan Kyne, Galway
James McCarthy, Dublin
John Small, Dublin
Jonny Cooper, Dublin
Keith Higgins, Mayo
Kevin McLoughlin, Mayo
Killian Young, Kerry
Lee Keegan, Mayo
Paddy McGrath, Donegal
Patrick Durcan, Mayo
Philip McMahon, Dublin
Robbie Kiely, Tipperary
Ryan McHugh, Donegal
Shane Enright, Kerry
MIDFIELD
Brian Fenton, Dublin
Colm Cavanagh, Tyrone
Gary Brennan, Clare
Mattie Donnelly, Tyrone
Paul Conroy, Galway
Peter Acheson, Tipperary
FORWARD
Aidan O'Shea, Mayo
Andy Moran, Mayo
Ciarán Kilkenny, Dublin
Cillian O'Connor, Mayo
Conor Sweeney, Tipperary
Damien Comer, Galway
Danny Cummins, Galway
Dean Rock, Dublin

Football All-Star Nominees

Diarmuid Connolly, Dublin
Diarmuid O'Connor, Mayo
Kevin McManaman, Dublin
Michael Quinlivan, Tipperary
Niall Sludden, Tyrone
Paddy McBrearty, Donegal
Paul Geaney, Kerry
Paul Murphy, Kerry
Peter Harte, Tyrone
Seán Cavanagh, Tyrone

2017
GOALKEEPER
David Clarke, Mayo
Niall Morgan, Tyrone
Stephen Cluxton, Dublin
DEFENDER
Brendan Harrison, Mayo
Caolan Mooney, Down
Chris Barrett, Mayo
Cian O'Sullivan, Dublin
Colm Boyle, Mayo
Conor Devanney, Roscommon
Fintan Kelly, Monaghan
Jack McCaffrey, Dublin
John Small, Dublin
Jonny Cooper, Dublin
Keith Higgins, Mayo
Lee Keegan, Mayo
Michael Fitzsimons, Dublin
Padraig Hampsey, Tyrone
Paul Murphy, Kerry
Philip McMahon, Dublin
Tadhg Morley, Kerry
Tiernan McCann, Tyrone
MIDFIELD
Brian Fenton, Dublin
Colm Cavanagh, Tyrone
Enda Smith, Roscommon
James McCarthy, Dublin
Kevin Feely, Kildare
Tom Parsons, Mayo
FORWARD
Aidan O'Shea, Mayo
Andy Moran, Mayo
Ciarán Kilkenny, Dublin
Cillian O'Connor, Mayo
Con O'Callaghan, Dublin
Connaire Harrison, Down
Daniel Flynn, Kildare
Dean Rock, Dublin
James O'Donoghue, Kerry
Jamie Clarke, Armagh
Jason Doherty, Mayo
Kevin McLoughlin, Mayo
Kieran Donaghy, Kerry
Niall Sludden, Tyrone
Paddy McBrearty, Donegal
Paul Geaney, Kerry
Paul Mannion, Dublin
Peter Harte, Tyrone

2018
GOALKEEPER
Graham Briody, Laois
Rory Beggan, Monaghan
Stephen Cluxton, Dublin
DEFENDER
Che Cullen, Fermanagh
Drew Wylie, Monaghan
Eoghan Bán Gallagher, Donegal
Eoghan Kerin, Galway
Eoin Doyle, Kildare
Eoin Murchan, Dublin
Gavin White, Kerry
Jack McCaffrey, Dublin
James McCarthy, Dublin
Jonny Cooper, Dublin
Karl O'Connell, Monaghan
Michael McKernan, Tyrone
Padraig Hampsey, Tyrone
Peter Harte, Tyrone
Ryan Wylie, Monaghan
Seán Andy Ó Ceallaigh, Galway
Seán Kelly, Galway
Tiernan McCann, Tyrone
MIDFIELD
Brian Fenton, Dublin
Colm Cavanagh, Tyrone
Mattie Donnelly, Tyrone
Michael Murphy, Donegal
Niall Kearns, Monaghan
Thomas Flynn, Galway
FORWARD
Brian Howard, Dublin
Ciarán Kilkenny, Dublin
Con O'Callaghan, Dublin
Conor McManus, Monaghan
Damien Comer, Galway
Daniel Flynn, Kildare
David Clifford, Kerry
Dean Rock, Dublin
Ian Burke, Galway
Niall Scully, Dublin
Niall Sludden, Tyrone
Paul Broderick, Carlow
Paul Cribben, Kildare
Paul Mannion, Dublin
Rory Grugan, Armagh
Ryan McAnespie, Monaghan
Ryan McHugh, Donegal
Shane Walsh, Galway

2019
GOALKEEPER
Shane Ryan, Kerry
Shaun Patton, Donegal
Stephen Cluxton, Dublin
DEFENDER
Chris Barrett, Mayo
Colm Boyle, Mayo
Conor McGill, Meath
Conor Moynagh, Cavan
David Byrne, Dublin
Dónal Keogan, Meath
Jack McCaffrey, Dublin
James McCarthy, Dublin
John Small, Dublin
Michael Fitzsimons, Dublin
Niall Daly, Roscommon
Paddy Durcan, Donegal
Paul Murphy, Kerry
Ronan McNamee, Tyrone
Ryan McHugh, Donegal
Stephen McMenamin, Donegal
Tadhg Morley, Kerry
Tom O'Sullivan (Dingle), Kerry
MIDFIELD
Aidan O'Shea, Mayo
Brian Fenton, Dublin
Bryan Menton, Meath
David Moran, Kerry
Jarlath Og Burns, Armagh
Michael Darragh Macauley, Dublin
FORWARD
Brian Howard, Dublin
Brian Hurley, Cork
Cathal McShane, Tyrone
Ciarán Kilkenny, Dublin
Con O'Callaghan, Dublin
Conor Cox, Roscommon
David Clifford, Kerry
Dean Rock, Dublin
Jamie Brennan, Donegal
Jamie Malone, Clare
Mattie Donnelly, Tyrone
Michael Murphy, Donegal
Paddy McBrearty, Donegal
Paul Geaney, Kerry
Paul Mannion, Dublin
Rian O'Neill, Armagh
Seán O'Shea, Kerry
Stephen O'Brien, Kerry

2020
GOALKEEPER
David Clarke, Mayo
Raymond Galligan, Cavan
Stephen Cluxton, Dublin
DEFENDER
Aidan Forker, Armagh
Bill Maher, Tipperary
Chris Barrett, Mayo
Ciarán Brady, Cavan
David Byrne, Dublin
Eoghan McLaughlin, Mayo
Eoin Murchan, Dublin
Gerry Smith, Cavan
Iain Corbett, Limerick
John Small, Dublin
Kevin Fahy, Tipperary
Lee Keegan, Mayo
Michael Fitzsimons, Dublin
Oisín Mullin, Mayo
Padraig Faulkner, Cavan
Patrick Durcan, Mayo
Peadar Mogan, Donegal
Robbie McDaid, Dublin
MIDFIELD
Brian Fenton, Dublin
Colin O'Riordan, Tipperary
Gearóid McKiernan, Cavan
Ian Maguire, Cork
James McCarthy, Dublin
Matthew Ruane, Mayo
FORWARD
Aidan O'Shea, Mayo
Ciarán Kilkenny, Dublin
Ciarán Thompson, Donegal
Cillian O'Connor, Mayo
Con O'Callaghan, Dublin
Conor Sweeney, Tipperary
David Clifford, Kerry
Dean Rock, Dublin
Kevin McLoughlin, Mayo
Martin Reilly, Cavan
Michael Langan, Donegal
Niall Scully, Dublin
Paul Conroy, Galway
Ryan O'Donoghue, Mayo
Seán Bugler, Dublin
Shane Walsh, Galway
Thomas Galligan, Cavan
Tommy Conroy, Mayo